WESTMINSTER COMMENTARIES
EDITED BY WALTER LOCK D.D.
LADY MARGARET PROFESSOR OF DIVINITY
IN THE UNIVERSITY OF OXFORD

THE BOOKS OF THE PROPHETS
MICAH OBADIAH
JOEL AND JONAH

THE BOOKS OF THE PROPHETS
MICAH OBADIAH JOEL AND JONAH

WITH INTRODUCTION AND NOTES

BY

G. W. WADE D.D.

SENIOR TUTOR OF ST DAVID'S COLLEGE, LAMPETER,
CANON OF ST ASAPH

METHUEN & CO. LTD.
36 ESSEX STREET W.C.
LONDON

First published in 1925

PRINTED IN GREAT BRITAIN

DULCISSIMAE DILECTISSIMAE

PREFATORY NOTE BY THE GENERAL EDITOR

THE primary object of these Commentaries is to be exegetical, to interpret the meaning of each book of the Bible in the light of modern knowledge to English readers. The Editors will not deal, except subordinately, with questions of textual criticism or philology; but taking the English text in the Revised Version as their basis, they will aim at combining a hearty acceptance of critical principles with loyalty to the Catholic Faith.

The series will be less elementary than the Cambridge Bible for Schools, less critical than the International Critical Commentary, less didactic than the Expositor's Bible; and it is hoped that it may be of use both to theological students and to the clergy, as well as to the growing number of educated laymen and laywomen who wish to read the Bible intelligently and reverently.

Each commentary will therefore have

(i) An Introduction stating the bearing of modern criticism and research upon the historical character of the book, and drawing out the contribution which the book, as a whole, makes to the body of religious truth.

(ii) A careful paraphrase of the text with notes on the more difficult passages and, if need be, excursuses on any points of special importance either for doctrine, or ecclesiastical organization, or spiritual life.

But the books of the Bible are so varied in character that considerable latitude is needed, as to the proportion which the various parts should hold to each other. The General Editor will therefore only endeavour to secure a general uniformity in scope and character: but the exact method adopted in each case and the final responsibility for the statements made will rest with the individual contributors.

By permission of the Delegates of the Oxford University Press and of the Syndics of the Cambridge University Press the Text used in this Series of Commentaries is the Revised Version of the Holy Scriptures.

WALTER LOCK

PREFACE

THE existence of so many excellent books relating to the Minor Prophets, collectively or singly, may be thought to render the production of another work on the same subject superfluous. But a series of commentaries on the whole Bible, when once started, calls for completion; and this is perhaps sufficient justification for the present volume. Nevertheless its writer has not been content merely to preserve what in previous commentators appeared most worth preservation, but has endeavoured to supplement it, wherever expansion or addition seemed desirable. Possibly an apology is required for the sections in the Introduction dealing with *Messianic Prophecy* and *Hebrew Versification*. But Christology is attracting renewed attention now, so that a review of the Old Testament passages connected with it cannot be deemed altogether untimely or out of place; whilst the inclusion of a slight sketch of the principles of Hebrew poetic rhythm has its utility in a book which takes some account of the textual criticism of such of the prophetic writings as are here included.

In the preparation of the volume the writer has consulted the works of older scholars like Maurer, Caspari, Ewald, Pusey, Henderson, and various contributors to the Speaker's Commentary; but he is mainly indebted to more recent critics, such as Marti, Nowack, Sellin, Van Hoonacker, and Wellhausen on the Continent, and Bewer, Cheyne, Driver, Horton, Kirkpatrick, Lanchester, G. Adam Smith, J. M. Powis Smith, and W. Robertson Smith in this country or in America. Whilst, however, he has derived from his predecessors much of his material, he has sought (as in a previous work) to exercise an independent judgment in drawing conclusions from the *data* that have been collected.

For great assistance in the preparation of the manuscript the writer wishes to express his deep indebtedness to his wife. The book has been read in MS. and in proof by Dr Lock, the General Editor, and his meticulous care has caused the author, who fondly imagined himself to be something of an adept in condensation, to feel that, after all, he is but a mere novice in the art. Dr Lock, however, has done far more than recommend omissions; he has contributed a number of very valuable suggestions, for which the warmest thanks are due. Help with the proofs has also been received from the Rev. D. D. Bartlett, B.A., Lecturer in Theology at Lampeter College. His scrutiny of them has resulted in the discovery and removal of many oversights and blemishes which had previously escaped detection, and his kindly service calls for most grateful acknowledgment.

G. W. W.

CONTENTS

xii
CONTENTS

A LIST OF TRANSLATIONS, COMMENTARIES, AND OTHER WORKS CONSULTED (WITH ABBREVIATIONS).

Aq. Aquila's Greek Translation of the Old Testament (in Field's *Hexaplorum quae supersunt*).

A.V. Authorized Version of the Bible, 1611.

Bewer. Bewer's *Critical and Exegetical Commentary on Obadiah, Joel, and Jonah* (I.C.C.), 1912.

C.B. Century Bible.

Camb.B. Cambridge Bible.

Caspari. C. P. Caspari's *Der Prophet Obadja*, 1842.

Cheyne. T. K. Cheyne's *Micah, with Notes and Introduction* (Camb.B.), 1882.

Driver. S. R. Driver's *The Books of Joel and Amos* (Camb.B.), 1897.

" *Gen.* S. R. Driver's *The Book of Genesis* (West.C.).

" *LOT.* S. R. Driver's *Introduction to the Literature of the Old Testament*, 1891 and later editions.

E.B. Expositor's Bible.

Enc.Bib. Cheyne and Black's *Encyclopaedia Biblica*, 1899—1903.

Ewald. H. Ewald's *The Prophets of the Old Testament* (E.T.).

Expos. The Expositor.

Hastings, *DB.* J. Hastings' *Dictionary of the Bible*, 1898—1904.

Henderson. E. Henderson's *The Book of the Twelve Prophets*, 1858.

Horton. R. F. Horton's *The Minor Prophets Hosea...Micah* (C.B.).

I.C.C. International Critical Commentary.

JE. *The Prophetic Document of the Pentateuch.*

JTS. The Journal of Theological Studies.

Kirkpatrick. A. F. Kirkpatrick's *The Doctrine of the Prophets*, 2nd ed., 1897.

Lanchester. H. C. O. Lanchester's *Obadiah and Jonah* (Camb.B.), 1918.

LXX. The Septuagint Translation of the Old Testament, ed. Swete, 1894.

Marti. D. K. Marti's *Das Dodekapropheton*, 1904.

Maurer. F. J. V. Maurer's *Commentarius Grammaticus criticus in Vetus Testamentum*, vol. II., 1838.

Nowack. W. Nowack's *Die Kleinen Propheten*, 1903.

Old Latin. The Old Latin Version (cited from *JTS.* vol. v. 247 f., 378 f., VI. 67 f.).

P. *The Priestly Document of the Pentateuch.*

Pusey. E. B. Pusey's *The Minor Prophets*, 1860.

R.V. The Revised Version of the Bible, 1884.

Sayce, *HCM.* A. H. Sayce's *The Higher Criticism and the Monuments*, 1894.

Schrader, *COT.* Schrader's *The Cuneiform Inscriptions and the O.T.* (E.T.).

Sellin, *IOT.* E. Sellin's *Introduction to the O.T.* (E.T.).

Smith, G. A. Sir George Adam Smith's *The Book of the XII Prophets* (E.B.).

" *HGHL.*, Sir G. A. Smith's *Historical Geography of the Holy Land.*

Smith, J. M. P. J. M. Powis Smith's *Critical and Historical Commentary on Micah* (I.C.C.), 1912.

Smith, W. R. W. Robertson Smith's *The Prophets of Israel*, 1895.
"Speaker's Bible" (The). *The Holy Bible, with a Commentary* etc., 1871— 6.
Sym. Symmachus's Greek Translation of the Old Testament (in Field).
Syr. The Syriac Translation of the O.T.
Th. Theodotion's Translation of the O.T. (in Field).
Van Hoonacker. A. Van Hoonacker's *Les Douze Petits Prophètes*.
Vulg. Biblia Sacra Vulgatæ Editionis.
Wellhausen. J. Wellhausen's *Die Kleine Propheten*, 1898.
West.C. Westminster Commentaries, edited by W. Lock, D.D.

*** The use of Hebrew characters has been avoided, and Hebrew words and phrases, when reference to the original has been found necessary, have been transliterated. Readers who are unacquainted with Hebrew should observe (1) that all Hebrew letters are consonants, the accompanying vowels being originally transmitted by oral tradition only, and when eventually written down, being marked merely by "points"; (2) that the difference between several of the consonants is small, those which can be most easily mistaken for one another being *d* and *r*, *b* and *c*, *v* and *y*, *h* and *kh*, *b* and *m*, *g* and *n*, *n* and *c*; (3) that the same symbol served for *s* and *sh*; (4) that in the unpointed text doubled letters were indistinguishable from single letters, and aspirated labials, gutturals and dentals were indistinguishable from the corresponding unaspirated letters. Knowledge of these facts will enable the plausibility of various emendations of the Hebrew text to be more fairly estimated than might otherwise be the case. In the present work for the sake of convenience no distinction in transliterating has been made between the letters *he* and *kheth* (both alike being represented, as in the English Bible, by *h*), between *samech* and *sin* (the substitute for both being *s*), or between *teth* and *tav* (both appearing as *t*). The letters *aleph* and *ayin* are indicated by (') and (') respectively.

INTRODUCTION TO MICAH.

CHAPTER I.

THE TITLE AND CONTENTS.

WITHIN the volume which is entitled *The Book of the XII Prophets* the writings that are ascribed to Micah occupy in the Hebrew Scriptures the sixth place, following after Hosea, Joel, Amos, Obadiah, and Jonah; but the internal evidence of several of these books makes it probable that the order in which they are arranged departs widely from the true historical succession of the prophets whose names they bear. In the LXX. the order in two cases is different, Micah being placed third (after Amos) and Joel being transposed to the fourth position, immediately next to Micah. This rearrangement, though still failing to correspond to the chronological order (so far as it is ascertainable), has at least the advantage of putting Micah in his right place by bringing his book into closer relation with those of Hosea and Amos. For that Micah's activity fell within the same century as theirs appears not only from the heading of his book (which may owe its origin to an editor, p. 1) but from Jer. xxvi. 18, where it is expressly stated that the prediction contained in Mic. iii. 12 was uttered in the reign of Hezekiah (727 (or 720)—692).

In the opening verse of the book Micah's prophetic career is represented as beginning in the reign of Jotham and extending through that of Ahaz into that of Hezekiah. The limits thus implied cannot be decided with any certainty, for calculations based on the duration of the reigns of the rulers of Judah, as given in the books of Kings, lead to results regarding the accession-years of the three sovereigns named in Mic. i. 1 which are mutually inconsistent, according as the reckoning is made backwards from (*a*) the capture of Samaria by Sargon in 722, (*b*) the invasion of Judah by Sennacherib in 701, (*c*) the capture of Jerusalem by Nebuchadrezzar in 587; and consequently some or all of the figures upon which the calculations are based must be erroneous. In the following tables, which give the Biblical figures, the years for the duration of each king's reign are reduced by one, since the Hebrew historians generally, though not quite uniformly, reckoned inclusively[1],

---

[1] See, for instance, 1 Kgs. xv. 25 and 28, xvi. 8 and 15.

so that the year of a king's death and of his successor's accession was by them comprised within the reign of each and, in the sum of the years of two consecutive reigns, was counted twice over.

(a)		(b)		(c)	
Jotham (15)	757	Jotham (15)	744	Jotham (15)	750
Ahaz (15) ...	742	Ahaz (15) ...	729	Ahaz (15) ...	735
Hezekiah (28)	727	Hezekiah (28)	714	Hezekiah (28)	720
Fall of Samaria *in H.'s 6th year* }	722	*Sennacherib's* *Invasion in H.'s* *14th year* }	701	Manasseh (54)	692
				Amon (1) ...	638
				Josiah (30)	637
				Jehoahaz ($\frac{1}{4}$)	607
				Jehoiakim (10)	607
				Jehoiachin ($\frac{1}{4}$)	597
				Zedekiah (10)	597
				Fall of Jerusalem	587

It will be seen from these tables (a) that if, according to 2 Kgs. xviii. 10, the Fall of Samaria occurred in 722 in Hezekiah's 6th year, the invasion of Judah by Sennacherib in 701 must have happened in his 27th year and not (as stated in 2 Kgs. xviii. 13) in his 14th; (b) that if Sennacherib's invasion took place in Hezekiah's 14th year, Samaria must have fallen, not in that king's 6th year, but in the 8th year of his father Ahaz; (c) that if Hezekiah came to the throne in 720 (the figure reached by calculating from the Fall of Jerusalem in 587), the Fall of Samaria must have occurred in Ahaz's 14th year, and Sennacherib's invasion in Hezekiah's 20th year. In view of these inconsistencies, it is only possible to form a more or less conjectural scheme of chronology for the reigns of the sovereigns mentioned; and one which is perhaps as plausible as any other is the following, which assigns to each king a length of reign differing, indeed, from that given in 2 Kings, but at least consistent with the dates fixed in the Assyrian inscriptions for certain events that happened within the reigns in question[1]:—

Jotham (3)	738
Ahaz (8) ...	735
Hezekiah (35)	727—692

The view that Ahaz was succeeded by Hezekiah in 727 may perhaps derive some confirmation from an oracle addressed to the Philistines, contained in Is. xiv. 28—32, which is assigned to the year of Ahaz's

---

[1] The events referred to are (a) the payment of tribute by Ahaz to *Tiglath-Pileser*, who died in 727; (b) the capture of Samaria in 722 by *Sargon*, who reigned from 723 to 705; (c) the invasion of Judah in 701 by *Sennacherib*, whose reign lasted from 705 to 681. See Schrader, *COT*. I. pp. 249, 264, 286.

death; for it was in 727 that there occurred the death of the Assyrian king Tiglath-Pileser, and it is very probable that Tiglath-Pileser is the "rod" alluded to in *v.* 29 which had smitten Philistia, but was then "broken." The scheme given above adopts the statement of 2 Kings that Samaria was destroyed in Hezekiah's 6th year; but from this it follows that Sennacherib's invasion occurred in Hezekiah's 27th, so that the statement in 2 Kings that it took place in his 14th year must be rejected as an error. It has been suggested that the figure 14 has been mistakenly deduced from the fact that Hezekiah's illness recorded in 2 Kgs. xx is represented as following close upon Sennacherib's invasion and occurring 15 years before the end of Hezekiah's reign, which lasted 29 years[1]. Some of the discrepancies between the dates given or implied by the historian of the books of Kings in connection with Hezekiah may be reduced, though not removed, by the supposition (lacking explicit support in the O.T.) that during the latter part of his father's reign he acted as regent for Ahaz, or was associated with him in the government: if so, 727 may be the beginning of his joint reign with Ahaz and 720 that of his rule as sole sovereign. If this supposition commends itself, the last table must be amended thus:—

Jotham (3)	... ...	738
Ahaz (15)	... ...	735
Ahaz ⎫ Hezekiah ⎬ jointly		727
Hezekiah sole king (28)		720—692

According to the scheme suggested above, Micah's prophetic activity (if the statement in i. 1 be accepted) began before 735, and lasted at least until after 722, for though some of the contents of ch. i. must date from before the overthrow of Samaria in 722 (perhaps between 725 and 723), the use of *Israel* to denote *Judah* in ch. iii. proves that when the oracles which this later chapter contains were delivered, the Northern kingdom must have come to an end. It is, however, not easy to feel much confidence in the assertion in i. 1 that the prophet began his ministry in the reign of Jotham (738—735?), for the earliest of his oracles seems to have in view the *impending* destruction of Samaria in 722. And inasmuch as there is no allusion in his writings to the Syro-Israelite alliance against Judah at the beginning of Ahaz's reign (2 Kgs. xvi. 5, Is. vii. 1 f.), or to the Assyrian invasion of the district of Galilee in 734 (2 Kgs. xvi. 9), it seems unlikely that any of his surviving

---

[1] See Van Hoonacker, *Les Douze Petits Prophètes*, p. 343.

prophecies dates from the reign of that king either (unless the Fall of Samaria really occurred whilst Ahaz was still on the throne). The only internal argument for assigning part of the book to the reign of Ahaz must be based on the belief that the passage iv. 1—3, which appears also in Is. ii. 2—4, was borrowed by Isaiah from Micah, and that since Is. ii. 5—21 (22) belongs to the time of Ahaz, the preceding passage common to both prophets must have been composed by Micah in that king's reign at latest. But since it is far more probable that the passage in question proceeds from neither prophet (p. 28), it follows that this argument falls to the ground. The contents of ch. iii. are shewn by Jer. xxvi. 18 to be contemporary with Hezekiah, and the utterances in chs. i., ii. are so similar in tenor that they are not likely to be far removed in point of time. Accordingly it may be affirmed without much hesitation that the reign of Hezekiah is alone known *for certain* to have included within it a considerable portion of Micah's prophetic ministry. As to how far into that reign his career lasted, it is impossible to form any trustworthy conclusion.

Of the personal history of Micah nothing is recorded, or capable of being inferred, beyond an allusion to his home (i. 1) and some more or less plausible deductions about him drawn from the contents of his prophecies. His name was apparently a shortened form of *Micaiah* (*Michāyāhu, Michāyhu, Michāyah*), another variation being *Mica* (*Michā*): the equivalents in the LXX. are Μειχαίας and Μιχά. The appellation was not uncommon, a dozen other instances of it occurring in the Hebrew O.T. and in the Apocrypha[1]. In one passage (2 Ch. xiii. 2) it appears to be feminine, but here the name is probably an error for *Maacah* (see 2 Ch. xi. 20). Its signification is "Who is like Jehovah?" (cf. Ex. xv. 11), so that it resembles in sense the name *Michael*, "Who is like God?" Analogous formations are found in Assyrian, e.g. *Manna-ki-du-rabu*[2]. The abbreviation *Micah* or *Mica* is paralleled by *Abda* for *Abdiah*. As has been seen, the prophet began his activity later than his contemporary Isaiah (who received his prophetic call as early as the end of Uzziah's reign). He was a native of, or a resident in, Moresheth-gath, a small town or hamlet in the Lowland (constituting the south and south-west of Judah), and usually identified with the modern *Beit-Jibrin*. According to tradition the locality was not only his birthplace but his place of burial also. His home was

---

[1] See Jud. xvii., xviii., 1 Kgs. xxii., 2 Kgs. xxii. 12, 1 Ch. v. 5, viii. 34, xxiii. 20, 2 Ch. xvii. 7, xxxiv. 20, Neh. xii. 35, 41, Jer. xxxvi. 11, Judith vi. 15.

[2] See Gray, *Hebrew Proper Names*, p. 157.

thus in a rural district, and not, like that of Isaiah, in the capital. As a dweller in the country and probably occupying a humble position (it is noteworthy that his father's name is not mentioned[1]) he was not likely to be in touch with state policy in the same degree as Isaiah; and there are no references in his book to any advice proffered by him to the king and his council similar to that given by Isaiah, first to Ahaz, and secondly to Hezekiah. Nevertheless he must have been acquainted with the capital, to the inhabitants of which several of his denunciations are expressly addressed (i. 5, iii. 9). His oracles had in view solely the defective religious and moral conditions of the time; and though he asserted that the sins which he denounced would, if not repented of, bring about the political subversion of the country, he did not intimate the name of the power which was to be the agent of the Divine judgment. It is true that in one prophecy included in his book (v. 5, 6) there are allusions to *Assyria* and *the Assyrian*; but these occur in a section which appears to be of later date than Micah's time (p. 39). In another oracle (iv. 10) mention is made of *Babylon* as a place whither the people for their offences were to be deported, and Babylon in the last quarter of the 8th century was subject to Assyria; but there are reasons rendering it probable that this section, too, is not by Micah (p. 35).

Micah's literary qualities must be judged by those parts of the book which alone can be indisputably regarded as proceeding from him (see pp. 1, 28). His style is forceful and impetuous, and is marked by the frequent use of rhetorical questions and commands (i. 5, 11, 13, 16, iii. 1); and like most Hebrew writers, he employs a number of vivid figures of speech (ii. 3, iii. 2, 3, 10), and is fond of alliteration and assonance. The last feature is especially noteworthy in a passage (i. 10—15) where he plays upon the appellations of various localities which he expected to be overrun by an enemy, and finds in their names allusions to occurrences which are soon to happen in connection with them.

The contents of the book fall into three divisions: i.—iii., iv.—v., vi.—vii. The first three chapters, with the exception of a very small section in ch. ii. (*vv.* 12, 13), consist of denunciations of iniquities marking both branches of the Hebrew people, and announcements of the fate destined to befall them by way of penalty; though the

---

[1] This is the case with Amos, Obadiah, Nahum, and Habakkuk, but not with Isaiah, Jeremiah, Ezekiel, Hosea, and some other prophets.

prophet's attention is concentrated chiefly upon the many forms of social wickedness abounding in his own country of Judah, and upon the vengeance impending over the offenders in it. From ch. iv. onwards the contents are very mixed, though chs. iv. and v. are distinguished from chs. vi. and vii. by the fact that in the former there predominate prophecies of future dignity and felicity in store for the Jewish people after a period of humiliation and affliction, deliverance from which is to be followed by external triumphs accompanied by internal purification. In the final pair of chapters the prevailing tone is more subdued, though the general sombreness of them is not unrelieved. A remonstrance against a misapprehension of what God desires from men is succeeded by a renewed denunciation of social offences and an announcement of the retribution which will overtake them; and this is followed by a confession of sin from the community *already* enduring the penalty of its wickedness, but nevertheless confident of eventually experiencing God's mercy. It will be seen from this that the book as a whole lacks any systematic structure; that its contents comprise a number of sections of which many stand in no logical or orderly relation to one another; that various oracles included within it must have been delivered on distinct occasions; and that the situations implied in several of them appear to be so widely sundered in respect of time that the book must contain the utterances of several prophets.

A clearer comprehension of the contents of the book and of the problems to which they give rise will be gained through a somewhat fuller analysis:—

I. (*a*) i. 2—16. A description of the descent of Jehovah in judgment, and a declaration in general terms that the transgressions of Israel and Judah occasioning it are concentrated in their respective capitals. Samaria is to be punished with the demolition of its buildings and the destruction of its idols; but retribution (seemingly through the same agent) will extend to Jerusalem also, and distress and despair are to befall numerous towns in the Lowland of Judah.

(*b*) ii. 1—11. A denunciation of the specific sin of Judah—the deliberate and violent spoliation of the weak by the powerful; and an announcement (received with incredulity by those addressed) of a corresponding nemesis planned by Jehovah for the spoilers, whose lands will be divided by foreign enemies and who will themselves be driven into exile.

(*c*) ii. 12—13. A declaration of Jehovah's purpose to re-assemble the remnant of His people, and to lead them forth from the place within which they are confined.

(*d*) iii. 1—12. A description, parallel to that of ii. 1—11, of the devouring of the people by their rulers, who abuse their authority, and whose appeals to Jehovah, when vengeance reaches them, will be unheeded; a warning to mercenary prophets that there will be withdrawn from them all prophetic faculty to which they lay claim; and a prediction that the perversion of justice by corrupt judges and self-complacent priests will be avenged by the razing of Zion to the ground.

II. (*e*) iv. 1—5. An announcement of the future elevation of mount Zion above all other heights; of the convergence thither of many peoples to seek from thence knowledge about Jehovah; and of their acceptance, in disputes, of His arbitration in lieu of war.

(*f*) iv. 6—8. A prediction of the re-assembling of dispersed Jews, and the restoration to Zion of the dominion that had formerly been hers.

(*g*) iv. 9—10. A derisive address to the inhabitants of Zion (here conceived as distressed and resourceless) who must evacuate their city and experience deportation to Babylon, whence they will be eventually rescued.

(*h*) iv. 11—13. A passage breathing a different spirit from the preceding—Zion being represented as assaulted by many nations, but receiving an assurance from Jehovah that He will enable her to destroy them, and to consecrate their spoil to Him.

(*i*) v. 1—6. The standpoint again changing, an ironical command is addressed to the populace of Jerusalem to raid as they had been wont to do[1], followed by an announcement that Jehovah's abandonment of the city to siege and her king to humiliation will last only until the emergence from Bethlehem of a Ruler, who, through Divine help, will ensure his people's security from future invasion.

(*j*) v. 7—9. A prophecy of the superiority which (through the power of God) the remnant of Israel is to manifest over other peoples.

(*k*) v. 10—15. An announcement of Jehovah's purpose to remove from among His people their military resources, their superstitious devices, and their idolatrous emblems.

III. (*l*) vi. 1—8. A controversy between Jehovah and His people, in which the former explains to the latter what His real requirements from them are—namely, not costly sacrifices but the practice of justice, mercy, and humility.

---

[1] The reading and meaning are very doubtful.

(*m*) vi. 9—vii. 6. A charge against the people of dishonesty, violence, and deceit; a prophecy of retribution inflicted through the ravage of the land by invaders; and a lament over the extinction of the good, and the universal prevalence of bloodshed, treachery, corruption, and domestic feuds.

(*n*) vii. 7—13. A humble confession, by the collective community (the true Israel), unprotected and distressed, that its affliction has been deserved by its offences; followed by an announcement from God of an approaching day for the rebuilding of the walls of Jerusalem, and for the return of its members still in exile.

(*o*) vii. 14—20. An entreaty to God from the prophet to tend His people and to enlarge their narrow boundaries; and an expression of confidence that, through His mercy, relief will come.

The sections marked (*a*), (*b*), and (*d*) are together of a tenor that creates no suspicion of their genuineness as utterances of Micah; and in sections (*k*) and (*m*) there is nothing incompatible with his authorship, though the conditions described were not peculiar to his age. But it is otherwise with regard to the remaining sections. Several, to all appearance, imply situations which were not realized until long after the 8th century had closed, and the impression produced by such sections is not adequately explained by the supposition that the book, whilst proceeding from a single prophet living in the 8th century, contains discourses delivered in a variety of circumstances falling within one man's lifetime, and calling now for threatenings and now for consolation. For though there are instances in prophetic literature of a remarkable capacity of prevision on the part of the Hebrew prophets, yet these sections of the book of Micah seem to *presuppose* conditions belonging to an age later than that prophet's, and not to *predict* their occurrence; so that doubts about his authorship of them are inevitably occasioned. An examination of such will be undertaken in the course of the commentary, whilst some general considerations bearing on the subject will occupy the next chapter.

CHAPTER II.

THE DISPUTED UNITY OF THE BOOK.

BEFORE an attempt can be made to describe in some detail the purport of Micah's prophecies, it is necessary to determine whether all portions of the book designated by his name are his; and if not, what parts can be reasonably regarded as proceeding from him, and what must, in all probability, be assigned to another or others. The review of the contents just furnished shews that there is much diversity of subject-matter; that, whilst some chapters denounce prevalent sins and foretell retribution for such, certain others assume that chastisement has already fallen, and that the chastened people need comfort and consolation, so that these latter are full of encouraging promises of deliverance. In considering whether the chapters, or sections of chapters, distinguished in this way are of different origin from those arraigning the people for numerous forms of crime, and foretelling their punishment, account must be taken of the fact that the predictions of ill, since they were designed as *warnings*, tended, so far as they produced an impression upon their hearers' consciences, to bring about their own non-fulfilment. Such predictions, though often absolute in form, were usually in essence conditional; and it was implied that the penalties announced in them could be averted by the repentance of the offenders. That this happened in the case of one of Micah's prophecies appears from Jer. xxvi. 17—19, where it is expressly stated that Micah's declaration that Jerusalem would be reduced to complete desolation caused the king (Hezekiah) to fear Jehovah and entreat His favour; and that a change of disposition on the part of sovereign and people led God to relent. It is therefore intelligible that prophets, who at one time prophesied evil, should at another, when signs of reformation became manifest, deliver oracles of quite a different tone; or, since they believed their race to be Jehovah's chosen people, should, even when affirming the certainty of Divine vengeance, yet hold out hopes of ultimate mercy. Brief summaries of such diverse prophecies, if they were copied on the same roll, or became otherwise united, would inevitably, since the circumstances in which they were originally delivered were not preserved, appear mutually contradictory. In view of this, it cannot immediately be inferred that a striking unlikeness in the contents of two contiguous passages involves difference of authorship: it is necessary to enquire whether the unlikeness can be sufficiently accounted for by a changed situation within the limits of a single prophet's ministry, or by an alteration in his attitude and outlook; or whether the matter and manner of the passages in question are so different as to render this explanation inadequate.

The passages which most acutely raise the question whether they proceed from Micah are those in which announcements about the future presume the existence of conditions very different from those of Micah's time, without any explanation of the way in which these conditions have been brought about. Thus in the case of the prophecy in iv. 1—5, which foretells that the Temple hill is to enjoy pre-eminence over all other hills and to become the seat of religious instruction for the heathen nations, it may be observed that it follows a prediction of doom for Jerusalem and (necessarily) of death or captivity for its inhabitants (iii. 12). But the sequel (in iv. 1—5) of this prediction of overwhelming disaster does not announce *first* a return of Jewish captives from exile and *then* their exaltation to a position of dignity among the surrounding peoples, but presupposes that they are already re-established in their own land. There is nothing in the earlier part of the book to explain this change of situation, except the short section ii. 12—13, which is isolated in its present context; and even this, though it predicts a re-assembling of a remnant of the people (seemingly from captivity), says nothing about the impression produced, by the restoration of the Jews, upon the heathen who witness it, or hear of it, leading them to seek to learn about the God who had effected it. A second prophecy out of harmony with its preceding context occurs in vii. 7—20. The previous section vii. 1—6 deplores the disappearance of the righteous from the land, and the prevalence of violence and strife, whilst intimating ($v.$ 4[b]) that a judgment from God is imminent. But the passage that follows (vii. 7—20) consists partly of penitential utterances from a community already experiencing grievous adversity, and partly of consolatory predictions from a prophet that the walls of Jerusalem are to be rebuilt, that the limits checking the expansion of its people are to be removed, and that there is to be a return of numbers that are still in exile. The passage plainly takes for granted that the offending land has already endured punishment through the dismantling of its capital and the deportation of many of its citizens: it *assumes* that chastisement has induced penitence; but that the city's walls are still in the condition to which foreign conquerors had reduced them: what it *predicts* is the reconstruction of the walls, and an augmentation of the community's territory and population. If the section proceeds from Micah, it must be supposed that besides foretelling his countrymen's exile, he foresaw both their rescue from it and the circumstance that Jerusalem, after the return of its citizens to their own soil, would long remain unwalled, and the re-occupied land would be circumscribed in area; but that he did not explicitly foretell the *occurrence* of these conditions, leaving this to be inferred from a prediction that in such conditions (the existence of which is presumed) a change for the better would eventually take place. This is so violent an assumption that it is preferable to conclude that the section really originated with a prophet who lived some 70 or 80 years after the

Return, was acquainted with the small numbers and defenceless situation of the repatriated exiles, and delivered the oracle contained in this section in order to cheer them with the prospect of relief.

The high probability that at least two sections of the book are not the authentic productions of Micah prepares us to entertain with less hesitation doubts that *prima facie* may arise respecting the genuineness of others also. Those which, next to iv. 1—5 and vii. 7—20, create suspicion are ii. 12—13, the remainder of ch. iv., and large parts of chs. v. and vi. The grounds for questioning their genuineness are not quite so cogent as those which have been adduced in disproof of the authenticity of iv. 1—5 and vii. 7—20, though they have considerable weight, for the evidence is cumulative, and the reasons advanced for denying to Micah other sections beside those just cited, if not very conclusive when taken by themselves, appear in a different light and assume greater importance when once it is seen that the book contains at least two passages of which the later origin is fairly patent.

If it appears probable that all or most of these sections did not originate with Micah in the 8th century, various explanations suggest themselves to account for their presence in a collection of his prophecies. One is the possibility that more than one prophet whose utterances have been preserved bore the name of Micah; if so, then there would inevitably be some risk of confusion, and oracles really emanating from two or more persons would come to be ascribed to a single prophet. Another is the circumstance that rolls of leather or papyrus were valuable enough to make it desirable that, if one were begun, it should be filled; so that any blank space in a roll only partially occupied by the oracles of Micah would readily be utilized for recording some delivered by other prophets, without any mark being appended to testify to their separate origin. For in this connection it has to be remembered that amongst the Hebrews little or no care was taken to preserve the names of the authors of literary compositions. They had no sense of the value of literary property or literary reputation, such as prevails amongst ourselves. Almost all the historical works of the O.T. are of unknown authorship. The poem of Job is anonymous; Ecclesiastes is pseudonymous; and among the prophetical writings a large part of the book of Isaiah (including chs. xl.—lv. and lvi.—lxvi.) and the last six chapters of the book of Zechariah have been shewn by internal evidence to proceed from writers of whose names we are absolutely ignorant. Accordingly, the hypothesis, to which various facts point, that within the book of Micah there have been included a number of isolated oracles delivered by some unknown writers living at different times is not an extreme one, but is justified by parallels forthcoming from other quarters.

CHRONOLOGICAL TABLE OF THE PROPHECIES IN THE BOOK OF MICAH.

(*a*)	ch. i.	8th cent. (second half, shortly before 722), Micah's.
(*b*)	ii. 1—11, iii.	8th cent. (between 722 and 701), Micah's.
(*c*)	vi. 9—16	8th cent. (perhaps Micah's) or 7th cent.
(*d*)	vii. 1—6	
(*e*)	vi. 1—8	7th cent. (second half).
(*f*)	iv. 9—10	
(*g*)	iv. 11—13	
(*h*)	v. 1—9	7th cent. (end) or 6th cent. (beginning).
(*i*)	v. 10—15	
(*j*)	ii. 12—13	6th cent. (middle, 587—537).
(*k*)	iv. 6—8	
(*l*)	iv. 1—5	6th cent. (second half, after 537).
(*m*)	vii. 7—20	5th cent. (first half).

CHAPTER III.

THE CONDITIONS OF MICAH'S AGE AND THE TENOR OF HIS TEACHING.

MICAH'S authorship of the opening oracles (i.—iii., apart from ii. 12—13) cannot be questioned; but though he was a prophet of Judah, these utterances include a denunciation of Northern Israel and its capital Samaria, as well as of Judah and its capital Jerusalem. It soon, however, becomes apparent that the prophet's thoughts were chiefly centred upon the conditions and destiny of his own country; and that he alluded to Samaria merely, or at least principally, because its impending fate conveyed a warning to Jerusalem. Consequently it is upon the internal situation of Judah that the contents of the first three chapters really throw light and focus attention.

Independent evidence for the religious and social state of that country is furnished by Micah's elder contemporary Isaiah. The prophetic activity of Isaiah much exceeded in length (so far as can be judged) that of Micah, for it extended (according to Is. i. 1, vi. 1) from the last year of Uzziah, through the reigns of Jotham and Ahaz, into the middle, at least, of the reign of Hezekiah; and the statements prefixed to chs. i. and vi. are confirmed by the internal evidence of the book; whereas it seems probable that Micah's ministry was confined to the reign of Hezekiah (p. xviii). And the circumstance that some of the former prophet's utterances were delivered during the lifetime of Jotham and Ahaz, both of whom in character were inferior to Ahaz's successor, and that by the latter king much-needed reforms were instituted, may suggest, at first sight, that the conditions subsisting in Judah under Hezekiah cannot have been quite so bad as Micah describes. In point of fact, however, though Hezekiah made an effort to put an end to religious and moral disorder, yet there is enough evidence to shew that the reformation effected was more tardy and superficial than might be concluded from the representation of the historian in 2 Kgs. xviii. 4. Various statements in the writings of Isaiah imply that much that was corrupt continued to exist even as late as the Assyrian invasion of 701, so that in using the testimony of Isaiah generally to substantiate the assertions of his younger contemporary, there is no need to discriminate very narrowly between statements applying to different reigns. All alike shew that the sombre colours in which Micah depicted the conditions of the country in his days were not darker in hue than the facts justified; and that no erroneous inferences will be deduced, if his account of the superstitions, injustices and disorders rife under Hezekiah is supported and illustrated by passages from Isaiah dating not only from that king's reign but also from the reigns of his two immediate predecessors.

Since reasons have already been given for concluding that two sections of the book of Micah are not the work of that prophet, and since arguments will be furnished later for thinking that various others are likewise not among his genuine productions, it is important, in considering his strictures upon the contemporary situation in Judah, and in summarizing his announcements about its people's future, to draw testimony only from those portions of the book of which his authorship is undisputed. These are confined to chs. i.—iii. (except ii. 12—13); but since a few passages in the rest of the book are not inconsistent with the conditions implied in the first three chapters and may come from Micah these will also be taken into account.

Isaiah's indictment of his countrymen included charges of idolatrous and superstitious practices (i. 29, ii. 8, 20, xxx. 22), of oppression, violence, and bloodshed (i. 15, 17, iii. 14, 15, v. 7, 8, xxx. 12, xxxiii. 15), of widespread intemperance (v. 11, 12, 22, xxviii. 7), of insubordination to authority (iii. 5), of venality among the classes most responsible for upholding morality, order, and justice (i. 23, v. 23), and of arrogant reliance upon material resources and political intrigues (xviii., xx., xxii. 9—11, xxx. 1—3, xxxi. 1). As Isaiah was a states-

man, he included in his censures not only social crimes and delin-
quencies, but also various features of the foreign policy of his country;
and he attributed many of the evils, of which he complained in his
early utterances, to the character of the reigning king and his court.
Micah's outlook was far less comprehensive. As he belonged perhaps
to the yeoman class, and, at any rate, was a resident in a small provincial town (though not unacquainted with the capital), his observations and reflections were confined to the ills from which the poorer
and weaker ranks of the population were suffering at the hands of
their social superiors (see especially iii. 1—3): questions of foreign
alliances and entanglements were beyond his range, and he did not
seek to influence the external relations of the state. But apart from
this difference distinguishing the two prophets, there is a singular
agreement between them as regards alike the worship of idols, the
wrongs inflicted upon the poor by the opulent, the dishonesty of the
judicial authorities, enabling evil-doers to escape human justice, and
the self-delusion (based on the belief that Jehovah and Israel were
indissolubly united) that led them to deem themselves safe from Divine
justice also. In the minds of the prophets as a body, from the earliest
to the latest, religion and social morality were solidly bound together.
Thus Micah denounced, just as Isaiah did, the seizure of houses and
lands by the rich and powerful, who in this way gratified their pride
and covetousness where they were able to do so. Robbery by violence
was committed on the highways, peaceful travellers being stripped
even of the garments they wore[1]. Women and children were evicted
from their homes and driven to seek refuge outside their own country,
which was Jehovah's land. The upper classes lived on the lower, either
through oppressive exactions of money and produce, through the con-
scription of their labour, or through the unrelieved pressure of economic
conditions; so that they are represented by the prophet as plucking
the skin from the flesh and the flesh from the bone. By such as did
not resort to open violence, dishonest gains were acquired through the
use of false weights and measures, and by fraudulent representations
(vi. 10, 11). And the exploitation of one class by another was accompanied by distrust, disunion, and strife amongst the members of the
same household, where the authority of the elders over the younger
was defied, and the loyalty expected from servants towards their
masters was replaced by open hostility (vii. 5—6). Nor was redress, or

---

[1] The passage (ii. 8) is possibly corrupt.

even a hearing, for their grievances obtainable from those—the magistrates, priests, and prophets—who were expressly commissioned by God to afford justice to the wronged, for their decisions about the complaints made to them were determined not by equity but by self-interest; judgment was wrested and the oracles of God perverted in favour of such as paid them best. All apprehension of Divine resentment for such conduct was removed by the reflection that no ill could befall those who had Jehovah and His Temple in their midst (cf. Jer. vii. 4); and the only prophets popularly deemed to be His spokesmen were persons whose utterances encouraged the magnates to indulge their vices.

Some of the causes that produced among the higher ranks of Judah, during the times of Ahaz and Hezekiah, a pride in luxury, a love of display, and a passion for the expansion of estates, which could only be gratified through the unscrupulous exercise of power and influence, are traceable without much difficulty. One was the return of prosperity to the Southern kingdom in the reign of Uzziah. In particular, there had probably been a renewal of maritime trade through the re-acquisition of Elath, the seaport on the gulf of Akaba (2 Kgs. xiv. 22)[1]. Though it was lost again under Ahaz (2 Kgs. xvi. 6, mg.), it must, during the period of its retention, have fostered considerably the development of commerce with the East; and the resultant introduction into the country of unfamiliar products from Arabia and elsewhere was calculated to create among the classes who profited by the promotion of such traffic a materialistic spirit and self-indulgent habits. Moreover Uzziah is also credited by the author of Chronicles with successes obtained over the Philistines, the Arabians, and the *Meunim* (or Minæans), and with the receiving of tribute from the Ammonites; so that if these representations have any truth behind them, an attitude of self-confidence was likely to be engendered in Judæan statesmen. A second cause also tending to bring about the conditions of which Micah and his contemporary Isaiah complained may be discovered in the closer relations which Judah was now entering upon with the empires that lay to the N.E. and S.W. of it. Hitherto the nations with which the two Hebrew kingdoms had been most nearly associated, either in peace or war, were the Moabites, the Edomites, and the Syrians (Arameans) of Damascus. But the danger with which the last-

---

[1] It must have been lost when Edom threw off the control of Judah in the reign of Jehoram (2 Kgs. viii. 20, 22).

named people, in alliance with Northern Israel, threatened Judah in the time of Ahaz, had led the Judæan king to seek help from Assyria (2 Kgs. xvi. 7); and envoys sent to Nineveh must have brought back reports of its greatness and splendour calculated to stir the imaginations of the chief citizens of Jerusalem. And rather later, from a different quarter, Egypt, which was the chief antagonist of Assyria, no doubt exerted similar influence, for, having motives of her own for desiring to detach Judah from the side of her rival, she both despatched to Hezekiah, and received from him, embassies (see Is. xviii., xxx. 1—6, xxxi. 1—3), which must likewise have contributed to stimulate tastes and aspirations that rapidly corrupted the simplicity of life that had previously prevailed. The propensities thus fostered were accompanied by a lowered sense of social duty and a decay of considerateness towards the poor and needy; so that injuries of the worst kind were perpetrated upon them without interference or relief from the officials who should have been the protectors of the defenceless.

It is reasonable to conjecture that the intense and concentrated indignation of Micah was fanned by scenes he had actually witnessed in country places. So far as can be judged from his utterances, he was a man of impressionable character and strong emotions, whose indignation was easily roused by the sight of hardship and wrong. Isaiah, too, no doubt, uttered his denunciations of contemporary iniquities from fulness of knowledge; but as he was a dweller in Jerusalem, his feelings of resentment could hardly have been as acute as those of a native of Moresheth-gath, who had personally seen the cruelty committed on the helpless peasantry by the avaricious and tyrannical. In affirming that chastisement awaited such offences, Micah refrained from specifying the agency by which it was to be inflicted: at least in those prophecies which can be confidently attributed to him, there is no express mention of Assyria, the mighty empire on the Tigris that menaced the independence of the small Palestinian states, as is the case with Isaiah (see x. 5 f., 24 f., xiv. 24—27). Nevertheless his declaration that the fatal blow impending over Samaria threatened Jerusalem also could only point to Assyria as God's instrument for the chastisement of Judah. The prospect of the speedy overthrow of the Northern kingdom, having (as it seemed) its certain sequel in the invasion of his own land, filled him with the profoundest distress (i. 8, 9). His anticipations of retribution for both countries were definite and precise. The sites of the offending capitals of Israel and Judah were to become unoccupied ground; the buildings of the two cities were to be demolished, and reduced to scattered heaps of stones; whilst the summit of Zion upon which the Temple of Jehovah stood was to be made as bare as the top of a forest-clad hill, where ground had been cleared for a "high place." The objects of false worship, the numerous idols of wood and stone, were to be destroyed; the classes that had driven others from their homes in order to augment their own possessions would themselves be carried into exile in foreign lands; and in the time of their distress Jehovah would be as deaf to their appeals to Him as they had been callous to the appeals of their victims. The law of equivalent retaliation would be imposed upon them: the evictions which they had enforced would be avenged by their own deportation. If some of the predictions of the book fore-telling in the end a brighter future for the nation are really Micah's, the realization of such was only looked for after the moral evils of the state had been purged out by a chastisement of the most drastic kind.

The activity of the Hebrew prophets often paved the road to organized reforms set on foot by secular or religious administrators, who could embody in statutes and institutions the principles affirmed in prophetic oracles. Jeremiah's utterances promoted the religious re-formation carried out by Josiah; and the teaching of Ezekiel laid the ground-plan of the system of law and ritual embodied in the Priestly code of the Pentateuch. In the same way it is reasonable to suppose that in an earlier age Micah and Isaiah were potent influences in leading Hezekiah to undertake in the course of his reign the abolition of some of the worst of contemporary corruptions prevailing amongst his subjects, which is briefly recorded by the historian of the books of Kings (2 Kgs. xviii. 4).

INTRODUCTION TO OBADIAH.

CHAPTER I.

The Title, Contents, and Structure.

The book of Obadiah (unlike the books of Hosea, Amos, Micah, and some others of the Minor Prophets) has no superscription, explaining when it was composed. It stands in the Hebrew Bible fourth in the order of the Twelve, being next to Amos and followed by Jonah, though in the LXX. it occupies the fifth place between Joel and Jonah (the book of Micah following immediately upon Amos); and its position in the Hebrew Canon has been appealed to as evidence of its date, it being supposed that the Minor Prophets have been arranged in approximately chronological order, and that consequently Obadiah in point of time cannot be far removed from Amos. But since both Joel, which precedes Obadiah in the Canon, and Jonah, which succeeds it, are probably later than Haggai (520 B.C.), standing tenth among the Twelve (pp. lxxii, lxxxv), any such inference is precarious. The circumstance that Obadiah in the Hebrew is put next to Amos is perhaps due to the fact that it relates to the doom of Edom, the occupation of which country by Israel is predicted in the concluding section of Amos (ix. 12). The book presumably derives its title from the name of the writer (if it is a unity) or of one of the writers (if it is composite). The name *Obadiah* (which might be merely a description, "servant of Jehovah") occurs as a designation of at least twelve individuals mentioned in the O.T.[1], though of only three are any particulars given. Of these the most notable was the steward of Ahab's household (1 Kgs. xviii.), who preserved the lives of a hundred prophets of Jehovah, when they were persecuted by Jezebel; but there is nothing to connect the book with him or any of the other Obadiahs elsewhere mentioned. Even the form of the name which serves as its title is not quite certain. The Heb. text of Ob. 1 has '*Obhadhyah*; and this is the way in which the name is written everywhere in the Heb. except in 1 Kgs. xviii., 1 Ch. xxvii. 19, and 2 Ch. xxxiv. 12, where it is pointed '*Obhadhyāhu*[2]. But whilst

---

[1] 1 Kgs. xviii. 3 f., 1 Ch. iii. 21, vii. 3, viii. 38 (=ix. 44), ix. 16, xii. 9, xxvii. 19, 2 Ch. xvii. 7, xxxiv. 12, Ez. viii. 9, Neh. x. 5 (6), xii. 25.
[2] Similar variations are found in connection with the names *Amaziah*, *Elijah*, *Hezekiah*, *Isaiah*, *Jeremiah*, etc.

in Ob. 1 the Vatican codex of the LXX. has ʼΟβδίου (cf. 1 Ch. iii. 21),
the Alexandrine codex has ʼΑβδίου, as also in 1 Kgs. xviii. 3 f.,
1 Ch. xxvii. 19; and since in other cases the LXX. generally represents
the name by ʼΑβδίας or ʼΑβδία, it is possible that the title of the book
should be written *Abdiah*[1] (cf. *Abdiel*, 1 Ch. v. 15, and the Arabic
Abdullah) instead of *Obadiah*.

The theme of the book is the pride and self-confidence of Edom, the
malice shewn by it towards the Jewish people (in spite of ties of blood)
on the occasion of a great calamity sustained by the latter, the deserved
retribution it has already undergone at the hands of its own allies (in
accordance with an earlier prophecy which is quoted in whole or in
part), and the prospective vengeance which is to overtake it from those
whom it has wronged, when the expatriated Jews, restored to their
former possessions, will enlarge their territory at the cost of the Edomites and other heathen neighbours. The fact that the book is thus
almost wholly concentrated upon a single subject, and its limited
extent (it is the shortest of all in the O.T.), create the expectation
that the questions presented by it will be confined to discovering what
the occasion was on which the Edomites exhibited the malice complained of, and whether the book was written prior to it or after it. But
its simplicity is illusory, and the problems to which it gives rise are both
more numerous and more involved than at first sight appears. Thus:—

(1) The circumstance that a portion of Ob. (*vv.* 1—5) is almost
identical with a passage in Jer. (xlix. 14—16, 9) makes it necessary
to determine the relation between them, and to settle whether the
writer of Obadiah has borrowed from the author of Jeremiah or the
reverse, or whether both are indebted to an earlier oracle.

(2) The fact that there is a sudden transition in *v.* 15 from the topic
of a judgment upon Edom alone to that of a judgment upon all the
heathen renders it questionable whether such an abrupt change of
subject-matter is compatible with unity of authorship.

(3) The variation in the use of the tenses (themselves susceptible
of more than one meaning) makes it uncertain whether the book is
consistently a prophecy, or, if not, to what extent it is partly a prophecy
of the future and partly a description of the past.

The small compass of Obadiah naturally creates an antecedent presumption that it is the production of a single mind. But in view of the fact
that so many of the prophetical writings are composite, the possibility

---

[1] In 1 Kgs. iv. 6, Neh. xi. 17 *Abda* stands for *Abdiah* (as *Mica* does for *Micaiah*).

that the book contains the work of more than one writer cannot be disregarded. The assumption that it is a unity may involve putting an unnatural interpretation upon certain passages in it, in order to bring them into harmony with the rest; and if the hypothesis of a composite origin affords the best solution of the questions which its contents occasion, its small size becomes a negligible consideration. Some of the problems which arise especially in connection with the concluding portion of the book are rendered all the harder by the state of the text, which in one or two places appears to be too corrupt to be interpreted or corrected with any confidence.

The sharp transition at *vv.* 15^a, 16 f. from the subject of Edom singly to that of the nations at large (the 2nd pers. sing. giving place to the 2nd pers. plur., and the predicted retribution embracing other peoples beside the Edomites) divides the book into two distinct parts. Of these the first describes an overthrow of Edom which is either impending in the near future or is in process of happening; whilst the second is a prediction of calamities yet to come upon the oppressors of Israel, including, but not confined to, the Edomites. But within the first fifteen verses are a certain number (*vv.* 1—5) which occur also in Jer. xlix.; and if, as will appear presently, these verses are probably derived by both prophets from an earlier source, there are three sections of the book, of which the origin and date require independent investigation.

CHAPTER II.

THE PASSAGE COMMON TO OBADIAH AND JEREMIAH.

THE relations subsisting between several verses of Ob. and Jer. xlix. create a problem of some difficulty and no little interest.

The opening verses of Ob. (1—5) so closely resemble Jer. xlix. 14—16, and 9, not only in substance but in actual phraseology, that it is impossible to suppose that the two passages are independent. Either, then, (i) Ob. has borrowed from Jer., or (ii) Jer. has borrowed from Ob., or, if neither of these alternatives proves admissible, then (iii) both are indebted to an earlier oracle.

(i) The prophecy against Edom in Jer. xlix., in which the verses common to both Jer. and Ob. are included, is not dated[1]; but since *v.* 12

---

[1] Within the group of chapters xlvi.—xlix. the prophecy against Egypt (xlvi.) was delivered in 604 B.C.; but this alone is precisely dated, and the occasion of some of the remaining predictions comprised in these chapters is disputed (see Driver, *Jer.* pp. 270, 271, note; Binns, *Jer.* pp. 318, 319 (West.C.)).

of that chapter seems to imply that the cup of suffering had not yet been drunk by Jehovah's people, it is probable that the prophecy was uttered before the Fall of Jerusalem in 587; and since Ob. was almost certainly written after that date (p. xliii), the possibility of borrowing on the part of the latter is manifest. Nevertheless against the conclusion that Jer. is the original source of the verses that appear in both there are two considerations of much weight.

(*a*) In Ob. the consecutiveness of the verses is less interrupted, and the sequence of thought is better observed, than in Jer. In Ob. these verses constitute a well-organized whole. The only break in the connection is a parenthetic exclamation, whilst the opening verse is an appropriate introduction to the verses which follow. On the other hand, the verse which so aptly begins the prophecy in Ob. is in Jer. preceded at some distance by a verse which in Ob. is the last of the five; whilst of the verses which in Jer. are peculiar to that book and come between this verse and the rest that are common to the two prophets, some relate to a distinct subject. There is thus a presumption that, if one of the two prophets has borrowed from the other, it is not the author of Ob. who is the borrower, since in his pages the verses in question are more coherent than in the other work which contains them.

A comparison of the two passages in Ob. and Jer., arranged in parallel columns, and rendered literally, will shew clearly both the divergence in the order of the verses and the resemblance in matter and wording.

Ob.	*Jer.*
1 A communication have we (LXX. I) heard from Jehovah, and a messenger has been sent among the nations, 'Rise ye, and let us rise against her to war.'	14 A communication have I heard from Jehovah, and a messenger is being sent among the nations, 'Gather yourselves, and go against her, and rise to war.'
2 "Lo, I make thee small among the nations: thou art despised greatly.	15 "For, lo, I make thee small among the nations, despised among men.
3 The pride of thine heart hath deceived thee[1], dweller in the clefts of (the) rock, the height of his abode; saying in his heart, 'Who will bring me down to the earth?'	16 Thy terribleness hath deceived thee[1], the pride of thine heart, dweller in the clefts of the rock, holder of the height of the hill:
4 If thou makest on high as a vulture, and if thy nest is set (LXX. if thou settest thy nest) among the stars,	though thou makest on high as a vulture thy nest,

---

[1] There is a slight difference in the Hebrew here.

Ob.	*Jer.*
from thence will I bring thee down," is the utterance of Jehovah.	from thence will I bring thee down," is the utterance of Jehovah.
5 If thieves came to thee, if marauders of the night (How art thou brought to naught!), would they not steal (only) till satisfied? if vintagers came to thee, would they not leave gleanings?	9 If vintagers come to thee, they will not leave gleanings; if thieves by night, they will destroy till satisfied.

(*b*) In the verses common to both writers there are none of the turns of speech to which Jeremiah is partial, whereas these are found in the immediate context in which the verses in question appear in his book.

Thus within the ten verses included in Jeremiah's prophecy against Edom (xlix. 7—22) that have no equivalent in Ob. 1—5, the following contain features which are met with elsewhere in Jer.:—

v. 8, *flee...turn back*; the same verbs are conjoined in xlvi. 5, 21, xlix. 24:

the time that I shall visit (or *the time of visitation*); see vi. 15, x. 15, xlvi. 21, l. 27, 31, cf. also xlviii. 44:

c. 13, accumulated synonyms expressive of conditions provoking contempt and scorn; see xxiv. 9, xxv. 9, 11, 18, xxix. 18, xlii. 18:

v. 17, *be astonished...hiss*; see xviii. 16, xix. 8, l. 13:

v. 18, *the overthrow of Sodom and Gomorrah*; see l. 40:

no man shall dwell therein; see xlix. 33, l. 40, li. 43:

v. 19, *the pride of Jordan*; see xii. 5, l. 44:

v. 20, *to purpose purposes* (or its equivalent); see xi. 19, xviii. 11, 18, xxix. 11, xlix. 30, l. 45:

the little ones of the flock; see l. 45:

v. 22, *fly as the eagle and spread out his wings*; see xlviii. 40.

This circumstance is even more decisive against the view that the verses in Ob. have been borrowed from Jer. than the one noticed under (*a*); for it is extremely improbable that a writer, in drawing upon another's work, should have selected from a single chapter just those verses which contain none of the original author's favourite expressions. If borrowing has occurred between the two writers, the fact that the verses in dispute do not exhibit any of Jeremiah's phrases amid a context which has several is only consistent with the supposition that they have been derived by Jeremiah from Obadiah.

(ii) It is, however, almost equally clear that Ob. is not the original source of the verses in question. This conclusion is suggested, to begin with, by the fact that only these five verses recur in Jer., although the subject-matter of them (the sin of Edom and its retribution) is further pursued by Obadiah; and the remainder of his book would have afforded material for additional borrowing if he had been previously drawn upon.

But it is decisively confirmed by an investigation of the metre in which the verses common to the two writers are composed. The passage Jer. xlix. 14—16, 9 consists of almost perfect elegiac (or *Kinah*) lines (see p. cxlii). So slight are the departures from this rhythm that it is reasonable to infer that the original passage was constructed according to this metrical scheme, and that any irregularities discernible in the existing text are due to some slight corruption. In the corresponding passage in Ob. the same metrical system can be detected here and there (see *v.* 5ª); but in various places it is disorganized, partly by the absence of words needed to complete the metre, partly by the presence of words that are metrically superfluous, and are not required by the sense. Comparison between the two parallel sections affords means of reconstructing with much plausibility the original passage; and from such reconstruction it becomes tolerably clear that the version in Ob., though preserving more closely than the version of Jer. the probable *order* of the verses as they were at first arranged (p. xxxv), reproduces less accurately than Jer. the authentic form of the separate verses, and that consequently Ob. cannot be the source from which Jeremiah has borrowed.

(iii) There remains, then, the alternative that the writers have drawn upon a third source, namely an oracle by an earlier prophet. Of the use of portions of earlier prophecies by later writers there are several probable examples in the O.T. Apart from short quotations (such as Num. xxi. 28, 29, included in Jer. xlviii. 45, 46), instances of the incorporation of comparatively long passages are furnished by the identity of Is. ii. 2—4 with Mic. iv. 1—3, and the identity of Is. xv. 2—6 and xvi. 6—11 with Jer. xlviii. 29—34, 36, and in each of these cases the passage common to the two writers named has almost certainly been derived by both of them from a prior author[1]. A reason for the use by Obadiah of the work of a preceding prophet may be readily suggested. He witnessed, as he believed, the fulfilment of the earlier prediction, and quoted it in connection with his own description of the event which confirmed its truth.

---

[1] In the N.T. an instance of the use of an earlier work by two later writers is furnished by the appropriation of Mk. in whole or in part by both Mt. and Lk., though they have handled it with great freedom.

CHAPTER III.

The Date.

The book of Obadiah having been provisionally analysed into the three sections (I) *vv.* 1—5; (II) *vv.* 6—14, 15^b; (III) *vv.* 15^a, 16—21, of which (I) has been shewn to be derived in all probability by the author of (II) from an earlier writer, it remains to consider more at length the justification of this analysis, and the date to which the several sections can most plausibly be assigned.

(I) In *vv.* 1—5, an oracle from Jehovah announces, at a time when a confederacy is being organized against Edom, that it is the Divine purpose to humiliate that nation; that its pride in its security among inaccessible rocks is ill-grounded; and that its spoliation and destruction will be complete. The tenses vary between perfects and futures; but future tenses are predominant; and the general impression produced by the passage is that it is not a description of events that have already happened but a prophecy relating to the future. Owing to the vagueness of the language, there is no positive indication of the time when it was written; but there is some negative evidence which seems to exclude a post-exilic date. The self-confident attitude attributed to Edom suggests that the country was at the time unmolested and prosperous; and the fact that a Hebrew prophet was prompted to predict for it disaster seems most naturally explained by assuming that some success had recently been gained by the Edomites to the prejudice of its neighbour, but the prophecy does not breathe the feeling of bitter resentment marking the rest of the verses down to *v.* 15, and evoked by the conduct of the Edomites on the occasion of the overthrow of Jerusalem in 587. The situation implied would correspond to the condition produced through the Edomites' re-acquisition of their independence in the reign of Jehoram (2 Kgs. viii. 20—22)[1]; or by their recovery, in the reign of Ahaz, of the harbour of Elath, which had so far remained in Jewish hands, but was then restored to Edom by Rezin of Syria (2 Kgs. xvi. 6, marg.), on which occasion, according to 2 Ch. xxviii. 17, the Edomites entered Judah and carried off some of its inhabitants as prisoners. Consequently, though the precise date of the prophecy must be a matter of conjecture, it may be regarded with some confidence as pre-exilic.

---

[1] Some have thought that the Edomites may have participated in the raid made by the Philistines and the Arabians related in 2 Ch. xxi. 16, 17.

(II) The section comprised in *vv.* 6—15 (or, in strictness, 6—14, 15[b], for 15[a] belongs to the succeeding section) must have been composed at a date subsequent to the later of two events:—(1) the forcible entry made into Jerusalem by an unnamed foreign people on an occasion when the Edomites had exulted at the capture of the city and taken part in the accompanying rapine and slaughter (*vv.* 11—14); (2) the ravage of Edom at a later period by an inroad of tribes previously friendly, in which the Jews (as represented by the writer) saw a meet recompense for the wrong previously perpetrated by the Edomites on themselves. The first of these two events is generally identified with the capture of Jerusalem by the Babylonians, when the Edomites exhibited the utmost delight at the calamity sustained by their kinsmen, and in consequence created in the Jews feelings of the most intense indignation. Jerusalem, indeed, is recorded in the O.T. to have been entered by an enemy no less than five times[1]; but the only occasions on which Edomites are known to have participated in, or rejoiced at, the assault were the last two—the siege and capture of the city by the Babylonians, first in 597 and again in 587, as related in 2 Kgs. xxiv., xxv. Both times the capital was plundered, and numbers of the citizens deported; but manifestly it is the second of these occasions, rather than the first, that suits the language of Obadiah best. The account in 2 Kings, indeed, does not enumerate Edomites in connection with the overthrow of the Jewish capital; but their presence and the malicious satisfaction which they expressed are attested by Ps. cxxxvii. 7, Ezek. xxxv. 5 (cf. xxv. 12, Lam. iv. 21, 22). The magnitude of the disaster, and the bitter resentment felt by the Jews towards the Edomites for the malevolence which they then displayed, answer sufficiently closely to the description in Obadiah (especially the expressions in *vv.* 12, 13) for this event to be accepted as the one which the writer had in mind when he discerned in the Edomites' conduct towards his countrymen an explanation of their own subsequent misfortune.

But though there is a general agreement that this section of Obadiah has in view the events of 587, it has not been universally admitted that it was written *after* them. Caspari, for instance, holds that it is a *prediction* of the fall of Jerusalem (the past tenses in *vv.* 11, 16 being explained as prophetic perfects). He is led to this conclusion partly by the position of Obadiah in the Canon after Joel and Amos (see p. xxxii),

---

[1] See (*a*) 1 Kgs. xiv. 25, 26, 2 Ch. xii. 2—9; (*b*) 2 Ch. xxi. 16, 17; (*c*) 2 Kgs. xiv. 8—14, 2 Ch. xxv. 17—24; (*d*) 2 Kgs. xxiv. 10—16; (*e*) 2 Kgs. xxv. 1—21.

by the supposed use of Obadiah by Jeremiah (see p. xxxv), and by the absence of any indebtedness to confessedly post-exilic writings like Is. xxxiv. and 3 Is. lxiii. But he lays most stress on the two facts (*a*) that warnings to the Edomites (such as those contained in *vv.* 12—14) to refrain from a certain line of conduct are unintelligible if the deeds against which they are cautioned had already been committed by them; and (*b*) that the denunciation of the Edomites alone for their crime against Judah is irreconcilable with the supposition that the passage was written after the Fall of Jerusalem, it being inconceivable that the writer could then have ignored the Babylonians, the chief perpetrators of his country's ruin, or confined his attention to those who took only a subordinate part in the tragedy. In connection with the latter of these two contentions, it is argued that, if the writer lived before 587, the features manifested by the prophecy are natural enough; for whereas prophetic foresight might not enable him long beforehand to specify the destined chastisers of his country except by the vague description of "strangers," he could easily anticipate the attitude of the Edomites on the occasion, owing to the hostility which they had displayed towards the Jews previously (cf. Am. i. 11). With regard to the argument based on the imperatives in *vv.* 12—14, though the use of them may be admitted to be remarkable, it can be fairly accounted for by the writer's imaginative power: he transports himself into the past, envisages the scene of the city's capture, and dramatically addresses the Edomites as though he saw them in the act of doing what he knew they actually had done. In respect of the omission of all mention of the Babylonians, the argument is of still less weight. Even in a writing composed shortly after 587 there would be nothing surprising if, in a denunciation of Edom for participating with foreigners in despoiling a kindred people, the foreigners in question should not be alluded to by name, for the guilt of the accomplices was independent of that of the principals in the crime, and it could occupy the writer's thoughts to the exclusion of anything else (cf. Ezek. xxv. 12—14, xxxv., Lam. iv.). But the circumstance becomes perfectly natural if (as is probable for reasons given below) the composition of this section of Ob. was separated from the events of 587 by a considerable interval, during which the Babylonian empire had perished, whereas the Edomites had still a country.

The occasion of the Edomites' display of malice towards the Jews is easier to determine than the later occasion which brought a nemesis upon them for their misconduct and upon which the writer looks back with satisfaction (*v.* 7). A conquest of Edom shortly after 587 by the Babylonians with whom the Edomites had co-operated previously would satisfy Obadiah's language in *v.* 7, and cannot be dismissed as impossible. Not long before 587 Edom was seemingly leagued with Moab, Ammon, Tyre, and Zidon (see Jer. xxvii. 3, 6); and since, according to Josephus (*Ant.* x. 9, § 7), Moab and Ammon were subdued by the Babylonian Nebuchadrezzar when he invaded Egypt in 582, five years after his subjugation of Judah, Edom may have undergone the same fate. The absence, however, of any explicit historic evidence that Nebuchadrezzar invaded and spoiled Edom on the occasion alluded to renders this explanation very doubtful. Much more may be said in favour of the view which identifies the calamity suffered by Edom with some phase in the dispossession of its people by the Nabatæans, who were in occupation of Edom in 312 B.C. (see Diod. Sic. xix. 94). The Nabatæans are described as Arabs by Josephus (*Ant.* i. 12, § 4, xiii. 1, § 2, cf. Strabo, xvi. 2, § 34, 4, §§ 2, 21); and the terms applied in Ob. 7 to the assailants of Edom would probably be as appropriate to them as to the Babylonians. Their establishment at Petra, the Edomite capital, at the date mentioned is likely to have involved the expulsion of large numbers of the native inhabitants. At the time when the book of Malachi was composed (*circ.* 450 B.C.) Edom had already undergone desolation (see Mal. i. 3, 4); and though the devastators of the country are not named, it is probable that they were the Arabian people just referred to. If this identification is correct, it is clear that the Edomites had already suffered from the inroads of the Nabatæans by the middle of the 5th century. And the condition which raids would produce seems adequate to explain the language in which the calamity experienced by the Edomites is described by Obadiah. If his words are not unduly pressed, and allowance is made for rhetoric, his description is scarcely too dark for the state of a land ravaged by marauders, even though it had not permanently passed into their hands. How early the Nabatæans had begun to raid Edom cannot be ascertained; but there are indications that the Edomites were pushing northwards into Judah shortly after 587 (see Ezek. xxxv. 10, xxxvi. 5). This movement may have been due to hostile pressure already driving some of the inhabitants of Edom to seek a new abode. Knowledge of the cause that forced the Edomites to leave their own country could not fail to become disseminated among the neighbouring peoples; and to a Jewish prophet their expulsion from their homes would seem a fit requital for the injury which no long while before they had inflicted on their neighbours. There thus seems to be no serious difficulty in the way of assigning the heart of the book to the interval between 587 and the date of Malachi (the middle of the 5th century), though it is quite possible that it may have been composed during the half-century following Malachi.

(III) The final section (vv. 15ᵃ, 16—21) predicts renewed calamity for Edom. But the passage differs in tenor from what has gone before. In the previous part of the book Edom alone is in mind, but here the punishment of the Edomites is viewed as an episode in a Divine visitation upon the nations at large, who are all represented as destined to drain the cup of Jehovah's vengeance. And this change of outlook, coupled with the circumstance that the 2nd pers. sing. is here replaced by the 2nd pers. plural, suggests the work of another author. This conclusion is confirmed by a difference in style. The vigorous and varied diction of the anterior portion of the book gives place to a much less impressive phraseology; the tone is less animated and the figures of speech are trite. The spirit in which the author writes is less that of a Prophet than of an Apocalyptist. The situation, too, in which the section was written differs to some extent from that implied previously. When it was composed, the Edomites were apparently settled in the *Negeb* (or South) of Judah and were a source of annoyance to their Jewish neighbours. But there is no expectation of punishment impending over the Edomite wrongdoers from any contemporary power: the writer looks for retribution to fall upon them in a general judgment which will come on the whole heathen world from Jehovah, and after which the exiles of both branches of Israel will regain their former possessions, and consume, like a fire, their injurious neighbours. Any precise determination of the date is unfortunately precluded by the absence of all references to contemporary conditions admitting of definite identification. The one supplied by the mention of Sepharad as a locality where there was a body of Jewish exiles is useless, since the place intended is extremely doubtful. The view that the writer has in mind a settlement of Jews in Lydia and Phrygia established by Antiochus the Great (224—187), as related by Josephus (*Ant.* XII. 3, § 4), and that the section consequently was written at a comparatively late date in the Greek period is difficult to reconcile with the inclusion of the book among the Twelve Minor Prophets, for allusion is made to these in Ecclus. xlix. 10, so that the collection must have been completed before 180 B.C. and the separate books in it written still earlier. And a further fact opposed to this late origin is the circumstance that Ob. is probably quoted in Joel, for in

Joel ii. 32 (Heb. iii. 5) the words "In mount Zion and in Jerusalem there shall be those that escape, *as Jehovah hath said*" seem to be a citation of the prediction in Ob. 17, "In mount Zion there shall be those that escape." If really so, then a date in the latter half of the Persian period, perhaps between 450 and 400 B.C., will be the latest to which this part of the book can with any plausibility be attributed. The writer appears to include himself among, or at least to be in contact with, a body of Israelites referred to in *v.* 20 (*this host* or *fortress*), though who they are is quite obscure.

Little or no light is thrown upon the date of Ob. by the language in which it is written; and though there is some difference of style between the various parts of it, there are virtually no indications, in the words or forms used in them, that they were composed at widely separated periods. There are, indeed, certain words that occur only here, or are very rare, or are used here in a sense not found elsewhere. Such are (rocky) *clefts* (*hăghăvim*), *hidden treasures* (*matspōnim*), *snare* (*māzōr*), *slaughter* (*keṭel*), *disaster* (*nōcher*), *crossway* (*perek*), *swallow down* (*lū'*). But ἅπαξ λεγόμενα are met with in most books of the O.T.; and of the rare words enumerated above *keṭel* is the only one that is at all suggestive of a late period in the Hebrew language.

It will be convenient to summarize here the conclusions reached in regard to the probable dates of the several divisions of the book.

I.   Verses 1—5, eighth century?
II.   „   6—14, 15[b], middle of the fifth century.
III.   „   15[a], 16—21, last half of the fifth century.

As the book comprises sections seemingly proceeding from three distinct writers separated in point of time, it is uncertain to which of them the name *Obadiah* properly belongs. If it is worth while to hazard a conjecture, it is perhaps most likely that the book is called after the prophet who composed the portion of it comprised in *vv.* 6—14, 15[b] and who incorporated the prophecy (*vv.* 1—5) of a predecessor; and to whose own work there was afterwards appended an oracle delivered at a subsequent date, perhaps by a Judæan prophet resident somewhere within the former territory of the Ten Tribes, if not in the actual neighbourhood of Samaria (see p. 85).

CHAPTER IV.

EDOM AND THE EDOMITES.

THE region to which the name *Edom* was especially applied was the mountain-ridge, red in colour, called Seir, on the east side of the Arabah, i.e. the deep gorge that extends from the southern extremity of the Dead Sea to the gulf of Akaba (see Gen. xxxii. 3, xxxvi. 8). But at the time of the Exodus and the Wanderings of Israel the Edomites also occupied the plateau on the west side of the Arabah, as far as Kadesh (which is described as being on the border of Edom (Num. xx. 16, JE)). Hence Edom stood in the way of any approach from the Sinaitic peninsula towards the country east of the Jordan; and accordingly the Israelites collectively, or at least some of the tribes, had to compass the Edomite territory. On the north Edom was contiguous to Moab, being separated from it probably by the *Wâdy-el-Ahsa*, which is usually, though not with certainty, identified with the torrent Zered (Dt. ii. 13). On the south it extended to the northern end of the gulf of Akaba, where Elath served as a port. In length it did not exceed 100 miles; in breadth its limits are less easily defined, but its greatest extent from east to west probably fell considerably short of 50 miles, and it doubtless varied at different periods. Its physical features are diversified. Though Seir consists in the main of bare cliffs, which rise to an average elevation of 2000 ft., these are cut by glens and ravines capable of producing abundant vegetation; and the name itself ("hairy") is probably due to the brushwood covering it. "The country (writes Professor Palmer) is extremely fertile, and presents a favourable contrast to the sterile region on the opposite side of the Arabah. Goodly streams flow through the valleys, which are filled with trees and flowers; while on the uplands to the east, rich pasture lands and cornfields may everywhere be seen. With a peaceful and industrious population it might become one of the wealthiest, as it is certainly one of the most picturesque, countries in the world[1]." Hence it is possible that the ambiguous language of Isaac's Blessing upon Esau in Gen. xxvii. 39—40, which is generally regarded as descriptive of Edom, is to be understood in a sense as favourable as that of *v.* 28; and there still exist many traces of former cultivation. On the other hand, at the present day the condition of the country exhibits the inevitable result of insecurity and

---

[1] Quoted in Harper, *The Bible and Modern Discoveries*, p. 343.

neglect. "The gifts of nature are lavished in vain, and what little corn the half-savage Fellahin can produce serves scarcely any other purpose than to excite the cupidity of the Bedawîn." In ancient times the principal towns were Sela (or Petra) and Bozrah (the modern Busairah), whilst others that are mentioned are Dinhabah and Avith.

The people that inhabited the country before the occupation of it by the Edomites were the Horites (Gen. xiv. 6, Dt. ii. 12). The name is generally taken to mean "cave-dwellers," from *hōr*, "a hole," though Sayce[1] connects it with the root *hăvar*, "to be white," and supposes that it designated a white race in contrast to the "red"-skinned Edomites who succeeded them. The cliffs, which are a conspicuous feature of mount Seir, abound in caves ; and the Horites were presumably an aboriginal race that had in these their dwellings. They were subsequently dispossessed or absorbed by the Edomites, whom Hebrew traditions represent as descended from Esau, a brother of their own eponymous ancestor Israel or Jacob, the father of the brothers being Isaac, the son of Abraham. It is not necessary to consider here whether any historic personalities lie behind these names; but it is generally agreed that the relationship represented as subsisting between the patriarchs that figure in early Hebrew tradition reflects current beliefs respecting the ties of kinship, near or remote, uniting the tribes or peoples reputed to have sprung from them. On this principle the Israelites were more closely connected with the Edomites than with the Moabites and Ammonites, for whereas the two latter peoples are depicted as sprung from Lot, Abraham's nephew, Israel and Edom are both described as descended from Abraham's son Isaac. Of Isaac's children, Esau, the traditional progenitor of the Edomites, is represented as the elder, a circumstance probably embodying the conviction that the Edomites were firmly established in their historic home in mount Seir before the Israelites were settled in Canaan. The belief implied in the traditions preserved in the book of Genesis that Edom was more nearly related to Israel than either Moab or Ammon finds confirmation in the fact that, although all three nations were generally hostile to the Israelites, yet it was Edom which by its conduct on the occasion of the Fall of Jerusalem evoked the bitterest resentment. The view that the tradition, by describing Esau as the elder brother, meant to imply that the Edomites were the older nation, is borne out by the notices of their early history. They were in possession of mount Seir and the adjoining

---

[1] See *HCM.* p. 204.

district on the west of the Arabah when the Israelites were yet in a nomadic stage of civilization; and they were in the enjoyment of a settled form of government before their kinsmen attained to such. They appear to have been ruled first by tribal or clan chiefs (termed in the R.V. *dukes*, from the Vulg. *duces*), and subsequently by kings. These kings can scarcely have reigned by hereditary right, since, in the list of them given in Gen. xxxvi. (if this is trustworthy), none is represented as the son of his predecessor; and it is possible that the monarchy was elective. But in view of the fact that a succession of *chiefs* both preceded and followed the kings, it seems more likely that the rule of a single sovereign was dependent upon the ability of some particular chief to become paramount over the rest. The beginnings of monarchy in Edom seem to have occurred when Israel was still wandering in the desert, if importance can be attached to the circumstance that in the "Song of Miriam," on the occasion of the Exodus, allusion is made to the "chiefs" of Edom, whereas when the Israelites were preparing to enter Canaan, it was to a king that application was made for leave to traverse the Edomite territory. But though Edom reached a settled condition before Israel, the ancient blessing of Isaac, predicting that Esau should live by his sword, probably reflects the warlike and predatory habits of the people, who depended largely for their support upon the chase and upon plunder.

As regards the language of Edom the only evidence is that supplied by the few names of persons and places that have been preserved. These confirm the inference, drawn from the traditional relationship subsisting between Edom and Israel, that it resembled Hebrew, since most of the names admit of being interpreted from Hebrew roots.

Of the religion of Edom little is known. Among the names of Edomite gods mentioned in inscriptions or deduced from other sources are *Hadad* (not definitely known as an Edomite deity, but inferred to have been such from the royal names *Hadad* and *Benhadad* (cf. *Benaiah*)), *Kaush* (occurring in certain seemingly theophoric names like *Kaush-malak, Kaush-gabr*) and *Koze* (Jos. *Ant.* xv. 7, § 9). From the proper name *Obed-edom*, it may be concluded with some plausibility that *Edom* was also the appellation of a deity, who was presumably worshipped by the Edomites; but there appears to be no independent evidence to corroborate the conclusion. The occurrence of various animal names amongst the Edomites in Gen. xxxvi., such as *Aiah* (vulture), *Achbor* (mouse), and *Zibeon* (hyæna), suggests that there once prevailed in Edom a totemistic stage of culture, in which families and clans were believed to be akin to certain animals after which they were called (see p. 120).

As has been already said, the occupation of mount Seir by the Edomites barred the way of Israel when the latter, either in whole or in part, attempted to enter Canaan from the east. The sources of the Pentateuch give conflicting accounts of the relations between the two peoples on the occasion. According to the principal narrative, the Israelites asked for leave to cross Edom, but being refused, avoided any violation of it by making a détour to the south, traversing its western border as far as the head of the gulf of Akaba, and then turning northward along its eastern frontier (Num. xx. 14—21, xxi. 4, JE). But there are other passages which imply no such circuit, but represent the Israelites as crossing the intervening country from mount Hor (probably Jebel Madurah, N.W. of Ain Kadîs) to the borders of Moab (see Num. xxxiii. 37 f., P, cf. xxi. 4ᵃ, 10, 11, P), though there is nothing to decide whether they are conceived as having done this by permission of the Edomites or whether they pursued a route which at the time was outside the Edomite territory. During the conquest of Canaan and the period of the Judges nothing is recorded of the relations between the two peoples. But there are not lacking indications that there was some intermingling between them. Othniel, one of the earliest Judges, is described as a son of Kenaz, and the latter is represented as a grandson of Esau. The Kenizzites were settled in Judah, the Chronicler appearing to reckon Kenaz among the descendants of Judah (1 Ch. iv. 13, 15); and as there is reason to think that Judah entered Canaan not from the east but from the south, it is probable that there was some intermixture between Israelite and Edomite clans during the wanderings of the former in the wilderness. After kingly government was established in Israel and the people began to increase in strength and to extend their borders, it was inevitable that grounds of quarrel should arise between them and their neighbours. The Mediterranean seaboard was closed by the Philistines (p. 82); and if the Israelites were to possess a port, it was on the Red Sea littoral that they had to find it. Hence a protracted struggle, marked by varying fortune, ensued between the two nations. Saul is recorded to have been successful over Edom (1 Sam. xiv. 47); and the country was subjugated by his successor David (2 Sam. viii. 13, mg., 1 Ch. xviii. 11, 12). A great victory was obtained in the Valley of Salt (presumably the plain immediately to the south of the Dead Sea) and the country was garrisoned. But the success of Joab, David's general, cannot have been as great as is represented in 1 Kgs. xi. 15, 16, where he is alleged to have exterminated the Edomite male population; for the Edomites even in the next reign seem to have given much trouble to the conquerors. Hadad, of the Edomite royal house, who had married an Egyptian princess, after having taken refuge in Egypt during the invasion of his country in David's reign, returned when Solomon ascended the Israelite throne, and (according to 1 Kgs. xi. 25, LXX.) became king of Edom. But Solomon (who included Edomite women in his harem) was able to retain Ezion-geber, a port on the gulf of Akaba, and was then in a position to take part in the profitable trade to Ophir (variously considered to have been situated on the east coast of Africa, in S.E. Arabia (cf. Gen. x. 29), in India, or even in the Malay peninsula); and it seems probable that Hadad's restoration to the throne of Edom did not secure for the country complete independence. After the disruption of the Hebrew kingdom, Judah succeeded in maintaining suzerainty over Edom for some period. According to 1 Kgs. xxii. 47 there was no king in Edom during the reign of Jehoshaphat (who, like Solomon, made use of Ezion-geber) and the land was governed by a deputy. In the reign of Jehoram, however, Edom seems once more to have had a native ruler, for an Edomite king took part in the war conducted by Ahab of Israel and Jehoram against Moab (2 Kgs. iii. 9); but he was probably at the time a vassal. Later in Jehoram's reign the Edomites recovered their independence (2 Kgs. viii. 20—22), but they seem to have been unable to eject the Judæans from Elath, a port a little to the south of Ezion-geber; and it was not until the reign of Ahaz that it was regained for them by Rezin of Syria (2 Kgs. xvi. 6ᵇ mg.). According to the Chronicler (2 Ch. xxviii. 17), the Edomites took advantage of the attack of Rezin upon Ahaz to invade the southern borders of Judah and carry away captives. The struggle for national freedom which this history implies was doubtless marked by much savagery, and the prophet Amos denounces Edom for its relentlessness (Am. i. 11). The Edomites not only pursued their own wars mercilessly, but bought captive Judæan slaves from the neighbouring Philistines (Am. i. 6). Their conflict with Judah did not cease with the acquisition of their independence in the reign of Jehoram, for the Judæan king Amaziah, about fifty years later, attempted to reconquer the country, inflicted a severe defeat upon its people, and captured Sela, which he called Joktheel. Elath, as has been said, still remained in Judæan hands and must have been accessible from Judah by a secure road, if it was to be of any value; so that possibly the part of Edom which had effectually thrown off Judæan authority was small. But with the loss of Elath in the reign of Ahaz Judæan sovereignty over Edom seems to have come to an end; and even Hezekiah, though he was stronger than his father, is not recorded to have attempted the re-subjugation of the country. In point of fact all the small Palestinian states were now menaced by Assyria; and the names of Edomite kings appear with those of others in the cuneiform inscriptions who paid tribute to Assyrian rulers. Kaush-malak was tributary to Tiglath-Pileser III (744—727), Malik-ram to Sennacherib (705—681), and Kaush-gabr to Esarhaddon (681—668) and Asshur-banipal (668—626).

It might have been expected that a common danger would have lessened the animosity prevailing between two nearly-allied peoples; but such was not the case when the Babylonians, having aided in the destruction of the Assyrian empire in 612, attacked Judah early in the following century. Although the menace from Babylon led for a moment to an attempt on the part of Edom and others of the states bordering on Judah to form a coalition with the latter for combined defence (Jer. xxvii. 3), nothing was effected; and when in 587 Nebuchadrezzar, the king of Babylon, took Jerusalem, the Edomites not only manifested the utmost satisfaction at the overthrow of their neighbours, but, according to the statements of Judæan writers, behaved with great barbarity to the unhappy Jews, sharing both in the plunder of the city and in the slaughter of its citizens. Their conduct on this occasion made an abiding impression on the surviving Jewish people; predictions of calamity for Edom and the Edomites are frequent in post-exilic prophecies (3 Is. lxiii. 1—6, Joel iii. 19, Mal. i. 4); and even the author of Ecclus., writing about 180 B.C., displays his hatred for them, if the Heb. of l. 26 (see mg.) preserves a correct reading. And not only did the Edomites exult over the Fall of Jerusalem, but they occupied part of the territory of Judah, settling in the *Negeb* (or South) and taking possession of Hebron, which remained in their hands (whether continuously or not, does not appear) until the time of the Maccabees. Their inroad into the south of Judah, however, was probably due to disasters of their own. The Nabatæans (see p. xli) are related by Diodorus Siculus (XIX. 98) to have been in occupation of Petra in 312 B.C.; and this seizure of their capital must have resulted in the withdrawal of numbers of Edomites from their own country into neighbouring lands; amongst which Judah, now thinly populated, would offer many advantages as a place of refuge. Here they remained

w. *d*

until the rise of the Maccabees and the renewal of a warlike spirit among the Jews, when they were expelled from the places which they had seized. Judas Maccabæus inflicted a severe defeat upon them at Akrabattine (in the neighbourhood of the ascent of Akrabbim, south of the Dead Sea) and likewise attacked them successfully at Hebron (1 Macc. v. 3, 65). John Hyrcanus in 128 B.C. drove them from Adora and Mareshah (Jos. *Ant.* XIII. 9, § 1, *B. J.* I. 2, § 6), and so completely subjugated them that he was able to impose upon them acceptance of the Jewish Law and the rite of circumcision. Edom thus became amalgamated with Judah; and it was by a family of Edomite origin that the Jews were eventually ruled. This was the house of Herod, which first became prominent under Antipater, who was made governor of Edom (called in Greek *Idumæa*) by Alexander Jannæus (104—78). His son, likewise named Antipater, was appointed procurator of Judæa by Julius Cæsar, and was the father of Herod the Great. The latter was made king of Judæa by the Roman senate; and after Actium (39 B.C.) received from Octavianus an extension of his dominions by the inclusion of Trachonitis. One of his sons, Herod Antipas, became, under his father's will, tetrarch of Galilee and Peræa, and married a daughter of Aretas, king of *Arabia Petræa* (the title by which the kingdom of Edom was known to the Romans). The country was devastated by Simon of Gerasa shortly before the siege of Jerusalem by Titus (Jos. *Ant.* XVI. 8, § 5; 14, § 4; XVIII. 2, § 1; *B. J.* IV. 9, § 7). Its independence came to an end in 105 A.D., when the Roman emperor Trajan reduced it to a province, its capital Petra being re-named *Hadriana* (after Hadrian, the general who captured it, and who became Trajan's successor).

INTRODUCTION TO JOEL.

CHAPTER I.

THE TITLE AND CONTENTS.

THE book of Joel affords little information respecting its author. The *name* is not rare[1], and is usually interpreted to mean "Jehovah is God," being related to *Elijah* ("My God is Jehovah") as *Joab* ("Jehovah is father") is to *Abijah*. But though the name must have had for Jews the significance stated, it is questionable whether this was its original meaning, since the occurrence of it in certain Phœnician inscriptions throws some doubt on its connection with *Jehovah*[2]. Nothing is known concerning the prophet; and the only information obtainable about the period in Hebrew history which witnessed his prophetic activity has to be inferred from the internal evidence of the book. Even the precise form of his father's name is uncertain, since the Hebrew gives it as *Pethuel*, whereas the Versions have *Bethuel*[3] or *Bathuel* (see p. 88). He is said by Epiphanius to have belonged to the tribe of Reuben; but he must in any case have been a resident at Jerusalem, and was identified with its interests (ii. 1, 15, 23, iii. 1, 16, 17, 20), since he not only repeatedly refers to that city, but also speaks of the offerings made in the Temple, and of the ministrations of the priests there. Where the term *Israel* occurs in the book (as in ii. 27, iii. 2, 16), it clearly refers to Judah.

The occasion of the prophecy which the book contains was the appearance in the land of extensive flights of locusts, accompanied by extreme drought, the two together involving an unprecedented destruction of vegetation, and consequent scarcity and distress for both man and beast. Through the ravages of the locusts the harvest, the vintage, and the other products of the soil were consumed; the supply of food for the support of life, and of cereal and wine offerings for the service of religion, was cut off ; and the devastation of the crops, the trees, and the herbage caused by successive swarms of the insects for several years

---

[1] It is the appellation of at least a dozen different persons in the O.T.: see (1) 1 Sam. viii. 2 (1 Ch. vi. 33), (2) 1 Ch. iv. 35, (3) 1 Ch. v. 4, (4) 1 Ch. v. 12, (5) 1 Ch. vii. 3, (6) 1 Ch. xi. 38, (7) 1 Ch. xxvii. 20, (8) Ezra x. 43, (9) Neh. xi. 9, (10) 1 Ch. vi. 36, but see mg., (11) 1 Ch. xv. 7, 11, (12) 2 Ch. xxix. 12.

[2] See Oxford Heb. Lex. p. 222: cf. Gray, *Heb. Proper Names*, p. 153.

[3] Cf. Gen. xxii. 23.

(ii. 25) had been augmented by a deficiency of the usual rain. This calamitous situation drew from the prophet counsel for the people's need. Interpreting the visitation as a prelude to, or perhaps as a phase of, Jehovah's Judgment Day, he urged his countrymen to seek, by sincere repentance and every token of contrition, to prevail upon their God to save them from the worst, and so preserve His worshippers from becoming the scorn of the heathen (ii. 17, mg.).

The book falls into three parts. The first section (i. 2—ii. 17) consists of a description of the sufferings of the country and of the resistless advance of the locusts, followed by the appeal of the prophet to both priests and people to make supplication to Jehovah to spare them. This first section is separated from the next by a brief narrative (ii. 18, 19^a), which is followed by a second address from the prophet (ii. 19^b—27). Between ii. 17 and the succeeding verse an interval of time must be supposed to have elapsed, during which Jehovah's acceptance of His people's prayer has been manifested by a turn for the better in their position. He has already sent rain; and in the second section (ii. 19^b—27) the prophet conveys God's promise that the locusts will be removed, and comforts the afflicted community with the prospect of such ample upplies of corn and other fruits of the earth as will make good what the insects had devoured. Upon this second section, which is limited to assurances of physical blessings, there ensues a third (ii. 28—iii. 21 (Heb. iii. 1—iv. 21)) containing predictions that at some later date Jehovah's material bounty will be followed by the gift of His Spirit, in virtue of which all classes of the people will become prophets. This will be a sign, amongst others, of the imminence of the judgment, from which those who shall invoke His name (i.e. the Jews) are to be saved in Jerusalem, but which will be executed upon the heathen. After the recall of those Jews who are still in exile, all nations will be brought together and be judged by God in the vicinity of Jerusalem for their treatment of Judah and its population. The Phœnicians and Philistines, in particular, because they have sold Jewish captives as slaves, will themselves be enslaved. The nations in general, assembled in the valley of Jehoshaphat, will there be trampled by Jehovah's hosts like grapes in a winepress. Such an issue will confirm the faith of the Jews in their God and in the future inviolability of their country. The fertility of its most barren localities will be ensured; Egypt and Edom are to be doomed to desolation for violence committed on the Jews; and Zion will become Jehovah's dwelling-place. With this section the book closes.

Though there is a break after ii. 17 which implies the lapse of an interval, the most important division of the book occurs at ii. 27, where there is a change of subject-matter, so that the book falls into two main halves, each with an interest of its own. The first half, i. 2—ii. 27, is concerned solely with the disasters occasioned by the locusts, with Jehovah's promise to remove the plague, and with His assurance of renewed fertility for the land, and material blessings for its people. But in ii. 28—iii. 21 the subject is exclusively a universal judgment, resulting in the deliverance and felicity of the Jews and the punishment of the heathen who have maltreated them. But though the two halves are thus contrasted in respect of their subject-matter, there is no real severance between them. The spiritual endowment of the Jews pre-announced in ii. 28—29 is the counterpart of the material plenty foretold in ii. 19—27 (note *afterward*, *v.* 28). And all through the section relating to the locust-plague (i. 2—ii. 17) the locusts are represented as forerunners of the Judgment Day, and their devastation of the land of Israel is described as accompanied by all the terrifying portents in nature that are destined to attend the predicted annihilation of the heathen (cf. ii. 1^b, 2, 10, 11 with ii. 31, iii. 15, 16). Such portents in the account of the locusts cannot be satisfactorily explained as due to features noticeable in connection with the actual movements of these insects, for though they constitute a very serious plague, they are not an unusual one in Palestine (cf. Dt. xxviii. 38, 1 Kgs. viii. 37, Am. iv. 9). There are, indeed, present in the prophet's narrative traits which, though startling, doubtless reflect a real experience of a locust-plague (e.g. ii. 3, 5, 6). Travellers relate that flights of locusts are sometimes so extensive that they even obscure the sky. But the shaking of earth and heaven, the pealing of thunder, and the withdrawal of the light of the sun, moon, and stars cannot be thus explained. And the fact that the same features figure both in a description of a destructive swarm of locusts and in a prediction of a comprehensive judgment executed upon the assembled heathen nations, thus bringing into relation with one another two events which to modern minds are incommensurate, has occasioned a very serious difficulty in the interpretation of the book, of which a solution has been sought in various ways.

CHAPTER II.

THE INTERPRETATION OF THE BOOK.

OF the two subjects with which the book is concerned, a disastrous plague of locusts in Palestine, and a Divine judgment upon the whole heathen world, the first is represented as actually being experienced when the work opens, and is looked back upon as past, as the book proceeds, whilst the second is still in the future, and its occurrence only predicted; yet the two are described in such similar language, that they appear to be successive stages of one process, the first as well as the second realizing the terrors of *the day of Jehovah*. From the terms used in ii. 1, 2, indeed, the locusts might be taken to be mere precursors of the Day of Jehovah, with its accompaniment of gloom and darkness, thunder and earthquake; but in ii. 10, 11 the same portentous signs in nature attend the locusts as are manifest when the heathen are gathered for their doom in the Valley of Decision (iii. 15, 16, cf. ii. 31). The fact that two events seemingly so different in character and importance are thus co-ordinated and treated as though they were on the same plane has been accounted for in different ways.

Formerly attempts were made to lessen the unnaturalness of painting in the same colours a destructive locust-plague and the final judgment upon the heathen, by interpreting the locusts allegorically. The successive swarms of locusts were explained as denoting successive invasions of heathen enemies; and since four distinct names are used for the locusts, they were taken to represent either assaults upon Palestine by four different nations[1], or four assaults at different times by the same nation[2]. Support for this view that the locusts are figures for hostile hosts was obtained from (*a*) the circumstance that the locusts are actually described as a *nation* and a *people* (i. 6, ii. 2); (*b*) the fact that they are termed Jehovah's *army* and *camp* (ii. 11, 25); (*c*) the charge preferred against them of overweening conduct, with its implication of moral accountability (ii. 20, end); (*d*) the epithet *the northerner* (ii. 20) applied to them, for whereas locusts rarely come to Palestine from a northerly direction (since the chief breeding-ground of the

---

[1] In the margin of Codex Marchalianus (6th century) of the LXX. there is a note to ii. 25 explaining the four names for locusts there given as standing for Αἰγύπτιοι, Βαβυλώνιοι, Ἀσσύριοι, Ἕλληνες, Ῥωμαῖοι, the Assyrians and Babylonians being perhaps reckoned together.

[2] Hilgenfeld took the four swarms to represent Persian invasions (1) under Cambyses, 525; (2) under Xerxes, 484; (3) and (4) under Artaxerxes I, 460—458 (see Van Hoonacker, *Les Douze Petits Prophètes*, p. 133).

swarms that devastate Western Asia is Arabia, whence they are carried to Palestine by *southerly* winds), it was from the north that the expected advance of the nations hostile to Israel was looked for (Jer. i. 14, Ezek. xxxviii. 6, 15, xxix. 2); (*e*) a possible translation of ii. 17 as given in the R.V. text, which interprets it as a prayer that the nations may not *rule over* Jehovah's people; (*f*) the magnitude of the terror and destruction caused by them, exceeding the results produced by real locusts; (*g*) the connection of the scourge with *the day of Jehovah*, which elsewhere is often associated with the invasion of Israel by hostile forces. But such an allegorical explanation is totally inconsistent with the natural significance of the writer's language. That the locusts are meant to be understood as real locusts and not as human invaders appears from the facts (*a*) that they are compared to an invading army, and therefore must be really distinct from such; (*b*) that the damage which they inflict is wrought solely through the destruction of *vegetation*; (*c*) that the comparison of their entry into the city to that of a thief, though suitable for a swarm of locusts penetrating into houses through the windows, is inappropriate for a victorious host; (*d*) that the manner of their destruction (ii. 20) is one which is not uncommon in the case of locusts (cf. Ex. x. 19), but is unnatural in the case of soldiers; (*e*) that the calamity occasioned by them is repaired by the revival of vegetation and the renewal of bountiful harvests; (*f*) that the Hebrew of ii. 17 admits of a different rendering (see mg.). The writer, indeed, depicting them poetically, invests them with certain human qualities, and even (if the last clause of ii. 20 is genuine, see p. 105) ascribes to them human responsibility. But human qualities are often attributed to the lower creatures by Hebrew writers (as well as by others), see Job xxxix. 7, 22, xl. 23; and it cannot seriously be doubted that Joel has in his mind not men but insects, which, though personified and likened to warriors, are meant to be understood literally. And though there is an element of hyperbole in his language, yet much of it is extraordinarily true to experience. Accordingly, the violence that is felt to be done to the plain sense of the book by the allegorical interpretation has led to another view, which maintains that whilst the locusts are intended to signify insects, they signify not ordinary but *supernatural* locusts, agents designed to take part in the execution of the Divine judgment in the Day of Jehovah (cf. Rev. ix. 3—11). But this explanation is a desperate expedient, and can only be justified if failure attends all other methods of rendering intelligible the relation of the locusts to the great and terrible Day.

More recently it has been sought to cut the knot by a process of critical analysis. One solution dissects the book into two different *works* occupied with distinct subjects, each part being the production of a separate author. A second solution is found in the hypothesis that the book consists of two originally disconnected *parts* of a single work, both proceeding, in the main, from the author whose name the book bears, but differing in subject-matter; and that the first has been assimilated to the second by a number of interpolations designed to interpret the locust-plague, which it describes, in the light of the comprehensive judgment predicted in the latter half of the book. Instances of such supposed interpolations are i. 15, ii. 1^b, 2^a, 6, 10, 11 (cf. iii. 14—16). These verses or parts of verses contain parallels with other books; and this fact has also been held to favour the view that they are insertions.

The question whether the features of the work really require either its partition, or the less disruptive hypothesis of extensive interpolation, is considered in the next chapter. The parallels between Joel and other O.T. writings, with the inferences to be drawn from them with regard to priority, are reserved for discussion in ch. IV. in connection with the date. If it can be shewn that the priority probably rests not with Joel but with the other writings that are compared with it, it need not follow that the passages in Joel have been introduced by an editor; they may reflect the influence of the earlier compositions upon the author himself. There is, however, in the book one group of verses, viz. iii. 4—8 (Heb. iv. 4—8), the authenticity of which is suspected for reasons of a special nature; and the arguments against its genuineness have considerable weight (see p. lx).

CHAPTER III.

THE UNITY OF THE BOOK.

THE disparity in importance between the subjects of the two halves of the book, and the occurrence in i. 2—ii. 27 (where the main interest is the scarcity caused by the locusts) of expressions which appear appropriate only to the catastrophe that is to overtake the heathen nations as predicted in ii. 28—iii. 21, have led (as has been seen) to the denial of its unity (i. 2—ii. 27 being the original work by a pre-exilic author and ii. 28—iii. 21 being a supplement by a post-exilic writer[1]),

---

[1] See Driver, *LOT.*[6] p. 311, note.

or to a theory of interpolations. Consideration, however, of the place which *dearth* occupies amongst Divine judgments in the O.T., and of the way in which the term *the day of Jehovah* is employed in the prophetic writings, will shew that the two sections of the book are not as irreconcilable as is represented. The similarity in the treatment of the subject-matter of the two parts becomes intelligible if the conditions of Eastern life at the time are adequately appreciated, and if the writer's language is not interpreted in too prosaic and literal a fashion.

In a country and in an age in which external trade cannot have been highly developed, and in which facilities for the transport of commodities from abroad must have been meagre, any occurrence which diminished or destroyed the harvest was bound to wear a serious aspect. Amongst a people to whom anything unusual presented itself as a direct intervention of the Deity, a succession of locust swarms, occasioning complete failure of the crops, must have inevitably appeared to be a Divine judgment upon the nation for its offences. And the light in which such a chastisement was regarded, and the gravity of the affliction which it involved, can be judged not only by the prominence given to instances of dearth in the historical books (Gen. xli. 54, 2 Kgs. iv. 38, Neh. v. 3), but also from the inclusion of it in the list of Jehovah's four sore judgments in Ezek. xiv. 12—23. From all of these—sword, famine, wild beasts, and pestilence—the land of Judah was liable to suffer during the period prior to the Exile. But from that event onwards Judah for many centuries enjoyed no national independence, being incorporated within the dominions of a great empire, first Babylon, and afterwards Persia, under whose rule, though it was humiliated, it was practically free from hostile ravage. Accordingly the sword was no longer to be feared in the same degree as during the pre-exilic age; and by the diminution, if not the elimination, of this source of danger, with its attendant evils of carnage and rapine, the calamities of famine and pestilence to which the country continued to be exposed, would become proportionately more impressive. And it is noteworthy that in the prophetic writings of the Persian period, like Haggai and Malachi, it is dearth which is represented as the penalty that punishes the Jews for their offences (Hag. i. 6 f., Mal. ii. 3). And if, as will be seen, Joel is not earlier than the Persian period, it is to be expected that the destruction of the harvest and vintage by an exceptionally severe visitation of locusts would inspire intense alarm, as indicating a terrible outbreak of Divine wrath against the people.

It was such a manifestation of Divine resentment that *the day of*

Jehovah was conceived by the prophets to usher in. In their expectation the Day was some decisive event bringing to a close the contemporary age which was so distressful to the pious among their countrymen, and introducing another age fraught with felicity for such as were deemed worthy to survive the impending crisis. But whilst the expression conveyed the idea of a conclusive judgment, settling, as it were, the long-standing account which Jehovah had with the sinful both within and outside Israel, its significance was not limited to a single experience. If the people, by opportune repentance, averted for a while the punishment that had threatened them, a relapse into sin might revive forebodings that had passed into the background. Moreover, a calamity that had already overtaken the nation for earlier transgressions could then be regarded by the conscience-stricken as a mere instalment of a retribution which in its full severity was still to come. And it is from this point of view that the references to *the day of Jehovah* in Joel i. 2—ii. 27 are to be understood. The acute distress caused by the plague of locusts was a symptom of the Divine anger, and a premonition of worse disasters yet in store. But the intensity of Jehovah's indignation was not, in fact, experienced. In consequence of the response to the prophet's summons to repentance, the destruction that menaced the people was removed; the fruits of the earth were once more granted to them; and the signs of the Day's approach, which had worn such a threatening aspect to Israel, disappeared. It was then predicted that these tokens would be succeeded by others, heralding the annihilation of Israel's enemies. For Jehovah's chastisement of His people did not terminate His relations with them. He remained their God; and now that they had amended their ways, their wrongs required to be redressed. The Day would therefore reach its consummation in vengeance upon the heathen who had so long exercised domination over them. The circumstance that the conception of the Day has a place in each of the two halves of the book is explained by its having two aspects; and the fact that in the second half it is regarded as finally to be realized in a future overthrow of all the heathen nations in the valley of Jehoshaphat is not inconsistent with an earlier phase being thought of as exemplified in the impoverishment of Israel through swarms of locusts. The view which considers the account of the plague of locusts and the prediction of the universal judgment upon the nations to proceed from the same author, but seeks to remove from the former all reference to the Day of Jehovah, does so because of the celestial portents represented as accompanying the locust swarms. In an imaginative picture of the destruction, by Jehovah in Person, of the heathen hosts, disturbances and convulsions of nature, the darkening of the luminaries, the quaking of the earth, and the trembling of the heavens, are deemed to be features which are not inappropriate; but their presence in even a poetic description of so ordinary an occurrence as a plague of locusts (though of abnormal proportions) is, it is contended, out of place. But this contention ignores the evidence for hyperbolical diction, inspired by religious emotion, which is supplied by Hebrew literature in general. Other prophets, in their representation of events as familiar as a locust-plague, or at least, of events not greatly transcending common experiences, afford ample parallels to the phrases used in Joel. The event, for instance, which is anticipated in Amos v. 20 is an invasion of the land by Assyria, and the deportation of its people to another country (v. 27); but the language used in connection with it suggests, if it is interpreted literally, an accompanying obscuration of the sky—"Shall not the day of Jehovah be darkness and not light? even very dark, and no brightness in it?" (v. 20, cf. Joel ii. 1, 2.) The writer of the prophecy contained in Is. xiii. 1—xiv. 23 has in view the overthrow of Babylon by the Medes; but he leads up to his account of the massacre of its inhabitants, in which neither age nor sex will be spared (probably no unprecedented feature in the sack of a hostile capital), by declaring "The stars of heaven and the constellations thereof shall not give their light: the sun shall be darkened in his going forth and the moon shall not cause her light to shine...I (Jehovah) will make the heavens to tremble, and the earth shall be shaken out of her place" (xiii. 10, 13). And, again, it is generally thought that the occasion which evoked Zephaniah's prophecy was the irruption into Asia of hordes of Scythians[1], but though the prophet anticipates a judgment for Judah through the instrumentality of such human agents, he describes it as "a day of darkness and gloominess, a day of clouds and thick darkness" (i. 15). There is thus in the language of Joel nothing that is seriously out of keeping with the habits of thought and modes of expression common amongst the prophetic writers generally. The celestial manifestations which are represented as attending certain disasters of no uncommon nature, though it may be of uncommon magnitude, are obviously figures of speech which were never meant by their authors to be interpreted with prosaic literalness.

Metaphors derived from gloom and darkness to express calamitous

---

[1] See Driver, *Minor Prophets*, II. p. 106 (C.B.).

and terrifying conditions are, indeed, so instinctive that the use of them by the prophets in connection with evils brought about by physical causes or human agents does not need to be enlarged upon. But it is not unlikely that the metaphors in question may also have had their source in eclipses, which, in an age ignorant of their origin, were calculated to be very alarming. The association, indeed, of the trembling of earth and heaven with darkness, in some of the passages just cited, may point to a further source from which the latter metaphor may come. The idea of a convulsion of the physical world is clearly drawn from the experience of an earthquake; and the memory of one which occurred in the reign of Uzziah of Judah was long preserved (Am. i. 1, 2 Zech. xiv. 5). And the clouds of dust raised by falling buildings, filling the atmosphere and discolouring the light of the sun, would add an additional element of horror; so that into mental pictures conjured up by the thought of an earthquake the obscuration of the luminaries might naturally enter. The purpose of these and similar figures of speech was to create in the mind of the hearer or reader conceptions of fear and agony, independently of any particular occasion. This is apparent from the analogous introduction of allusions to storm and hurricane into descriptions of martial conflict, as in Am. i. 14, 15 "I will kindle a fire in... Rabbah, and it shall devour the palaces thereof, with shouting in the day of battle, with a tempest in the day of the whirlwind: and their (the Ammonites') king shall go into captivity, he and his princes together." It is plain from such an example that there is nothing singular in the reference to the shaking of the earth and the darkening of the sky in Joel even in connection with the plague of locusts. The presence of these features in the prophet's description is designed merely to heighten the impression which he wishes to produce of the terrible nature of the calamity. The writer does not mean that the devastation caused by the locusts was actually accompanied by earthquake or eclipse, but that it was of a magnitude calculated to inspire alarm comparable to that arising from the latter causes, the expressions employed by him being customary, almost stereotyped, symbols of fearful conditions.

The only passage for the rejection of which as an insertion plausible reasons can be urged is iii. 4—8 (Heb. iv. 4—8). The passage is a denunciation of injuries committed upon the Jews by the people of Tyre, Zidon, and Philistia, and an assurance that such injuries will be avenged. The grounds for questioning its authenticity are as follows. (*a*) The passage is written in prose, whereas the context on either side is in verse. (*b*) It is a digression, interrupting the connection between the subject-matter of iii. 3 and of iii. 9 f. In these groups of verses the subject is the prediction of vengeance against all the nations; and the singling out, in the intervening section, of Phœnicians and Philistines for special denunciation disturbs the current of thought very awkwardly. (c) The statement that these people had sold Jews as slaves (v. 6) repeats a charge already directed in general terms against the nations at large (v. 3). (d) The retribution which is to overtake them differs from that which awaits the collective heathen nations. These are to be exterminated by Jehovah and His celestial hosts; whereas the two peoples who are the subjects of consideration in vv. 4—8 are to be sold into slavery, thereby undergoing the same experience which they had inflicted on others. The date of the interpolation need not be much later than that of the rest of the book: a suggestion as to the occasion which produced it is offered on p. 114.

CHAPTER IV.

THE DATE OF THE BOOK.

OF the time when the book was written there is given in the opening verse no indication, such as occurs in Isaiah and Jeremiah among the Major prophets, and Hosea, Amos, Micah, Zephaniah, Haggai, and Zechariah among the Minor. Nor is there any reference to the writer in the historical books, for though the name Joel occurs in them not infrequently (see p. li), there is nothing to identify the prophet with any of the individuals elsewhere mentioned. The circumstance that the prophecy is placed in the Canon between Hosea and Amos, which were both written in the 8th century, has been held to favour an early date; but the forward position amongst the Twelve occupied by certain prophetic works which for cogent reasons have come to be regarded as of relatively late origin (e.g. the book of Jonah) deprives the consideration of any importance. Moreover the arrangement by which Joel is followed by Amos can be explained by certain features in the two books; for Joel ends with the announcement of a comprehensive judgment upon all heathen nations, specific mention being made of Tyre, Zidon, Philistia, Egypt, and Edom; whilst Amos begins with a series of predictions against a number of heathen powers including Tyre, Philistia, and Edom; and moreover the phrase "Jehovah shall roar from Zion, and utter his voice from Jerusalem" occurs near the conclusion of Joel (iii. 16), and forms the opening of Amos. Consequently the date of the book has to be determined indirectly from internal evidence. This consists of

(i) the historical allusions found in the work, and the social and religious condition of the people which is implied; (ii) the parallels offered to its more distinctive ideas by other prophecies of more or less certain date; (iii) the literary relations between it and other writings, as either quoting or quoted; (iv) the style and diction.

(i) The occurrence which evoked the prophet's utterances was (as has been seen) a calamitous plague of locusts, productive of extreme dearth, an incident too common in the East to afford any clue. The places and peoples named in the course of the book are Tyre and Zidon, Philistia, the Greeks, the Sabeans, Egypt, and Edom; but the allusions are vague, nor are the references to contemporary internal conditions very illuminating. The relevant criteria may be conveniently divided into positive and negative.

(1) POSITIVE.

(*a*) The population of Judah is represented as scattered among the nations, who have parted among them its lands. One phrase, indeed, as commonly rendered, refers to the "captivity of Judah and Jerusalem," which Jehovah purposes "to bring again" (iii. 1); but as the expression is of somewhat doubtful significance, it cannot by itself be deemed decisively to imply the Exile or to predict the Return. But that the country had been occupied by invaders and its inhabitants (wholly or in part) had been despoiled and enslaved is clearly stated (iii. 2, 3).

(*b*) Tyre, Zidon, and Philistia are described as having taken away Jehovah's silver and gold (an expression which may mean the spoliation of the country in general or of the Temple in particular), and as having sold Jewish slaves to the Greeks (iii. 4—6).

(*c*) Egypt and Edom are threatened with desolation because they have done violence to the people of Judah and have shed innocent blood in their land.

(*d*) Mention is made of a locality called the valley of Jehoshaphat, recalling the king of that name who reigned *circ.* 876—851.

(*e*) The due maintenance of the Temple worship is a matter of deep concern, with which the prophet appears to sympathize (i. 9, 16); and the prospect of the suspension of the meal offering and the drink offering through the ravages of the locusts occasions great distress.

(*f*) In the national appeal to Jehovah for deliverance from the plague, the priests are described as taking the leading place.

(*g*) To render the appeal more effectual the prophet exhorts the people to hold a public fast.

(2) NEGATIVE.

(*a*) The kingdom of Northern Israel (the Ten Tribes) is not mentioned. The name Israel, indeed, occurs in the book (ii. 27, iii. 16), but the context makes it plain that the word is only a title for Judah (cf. p. 107).

(*b*) There is no allusion to the Syrians, the Moabites, the Ammonites, the Assyrians, the Babylonians, or the Persians.

(*c*) There is an absence of references to any special national vices. That the people are sinful, and that the locusts are viewed as a judgment for their sins, is implied by the exhortation to repentance; but neither idolatry, nor social injustice, nor gross sensuality is specified as having provoked Jehovah's anger.

(*d*) No mention is made of a contemporary king or of princes, the only officials alluded to (besides the priests) being perhaps *elders* (i. 14 mg., ii. 15 mg., though see p. 88).

Of the positive criteria here enumerated all, with one exception, can be shewn to be indecisive. The Phœnicians, who constituted the population of Tyre and Zidon, are nowhere recorded in the O.T. to have actually invaded Judæan territory (which their situation did not render easy), though in Jud. x. 12 the Zidonians are reckoned among the nations who had oppressed Israel before the time of Jephthah; so that the reference to them is most naturally interpreted to mean not that they had themselves participated in the robbery and enslavement of Judah, but that they had bought valuables and slaves from some unnamed despoilers and enslavers of the Jews, and disposed of them to more remote purchasers. The Phœnicians were known to the Hebrews as active traders as early as the reign of Solomon; and they were doubtless at all times ready to engage in the slave traffic. Tyre was expressly denounced in the 8th century by Amos (i. 9, 10), apparently for selling slaves (though not necessarily Jewish slaves) to Edom; and in the 6th cent. was described by Ezekiel (xxvii. 13) as purchasing "the persons of men and vessels of brass" in exchange for its own wares. Prophecies against both Tyre and Zidon also occur in Is. xxiii.[1], Jer. xxv. 22[2], 2 Zech. ix. 2—4[3]. The Philistines, on the other hand, were close neighbours of Judah, and a constant source of injury and annoyance from the time of the Judges onwards; and their successful raids were sure to have resulted in the enslaving of captives.

---

[1] Perhaps between 597 and 587 B.C.
[2] Between 626 and 586 B.C.
[3] Probably later than 333 B.C.

Their wars with Judah in the reigns of Saul and David before the Disruption, and in those of Jehoram and Ahaz after it, during the 9th and 8th centuries, are related in the books of Samuel and Kings. The people of Gaza, one of their cities, were denounced by Amos in the 8th cent. for carrying away captives from Jewish border towns and delivering them up (doubtless as slaves) to Edom, in the same manner as the Tyrians; the inhabitants of Ashdod took part in the hostility of Sanballat against Jerusalem in the time (5th century) of Nehemiah (Neh. iv. 7); and Philistines participated in attacks upon Judah as late as the 2nd century (1 Macc. iii. 41). Oracles against them were uttered by Isaiah (xiv. 28—32), Jeremiah (xlvii.), Zephaniah (ii. 4—5), Ezekiel (xxv. 15—17), Deutero-Zechariah (ix. 5—7), and the author of Is. xi. 11—14. Even the reference to the Greeks (*Javan,* the Ionians) cannot be regarded as pointing conclusively to a particular period, though it suggests a late rather than an early date. They are not named, indeed, in the O.T., before the time of Ezekiel (xxvii. 13, 19); but the early intercourse between Judah and Phœnicia makes it quite possible that the Jews were acquainted with the name of the Ionian Greeks long before the date when it is first found in their Scriptures. The Sabeans (Heb. *Shĕbhā'im,* a people of S. Arabia), mentioned as a distant nation to whom Phœnicians and Philistines in retaliation are to be sold into slavery, were known to the Hebrews in the time of Solomon; and allusions to them or to their country occur in Jer. vi. 20, Ezek. xxvii. 22, xxxviii. 13, 3 Is. lx. 6, Job i. 15, vi. 19. Egypt came into relation with Judah both at an early and at a late period. The memory of the oppression in Egypt was never erased from Jewish minds (cf. Mic. vi. 4, Ps. cv., cvi., cxiv.), and the Egyptians had invaded Judah both in the reign of Rehoboam (about the close of the 10th century) and in the time of Josiah (at the end of the 7th). Utterances against Egypt appear in Is. xxx., xxxi., Jer. xlvi., Ezek. xxix.—xxxi., and Is. xix. Edom, like Philistia, was continually hostile to Judah, and for some period was subject to it. The Edomites were conquered by David, revolted in the reign of Jehoram (851—843), carried away captives in the reign of Ahaz (according to 2 Ch. xxviii. 17), and earned the unrelenting hatred of the Jews by their malicious satisfaction on the occasion of the Fall of Jerusalem in 587 (p. xxxix). They are denounced in Am. i. 11, 12, Jer. xlix. 7—22, Ezek. xxv. 12—14, xxxv., Ob. 8—14, Is. xxxiv. 5, lxiii. 1 f., Mal. i. 2—4, Ps. cxxxvii. 7. Mention of the Valley of Jehoshaphat, even if it was originally named after that king, only proves that the book was written later than his reign, which has never been questioned;

whilst it is probable that in reality the name has only a symbolic
sense. In regard to the reference to the Temple and its worship, there
is nothing to determine whether the temple in the prophet's thoughts
is the first or the second. And if his attitude towards ritual observances contrasts with that of the First Isaiah (8th century), it likewise
contrasts with that of the Third Isaiah (5th century). Public fasting, too,
was a religious practice amongst the Hebrews in both early and late times
(1 Sam. vii. 6, 1 Kgs. xxi. 9, Neh. ix. 1). Nor were meal offerings and
drink offerings exclusively of late institution; for they are mentioned
together in the account of the sacrifices of Ahaz whose reign fell within
the 8th century (see 2 Kgs. xvi. 13).

The negative evidence is equally ambiguous. Inferences from silence
are generally precarious, and in regard to the kingdom of Northern
Israel, to Syria, to Moab, and to Ammon the writer of the book may
have had, from the immediate circumstances of his time, no occasion
to mention them. The case is rather different with his silence respecting
Assyria and Babylon. Each of these two states during its period of
supremacy in Western Asia so completely dominated the political
situation that it represented for contemporary Hebrew prophets the
hostile world-power of the age; and it is difficult to suppose that Joel
could fail to refer to one or the other if either was, at the time that
he wrote, prominent. But his silence is compatible with one of two
alternatives; he may have written *before* the rise of Assyria (*circ.* 850)
or *after* the fall of Babylon in 538. On the other hand, omission of all
reference to Persia is not inconsistent with the hypothesis that the
book was written during the period of Persian predominance, since the
Persians, from the seventh decade of the 6th century (when they replaced the Babylonians as Israel's lords) to about the middle of the
4th century, usually treated the Jews with leniency. The circumstance
that the prophet, though exhorting his countrymen to repent and
turn to their God, does not charge them with specific sins is noteworthy; but if it is an exception to the general practice of the prophets, it does not point to one age more than to another. But his
silence respecting any individual ruler of the country, in connection
with the appeal to Jehovah, really seems to *exclude* as a possible date
for the book *every period in pre-exilic times save one*. The only
occasion before the Exile when the absence of all reference to the king
is intelligible is the comparatively short interval in the 9th century
when the *de jure* ruler of Judah was a minor.

This occurred in the reign of Joash, the son of Ahaziah, who was

w.   e

7 years old at his accession (2 Kgs. xi. 21); and it is to this date
(a few years following 836) that the book has been assigned by many
scholars, who thus regard it as the earliest of the prophetical writings.
If this view is correct, the prominence given to the priests and the
absence of all mention of the sovereign is fairly accounted for, since
the chief authority during the minority of Joash rested with the high
priest Jehoiada. On the same assumption some other features of the
book likewise receive an explanation. Prior to the reign of Joash there
had taken place in the reign of Rehoboam the invasion of Judah by
the Egyptian Shishak (1 Kgs. xiv. 25, 26), which can be regarded as
occasioning the prediction of Egypt's desolation and the promise that
foreigners should pass through the land no more (iii. 17). Moreover,
although before the time of Joash Assyria had so far become a danger
to the Northern kingdom that Jehu paid tribute to it in 842, yet it
had not begun to menace Judah; and though the Syrians spoiled
Judah and Jerusalem in the reign of Joash himself, this was seemingly
after he had taken the control of the kingdom into his own hands, and
the event would thus befall later than the origin of the book, if this
was composed shortly after his accession. The revolt of Edom from
Judah in the reign of Jehoram (2 Kgs. viii. 20—22), in the course of
which, no doubt, many Jews were killed, would account for the retribution declared to be in store for the Edomites. Moreover in the
reign of Jehoram (according to 2 Ch. xxi. 16, 17) Philistines and
Arabians had raided Judah, despoiled the royal possessions, and carried
away as prisoners the king's wives and sons; and it is natural to
assume that many of these captives were sold as slaves.

But whilst this view satisfies many of the conditions of the problem,
there is one feature in the book which is sufficient to negative the
hypothesis of a pre-exilic date. This is the representation (iii. 2) that
Jehovah's people had been scattered amongst the nations, and that His
land had been parted by lot. Such a statement cannot be adequately
explained by any event except the overthrow of Judah by the Babylonians in 587, the destruction of its independence, the occupation of
its territory, and the dispersal of its people. The language is not satisfied by the sale of slaves, following upon a raid, and plainly implies
more than a temporary inroad, like that made by the Philistines and
Arabians. And confirmation of this is supplied by the real significance
of the ambiguous words *when I shall bring again the captivity* (or *turn
the fortune*) *of Judah and Jerusalem* (iii. 1). Though the words can
be used of recovery from disaster other than expatriation (see Ezek.

xvi. 53, Job xlii. 10), they are employed only of restoration from *great disaster*; and, in relation to Israel, customarily mean *restoration from exile* (see Jer. xxix. 14, xxx. 3, 18, xxxii. 44, xxxiii. 7, 11, Am. ix. 14, Dt. xxx. 3). And whilst the remaining features of the book are compatible with a pre-exilic date, some are quite as intelligible, and others are more natural, on the assumption that the book was composed *after the Exile.* Silence respecting Northern Israel and Damascus, and the empires of Assyria and Babylon, with the omission of all mention of a king or princes of Judah, is most simply explained by the hypothesis that the four kingdoms or empires just enumerated, together with Judah, had, as independent nationalities, all come to an end. Although allusion is made to particular heathen peoples (iii. 4, 19) as destined objects of Jehovah's vengeance, the general tone of the book suggests that the writer's countrymen regarded as their foes *the heathen world at large,* an attitude most intelligible after they had experienced a long term of uninterrupted subordination to successive heathen powers. The animosity displayed against Edom is most fully accounted for by the delight manifested by the Edomites on the occasion of the Fall of Jerusalem in 587. The Egyptians, under Pharaoh Necho, had killed one Jewish king in battle and dethroned another (2 Kgs. xxiii. 29, 33) shortly before the close of the 7th century. The allusion to the Greeks, though it is admittedly possible that they were known by name to the Hebrews in pre-exilic times, is paralleled within the O.T. only in exilic and post-exilic writings (see on iii. 6). The gathering of the Jewish people by the sound of a trumpet blown in *Zion* (ii. 1, 15) suggests the small post-exilic community, rather than the larger pre-exilic kingdom (contrast Jer. iv. 5). The importance of the priests (ii. 16, 17)[1] is also more in keeping with a post-exilic than with a pre-exilic date. The prominence given to the Temple offerings and the distress occasioned by the cessation of them through the locusts are consistent with the care displayed about them in the age of Nehemiah (see Neh. x. 32, 33). And the absence, in the prophet's exhortation to repentance (ii. 13), of any sense of disloyalty on the people's part to Jehovah in the immediate past through idolatry, and the omission of any warning against that particular sin (such as appears not only in the prophetical writings of the 8th century, but even in Deuteronomy, a book of probably 7th century date) are more in accordance with an age when the inclination to idol worship had been more or less eradi-

---

[1] Cf. Is. xxiv. 2, a passage probably not earlier than the 4th century.

cated from the people than with one in which it was constantly exhibited.

(ii) The resemblance between certain peculiar conceptions that are common to Joel and some other prophets raises questions of priority, though such are difficult to settle with much confidence. The conceptions referred to are those relating to (*a*) Jehovah's gathering of all nations to the vicinity of Jerusalem to fight, and His destruction of them there; and (*b*) the issuing from the Temple of a fountain which is designed to water an unfertile valley in the neighbourhood, and (by implication) to render it fruitful. Parallels to the first occur in Ezek. chs. xxxviii., xxxix., and 2 Zech. xii. 1—9, xiv. 1—7 (cf. also 3 Is. lxvi. 18); and to the second in Ezek. xlvii. 1—12 and 2 Zech. xiv. 8. The date of the concluding chs. of 2 Zech. (xii.—xiv.) is debated; but there is much plausibility in the view that they were composed in the 4th century[1]; and certainly Ezekiel did not write earlier than the beginning of the 6th century, after the first deportation of Jews to Babylonia. The nations whose hosts Ezekiel represents as destined to be gathered against Judah after it has been restored from exile are arrayed under Gog, of the land of Magog, and include the Persians and a number of distant peoples dwelling in Western Asia and Northern Africa. The similar passage in Joel does not specify any particular peoples, but describes *all nations* as brought down into the valley of Jehoshaphat. It seems most likely that Ezekiel is the more original of the two parallel passages, and that in Joel, the more detailed representation of the other prophet has been compressed and generalized. If so, this determines the posteriority of Joel to Ezekiel. The same conclusion is favoured by a comparison of their respective predictions of the stream of water that is to issue from the Temple. The purpose which the stream is to serve is in Ezekiel clearly explained; the water is to flow into the Dead Sea and to heal its saltness, whilst upon the banks are to grow all manner of useful and health-giving fruit-trees. In Joel the stream is doubtless meant to promote a similar end, but its purpose is expressed obscurely and enigmatically. Hence the author of the latter book is likely to have written for readers who were familiar with the idea and would understand his meaning in spite of the obscurity of his words. The chronological relation which is thus established between the two prophets confirms for Joel the post-exilic date probable on other grounds.

---

[1] See Driver, *Minor Prophets*, II. p. 230 f. (C.B.).

(iii) The parallels in phraseology and expression which subsist between Joel and other O.T. writings are extremely numerous. If those which may be regarded as mere coincidences are left out of account, there still remain enough to shew that "either Joel was greatly influenced by earlier writers, or, himself living early, his prophecy was remarkably influential over a large number of other writers[1]." The following are the most striking parallels :

Joel i. 15, For near is the day of Jehovah, and as destruction from the Destroyer (*Shaddai*) shall it come.

Is. xiii. 6, For near is the day of Jehovah, and as destruction from the Destroyer (*Shaddai*) shall it come.

Joel ii. 2, A day of darkness and gloominess, a day of clouds and thick darkness.

Zeph. i. 15, A day of darkness and gloominess, a day of clouds and thick darkness.

Joel ii. 6, All faces gather colour.

Nah. ii. 10 (11), The faces of all of them gather colour.

Joel ii. 27, And ye shall know that I am in the midst of Israel, and that I am Jehovah your God, and there is none else.

Ezek. xxxvi. 11, And ye shall know that I am Jehovah.

Ezek. xxxix. 28, And they shall know that I am Jehovah their God.

2 Is. xlv. 5, I am Jehovah and there is none else.

Joel ii. 28, I will pour out my spirit upon all flesh.

Ezek. xxxix. 29, When I have poured out my spirit upon the house of Israel.

Joel ii. 31, Before the great and terrible day of Jehovah come.

Mal. iv. 5, Before the great and terrible day of Jehovah come.

Joel ii. 32, For in mount Zion and in Jerusalem shall be they that escape, as Jehovah hath said.

Ob. 17, And in mount Zion shall be they that escape.

Joel iii. 2, And I will plead with them (*'immām*) there.

Ezek. xxxviii. 22, And I will plead with him (*'itto*), i.e. with Gog (p. lxviii).

Joel iii. 3, And for (*'el*) my people they cast lots.

Ob. 11, And upon (*'al*) Jerusalem they cast lots[2].

Joel iii. 10, Beat your mattocks (*or* coulters) into swords and your pruning-hooks into lances.

Mic. iv. 3 (=Is. ii. 4), They shall beat their swords into mattocks (*or* coulters) and their spears into pruning-hooks[3].

Joel iii. 16, And Jehovah shall roar from Zion and utter his voice from Jerusalem.

Am. i. 2, Jehovah shall roar from Zion and utter his voice from Jerusalem.

Joel iii. 18, The mountains shall

Am. ix. 13, And the mountains shall

---

[1] See G. B. Gray, *Critical Int. to the O.T.* p. 209, and *Expositor*, Sept. 1893, p. 208 f.; Driver, *Joel and Amos*, pp. 19—22 (Camb.B.).

[2] Cp. also Nah. iii. 10.

[3] A similar inversion of a phrase occurring in other prophetic writings is found in Joel ii. 3 compared with Ezek. xxxvi. 35, 2 Is. li. 3.

drop sweet wine, and the hills shall run with milk.	cause sweet wine to drop, and all hills shall be dissolved.
Joel iii. 19, For the violence done (by Edom) to the children of Judah.	Ob. 10, For the violence done (by Edom) to thy brother Jacob.

Further instances where there is identity or close resemblance between Joel and other O.T. books are cited in the commentary. The above are selected because they are parallels between Joel and a number of prophetic oracles all of which except Amos probably originated not earlier than the second half of the 7th century and several after 587. It is clearly more likely that the author of Joel lived late enough to be familiar with, and to draw upon, the writings enumerated above than that he lived before their authors, who all made use of his small book. An examination in detail of some of the parallel passages confirms the conclusion that Joel is the borrower. Thus in Joel ii. 32, if placed by the side of Ob. 17, the writer seems expressly to refer the words he uses to another by attaching to the passage common to himself and Obadiah the addition "as Jehovah hath said." And similarly Joel iii. 10 is more likely to be modelled on Mic. iv. 3 (= Is. ii. 4) than the reverse; as Van Hoonacker remarks, though the transformation of weapons of war into implements of labour is an appropriate characterization of a reign of peace, the converse idea would only be natural to a people lacking arms (cf. 1 Sam. xiii. 20—22). And this conclusion becomes the more convincing from the fact that in certain cases the phrases common to both him and other writers are almost frequent enough in the latter to be styled characteristic. Thus, for example, *Ye shall know that I am Jehovah* recurs constantly in Ezekiel, whilst *I am Jehovah and there is none else* occurs three times in 2 Isaiah. It is manifestly improbable in the extreme that each of these two writers should have derived a *favourite* expression from one and the same work. Hence an examination of Joel and other prophetic writers in respect of the phraseology which they employ in common corroborates the inference already reached that the former did not live before the Exile; and if he has borrowed from Malachi, whose prophecy belongs to the age of Ezra and Nehemiah, he cannot have been earlier than the middle of the 5th century.

(iv) There is little, it is true, in Joel's style to suggest that he is not a writer belonging to the best period: his syntax is distinctive of good Hebrew. But in his vocabulary he shews affinity with writings composed comparatively late in Hebrew literary history; and some of the words he uses are rare in Hebrew but common in Aramaic.

The following is a list of words occurring in Joel but found elsewhere in the O.T. only in writings not earlier than Jeremiah, or in passages of uncertain but probably late date. The importance of these varies, since the absence of some from early books may be due to the fact that the subject-matter of such books afforded no occasion for their use; but on the whole, the list confirms the assignment of Joel to a post-exilic date. The English equivalents are those that are given in the R.V.:—*jaw teeth* (*mĕthallʻoth*, i. 6[1]); *the Lord's ministers* (*mĕshā-rĕthē Yehōvah*, i. 9, ii. 17); *apple tree* (*tappuah*, i. 12); *groan* (*ʼānah*, i. 18); *be perplexed* (*būch*, i. 18[2]); *weapon* (*shelah*, ii. 8[3]); *hinder part* (*sōph*, ii. 20[4]); *spring up* (*dāshāʼ*, ii. 22[5]); *spear* (*rōmah*, iii. 10[6]); *sickle* (*maggāl*, iii. 13).

The following occur in Heb. only in Joel:—*barked*, literally *a splinter* (*kĕtsāphah*, i. 7); *lament* (*ʼālah*, i. 8); *seed* (*pĕrudhah*, i. 17); *rot* (*ʼābhash* i. 17); *clod* (*mĕghrāphah*, i. 17); *barn* (*mamghurah*, i. 17); *break* or *entangle* (*ʼābhat*, ii. 7); *ill savour* (*tsahănah*, ii. 20); *haste* (*ʻūsh*, iii. 11).

Joel, like late writers in general, uses the pronoun *ănī* instead of *ānochī*; and in disjunctive questions (i. 2) follows late and not early practice. He has the combinations *generation and generation* (ii. 2, iii. 20) and *all flesh* (ii. 28), which occur first in Deut., but are only frequent in exilic and post-exilic writings; and he employs *the sons of the Greeks* (iii. 6), where *the Greeks* or *the sons of Greece* might be expected, his usage being paralleled only in Chron. He likewise inverts (ii. 13) after the fashion of post-exilic writers the order of the epithets *full of compassion and gracious*, occurring in Ex. xxxiv. 6.

The circumstance that Joel uses a number of late words and phrases and yet writes for the most part in the manner of the best Hebrew authors finds a satisfactory explanation in the assumption that he was very familiar with the earlier literature of his country. He absorbed sufficient of its spirit to enable him to write in the smooth and flowing style of the best of his predecessors, whilst the linguistic usage of his own age here and there coloured his diction. It is observable that even in expressions and phrases which appear to be borrowed from, or at least influenced by, earlier models, words employed in the parallel passages are sometimes replaced by others that are characteristic of a

---

[1] Elsewhere only in Job and Prov. (xxx. 14).
[2] Elsewhere only in Ex. xiv. 3 (P) and Esth. iii. 15.
[3] See note on ii. 8.
[4] Elsewhere only in Ch. and Eccles. and the Aramaic of Daniel.
[5] Elsewhere only in Gen. i. 11 (P), in a causative form.
[6] See note on iii. 10.

late period (see notes, pp. 100, 115). This would occur all the more naturally if his reproductions of earlier writers were due not so much to direct quotation as to the impressions left upon his mind by constant reading[1].

The conclusion to which the preceding lines of investigation point is that the book of Joel cannot have been written before the Exile; and as its writer plainly lived in Jerusalem, it follows that his work must have been composed after the Return. Since it is implied that the (second) Temple was in existence, the book must be later than Haggai and Zechariah (*circ.* 520); and since it also seems to be implied that the city was walled, it is probably later than the erection of the fortifications of Nehemiah (*circ.* 444). On the other hand, there is no suggestion in it of suffering caused by the rigour of an oppressive power; so that it is scarcely likely to have been written during or after the reign of Artaxerxes Ochus (358—337), who was the first Persian king to ill-treat his Jewish subjects. On the whole, the date of it (apart from iii. 4—8) may be conjecturally fixed at about 400 B.C.[2].

If the section iii. 4—8 is really an insertion (see p. lx), it must be later than its context. Nothing is known from other O.T. sources of any action by Phœnicians or Philistines in connection with the Fall of Jerusalem in 587 to justify the charge here brought against them. It has been suggested that these two peoples may have taken advantage of the punishment inflicted on the Jews by Artaxerxes Ochus to make purchases of treasure and slaves. Whatever may have been the occasion which caused the writer's complaint against them, a fulfilment of his prediction about them may be seen in the capture of Tyre and Gaza and the enslavement of their populations by Alexander in 322, unless, indeed, this prophecy is a reflection of those events.

CHAPTER V.

JOEL AND ESCHATOLOGY.

THE conclusion just reached that Joel was composed after the Return of the Jews from exile obtains additional corroboration from the fact that a relatively late origin accounts best for a certain element in it which would otherwise be difficult to explain. This element is the element of Apocalyptic. Apocalyptic prophecy is linked to the prophecy current in

---

[1] See G. B. Gray, *Expositor, l.c.*, p. 223 f.
[2] "The book as a whole is later than Malachi," Sellin, *IOT.* p. 164.

the ages of Assyrian and Babylonian supremacy by the common idea of an approaching *day of Jehovah*, for though the actual phrase is not always employed, the thought of a Divine judgment is never far from the minds of most of the prophetic writers, both early and late. But there is a significant difference in the emphasis which is placed by the late writers upon the two sides which a Divine judgment, as explained by their predecessors, presented. The term *the day of Jehovah*, which had been prevalent in Israel before the time of Amos to describe the desired intervention of Jehovah in the perennial struggle between Israel and its foes, was taken up by that prophet and declared to involve a crisis which would be determined by ethical principles. When it came, it would set on foot a process of discrimination between the righteous and the unrighteous which would begin with Israel itself. The elimination from the latter of all the corrupt and corrupting elements in it would, indeed, be followed by the removal, or the destruction, of the foreign agencies employed in the work of purification; but the principal stress was laid upon the chastisement merited by the sins of the people and not upon the eventual blessings which were in store for a humbled and repentant remnant. When the prophets saw the religious and moral evils that were rife among their countrymen, it was natural that, in order to awaken them to a sense of their guilt and to bring about their amendment, they should insist more upon the threatening, than upon the cheering, aspect of the Day of Jehovah. With their successors after the Exile it was largely the reverse. The capture of Jerusalem, the overthrow of the Jewish state, and the deportation of the flower of its people by a nation which was devoted to idolatry, inevitably had the effect of altering, in the minds of Hebrew contemporary thinkers, the balance of national deserts and fortune. The return of a section of the exiles to their former homes did not redress the balance. Judah and Jerusalem still remained under alien rule, and the material conditions of the people failed to correspond to the prospects that had been held out by Deutero-Isaiah and other prophets of the exilic period, and were, indeed, the more depressing by the force of contrast. Accordingly, the post-exilic writers were led to emphasize less the retribution deserved by their countrymen for their repeated offences than the retribution merited by the heathen for their prolonged supremacy over God's own people.

The external situation of Israel in the post-exilic age would not have exerted upon the spiritual leaders of the nation the particular influence it did apart from the fact that monotheism had by this time acquired a firm hold over the people at large. That Jehovah alone controlled the forces of nature and the fortunes of men had been a doctrine urged by the prophets ever since the 8th century. But it was only after a considerable interval that this monotheistic belief came to prevail generally. So far as can be judged, it was the experience of the Exile that alone detached the bulk of the people finally from idolatry: at any rate, a section that did not undergo that experience but remained on the soil of Palestine continued to be addicted to it[1]. With those, however, who had shared the Exile in Babylon, and who preserved its memories, monotheism became a settled religious conviction. The elaboration of the sacrificial system by Ezekiel and the codification of the Law by Ezra and other scribes must have deepened, even for many who were fully alive to the moral deficiencies of the nation, their consciousness of the religious gulf separating Israel from the rest of the world. But the belief that they alone of all the peoples of the earth worshipped the one true God became, in the circumstances in which they were placed, a source of painful perplexity. As the recollection of their past apostasies faded, their monotheistic faith rendered their continued subordination to Gentile powers the more unintelligible and intolerable. Hence refuge was sought in the consideration that God was bound in the end to avenge His people, and that the overthrow of the heathen world would be all the more complete in proportion to its long postponement. Apocalyptic prophecy was thus the product of a particular age and situation; and the presence of Apocalyptic features in a prophetical writing is almost incomprehensible apart from an exilic or post-exilic date.

The fact that Apocalyptic prophecy resulted from the reaction of the Hebrew mind, not to some temporary calamity, but to a protracted period of national humiliation, affected the form which it assumed. The hopes which at the Return had attached to Zerubbabel had come to nothing (cf. p. cxxiii); and there was no longer anything to encourage the expectation that there would emerge from the nation a great leader destined to right all wrong (although, as appears from the Psalms of Solomon, the expectation survived in certain circles until the 1st century B.C. (p. cxxvi)). Whatever anticipations were entertained of a retrieval of the national fortunes tended to be independent of contemporary circumstances, and to be moulded exclusively by theological considerations. They did not reproduce in an idealized shape past history and experience, but represented what the imagination deemed to be most appropriate to the power and majesty of the Almighty. In

---

[1] See 3 Is. lvii.

consequence, the descriptions of the future which was to make amends for the unhappy present were more than ordinarily out of touch with mundane reality. Instead of the overthrow of some single oppressive power to whom retribution might seem due either for actual aggression, or, if the power in question could be viewed as commissioned by Jehovah to chastise Israel, for exceeding His mandate, there was predicted the extermination of the whole, or the greater portion, of the Gentile world. The heathen were depicted as moved by Jehovah to muster against Israel, and to court the destruction designed for them. Sometimes Israel was represented as taking part in the slaughter of them; but more commonly their annihilation was thought of as effected by Jehovah alone, or by Him in company with His celestial armies. In the details of the descriptions alike of the catastrophe in store for the heathen and of the subsequent felicity of Israel the exuberance of Hebrew rhetoric reached its climax, and the imagery became weird and bizarre in an unusual degree.

The time when the hoped-for redress would be realized was left vague and undefined, though in this respect Apocalyptic prophecy did not depart from the usage of Hebrew prophecy in general. The expression *in the latter days* (literally, *in the sequel of days*, see Mic. iv. 1), which was sometimes employed to denote the period when the depressing conditions of the present were to be replaced by happier circumstances, is apt to suggest associations which do not properly belong to it. It marks *relative finality* only, introducing a phase of the future which is final only in the sense that the speaker's thoughts at the time do not extend beyond it. It is, in fact, little more than an equivalent for *afterwards* (see Hos. iii. 5 and cf. Jer. xlviii. 47 with xlix. 6); and it is this latter term which is used by Joel in connection with the outpouring of the Spirit, which is the prelude to the Apocalyptic scene with which his book ends. His closing prophecies are consequently eschatological only in a relative sense. There is nothing to suggest that either the Prophets or the Apocalyptists of the O.T. expected that what they announced was far distant in point of time; the date at which their prophecies were to be fulfilled was left undefined, and their ruling tendency was greatly to foreshorten the interval separating that fulfilment (so far as it occurred) from their own age. And there is equally little reason to suppose that the conditions to which they looked forward were regarded by them as fixed and absolute. The future which the Hebrew prophets were wont to describe was a constantly shifting future, as each successive generation of them found the anticipations of their predecessors to be only imperfectly realized; and they cannot have credited their own representations about the consummation that was yet in store for God's people with any greater quality of finality than marked those of earlier days, however much their language seems to us to convey that impression. What was really permanent and unvarying was their religious faith, to which they gave concrete embodiment through the transient creations of their imagination.

NOTE ON LOCUSTS.

According to the classification of insects by reference to their wings or their lack of wings, locusts belong to the order *Orthoptera*, in which the wings are four in number, the anterior pair being small and straight and the posterior large, and, when at rest, folded under the others. This order embraces two divisions, *Cursoria* and *Saltatoria*; and the latter division comprises three families, the *Gryllidae* (represented by crickets), the *Locustidae* (exemplified by grasshoppers), and the *Acridiidae*, which include the various kinds of true locusts. Only those species are usually accounted true locusts which are both migratory and destructive. Of these there are several varieties, but here it is unnecessary to mention any except those that are most common in Palestine. These are the *Oedipoda migratoria* (or *Pachytylus migratorius*) and the *Acridium peregrinum*. The first of these is grey or green in colour, and varies in length from 1½ to 2 inches. The second is yellow or reddish, and is rather larger than the first-named. Both of these varieties ravage Asia, but only the *Oedipoda migratoria* extends its devastations to Europe, being very destructive in S. Russia. The extent of their migrations, their numbers, and their voracity make them one of the greatest of scourges to the lands which they infest. Of the distance that their flights may cover, a thousand miles is said to be a moderate calculation. The size to which their swarms can attain may be estimated from the accounts of observers, modern as well as ancient, when they describe their approach as sometimes darkening the sky, compare the rustling of their wings to the sound of many waters, or of wind-tossed trees, and state that they often advance in clouds (if in the air) or in columns (if on the ground) that stretch for several miles. Their voracity is not confined to any one of the three stages of development through which they pass (the *larva*, the *pupa*, and the perfect insect) but is equally conspicuous in all of these. The destruction which they cause is such that, when a large swarm settles in any neighbourhood, all vegetation quickly disappears; and not only is the foliage of the trees (like the herbage of the fields) devoured, but even the very bark is attacked. The distress resulting to the population of the districts affected is very serious, owing to the ruin of the crops, and preventive measures appear to be attended with but indifferent success.

In the Hebrew of the O.T. there are nine names for locusts or insects similar to them. These are (1) *'arbeh*, (2) *sol'ām*, (3) *hargōl*, (4) *hāghābh*, (5) *gāzām*, (6) *yelek*, (7) *hāsīl*, (8) *gōbh*, (9) *tsĕlātsāl*. It is not likely that all these denote different varieties, or, indeed, that they all denote true locusts. The only passage in which *kinds* are expressly distinguished is Lev. xi. 22, where the first four of those enumerated above are mentioned; but since they are given as species of *leaping* insects, some of them may be crickets or grasshoppers. The name in commonest use is *'arbeh* (see Ex. x. 4, Dt. xxviii. 38, Prov. xxx. 27, Nah. iii. 15, etc.), and this is included in the list of four names occurring in Joel i. 4 (where it is represented in the LXX. by ἀκρίς). Joel manifestly describes true locusts, for he dwells upon their numbers, their onward movements, and their destructiveness; and inasmuch as *Acridium peregrinum* is the locust most frequent in Palestine, it is the one for which *'arbeh* seems the most appropriate term[1]. It cannot, however, be assumed that all or any of the names in Joel are meant to designate distinct species; and even if they are so meant, it is quite impossible to identify them with any confidence. It has been suggested that *hāsīl* is *Oedipoda migratoria*; but there are really no data for attaching to it this name rather than one of the others.

---

[1] Etymologically it is usually taken to mean "the multitudinous."

INTRODUCTION TO JONAH.

CHAPTER I.

THE TITLE, CONTENTS, AND PURPOSE.

THE book of Jonah, though included among the prophetical writings (being the *fifth* according to the Heb., the *sixth* according to the LXX., of the Minor Prophets) is, in form, an historical narrative, relating an episode in the life of the prophet whose name it bears. There is nothing in the contents to suggest that the prophet was the writer of it, and much to negative such a conclusion[1]. Probably, then, like Joshua, Ruth, and Esther, it derives its title from the character who is the subject of it, and of whom mention is made in 2 Kgs. xiv. 25. Jonah, the son of Amittai, was, like Hosea and Amos, a contemporary of Jeroboam II., king of Israel from 782 to 741 B.C., and belonged to Gath-hepher (or Gittah-hepher, Josh. xix. 13) in Zebulun, within the district of Galilee[2]; he was therefore not a Judæan but a Northern Israelite. The site of Gath-hepher is generally identified with El Meshhed, a village 3 miles N.E. of Nazareth, where a tomb of the prophet, according to tradition, still exists. All that is stated about him in 2 Kgs. is that he predicted the success of Jeroboam II. in recovering the lands taken from his predecessor Joash, and in restoring the borders of the Northern kingdom from the gorge between Lebanon and Hermon to the gulf of Akaba. In the book of Jonah there is no reference to this prediction, or to any circumstance connected with the reign of Jeroboam; but that the prophet whose experiences are described in it (see i. 1) is meant to be identified with the prophet named in 2 Kgs. xiv. 25 cannot reasonably be questioned in view of the fact that his own name and that of his father are found in combination only in these two passages[3].

---

[1] The mere fact that the prophet is referred to throughout in the 3rd person is, of course, no disproof that he was the author (as the *Commentaries* of Cæsar and the *Anabasis* of Xenophon shew).

[2] This circumstance contradicts the statement attributed to the Jews in Joh. vii. 52. Possibly, however, the true reading in this passage is preserved in the Egyptian Sahidic Version, "*The* prophet ariseth not out of Galilee" (Peake, *Comm. on the Bible*, p. 753).

[3] It has been maintained by Winckler that in 2 Kgs. xiv. 25 the words *son of Amittai* are a later addition, on the ground that, since mention is made of the prophet's home, mention of his father likewise is against usage. But, as Bewer points out, a parallel is furnished by 1 Kgs. xix. 16.

The book in its present shape narrates that Jonah was directed by Jehovah to go to Nineveh, the capital of Assyria, and warn its people that its destruction was imminent because of its wickedness; that he, believing that, if it repented, it would be spared, sought to evade the command by taking ship from Joppa to Tarshish, a distant port; that Jehovah caused the ship to be overtaken by a violent storm, leading the seamen to supplicate their gods for the preservation of their lives; that it was inferred by the crew that the storm was occasioned by the sin of some-one on board; that lots were drawn to decide who was the offender, and that, when the lot fell upon Jonah, he admitted his guilt; that after the sailors had vainly tried to reach the land, he, at his own suggestion, was thrown into the sea, which at once became calm; that he was saved from drowning by being swallowed by a great fish; that in the fish's belly, where he remained three days and nights, he prayed to Jehovah, giving thanks in a psalm for his preservation; that after Jehovah had directed the fish to disgorge him on to dry land, he was again commanded to proceed to Nineveh, and obeyed; and that in consequence of his announcement of the impending overthrow of the city, its people, before a prescribed period of respite expired, repented of their evil ways with every sign of sorrow; that God accordingly withheld the threatened vengeance, and that this clemency displeased Jonah, who from dis-appointment prayed for death; that, whilst he waited, under a booth which he had constructed, to see what would happen to the city, God made a shady plant to spring up in a night to shield him from the sun's heat, and then as speedily caused it to decay; that Jonah felt pity for it, thus dying, and was thereupon bidden by God to reflect whether He Himself had not more reason to feel pity for the vast number of human beings and cattle in the great city, whose preservation had offended Jonah.

But though the book is thus in form a history, comparable with the histories of Elijah and Elisha (1 Kgs. xvii.—xix., 2 Kgs. i.—ix., xiii.), and alluding, like these, to various historical localities, it is clear that its author did not relate the incidents recorded therein in the spirit, or with the aim, of an historian, but that he narrated them with a didactic purpose, and was only concerned with them so far as they served that purpose. This is apparent from his failure to furnish information upon a number of matters which for an historian could not but have interest; and from his omission to bring his narrative to a proper conclusion. Thus, in addition to the absence of other details, nothing is said of (a) the time when Jonah lived, or the place where he received his instructions to go to Nineveh; (*b*) the name of the contemporary king of Nineveh, who figures in the narrative; (*c*) the prophet's return to his own country. The book ends with Jehovah's address, conveying His rebuke to Jonah; and when the author has indicated the religious lesson which he sought to impart, he brings his recital to a close, leaving Jonah outside the walls of Nineveh. Hence the historical interest is altogether subordinated to the ethical and spiritual; and the work, though superficially a history and containing only one short oracle (iii. 4), finds its proper place among the prophetical writings.

The central object of the book manifestly is to reprove the spirit of religious exclusiveness and vindictiveness evinced by the Jewish race (personified by Jonah) towards the Gentiles. Along with this principal aim the narrative illustrates various religious conceptions; and some of these may have been consciously kept in view by the writer. Human inability to frustrate the Divine purposes; the control exercised by God over the physical forces of nature and the animate creation, and His utilization of them to further His ends; His desire to give to all men an opportunity of turning from their errors; the response which a Divine warning can evoke even from heathen hearts; the power of prayer and the efficacy of sincere repentance to influence the Deity and to avert His anger; the conditional character of prophetic predictions—all these are exemplified in the course of the history. But the illustration of none of these last conceptions constitutes the real intention of the book. This is to throw into relief and expose the hard and grudging disposition of those Jews who regarded with jealousy any mercy shewn by the God of Israel to the heathen world. Such an unlovely trait is exhibited in the person of one of their own prophets; it is represented as the motive of his avoidance, by flight, of his commission in the first chapter, and of his displeasure and complaints in the last; and it is set in effective contrast to the humaneness of the Almighty towards all His creatures alike, including even cattle (iv. 11). That God was not indifferent to the fate of the heathen, but cared for the Gentiles as well as for Israel, was not, indeed, a truth here presented to the Jewish people for the first time. Monotheism, when, by degrees, it had replaced henotheism in Israel, involved as a corollary the belief that Jehovah stood in the same relation to all mankind, and that the repentance which had repeatedly saved Israel from the destruction which its offences merited could avail to save the Gentiles also. Under these circumstances it was impossible for thinkers of a sympathetic and generous temper not to presume in the Deity a desire to induce repentance in all offenders alike, in order that all alike might be spared. And if, as history appeared to shew, Israel had been privileged to know the true God sooner than others, such a prerogative could only involve a corresponding responsibility to extend that knowledge to the rest of mankind. The idea that Israel was designed to be God's agent in making Him more fully and intimately known to the heathen was one which, on the assumption that Jonah is not of earlier date than the 5th or 4th century (p. lxxxv), had already been pressed upon the national conscience by prophets like the Second Isaiah and the writer of the "Servant Songs," whose compositions are incorporated in 2 Is.[1]. But the conviction that this was the national function was far from being universally held by the people. The experience of racial suffering and humiliation had embittered them; and the writings of some of their prophets had enhanced this bitterness, and had fostered the hope that retribution would eventually overtake the nations which had trampled them underfoot[2]. Belief, too, in a permanent distinction between Israel and the rest of the world had been much strengthened by the influence of the legalistic circle of Ezra and his successors. It was the popular spirit which could not tolerate the thought that God should grant to the heathen repentance and pardon that constituted the theme of the book of Jonah. The writer shews to his countrymen their own attitude mirrored in the conduct of the prophet, who, having received a Divine injunction to warn a heathen city of coming doom, with a view to inducing penitence, seeks to escape the execution of the command; and then, when he has at last performed it, grieves that God accepts the repentance which his own preaching has elicited. He appears all the more repellent by the side both of the heathen sailors (whose religious instincts are manifest alike in supplication and in thanksgiving for their rescue, and who, though believing it to be the Divine will that they should expose Jonah to destruction, do so with reluctance), and of the citizens of Nineveh (who respond so readily to the Divine summons to amend their lives). And the self-centred disposition of the prophet, and the lack of all sense of proportion in his estimate of things, are thrown into the boldest relief when he complains of God's pity in sparing thousands of human beings of whom He is the Creator, whilst his own pity is restricted to a plant upon the growth of which he had spent neither thought nor labour. The book of Jonah, in its protest against Israel's religious narrowness, and in its

---

[1] 2 Is. xlii. 1—4, xlix. 1—6, l. 4—9, lii. 13—liii. 12.
[2] See Ob. 1—18, Is. xiii. 1—xiv. 23, 3 Is. lxiii. 1—6, Ps. cxxxvii. 7—9, Jer. xlvi.—xlix.

effort to instil into the people a spirit of good will towards the Gentile world, does not (as has been pointed out) stand altogether alone in the O.T. (its closest parallel, in certain aspects, being the book of Ruth). But its teaching is certainly on a level with the most elevated that is found in the Hebrew Scriptures; and in breadth of view and generosity of temper it approaches as nearly as any, and nearer than most of them, to the comprehensive attitude of Christianity.

CHAPTER II.

The Date.

Light is thrown upon the date of the book by the traces in it of the influence of other writings and by the character of its language.

The writer seems to have been acquainted with the story of Elijah in 1 Kgs. xix., for some of the utterances attributed to Jonah bear a curious resemblance to those of the earlier prophet (see on iv. 3, 8). The peculiar combination of the names *Jehovah God* (in iv. 6) appears to betray knowledge of Gen. ii., iii. (where the addition of *God* to *Jehovah* is best explained as due to the compiler who united the Priestly and Prophetic narratives out of which Genesis has been constituted). And finally, use is made of quotations from the book of Joel (in iii. 9, iv. 2), which are also reminiscences of Ex. xxxiv. 6, and Ps. lxxxvi. 15. Of these several writings the history of Elijah may have been in existence for some time before the Exile; but even if the Priestly narrative of the Pentateuch dates from the Exilic period[1], the editor who combined it with the Prophetic narrative probably lived after the Exile. The date of Joel is disputed, but the probabilities are strongly in favour of its being a post-exilic work (see p. lxxii). Hence the use in Jonah of the writings cited points to the conclusion that, like the latest of them, it, too, was written in post-exilic times.

Again, the attitude of the writer to the Gentile world, as represented by Nineveh, is more natural in a comparatively late period of Hebrew history than at an earlier era. If his purpose was to create in his countrymen a kindlier and more generous feeling towards the heathen, such a sympathetic spirit is most intelligible in one who lived after, rather than before, the Exile. The broad humanity of the book has, within the O.T., a parallel, as already remarked, in the "Servant Songs" included in Deutero-Isaiah. In these the "Servant of Jehovah" most

---

[1] See Driver, *LOT.*[6], pp. 135—159.

probably personifies Israel, viewed from an ideal standpoint; and it is expressly affirmed that it is the mission of the "Servant" to be a source of religious enlightenment to the Gentile peoples (see especially xlix. 6). It is difficult not to think that the author of Jonah not only shared the temper of the writer of these "Songs," but had been influenced by them.

The same inference about the comparatively late origin of the book is deducible from its language. The diction of the narrative differs considerably from that which characterizes the prophetic writings of the 8th century (the age in which the historic Jonah lived), and a number of words, expressions, or meanings found in it occur elsewhere only or chiefly in works known, or reasonably believed, to be of post-exilic date, and to have originated in the 5th, or some still later, century (such as Chronicles, Ezra, Nehemiah, Daniel, The Song of Songs, and certain Psalms). The following are the principal instances:—

(a) *'āshath*, "to think" (i. 6), recurs only in Dan. vi. 4.

(b) *shāthak*, "to be calm, at rest" (i. 11, 12), is found again only in Ps. cvii. 30, Prov. xxvi. 20.

(c) *minnah*, "to appoint, prepare" (i. 17 (ii. 1), iv. 6, 7, 8), does not recur in this sense anywhere in the O.T. except in Job vii. 3, Ps. lxi. 7 (8), Dan. i. 5, 10, 11, and (in the passive) 1 Ch. ix. 29; though the form *mānah* has a signification approximating to it in 2 Is. liii. 12, 3 Is. lxv. 12.

(d) *ṭa'am*, "a decree, command" (iii. 7), is found with this meaning nowhere else, though the Aramaic *ṭě'ēm* occurs with the same sense in Dan. iii. 10, Ez. iv. 19, 21, vi. 14, vii. 23, etc.[1].

(e) *'āmal*, "to labour, toil" (iv. 10), occurs in Eccles. i. 3, ii. 11, 19, 20, 21, etc., Ps. cxxvii. 1, Prov. xvi. 26, but not elsewhere.

(f) *ribbo*, "myriad" (iv. 11), is found in Hos. viii. 12 (text as written, not read), Ps. lxviii. 17 (18), but otherwise only in late writings like 1 Ch. (xxix. 7), Ezra (ii. 64, 69), Nehemiah (vii. 66, etc.), Daniel (vii. 10, xi. 12). Three other features which are *rather* more characteristic of late than of early writings are the following:—

(a) A slight preponderance of *'ănī* over *'ānōchī*. (The former is predominant in late books like Ezek., Lam., Chr., Ez., Esth., Eccles.)

(b) The employment of *lě* for the accus. (iv. 6, if the text is sound). The use of it "occurs...rarely in the early and middle periods of the language, and with greater frequency in exilic and post-exilic writings" (Driver, *Heb. Text of Sam.* p. 146).

(c) The use of *shě* for *'ăsher* (i. 7, 12, iv. 10). This, though common

---

[1] Pusey considers that this Aramaic word (used at Nineveh) has been given by the author of the book a Hebrew pronunciation.

in late writings, is neither uniformly characteristic of, nor exclusively confined to, these. Amongst late compositions in which it is very frequent are Cant. and Eccles.; but it does not occur in Dan., Neh., or Esth. It is found only once in Ezra (viii. 20), and only twice in Chronicles, probably once in Job (xix. 29), and nineteen times in the Fifth book of the Psalms. In the earlier writings of the O.T. it occurs in Jud. v. 7 (The Song of Deborah), vi. 17, vii. 12, viii. 26, 2 Kgs. vi. 11, Lam. ii. 15, 16, iv. 9, v. 18 ; perhaps in Gen. vi. 3, xlix. 10 (LXX.); and probably in the names *Methushael* and *Mishael*. The range of its use seems best accounted for by the supposition that it did not become prevalent until a late period in Hebrew literary history, but existed as a dialectic peculiarity (probably North Palestinian) at a much earlier date[1].

Reference is sometimes made to the occurrence, in this book only, of the words *sĕphīnah* "decked ship" (i. 5) and *kĕrī'ah* "proclamation" (iii. 2), and to the circumstance that *mallah* "mariner" (i. 5) recurs only in Ezek.; but these facts throw little light on the time of the book's origin. In the case of the first and third, their presence here and their rarity elsewhere are sufficiently explained by the subject-matter of the work and the differing nature of the contents of most other O.T. writings.

The diction of the psalm in ch. ii. is not remarkable. The numerous resemblances, however, which it presents to various other psalms of different dates, some seemingly of late origin, render it likely that it is a late composition: the author, who appears to be distinct from the writer of the rest of the book (p. lxxxv), must have lived at a time when a considerable body of literature of this kind existed, and presumably drew upon it.

From this review of the literary allusions in Jonah and of its phraseology it is plain that both combine to support the belief that the book is not earlier than the post-exilic period of Ezra and Nehemiah (i.e. the 5th century B.C.). On the other hand, the mention of *the twelve* prophets in Ecclus. xlix. 10 shews that the composition of Jonah cannot be subsequent to the close of the 3rd century, since Ecclus. probably dates from the beginning of the 2nd century (*circ.* 180 B.C.). Mention is likewise made of the book in Tobit (xiv. 4), which is also, in all likelihood, a 2nd century work[2]. These limits give the period between the

---

[1] See Driver, *LOT.*[6], p. 322, cf. p. 188, note.
[2] See Hastings, *DB.* IV. p. 788.

end of the 5th and the end of the 3rd century as the extreme interval within which Jonah must have been written. If the book of Joel is a 4th century production, the limits will be somewhat narrower (between 350 and 200); but the almost complete absence in Jonah of references to historic persons or events of known date renders greater precision impossible.

CHAPTER III.

THE DEFECTIVE UNITY OF THE BOOK.

THE unity of the book has been questioned by several scholars. Perhaps the gravest doubts are raised by the psalm in ch. ii. This is really a thanksgiving, not a prayer; and in its existing position is meant to be understood as an expression of gratitude to God on the part of Jonah for his being preserved from drowning. The reasons for doubting its authenticity as an original constituent of the work are substantial; and it seems probable that it was neither composed by the author of the book nor inserted by him from another source. It appears too little suited to the prophet's case to be easily accepted as the composition of the author of Jonah, for it contains not even the remotest allusion to the peculiar way in which the prophet had been rescued; and its language might serve as a thanksgiving for anyone saved by the most ordinary means from a death by drowning, or might even voice the emotions of the collective Hebrew people in or after a time of national affliction[1]. Nor is its unsuitability as a thanksgiving composed for Jonah of an exclusively negative character, for the allusion to the Temple (v. 4) is inappropriate in the mouth of a prophet of the Northern Kingdom. These objections to its proceeding from the author of the book are perhaps not absolutely fatal to its being an integral part of it, since it is possible to suppose that, though it was not written by the author of Jonah, yet it was taken by him from another source, and inserted in his own work as being the best available for his requirements. Although intended for a different situation, and perhaps meant as a thanksgiving to God from one who on dry land expresses his gratitude for having been saved from perishing in the waters, it may have been deemed fit, *faute de mieux*, to be attributed to the prophet whilst he was in the belly of the fish, since the fish figures in the story as the agent of his deliverance from drowning.

---

[1] Cf. Cheyne, *Origin of the Psalter*, p. 127.

But the writer of Jonah in the rest of his book is so brief and compressed, and confines himself so closely to the object which he has in view (not even bestowing a thought upon the prophet's return from Nineveh as soon as, in the course of the narrative, the heart of its teaching is reached), that it seems extremely unlikely that he would have inserted a psalm in the middle of so concentrated a piece of work. Moreover, although the prophet is depicted in ii. 2 as conscience-stricken, the rest of the book does not present him in a favourable light, so that it is improbable that the writer of it would have depicted him as full of gratitude to God for the rescue which he had experienced. The most natural explanation of the psalm, therefore, is that it was interpolated in its present position by an editor or a reader who missed the prayer alluded to in ii. 1; though to modern minds a more appropriate place for a *thanksgiving* (such as the psalm is) would appear to be after *v.* 10. Before it was inserted, the verb *prayed* in *v.* 1 must have signified an actual petition for deliverance, to which *v.* 10, following immediately upon it, describes the response. Parallel instances of psalms being interpolated in narratives to which they are certainly or probably alien are the Song of Hannah (1 Sam. ii. 1—10, see Driver, *LOT.*⁶ p. 174), and the "Writing" of Hezekiah (Is. xxxviii. 9—20); cf. also the Song of the Three Children (inserted by the LXX. in Dan. iii.).

In the narrative portion of the book there are certain inconsistencies of representation, of greater or less importance, which require to be accounted for. It is possible that they are due to additions that have been made to the text, or to some dislocation which it has undergone; and they can be at least partly remedied by excision or transposition. But another explanation suggests itself, namely, that the book is composite, and has been constructed out of two versions of a single story. This explanation at first glance seems improbable in view of the brevity of the work; but the facts that countenance it at least deserve consideration. The principal are as follows:—

(*a*) In i. 3^{aa} Jonah flees of set purpose to Tarshish; but in i. 3^{aβ} his going there seems due to the circumstance that the place was the destination of the ship which he happened to find at Joppa. In this *v.* the words *from the presence of Jehovah* appear twice (once in each half-verse). The conjunction beginning the second half-verse can mean *but*.

(*b*) In i. 7 lots are cast to decide to whose sin the storm is due; but in i. 8 Jonah himself is asked to tell the sailors on whose account the trouble had happened.

(*c*) In i. 13 mention of the efforts of the sailors to bring back the ship to shore seems out of place after the appeal to the lot (*v.* 7), and after Jonah's direction to them to throw him overboard (*v.* 12). The *nevertheless* of the R.V. is not the only meaning of the Heb.; it can signify *and*. The last clause of this *v.* differs slightly from the similar clause in *v.* 11.

(*d*) In iii. 4 the Heb. text represents the respite granted to Nineveh as being *forty days*, but the LXX. B has *three days*; and both of these representations receive some support from the sequel (see *infra*).

(*e*) In iii. 5 the fast and other signs of repentance at Nineveh proceed from the spontaneous action of the people, and information of Jonah's preaching does not reach the king till afterwards (*v.* 6). This is unnatural, and looks as though two variant representations had been combined, *v.* 5 constituting one, and *vv.* 6—9 constituting the other. This is confirmed by a slight difference of phraseology between *v.* 5 and *v.* 6.

(*f*) In iv. 1—4 Jonah is at once aware of God's purpose not to destroy Nineveh; but in iv. 5 he is described as sitting outside the city (under a booth which he had made) in order to see what would become of it. The latter account is consistent only with the reading of the Heb. text in iii. 4; but the former is compatible with, if it does not actually demand, that of the LXX.

(*g*) In iv. 5 Jonah builds himself a booth to shield himself from the sun; but in iv. 6 God makes a shrub to spring up to afford him shelter. The booth and the shrub look like variant devices, derived from parallel accounts, for securing the same result.

(*h*) In iv. 8 the distress occasioned to Jonah through the heat striking his undefended head leads the reader to expect from him repinings on account of his own suffering; but in iv. 9—10 his complaints appear disinterested, and caused by a sentiment of pity for the sudden destruction of the shrub.

In some places there are repetitions, in different contexts, of the same phrase (i. 11[b] and i. 13[b], iv. 3 and iv. 8, iv. 4 and iv. 9); whilst one verse seems to contain a doublet varying in phraseology (i. 14), though whether significance attaches to these facts depends upon other features with which they are combined.

Of the inconsistencies enumerated some are not very serious. But there remain a sufficient number of substantial discrepancies to render the theory that the narrative is composite more plausible than it appears at first sight. Several critics who are sensible of them have sought to remove them by textual alteration. But in the light of the composite origin of so many Hebrew writings, the view that this book is also compiled from more than one version of the same story cannot be dismissed as fanciful; and in short it seems to afford a simpler solution of some real difficulties than the supposition of interpolation or displacement. The advantage of such a view is that by a single hypothesis numerous phenomena are accounted for, which otherwise have to be explained by a number of separate assumptions. Its chief defect is the absence of strongly confirmatory evidence from the phraseology (such as helps to establish the documentary analysis of the Pentateuch). No assistance, for example, is derivable from the fluctuations in the use of the Divine names *Jehovah* and *God* ('Elōhim). In i. 6, iii. 5, 8—10, *God* is appropriately put into the mouth of, or used in connection with, the heathen: in i. 14, 16 *Jehovah* is equally fittingly employed where the heathen are represented as praying and making vows to the God of the Hebrews; but in iv. 7—9 the use of *God* cannot be thus explained, and here it is manifest from the contents of *vv.* 7 and 9 that these verses must proceed from the same hand that wrote *vv.* 10, 11 (where *Jehovah* occurs). It is this circumstance that renders precarious any attempt to disentangle in minute detail the strands from which the narrative has, *ex hypothesi*, been woven. Nevertheless it may be expedient to outline a scheme of analysis here, if with no other aim than to illustrate the *kind* of solution which the literary problem of the book seems to require. The following scheme assumes that the constituent sources are two; and these are distinguished as *A* and *B*, wherever sufficient *criteria* appear to be present. Where such fail, it is inferred that the two sources were of one tenor; and this common matter is printed between them. See also p. 144.

A	Common	B	A	Common	B
	i. 1—2			i. 14ᵃ	
i. 3ᵃ			i. 14ᵇ		i. 14ᶜ
		i. 3ᵇ		i. 14ᵈ—iii. 4ᵃ	
	i. 4		iii. 4ᵇ LXX.		iii. 4ᵇ Heb.
		i. 5ᵃ	iii. 5		
i. 5ᵇ					iii. 6—9
		i. 5ᶜ—6	iii. 10—iv. 4		
i. 7					iv. 5
		i. 8—10ᵃ	iv. 6—7		
i. 10ᵇ					iv. 8ᵃ
		i. 11—12	iv. 8ᵇ—11		
i. 13					

The distinctive features of the two supposed sources are as follows:— According to *A* Jonah, on being sent to Nineveh, went by design to

Tarshish. In the storm the mariners first threw overboard the gear (or the cargo) of the ship, to lighten it; and then cast lots to discover on whose account the trouble had befallen them, that they might get rid of him. The lot falling on Jonah, they realized the significance of a previous confession made by him that he had fled from the presence of Jehovah; and they sought to return to the shore in order to land him. But since they could not do so owing to the storm, then, with a prayer to Jehovah, they threw the prophet into the sea. The episodes of the fish, of Jonah's journey to Nineveh, and of his announcement there were told on common lines by both sources; but in *A* the period of grace granted to Nineveh by Jehovah was three days (as stated by the LXX.). The people fasted and repented, and God spared the city, but Jonah was indignant and begged to die. To afford him shade in the heat, God caused to grow in a single night a shrub which He destroyed next day; and Jonah being angry through pity for the shrub, God asked Him whether He Himself had not more reason to pity the vast number of living creatures contained in Nineveh.

According to *B*, Jonah, being sent to Nineveh, went to Joppa and chanced to find there a ship bound for Tarshish. In the storm the mariners prayed to their gods, and Jonah, who had gone below to sleep, was bidden by the captain to pray to his God likewise. The prophet's withdrawal having directed attention to him, the crew put questions to him about himself, and on his declaring that he was a worshipper of Jehovah, the Creator of the sea and land, they were afraid. Asking him what they should do to him, that the sea might become calm, they were told by the prophet to cast him overboard, for he knew that the storm had occurred on his account. So, praying that they might not be guilty of innocent blood, they threw him into the sea. As already stated, this source recounted the incidents of the fish, Jonah's journey to Nineveh, and his announcement there in the same way as *A*, but it represented Nineveh's term of grace as 40 days. Information about Jonah's warning having reached the king, he issued a proclamation, urging his people to repent. Jonah went outside the city to await the issue, which would not be known until after an interval of more than a month, and built a booth to shelter him in the meanwhile. God caused an east wind to rise [and it destroyed the booth]. Probably this version ended with a description of Jonah's distress, similar to that in iv. 8[b], and a comment from God upon his plaint.

The statement in iv. 8 that God prepared an east wind is an incomplete one, for nothing is said about the purpose for which it was intended. But it is a plausible suggestion that it served a similar end to that served by the worm (*v.* 7) in the companion version, and tore down Jonah's booth as the worm destroyed the shrub. The construction of the booth clearly had in view a long interval of waiting, so that the source (*B*) which contained the account of it must have had in iii. 4 the *forty days* of the Heb. text. On the other hand, it seems not improbable that the parallel source (*A*) had the *three days* of the LXX., and that it supposed that Jonah became aware that Nineveh's repentance had averted its destruction by the time he had crossed the city from one side to the other (which he would spend three days in doing). In these circumstances there was no necessity for the prophet to build a booth; his departure for home would be almost immediate, and such relief as he needed would be appropriately supplied by the springing up of the shrub in a night.

The termination of the hypothetical version indicated by *B* seems not to have been incorporated. In the book as we have it *B* ends abruptly, and the tenor of God's final speech to Jonah, as contained in it, can only be conjectured. Possibly the concluding speech of the Almighty contrasted Jonah's selfish concern for his own individual distress, consequent upon the demolition of the booth, with the concern which He Himself had for the prospective suffering of the vast population of the threatened city (without specific reference to children or cattle).

It has been contended that, in the case of a book of so pronounced a didactic aim as Jonah, a composite origin is improbable; and that its scheme, in which details are so inconspicuous and so carefully subordinated to the special purpose of the work, bears the impress of a single mind. But this criticism does not seem fatal to the comparatively simple theory here sketched. No doubt the general plan really proceeded from a single mind; but it is not unlikely that the story, when once originated, became circulated in more than one form. So interesting a narrative could scarcely fail to be popular; and variations would tend to appear in it in the course of transmission. Subsequently, two versions of it were combined, most, though probably not quite all, of the variations in them being retained; and the result is the work in the condition in which we possess it.

CHAPTER IV.

THE CHARACTER OF THE NARRATIVE.

WHILST a didactic purpose is visible throughout the book, and there is a general agreement respecting the lesson which it is intended to convey (though the different features in its teaching have been variously emphasized by different commentators), there has been much diversity of view regarding the character of its contents. The historical form in which it is couched is not necessarily any proof that it is, or was intended by its writer to be considered, an actual history, but is consistent alike with its being meant either as a record of real events or as a work of fancy. A writer with a moral or religious end to serve may select and adopt, for his purpose of illustrating by analogy a spiritual truth, an account of some action or experience either familiarly occurring, or reported to have once occurred, or else he may invent, with the same object, a purely imaginary history. And in estimating the character of the contents of the book of Jonah, and in determining whether it is meant as a history or as a parable, it is not sufficient to decide whether or not it is a history according to modern notions of what is credible: it is necessary to consider whether it contains anything that would be deemed incredible as history in the age which saw it produced, and for which it was designed, since alleged experiences appear probable or improbable according to the acquaintance with nature and natural processes that prevails at different epochs. Should it be concluded, however, on good grounds that the narrative is not a history and was not intended for such, but was invented simply with a religious purpose in view, there will remain the further question whether it is a parable or an allegory. In an allegory all, or at least most, of the details have a symbolic meaning; in a parable the symbolism is to be sought in the general purport of the story, the incidental details only helping to bring out the desired significance or to render the representation more realistic.

That the contents of the book of Jonah are not as a whole historical if judged by modern ideas of what is intrinsically likely, ought not to require to be argued at length. The book has been classed by Budde with *Midrashim*, a Midrash being "an imaginative development of a thought or theme suggested by Scripture[1]"; and examples of such are

---

[1] Driver, *LOT.* p. 497.

the stories of Tobit and Susanna preserved in the Apocrypha. The writer of Chronicles refers to *Midrashim* (R.V. *commentary*) containing accounts of the actions and sayings of various Israelite kings (2 Ch. xiii. 22, xxiv. 27); and Budde regards the book of Jonah as a Midrash on 2 Kgs. xiv. 25, which included the record of Jonah's prediction there related, and followed it (after *v.* 27) with the narrative of the prophet's mission to Nineveh (the conjunction *And* with which, in the Heb., the book begins linking the two[1]). The suggested connection, however, with 2 Kgs. xiv. 27 is not really close enough to be plausible. Though Israel had come into contact with Assyria before Jonah's time (Jehu, the great-grandfather of Jeroboam II, being an Assyrian vassal[2]), and though the supposition that the book was once part of some larger whole accounts very well for the absence in it of any particulars respecting the prophet's home or date, there is no allusion in the history of Jeroboam II (2 Kgs. xiv. 23—29) to Assyria; whilst the first mention of Nineveh in the books of Kings does not occur until much later (xix. 36). Nevertheless whether the book belongs to the class of *Midrashim* or not, the estimate of it as, in the main, a creation of the imagination is sound. It is not impossible, indeed, that tradition actually attributed to Jonah a journey to Nineveh, and that around him and his experiences legends had accumulated. Indeed, in the absence of a satisfactory explanation afforded by the meaning of his name (see p. 120), it is difficult to understand why a prophet living at a definite time and place, but not otherwise very distinguished (as, for instance, Elijah and Elisha were), and not connected, in the books of Kings, with Nineveh, should have been selected by the writer to illustrate the purpose which he had in mind, unless some incident traditionally associated with him rendered the choice appropriate. Elisha is recorded to have gone to Damascus, the capital of Aram (or Syria) (2 Kgs. viii. 7); and it is not incredible that a prophet living in the Assyrian period of Hebrew history may, on some occasion, have travelled, or been conveyed, to a city as remote as the Assyrian capital. But that of such a journey, if any really took place, the book presents a true account is eminently improbable. The long interval separating the date at which the work was composed (see p. lxxxv) from the date of the events which it professes to record would impair its value as an authority for detailed occurrences, even if they were of a less miraculous character than those actually recounted. The

---

[1] But see note on i. 1.
[2] This is shewn by the inscription of Shalmaneser II on the Black Obelisk now in the British Museum.

title "king of Nineveh," to designate the king of Assyria, is said to be one which could never have been applied to him in Assyria itself[1]. There is no parallel in the historical books of the O.T. for a mission like that on which Jonah is represented as having been sent; and the success described as attending his preaching lacks plausibility[2]. Though a foreigner in Assyria and quite unaccompanied, he is represented as bringing to repentance the population of a city depicted as so large that it required three days' journey to cross. And the record of so extraordinary an achievement is accompanied by the recital of other wonders which are even more astonishing. Such marvels as Jonah's living for three days and nights within the belly of a fish, his ejection by the fish on to dry land, and the growth of a tree (or shrub) within a single night to a size sufficient to shield him from the sun, invest the narrative with an atmosphere like that of wonderland. These physical marvels constitute at the present day an insurmountable obstacle to a general belief in the book as a record of actual facts. The abstract possibility of the miraculous (admitted by most theists who hold that the uniformities of nature are only the expression of a Divine will, which has the power to vary them at pleasure) cannot, in the light of our long experience of the regularity of nature, render plausible the particular miracles here related. The credibility of a reported miracle has to be estimated by the weighing of testimony and a balancing of probabilities; and in the case of alleged occurrences so abnormal as those here in question, attested as they are by no evidence which is even approximately contemporary, there can be only one verdict.

Some theologians, indeed, in order to make the miracle connected with the fish easier of belief, have adduced examples, first of monsters capable of swallowing a man, and secondly of men being actually swallowed and afterwards disgorged alive. The fish that figures in the story is not necessarily to be identified with a whale; but there are even whales that are able to swallow a man. For instance, the gullet of the spermaceti whale or cachalot, a creature which has a length of 55 or 60 feet, is capacious enough to take down a man without difficulty[3]. Again it has been pointed out that the rorqual, the largest variety of which (the "blue whale") sometimes attains a length of

---

[1] See Sayce, *HCM*. p. 487.

[2] Assyriologists, however, have drawn attention to the circumstance that in the reign of Ramman-nirari III a monotheistic reform is represented to have occurred at Nineveh.

[3] F. T. Bullen, speaking of the sperm whale, says that it "can swallow morsels of truly heroic size, at least 6 ft. cube."

85 feet, though it has a gullet too small for a man to pass through, yet possesses longitudinal folds beneath its jaws and throat within which a man could lie at full length. Since, however, the Heb. expression is perfectly vague, and the Greek equivalent employed in the LXX. and the N.T. (κῆτος) is applied to various marine creatures of large size, a more likely monster to seize and swallow a human being is some variety of shark. Some specimens of the genus *Carcharias* reach a length of 25 feet, whilst of the genus *Carcharodon*, a native of tropical and subtropical seas, instances have been found with a length of 40 feet. One of the latter, measuring 36½ feet, had a jaw 20 inches wide (measured transversely). And examples are cited of sailors who have actually been swallowed by sharks and disgorged alive. But such examples, so far as they are genuine, do not really meet the difficulties involved in the narrative. For the prophet is not only represented as having been swallowed by the great fish; he is described as having remained alive and conscious within it for three days and nights; and as having been, at the close of that period, thrown up on the shore in a condition sound enough to allow him eventually to proceed on his mission to Nineveh. Consequently instances of "escapes" like those referred to could, even if authentic, do little to render the story more credible to modern minds.

Pusey (*Minor Prophets*, p. 258) quotes the following incident from Müller, *Vollständige Natursystem des Ritters Karl von Linné*, Th. III. p. 268. "In 1758 in stormy weather a sailor fell overboard from a frigate in the Mediterranean. A shark was close by, which, as he was swimming and crying for help, took him in his wide throat, so that he forthwith disappeared. Other sailors had leapt into the sloop to help their comrade while yet swimming: the captain had a gun, which stood on the deck, discharged at the fish, which struck it so that it cast out the sailor which it had in its throat, who was taken up, alive and little injured, by the sloop which had now come up. The fish was harpooned, taken up on the frigate, and dried. The captain made a present of the fish to the sailor, who by God's Providence had been so wonderfully preserved. The sailor went around Europe exhibiting it....The dried fish was 20 ft. long, and, with expanded fins, 9 ft. wide, and weighed 3924 pounds."

König (Hastings, *DB.* II. p. 750, citing the *Neue Luth. Kirchenzeitung*, 1895, p. 303 f.) relates that a whale-hunter named James Bartley was in Feb. 1891 swallowed by a whale, and that on the following day when the animal was killed, was taken alive out of its stomach. But Lukyn Williams, investigating the story, learnt that neither the owners of the ship nor the widow of the captain had ever heard of it: see *Exp. Times*, Aug. 1906, Jan. 1907.

It is sometimes urged, however, that belief both in the historical truth of the book as a whole and in the physical miracle of the fish is necessitated for Christians by Christ's allusions to them in the Gospels. It is contended that our Lord's declaration, that in the Judgment the men of Nineveh would rise up and condemn the Jews of His own generation (Mt. xii. 39, 41 = Lk. xi. 29, 30, 32), implies His own acceptance of the story of Jonah's mission; whilst His comparison of the prophet's imprisonment in the fish's belly to His own entombment in the earth (Mt. xii. 40) is evidence that He likewise regarded as true the narrative about the fish (which may have been the Scripture to which He referred as foreshadowing His rising again on the third day (Lk. xviii. 31—33, cf. 1 Cor. xv. 4))[1]. But the issue is not quite so plain as this suggests. His reference to the Ninevites, indeed, has good support behind it, occurring as it does both in Mt. and in Lk.[2]; but even so, it does not necessarily place the literal truth of the account in the book of Jonah beyond question. His treatment of the narrative as historical may have been a consequence inseparable from the conditions of His incarnation. Limitations of knowledge, equally with physical weakness and infirmity appear to be inevitable concomitants of a true humanity, and were manifested by our Lord on several occasions[3]; and the fact that He (in common with His countrymen at large) treated the book of Jonah as a record of actual facts can reasonably be considered a natural result of His being born a Jew at a particular era. His allusion to Jonah's detention in the belly of the fish for three days and nights, if a genuine utterance, admits of being accounted for on the same lines. But the authenticity of the statement thus attributed to Him is open to grave suspicion. It is found in Mt. alone, being absent from the parallel in Lk. xi. 29, 30, 32; and where it occurs in the First Gospel, it is out of keeping with its context. For the purport of our Lord's answer to those who requested a sign was that no sign of the nature desired, immediate and visible, should be granted. The sole sign that should be given to them was such as was involved in His preaching, of which Jonah's preaching at Nineveh was a counterpart. Only when *the sign of Jonah* in Mt. xii. 39 is thus understood to be the prophet's proclamation to the Ninevites does the argument that follows in *v.* 41 (= Lk. xi. 32) become intelligible; the Ninevites repented in response to Jonah's warnings, whereas the Jewish contemporaries of Jesus paid no heed to One among them who was greater

---

[1] More probably the Scripture in question is Hos. vi. 2.
[2] Certain narratives and discourses common to the First and Third Gospels but peculiar to them appear to be derived from an earlier source usually designated by the symbol Q.
[3] See Mk. v. 9, 30, vi. 38, ix. 16, 33, xi. 13.

than Jonah. It seems probable, therefore, that the allusion in *v.* 40 to Jonah's imprisonment in the belly of the fish was not really our Lord's, but originated after His Resurrection. When a belief in the physical resuscitation of His body from the grave had grown prevalent, a comparison between the Resurrection after a three days' entombment[1] and Jonah's release after spending three days and three nights within the fish became natural, and a corresponding interpretation of Christ's reference to the *sign of Jonah* seems to have been introduced into the latest of the Synoptic Gospels.

But whilst there is every reason for concluding that the marvels related in the book of Jonah are really unhistorical, there is no reason for classing the narrative amongst *fables* (like that contained in Jud. ix. 7—15). A fable, in contrast to a parable, is a story in which things happen that transcend the limits of what contemporary belief regards as possible in the place, or at the time, supposed; whereas in a parable these limits are respected. And such is the case here, for none of the incidents narrated in the book overstep the range of wonders deemed credible by Hebrew writers, as will be realized if only a few of the marvels that figure in the historical books of the Hebrew Scriptures be recalled[2]. The acquaintance which the Hebrews had with nature was not sufficiently wide and exact, and their ideas about natural law were not sufficiently thought out, to prevent them from imagining the occurrence of extraordinary and abnormal incidents through the interposition of God in the interest of His people or of His prophets. Moreover, such marvels are generally attributed to a distant past, and tend to secure a greater degree of credence than would be accorded to them if they were reported of a more recent age[3]. This is as true of the miracles narrated in the book of Jonah as of most others in the O.T. Jonah was a prophet who lived some three or four hundred years before the writer who here gives an account of him; and since he was "a man of God," represented as entrusted with a commission from the Almighty, who could not allow His purposes to be foiled by any act of man, no improbability would attach to a current tradition (if such was in circulation) ascribing such strange experiences to the prophet; nor would a Hebrew writer hesitate

---

[1] According to the Gospel narrative our Lord's Body lay in the grave only one whole day and parts of two others; but *on the third day* and *after three days* are regarded as equivalent expressions (Mt. xvi. 21, Mk. viii. 31).

[2] See Num. xvii. 8, xxii. 28, Josh. iii. 14—17, vi. 1—20, x. 13, 14, 2 Kgs. ii. 8, iv. 1—7, 42—44, vi. 1—7, etc.

[3] Cp. Verg. *Aen.* x. 792, *Si qua fidem tanto est operi latura vetustas.*

to introduce them as credible incidents into an edifying story of his own invention[1].

But whilst it is tolerably certain that there is nothing recorded in the book of Jonah which either its author, or the majority of his contemporaries, would find any difficulty in believing, so that the narrative is not a fable but a parable, it is not easy to determine whether the author, in seeking to convey a desired religious lesson, really utilized traditions associating Jonah with Nineveh, and availed himself of legends that had gathered round the prophet, or whether the story is altogether the product of his fancy. The narrative is certainly a parable in intention; and if there are actual traditions behind it, the historical interest is so subordinated that it is almost a parable in form. But the supposition that there previously existed a traditional nucleus of which the writer made use has the advantage of accounting for the choice of Jonah as the figure round which the story moves (see p. xcii). In the absence of such an explanation, it seems necessary to treat the narrative not as a parable but as a deliberate and elaborate allegory[2]. If it is regarded simply as a parable, the only real symbolic element in it is Jonah himself. The prophet is typical of the Israelite people, and his unwillingness to become the agent in saving Nineveh from destruction illustrates Jewish ill-will towards the heathen world. But to the other features in it no symbolism attaches; they are only the circumstances against which Jonah's character is displayed, or by which the development of the Divine purpose is helped forward. On the other hand, if the story is treated as an allegory, then the names of Jonah and his father Amittai, the stormy sea, the great fish, Nineveh, and the tree (or shrub) that sprang up in a night, all have a symbolic value. Jonah represents Israel; but the choice of him rather than of another prophet to typify his countrymen is accounted for by his name. The word *Jonah* signifies "a dove," a bird to which the Israelite nation is more than once likened, whilst *Amittai*, the name of the prophet's father, means "truthful" or "man of truth." Hence there would be some appropriateness in symbolizing Israel, the nation entrusted with the truth of God, by Jonah the son of Amittai. Jonah is naturally represented as a

---

[1] The miracles related in the book of Daniel, a work of the 2nd century, are associated with characters represented as living in the 6th century.

[2] The distinction between a parable and an allegory adopted in what follows is that of Jülicher: see *JTS.* Jan. 1900, p. 162 f. Examples of allegories occur in 2 Esd. ix. 38—x. 59 and xiii. In the N.T. the "parables" of the Sower and of the Wheat and Tares are allegorical in character; see Mk. iv. 3—8, 14—20, Mt. xiii. 24—30, 37—42.

prophet, inasmuch as Israel, in the writings of the Second Isaiah and elsewhere, was regarded as having a prophetic vocation amongst mankind (p. lxxxi). Nineveh, the capital of the greatest empire known to the Israelites in the age of the historic Jonah, was a fitting type of the heathen world, which Israel, personified by Jonah, was designed by God to bring to repentance. But Israel disregarded its duty, and whilst thus evading its true mission, was swallowed up by a hostile world-power (the Babylonian empire)[1]. Even the casting of Jonah into the sea could represent the overthrow of Israel as a nation, and its submergence beneath heathen domination. But no doubt the great fish that swallowed Jonah may be regarded as more decidedly typical of the empire that absorbed Israel. Nebuchadrezzar, king of Babylon, the power that extinguished Israel's national existence, is expressly likened by Jeremiah to a sea-monster; and Israel, in being carried into captivity, is figuratively declared to have been devoured and swallowed up (Jer. li. 34); whilst God in restoring Israel is similarly represented as bringing forth out of the mouth of Bel (the god of Babylon) that which he had swallowed (Jer. li. 44). It was only after the Captivity that Israel recognized that it had a duty to the Gentiles; but even then it had in general little sympathy with God's merciful purposes towards them, and its attitude is reflected in the conduct and temper of Jonah subsequent to his release from his imprisonment in the fish. The plant which raised in Jonah hopes that were quickly blighted has been taken as an emblem of Zerubbabel, designated by Zechariah as the *Shoot* or *Sprout* (iii. 8, vi. 12), of whom great expectations were at one time entertained, but who failed to fulfil them (p. cxxiii). This allegorical interpretation of the book is open to some serious objections. In the first place, there is comparatively little evidence within the O.T. itself that Israel was ever symbolized by a dove. It is often, indeed, from various points of view *compared* to one (Hos. vii. 11, xi. 11, 2 Is. lix. 11, lx. 8, Ps. lxviii. 13, see also Ps. lv. 6[2]), but so are other peoples (Jer. xlviii. 28, Nah. ii. 7[3]); and the only instance of a dove being treated as a *symbol* of the Israelite nation (perhaps in contrast to heathen powers, conceived as birds of prey) seems to be the title of Ps. lvi., where *Yonath 'elem rehōkim*, "the silent dove of them that are far off" (apparently the air to which the

---

[1] See G. A. Smith, *Book of the XII Prophets*, II. p. 523 foll. (E.B.).

[2] By Jewish interpreters Cant. ii. 14 (*O my dove*), iv. 1 (*thine eyes are as doves*), were applied to Israel (*Enc. Bib.* II. 2567). In Ps. lxxiv. 19 Israel is figuratively designated Jehovah's turtle-dove (*tōr*).

[3] Here *Huzzab*, if a title, probably denotes either the Assyrian queen, or the city of Nineveh.

psalm was to be sung) is rendered in the LXX. by ὑπὲρ τοῦ λαοῦ ἀπὸ τῶν ἁγίων μεμακρυμμένου ("on behalf of the people removed to a distance from the sanctuary"). Next, there is a decided lack of consistency in an allegory in which one heathen empire is symbolized by a sea-monster, whilst the rest of the heathen world is represented by an historical city that once formed part of that world. Thirdly, to explain the great fish as an emblem of Babylon, the destroyer of Israel's independence, is to misconceive the part played by it in the story; the fish is an agent not of destruction but of preservation, its function being to save Jonah from drowning, not to injure him. Fourthly, the explanation of the plant as an emblem of Zerubbabel is forced; for there is no verbal expression employed in the account of its growth which is suggestive of the term (*tsemah*) applied to Zerubbabel by Zechariah, although the cognate verb was available, if the writer had had the supposed signification in his mind (see Gen. ii. 5, 9). And finally, the effectiveness of the lesson which the book is designed to enforce is seriously impaired by the allegorical interpretation. Consideration of the import of the subordinate features in the story distracts attention from the two principal figures in it, the Almighty and Jonah; and the contrast between the compassionateness of God and the inhumanity of the Jewish people in the person of one of their prophets becomes obscured.

GENERAL SUPPLEMENT TO THE SEPARATE INTRODUCTIONS.

CHAPTER I.

THE THEOLOGY OF THE BOOKS OF MICAH, OBADIAH, JOEL AND JONAH.

SOME account of the message conveyed by the prophet Micah to his contemporaries has already been given, and attention will be drawn in the commentary to the teaching of the other oracles and prophecies that are comprised in this volume. Nevertheless it will not be inexpedient to treat collectively all the writings that are here united, and to bring under review their main theological and religious conceptions. As they all belong to a period when the prophetic order in Israel had arrived at a belief in Jehovah as the only existing God, whose exalted nature and character demanded a proportionately elevated standard of conduct and worship from His servants, it will be most convenient to begin by summarizing the principal attributes ascribed to God in the 8th and two or three following centuries, and then to consider how far these writings illustrate, enlarge, or modify the view of God by this time attained. The enquiry is best divided into three parts, relating to (I) the Being of God; (II) His dealings with mankind; (III) the duties of men towards Him.

I. No systematic or coherent exposition of the Divine nature is found in the O.T.; the ideas entertained about God have to be collected from incidental statements or implications occurring in writings of various dates, and reflecting lower and higher stages of intuition and inspiration, which are incapable of being fully harmonized. But if attention be concentrated on the teaching of the *writing* prophets, to the exclusion of the immature phases of belief prevailing in earlier times, some common religious convictions can be clearly discerned. The chief qualities ascribed to God which emerge from this teaching are Unity, Spirit, Wisdom, Goodness, and Power[1]. All these are inseparable from Personality; and it is obvious that by the Hebrews God was regarded as a Person. The Divine nature was conceived after the analogy of human nature, but was deemed to be free from the limitations that accompany

---

[1] Another quality is *Holiness* (see Otto, *The Idea of the Holy*); but this is not conspicuously illustrated in the Prophets here considered.

humanity. The ideas formed about God's attributes of mind and character had a history, primitive fancies about Him being shed in course of time as unworthy and untrue. But to trace the gradual disappearance of such primitive fancies is unnecessary here: what is important for the present purpose is to consider the conceptions about God cherished by the Hebrews when their religious progress during the period covered by the O.T. reached its culmination.

(a) The Divine Unity, belief in which only by degrees replaced a phase of thought that took the existence of a plurality of gods for granted, came to be the most fundamental conviction of Hebrew religious thinkers. It finds most emphatic expression in Dt. vi. 4, *Jehovah our God is one Jehovah*. The best rendering, however, of this passage and its true meaning are rather doubtful (as the variety of translations given in the R.V. mg. shews), for it may imply either that Jehovah is single and indivisible, in contrast to the multiplicity and variety of the gods of the heathen, or that He is unique and incomparable. Probably it combines the two ideas that He is intrinsically one and self-consistent; and that He exists without a rival, all other spiritual powers being subordinate to Him[1]. That Jehovah is the only existing Deity is not asserted as explicitly by any of the prophets with whom we are here concerned as it is (for example) by Deutero-Isaiah (see 2 Is. xliii. 10, xliv. 6, xlv. 14, 21, etc.), but the idea is implicitly present. He is the God of heaven, the maker of the sea and the dry land (Jon. i. 9); He controls the forces and agencies of nature, using them both to punish men, and to bring them relief and prosperity (Joel ii. 11, 19, 23—25, iii. 18, Jonah i. 4, 17, ii. 10); He is the Judge of all peoples (Mic. i. 2), and calls all nations to account for the wrongs done by them to Israel (Ob. 15, Joel iii. 2, 11). If His sole Godhead is not expressly affirmed by these prophets, the ascription to Him of such authority over the physical world and the races of men adequately attests their belief in it.

(b) That Jehovah was Spirit and not flesh was implied by Isaiah when he declared the Egyptians to be men and not God, and their horses flesh and not spirit (Is. xxxi. 3); and the desire to preserve (even at the cost of discouraging all graphic and plastic art) the belief in Jehovah as a spirit lacking corporeal form was one of the motives that led to the prohibition by the religious teachers of Israel of all material symbols of Him (cf. Mic. v. 13, 14, and see notes *ad loc.*). Nevertheless the Hebrews seem to have found great difficulty in conceiving God to be altogether

---

[1] Cf. Driver, *Deut.* pp. 89, 90.

immaterial, and it looks as if they were inclined to think of *spirit* as merely an extremely tenuous and impalpable form of matter[1]. The importance of safeguarding the belief that God in His nature is only spirit and not, like man, spirit and body lay in its connection with the belief in His omnipresence. From the limitations inseparable from a solid bodily frame a spiritual Being could be deemed to be free; so that if God were spirit only, His presence everywhere would be the more easily intelligible. Jehovah's ubiquity is implied in several passages of these prophets. He observes and punishes evil that is committed in Judah and Jerusalem (Mic. ii. 1—11); but with equal facility He gathers and redeems His chastened people from the distant lands where they have been dispersed (Mic. ii. 12—13, iv. 6). He requites wrong-doers alike in Tyre, in Zidon, in Edom and in Egypt (Joel iii. 4—8, 19). Perhaps the book of Jonah illustrates most vividly the conviction entertained of His omnipresence. He commands the prophet, whilst in the Holy Land, to depart on a mission to Nineveh; when His messenger disobeys and crosses the sea, He raises a storm ; and when Jonah is thrown overboard from the ship conveying him, He causes a monster of the deep first to swallow and then to disgorge him ; and when at last the prophet goes to Nineveh, God's activity there is manifested by the miraculous growth and equally miraculous destruction of the gourd. Nevertheless, though the Lord's omnipresence is thus conspicuously brought into mind, it is regarded as not incompatible with His having, in a special sense, His dwelling in Zion (Joel iii. 17, 21). It is thence that He roars against His adversaries (Joel iii. 16); thither heathen peoples, impressed by His might, will ultimately resort to be instructed about Him (Mic. iv. 2); and there the centre of His kingdom is to be (Ob. 21). The explanation of this seeming incongruity is to be found in the thought that, though God is nowhere absent from the world, yet He is most intimately present in the hearts of His servants and worshippers, and these were to be found chiefly, though not exclusively, in the Jewish capital.

(c) The greatness of God's Intelligence and Wisdom does not receive abstract emphasis in these prophecies as it does in some other of the O.T. books (Prov. iii. 19, Jer. x. 12, Job xxxvi. 5), but there is ample evidence therein of a belief in the boundless resources of His understanding. He devises evil against evil-doers, from which they can find no escape (Mic. ii. 3). He foils the plans of Zion's foes, and disappoints

---

[1] Cf. p. 108.

their expectations (*ib*. iv. 11, 12). He humbles the pride of the Edomites amid their inaccessible cliffs (Ob. 3); and threatens with destruction the great city of Nineveh (Jon. i. 2, iii. 2). That the fortunes of peoples are under His control is tacitly but none the less plainly affirmed wherever one nation, in the fancied pursuit of its own designs, is represented as being really the agent of Jehovah for chastising the offences of another (Ob. 7—14, Mic. i. 5 f., iii. 9—12). And equally impressive does the working of Divine Providence appear (though the fact is not explicitly proclaimed by the prophets but left to be read between the lines they have written) when the deportation of the Jewish race into a remote region and their subsequent wonderful restoration to their own home are seen to be events resulting in the bringing of heathen peoples to a knowledge of the God of Israel (Mic. iv. 1—4, vii. 16—17).

(*d*) God's Ethical Character is perhaps that aspect of Him which is most prominently thrown into relief by the Hebrew prophetic writers in general. The qualities entering into their conception of it are principally His justice, His compassion, His forgivingness, and His faithfulness. The first of these attributes is accentuated by the resentment represented as provoked in Him by the social wickedness prevalent in Judah—the oppression and spoliation of the poor, the corruptness of the governing classes, and the dishonesty practised in trade (Mic. ii. 1, 2, 8, 9, iii. 1—3, 9—11, vi. 10—12, vii. 1—4); and not less by His wrath against the Edomites for their unbrotherly conduct to Judah on the occasion of the latter's overthrow (Ob. 10—14). For all such iniquity retribution swift and heavy is predicted. But Jehovah's justice does not exclude compassion when due chastisement has been inflicted: from the exile which is destined to purify the Jewish people they are ultimately to be rescued; and from the humiliating conditions which continue to beset them even after their repatriation they are to be relieved (Mic. ii. 12—13, iv. 6—8, v. 2—9, vii. 11—12). Repentance for misdeeds speedily evokes the Divine pardon, and leads to alleviation of the troubles that have demonstrated the Divine wrath (Joel ii. 18 f.). Nor is His compassionateness confined to Israel. He manifests interest in the heathen; sends a prophet to warn the people of Nineveh of the destruction that their sins have provoked; spares them when they are penitent; and, rebuking Jonah for his displeasure at the city's reprieve, intimates His concern for its innocent children and even its cattle (Jon. i. 2 f., iv. 11).

It is observable that the prophets here under review regarded the existing world as the exclusive field for the retribution and the recompense meted out by God to the evil and the good respectively. And since they could not believe that God failed to govern His world with equity, they looked for wrongdoing to be requited without fail in this life (unless requital was averted by timely repentance); and when vengeance did not overtake the actual wrongdoers during their own lifetime, they supposed that it would eventually befall their posterity (the responsibility which we consider to attach to individual offenders being regarded by the early Hebrews as embracing their households and their descendants). Similarly when the innocent seemed to miss their reward, the apparent miscarriage of Divine justice was accounted for by the existence of some ancestral guilt which had escaped detection by man but was known to God. It was, however, recognized at last that this view was not really satisfactory; and so some Hebrew thinkers in the long run came to believe that the vindication of the righteous and the punishment of the unrighteous would be consummated in another sphere of life, though the scene and manner of the same were differently conceived by various minds (see Ps. xvi., xvii., xlix., lxxiii., Job xxv. 27, Dan. xii. 2, 3, Wisd. iii. 1—9). But this hope lay beyond the range of thought of our four prophets, in whose writings there is no hint of human immortality.

(e) That the prophets to whom these books are due considered that Jehovah possessed all the Power necessary for the execution of His designs is evinced by their attributing to Him as Author both present and past national catastrophes and deliverances (Joel ii. 11, Mic. iv. 6, 7, vi. 4, 5) and by their confident predictions about what He would accomplish both of good and of ill in the future. But there is a difference between the ancient and the modern conceptions of the Divine *method* of working in the natural world which here calls for brief notice.

The Hebrews so far emphasized the distinction between God and His universe that they were prone to represent Him as acting upon it from without. Concentrating their thoughts upon His transcendence in respect of nature, and having little interest in the scientific investigation of physical phenomena, they felt no difficulty in crediting marvellous stories of departures from common experience through the immediate intervention of God. Modern thought, on the other hand, accentuating the Divine immanence in natural processes, systematic and regular in their operation, finds it difficult to accept as historic many of the miracles recorded in the O.T., of which notable examples occur in Jonah (p. xciii). The Hebrew writers, of course, could not be blind to some of the regularities observable in nature. But they were more interested in the purposes which nature's Creator appeared to have in view than in the chain of secondary causes by which He brought results to pass; and in the study of the O.T. this difference of mental attitude between its authors and their modern readers has constantly to be kept in mind.

II. Jehovah was originally the God of Israel (or of some of the tribes that constituted Israel) just as Chemosh was the god of Moab, Milcom the god of Ammon, and Asshur the god of Assyria; and it was not until the 8th century that He was affirmed by the prophets of Israel to be the *only* God. It might have been antecedently expected that when a purely national god came to be declared the sole and supreme divinity in heaven and earth it would be likewise contended that He was not in any exclusive or peculiar sense the God of Israel merely, but was the God of all peoples alike, impartially interested in the welfare of the whole of mankind. This step, however, the prophets (including those here under discussion) did not fully take: whilst asserting that Jehovah directed the fortunes of Israel's neighbours as well as of Israel itself, and that He was the Judge of all nations equally, they continued to foster in their countrymen the conviction that He felt special concern for them, and gave them the foremost place in His love and care. They were His people and His heritage (Joel ii. 17, iii. 2), and Zion, their capital, was His holy mountain (*ib*. iii. 17, Ob. 16). The bond between Him and them went back to the age of their forefathers; and in their distress they could appeal trustfully to the sworn promise which He had made to the patriarchs Abraham and Jacob (Mic. vii. 20). The truth underlying this conception of a bond and covenant subsisting between Israel and the Almighty is to be sought in the signal privileges which certain races and nationalities seem to enjoy in comparison with others in regard to intellectual faculties and aptitudes, or to qualities of disposition and character. Familiar examples in antiquity of such gifted peoples are furnished by the Greeks and Romans, who were so remarkably endowed, the one with a genius for art and literature, and the other with a singular ability for government and organization, the artistic creativeness and the instinct for political order, which respectively characterized them, witnessing to the presence in them of an exceptional degree of what may reasonably be called inspiration. Capacities of another kind have been equally distinctive of certain other peoples. The Hebrews, if their prophets may be looked upon as the flower of their race, were pre-eminently distinguished by a special measure of insight into religious truth, which, at the same time, from a theological standpoint, implies, and can justly be represented to be, a unique revelation, imparted to them by God, of His moral attributes (according as we accentuate the human or the Divine factor co-operating in human history). It was from Israel, too, that our Lord Himself drew His human lineage, crowning the line of the prophets and likewise, as the Christ or Messiah, realizing the ideal of filial conduct in relation to God which a national king, concentrating in his own person the vocation of his race, had long been expected, but expected in vain, to fulfil (p. cxxx). But whilst the prophets believed themselves to be the channels of Divine oracles to their people, who were regarded by them as standing in an exceptional relation to the one true God, they recognized (though not all equally) that this privileged position carried with it certain responsibilities, and that if Israel was the depository of Divine revelations, it was entrusted with them for the eventual good of mankind. This conception of their race's function in the world takes more than one form. In many prophetic passages (2 Is. xlii. 6, xlix. 6, Zech. viii. 23, etc.), and not least conspicuously in Mic. iv. 1—3 (= Is. ii. 2—4), the prevalent idea is that Israel through its wonderful experiences of national extinction and subsequent revival would attract the attention of a multitude of peoples to the God of Israel who had wrought so marvellously for His votaries, and would induce the heathen to seek at Jerusalem for knowledge about so potent a Deity. But in one of the four books included in this volume, namely Jonah, this idea assumes a different shape. It is presupposed that Israel had a direct mission towards the rest of the world which it was its duty to execute. The chief character in the book is a personification of Israel; and the prophet is represented as expressly charged by God to warn the people of the heathen city of Nineveh (symbolizing the Gentile world) of their imminent doom unless they would repent and secure their pardon. The author thus illustrated what he took to be the vocation of Israel amongst mankind, whilst at the same time by depicting Jonah as first of all trying to evade his commission, and then as being displeased at the mercy shewn by God to the Ninevites when penitent, he held up a mirror to those of his countrymen who grudged to their Gentile neighbours any share in God's compassion, instead of lending themselves gladly to promote His saving purposes.

III. Since Jehovah was believed to be bound to Israel by a permanent and inviolable tie, since He was regarded as the owner of the and and as its people's Divine king, and since He was supposed, like human sovereigns, to take pleasure in honorific oblations and other tokens of homage, which in general there was no unwillingness on the part of the people to render (the mass of men at all times being ready to perform religious ceremonies), the early prophets (such as Elijah) found little to censure in their nation, save when a disposition was manifested by a contemporary ruler, followed by a section of his subjects, either to represent Jehovah by some material symbol, or else to abandon the exclusive worship of Him and to pay adoration to the god of a neighbouring state. But the deeper insight into the nature of God marking the prophets who appeared in the 8th century and their successors caused these to contend that no formal service of Jehovah, divorced from the discharge of moral duties, could ensure the retention of His favour; and that the multiplication of sacrifices by those who were guilty of social offences could only aggravate the Divine displeasure. Of the four prophets here dealt with Micah in Jehovah's name denounced with the utmost vehemence the violence and corruption of the more powerful classes among his contemporaries; and declared that under such conditions the trust reposed in the presence of Jehovah amongst them was a fatal delusion. In his surviving oracles, indeed, he does not, like Amos and Isaiah, directly assail the folly of imagining that God would be content with sacrificial offerings in lieu of social righteousness; but by a later prophet, whose utterances are included in the book bearing Micah's name, there is repudiated most impressively the thought that sin can be expiated by sacrifices however costly, since God's essential requirements from man are justice, mercy, and humility before his Maker.

CHAPTER II.

MESSIANIC PROPHECY.

THE occurrence in Mic. v. 2—6 of a prediction of the kind usually designated *Messianic*, and the citation of part of it in the New Testament (Mt. ii. 6), render it desirable to bring this oracle into relation with other prophecies of the same class. It is not proposed, indeed, to take account in detail of the whole field of Messianic prophecy; but it will be useful to review briefly such predictions as appear to be of earlier date than Mic. v. 2—6, and to distinguish in these certain common or contrasted features; whilst it will contribute to a better comprehension of the whole subject if some attention is paid to the directions in which prophetic anticipations developed during the centuries subsequent to the probable date of Mic. v. 2—6, and the realization which these received in our Lord Jesus Christ.

The term *Messiah* is a title meaning "anointed"; and, when not used
as an adjective, is followed in the O.T. by the genitive of the Divine
name *Jehovah* or an equivalent possessive pronoun (*my, thy, his*). It is
applied to various classes of persons, including Israelite kings (1 Sam.
ii. 10, xii. 3, xxiv. 6, 10, etc., 2 Sam. xix. 21, Lam. iv. 20), high priests
(Lev. iv. 3, 5, 16, vi. 22 (15), 2 Macc. i. 10, and perhaps Ps. lxxxiv. 9
(10)), the patriarchs (Ps. cv. 15), and collective Israel (Hab. iii. 13,
Ps. xxviii. 8). It was perhaps also applicable to prophets, for these
were sometimes anointed (1 Kgs. xix. 16); and though the term is not
actually employed in the O.T. in connection with them, yet it is probable
that the Hebrew patriarchs were denominated by the writer of Ps. cv.
Jehovah's anointed in virtue of their being accounted prophets (cf.
Gen. xx. 7). In one instance it is also used of a foreign ruler (Cyrus), regarded as an accredited agent to carry out Jehovah's designs (2 Is. xlv. 1).
The practice of anointing persons by way of investing them with
authority is perhaps a survival from a totemistic stage of religion, when
some animal or plant was taken to be the divine ancestor of a particular
tribe or clan, which, in consequence, bore its name (see p. 120), and
when its blood or fat (if the totem was an animal) or the oil obtained
from it (if it was a berry-bearing plant like the olive) was deemed, where
smeared upon a member of the tribe or clan, to be a means of imparting
to him some of the qualities of the sacred ancestor. Later, when the
totemistic stage of thought was outgrown and replaced by a more
enlightened form of religious belief, the ceremony of anointing and the
use of the term naturally became purely symbolical (see 3 Is. lxi. 1).

Although, as has been seen, the title *Messiah* was applied to more
than one class of official, it was predominantly used of *kings*. Both
Saul and David, as well as some of their successors, are severally termed
the Messiah of Jehovah (1 Sam. xxiv. 6, 2 Sam. xix. 21, Ps. ii. 2, xviii.
50, etc.); and the rite of consecration by means of oil is expressly
mentioned in connection with them (1 Sam. x. 1, xvi. 13, 1 Kgs. i. 39,
xix. 16, Ps. lxxxix. 20). It is the association of the term with the function
of kingship that has caused the epithet *Messianic* to be employed to
describe certain predictions, delivered by the prophets on occasions of
national disaster or depression, which foretold the advent of a king
destined to put an end to the distress of his people and to restore them
to greatness and glory (though to such an expected king the title
Messiah is not actually applied). But the term *Messianic* is also loosely
used to denote prophecies predicting for Israel conditions of peace and
prosperity without any reference to a human ruler; and it is likewise

applied to passages in the prophetic writings, wherein announcement is made of a future line of kings under whom the nation is to enjoy felicity, but without stress being laid upon any pre-eminent individual amongst them. Hence the nature of the prophecy in Mic. v. renders it expedient to confine detailed attention to those prophecies only which pre-announce, or appear to pre-announce, the advent of an individual prince of consummate qualities; but before considering these it will be desirable to begin with a more general survey, and to trace, as far as possible, the genesis of this expectation, in times of adversity, of a happier future, in descriptions of which a king of exceptional parts occasionally but not uniformly figures.

Some of the peoples of antiquity, in contrasting contemporary evils under which they suffered with a better time that their fancy painted, placed the latter in the prehistoric past, from which they supposed that there had been a continuous declension down to their own day. Thus the Greek poet Hesiod begins his account of the history of mankind with a Golden race, when the primitive god Kronos (the equivalent of the Latin Saturnus) held sway; and traces growing deterioration through the races of Silver, Bronze, and the Heroes until he comes to his own, which he calls the race of Iron, the last and worst. The retrospect is shared by the Roman Vergil, though in a less sombre spirit (*G.* I. 125 f.); and even when the latter (after the peace of Brundisium in B.C. 40) looked forward to the dawning, in the near future, of a happier age than that with which he had been familiar, he conceived it to be a return to the conditions of the earth's infancy:—

> *Magnus ab integro sæclorum nascitur ordo.*
> *Iam redit et Virgo* (Astræa), *redeunt Saturnia regna.*

But this was not the outlook of the Hebrews. For them the future held something better than there had ever been before; and so far as they drew upon the past in giving shape to their hopes, they did not recur to the myths current concerning the primæval world, but to a phase in their own historical experience, enhanced and magnified by a glowing imagination.

The confidence in its future which Israel retained throughout longer or shorter periods of affliction and humiliation, and which eventually took form in the Messianic hope, had its foundation in religion. Israel's religion, however, in its early character did not differ greatly from that of kindred and surrounding peoples. Like other nations the Israelites started with monolatry—a belief in, and the worship of, a single deity, without any accompanying disbelief in the existence of other divinities to whom their neighbours rendered allegiance, and who, in times of warfare, were the antagonists of their own God Jehovah. Their thoughts about Jehovah and their feelings towards Him were not dissimilar to those which the Moabites, for example, cherished concerning Chemosh. They were individually Jehovah's sons and daughters, or the collective community was His son (Hos. xi. 1, Dt. xxxii. 6), as the Moabites were the sons and daughters of Chemosh (Num. xxi. 29); in the conduct of their wars Jehovah took part; and He was as much concerned as they in the issue, since their success or failure in them redounded to His reputation or to His discredit (Ex. xv. 3, 4, Jud. iv. 14, v. 23, vii. 20, 2 Sam. v. 24, Ps. lxxix. 10).

In the case of the Semitic races generally triumph in war tended not only to foster national pride but also to develope a conviction that the national divinity was superior to rival gods. And in the instance of Israel the belief which came to be entertained about Jehovah's exceptional power in comparison with that of other deities can be traced to two definite events in their history. The first of these was the deliverance from bondage in Egypt, followed, as it was, by the conquest of Canaan. It was the escape from their Egyptian task-masters, through occurrences which seemed to be due to the providence of Jehovah, that especially caused the Israelites to deem themselves the objects of His paternal care, and to judge Him to be mightier than all the gods of Egypt (see Hos. xi. 1, xii. 9, Am. ii. 10, iii. 1, 2, Ex. xii. 12, Num. xxxiii. 4); and His graciousness and His strength were shortly afterwards as signally manifested by His ejection from before them of the tribes of Canaan and the bestowal upon His worshippers of the possessions of its inhabitants (Neh. ix. 24, Ps. xliv. 2, lxxviii. 55, lxxx. 8, cxxxvi. 17—22). A subsequent age sought to demonstrate that these wonderful experiences were the outcome of Jehovah's benevolent purposes towards their nation by representing them as having been predicted by Him long before to their ancestors when these were but lonely wanderers (see Gen. xii. 1—3, xiii. 14—17, xv. 13—16, 2 Sam. vii. 23, 24). The second event which made a deep impression on the national mind as attesting alike Jehovah's interest in, and love for, Israel, and His ability to give proof of both in the promotion of its fortunes, was the establishment of the monarchy. The need of a king to weld a loose aggregate of quarrelsome tribes into a nation became manifest when serious danger threatened from the Philistines (p. 82). The reign of the first sovereign, Saul, ended, indeed, in disaster; but his successor David shewed himself capable of consolidating his subjects into a unity, which lasted to the end of his own life and that of his son Solomon, and enabled the people not merely to defend themselves against aggression but to extend their territories in various directions. That the institution of the monarchy in Israel, with the resultant triumphs over peoples like Moab and Edom, obtained in the reign of David, was also regarded as predetermined in the counsels of Jehovah appears from a prophecy of it which is attributed to the seer Balaam and represented as delivered by him whilst Israel was yet in the wilderness (see Num. xxiv. 15—19), though the precision of it suggests that it is really a *vaticinium post eventum*, and originated after the monarchy had come into existence[1].

In this connection it is desirable to discuss here a passage which has often been deemed Messianic in the sense defined above, though probably erroneously. This is Genesis xlix. 10, part of the prediction about Judah included among the "Blessings" represented as pronounced by the patriarch Jacob upon all his sons[2]. These "blessings," in general, appear to date from the period of the Judges; but *v.* 10 may reasonably be suspected to be of post-Davidic origin. As will be seen from the various renderings of the passage offered in the text and margin of the R.V., both the meaning and the originality of the existing Hebrew are doubtful. The most obvious translation of the present text is the following (cf. the R.V. margin):

> "The sceptre shall not depart from Judah,
>   Nor the ruler's staff from between his feet,
> Until he come to Shiloh,
>   And unto him shall the obedience of the peoples be."

This is supported by the fact that everywhere else in the O.T. *Shiloh* is a place-name, and denotes the locality where all the congregation of Israel is recorded to have assembled after the invasion of Canaan by Joshua, in order to determine by lot what parts of the country should belong to each of the seven tribes that had not previously received their portions (Josh. xviii.). But historically it is very unlikely that the tribe of Judah gathered at Shiloh in the time of Joshua, even if there was an assembly of other tribes there (Judah and Simeon appear to have entered Canaan from the south[3]); and certainly nothing happened at Shiloh affecting the fortunes or position of Judah, as suggested in the verse under consideration. An alternative rendering of the existing Hebrew of the third line is that which is given in the text of the R.V., "Until Shiloh come"; and it has been widely assumed that by *Shiloh* is meant the Messiah; and the passage is taken as a real prediction that the regal associations attaching to the tribe of Judah, through the circumstance that the dynasty of David belonged to that tribe, would last until the Messiah's advent; and that He, at His coming, would receive the allegiance of the world. If this were really a probable inter-

---

[1] See Gray, *Numbers*, pp. 313, 314 (I.C.C.); Kennedy, *Numbers*, p. 332 (C.B.).
[2] See Driver, *Gen.* pp. 385, 386, 410—415 (West.C.).
[3] See Burney, *Judges*, pp. cv, 46.

pretation, the passage would be Messianic in the strict sense. But *Shiloh* is
not a name elsewhere in the Bible applied to the Messiah, and it does not
connote a meaning which would be appropriate to him, for the Hebrew root
with which it seems to be connected signifies "to be quiet," "to be at ease," or
even "to be easy-going," but not "to be peaceful" (in the proper sense). In
these circumstances, it appears necessary to conclude that the traditional
Hebrew text is faulty, and that the authentic text is preserved in the LXX.
and other Greek versions, in the Syriac, and in several of the Targums. All
these translations and paraphrases were made from a text that, instead of
Shiloh, had *Shelloh,* which can signify (as the R.V. notices in the margin)
either "that which is his" or "he whose it (the sceptre) is." But the first
of these significations, yielding the rendering "until that which is his shall
come," makes poor sense, for it is not easy to see how Judah's acquisition of its
own would mark the cessation of its previous authority. The second possible
signification—"until he shall come whose it (the sceptre) is"—has likewise
been taken to have the Messiah in view. It is assumed that the sceptre must
be an emblem of *royal* authority; and the passage has been understood to be
a prediction that a succession of kings belonging to the tribe of Judah would
not terminate until the coming of the Messiah, through whom the limited realm
possessed by previous sovereigns would be transformed into one of world-wide
extent. But a similar objection to that attaching to the alternative translation
presents itself here, for Judah, as the tribe of the reigning dynasty, would
acquire enhanced eminence through the replacement of a line of ordinary kings
by the Messiah himself, and would not experience a loss of importance (as the
word *until* suggests). These objections, however, are avoided if the passage be
interpreted of the termination of Judah's *tribal independence* through the firm
establishment of monarchical authority in the hands of *David.* When the
collective tribes became united into a kingdom under a single ruler, the
authority previously exercised by each tribe over its own members passed to
the king, and Judah would lose this, equally with the rest of the tribes. If such
be the right explanation (and though it is not free from difficulty, it seems
more plausible than the others) the import of the passage appears to be a
prophecy of the advent, not of the Messiah, but of the first sovereign springing
from the tribe of Judah; though it is perhaps less likely to be a real prediction
of that event, and to date from a time prior to it, than to be an oracle
composed *after* the occasion which it purports to foretell, originating either in
the reign of David himself or in that of Solomon, but put into the mouth of the
patriarch Jacob[1].

The success which, in spite of internal troubles, marked David's
reign—his expulsion of the Philistines from Israelite territory, his
capture of Jerusalem from the Jebusites, his conversion of it into a
capital for the nation which he had consolidated, and his victories over
Moab, Ammon, Edom, and other peoples—profoundly impressed the

---

[1] The passage seems to be referred to in Ezek. xxi. 27, where it appears to be
invested with a Messianic significance.

minds of his countrymen. His house came to be viewed as the nerve-centre of the state, the seat and mainspring of its activities, and the channel through which God had chosen to glorify Israel. In David and his line the filial relation which Israel was believed to occupy towards Jehovah (p. cx) was held to be concentrated. If the nation was Jehovah's son, as evidenced by the marvellous favour which it had enjoyed, the successive sovereigns of David's lineage could be deemed to represent in this respect their collective subjects; and in virtue of the fact that they were individual personalities, they were qualified to realize this conception the more vividly and effectually (see 2 Sam. vii. 12—16, Ps. lxxxix. 26, 27). Many Judæan kings, of course, in their character and conduct fell far below the ideal which such relationship involved, disregarding the administration of justice to their subjects, and fancying that formal acts of worship would satisfy Jehovah. Nevertheless repeated failures on the part of one monarch after another to exhibit the disposition, or to experience the fortune, appropriate to a ruler whom Jehovah graciously styled His son, could not destroy the conviction entertained by the prophets that it was through a descendant of David that the high destiny believed to be designed for Israel would be fulfilled. The retribution which was bound to follow moral and religious offences could not (it was thought) cancel Jehovah's promises. Consequently the national hope, if often disappointed, continually revived, for Jehovah would be faithful to His covenant. He was permanently Israel's spiritual King (1 Sam. xii. 12, Is. xxxiii. 22, Ps. xliv. 4, lxxiv. 12, xcviii. 6, 2 Is. xliii. 15), and it was through a human king, deriving his ancestry from the son of Jesse, and acting as Jehovah's vicegerent, that the Divine goodness towards Israel would finally be consummated.

For the purpose of reviewing the nature of the assurances respecting a glorious future with which the prophets sought to relieve the despondency of their fellow-countrymen in times of calamity, it is proposed here to divide them into classes according to their tenor, without respect to chronology, though within these classes regard will be paid to chronological order, so far as this is clearly ascertainable. In the first class will be included prophecies wherein no mention is made of a human king in connection with the felicity promised to the people. In the next there will be comprised those predictions in which the restoration of happy national conditions is associated with the rule of righteous kings belonging to David's house. The third will contain certain oracles which appear to announce with more or less definiteness the birth of an individual king of pre-eminent attributes, whose function it will be to ensure for his people both external security and internal integrity. The oracles constituting this last class, and alone properly deserving the title *Messianic*, will require to be considered at greater length than the others, which can be dismissed without much discussion.

1. Of the class of passages from which all stress upon, or even mention of, a king or kings of David's line is absent and in which Jehovah Himself is represented as being in Person His people's Protector and Ruler, illustrations may be taken from Is. iv. 2—6, xxxiii. 20—24, 3 Is. lx.[1]. Of these passages the first is probably Isaianic in origin (with the exception of *vv.* 5, 6, which contain some late features) but the other two are most likely post-exilic. Is. iv. 2—6 is a prediction that, after a severe judgment shall have eradicated impenitent offenders from the nation, the land will be clothed with luxuriant vegetation and will produce abundant crops, supplying the needs of, and reflecting glory upon, the surviving inhabitants, who will all be holy and pious in character, and who will be screened by Jehovah Himself from all distress arising from injurious conditions. In Is. xxxiii. 20—24 (seemingly a late conclusion appended to an Isaianic oracle) it is declared that Jehovah will abide with Israel, encompassing and safeguarding them in virtue of His being their Judge, their Lawgiver, and their King. 3 Is. lx., an oracle designed to comfort the Jews during the depressing years following their return from exile, when they were a small community impoverished and harassed, assures them of a speedy increase in their numbers and wealth, and predicts that violence and devastation will cease from the land, and that Jehovah Himself will be there to illumine and glorify His people. In prophecies like these the writers are content to emphasize Jehovah's loving care for Israel, notwithstanding its earlier offences, and do not concern themselves with explaining the agencies by which He will accomplish His gracious purposes.

2. But in another class of prophecies the contrast, material and moral, which it is anticipated that the future will offer to the unhappy present is associated with the rule of a royal dynasty that will ensure among the people the maintenance of justice, order, and true religion; and the restoration of the national fortunes is generally connected with the revival of the Davidic house, the traditions of David's reign being idealized by distance. An oracle looking to the authority of a righteous sovereign and just ministers as a condition of the attainment by the people of the standard of conduct required from them by Jehovah occurs

---

[1] See also Mic. iv. 7.

in Is. xxxii. 1—8. In the books of Jeremiah and Ezekiel, the authors of which witnessed the destruction of the Judæan monarchy, there are contained definite anticipations of the re-establishment of David's line on the throne, as God's destined agency for safeguarding the people from any relapse into the sins which had been so severely punished. To comfort their countrymen, confronted with captivity in a foreign land, these prophets, at the end of the 7th and the beginning of the 6th century, held out to them promises that the period of their servitude would be limited, that in the end they should return to their own soil with their proneness to apostasy eradicated by the bestowal of a new heart and spirit, and that in their former home they should dwell in safety, protected and wisely governed by a righteous descendant of David. The expected king is spoken of in the singular (as "a scion of David" or as "David"); but both prophets doubtless had in mind a succession of rulers who should reproduce the virtues, and renew the achievements, of their illustrious ancestor (see Jer. xxiii. 5, 6, xxx. 9, Ezek. xxxiv. 23). The use of the title *David* to designate a restored Davidic dynasty appears likewise in a passage which is probably an interpolation in the book of Hosea (iii. 4, 5); and an oracle added to the book of Amos (ix. 11 f.) after the termination of the Davidic monarchy announces in somewhat similar terms that Jehovah "will raise up the tabernacle of David that is fallen."

3. In the prophetic passages just considered, which contemplate the renewal of the monarchy after a period of affliction, there is nothing suggesting that the king, or the succession of kings, that the prophets had in mind, would be characterized by extraordinary attributes to which only unusual titles could do justice. But there are a few oracles in which a king whose advent is anticipated is portrayed in terms of a remarkable and startling kind; and though the import of them is not beyond doubt, they call for fuller notice. They occur in the book of Isaiah, and it is with these that the prophecy of Micah v. 2—6 falls into line.

Isaiah discharged his prophetic ministry in the kingdom of Judah during the reign of Ahaz (*circ.* 735—720 B.C.); and the occasion of the first of his prophecies (vii. 14—17) that must be here discussed was a coalition formed against his country by the kingdom of Northern Israel (or Ephraim) and the Syrians of Damascus. The leaders of these hostile powers were respectively Pekah and Rezin. The two allies had probably combined together with the view of forcing Judah to join them against Assyria, or of deposing Ahaz if compliance was refused. The Syrian army, after encamping on Ephraimite territory and drawing reinforcements from it, advanced to invest Jerusalem, causing the utmost consternation to both its king and its people. To reassure Ahaz the prophet Isaiah went to meet him, and bade him lay aside his fear. Neither of the two confederates (he declared) was really formidable: both were only like smouldering embers, more smoke than flame; and their threat of deposing the king and replacing him by a minion of the Syrian sovereign could be disregarded. But the condition of deliverance was tranquil faith in Jehovah, not the adoption of some political device, such as an appeal to Assyria for help. And to encourage Ahaz to repose trust in Jehovah Isaiah felt empowered to offer a sign, the occurrence of which would be an assurance that the prophet spoke by Divine authority. The sign might be anything that the king liked to choose, since Jehovah's power was universal. But Ahaz, having presumably decided to seek foreign aid, refused the offer: he would not (he said) put Jehovah to the test. Whereupon the prophet affirmed that Jehovah Himself would, unsolicited, indicate a sign, which is described in the three verses vii. 14—16, but of which the precise nature is the subject of some uncertainty. The word rendered in the R.V. by *virgin* means a woman of marriageable age whether actually married or not (for it is the feminine of a word denoting a youth or stripling), and does not connote virginity, a condition which would be expressed in Heb. by another term; and accordingly the word *virgin* would be better replaced by *damsel*. But the Hebrew of the passage admits of being rendered by both "a damsel[1]" and "the damsel"; and two divergent interpretations become possible. If the former translation be adopted, the sign consists in the bestowal in the near future by any young woman, pregnant at the time of the prophet's utterance, of the name *Immanuel* ("God is with us") upon her baby (when born) as a recognition of God's presence with His people, evinced by the withdrawal from Jerusalem of the menacing hosts of Syria and Northern Israel, as predicted by the prophet. Such an intervention by Jehovah, reflected in the name given to one, or more than one, infant born just after the people's experience of relief from their peril would be calculated to convince the king of Isaiah's authority to speak in Jehovah's name, and induce him to believe in the further prediction that the power of Judah's enemies to do subsequent injury would be crippled or wholly destroyed within a few years. This interpretation implies that by the "sign" is meant an occurrence in the near future likely to recall and

---

[1] See Davidson, *Heb. Syntax*, § 21 (e).

confirm a *previous* assertion, the truth of which had been doubted; and this explanation of it can be supported by the parallel in Ex. iii. 12 (where, before Israel's escape from Egypt, Jehovah affirms that the eventual safe arrival of the people at Horeb will be a sign that He had been with Moses in bringing that escape to pass). This interpretation, however, fails to account for the use of the word "a damsel" or "a young woman" (*'almah*) instead of "a woman" (*'ishshah*); for such a term suggests that the child who is to be named Immanuel will be his mother's first-born; whereas on this theory of the sign the name might be easily given, in the circumstances supposed, by *any* mother to her recently born child, whether she had previously had offspring or not. On the other hand, if the second possible rendering of the ambiguous term *hā'almah* be adopted and it be translated "*the* damsel," the prediction must refer to some particular birth already much in the thoughts and hopes of the people, and the sign must consist in the fact that the young woman predestined to be the mother of a wonderful child designed by God for sovereignty and high achievement will bear him very shortly, some marvel attending his entrance into the world marking him out as the fulfilment of the popular anticipations, and leading to the bestowal upon him, by his mother, of the name *Immanuel*[1]. This suggestion has in its favour (*a*) that it is not out of proportion to the range of choice submitted to Ahaz when bidden to ask a sign (for if the limits named are the height of heaven above and the world of the dead beneath, some marvellous event might be looked for as the sign proffered by the prophet in consequence of Ahaz's refusal to choose one); (*b*) that it accounts for the application of the term *hā'almah* to the mother of the child, who would naturally be expected to be her first-born; (*c*) that in viii. 8 the Hebrew text as pointed most obviously implies that the prophet there apostrophizes the as yet unborn Immanuel as being *the lord of the land*. Nevertheless this explanation, like the preceding, is not free from difficulty. (*a*) The currency in Israel of such an anticipation as is here described is an assumption lacking independent evidence to support it. (*β*) The passage in viii. 8 admits of being slightly modified so as to be rendered, not *the breadth of thy land, O Immanuel*, but *the breadth of the land. For God is with us.* (*γ*) About any circumstances destined to attend the child's birth and calculated to identify him with the looked-for king or deliverer, causing his mother to name him Immanuel, the narrative contains not a word. In the case

---

[1] See *JTS.* vol. x. pp. 580—584.

of various distinguished personalities figuring in earlier Hebrew history, certain unusual features are recorded to have been predicted about, and to have accompanied, their conception or their birth (e.g. Isaac, Samson, Samuel); but the present pre-announcement is silent concerning any corresponding marvel in connection with the birth of Immanuel. And although the term *'almah*, which is applicable to both married and unmarried women still in the flower of their youth, is expressly translated in the LXX. by παρθένος (reproduced in the account of our Lord's birth in Mt. i. 23), the other Greek translations represent it more correctly by νεᾶνις, so that the inference that Isaiah had in his mind the idea that the child whose advent he predicted would be the offspring of a *virgin-mother* cannot reasonably be drawn from the Hebrew text. In view, then, of the obscurity investing the prophecy, it would be indefensible to give to the passage a Messianic import if it stood in isolation.

This, however, is not the case. For, some 33 years after this, Isaiah uttered another oracle in which he, on a second occasion when the fortunes of his country were at a low ebb, again assured his fellow-countrymen that Jehovah would raise up for them a king of remarkable qualities of intellect and character, who, though he was not to be their actual deliverer from the danger encompassing them (that would be averted otherwise by God), would be their security in the future against any renewal of either external or internal ills.

The oracle in question was delivered, so far as can be judged, in 701, when, in the reign of Hezekiah, the son and successor of Ahaz, Judah was ravaged by the Assyrian king Sennacherib; and the prophet's words, contained in ix. 2—7, are marked by the parallelism characteristic of Hebrew poetry[1]. The language of the prophecy is for the most part couched in past tenses, as though the prophet was narrating occurrences that had already happened; but this is a feature often found in Hebrew descriptions of future events, the speaker or writer, in the fulness of his conviction that what he predicts will really take place, representing it as already realized.

The centre of interest lies in *vv.* 6, 7, the preceding part of the passage depicting the intensity of the satisfaction occasioned by the birth of the

---

[1] To the prophet's utterance has been prefixed a note in prose (constituting the first verse of the chapter) apparently emanating from a later scribe, who, being perhaps a native of Galilee and resident in exile, thought of the devastation brought, long before, upon his home by Tiglath-Pileser in 734, and who applied to his own land the consolatory prospect which was really intended by Isaiah for his fellow-Judæans.

ideal king, the relief from all oppression which will soon be experienced, and the destruction of the weapons and accoutrements of the hostile soldiery. After describing the removal of every trace of the occupation of the land by the Assyrian troops, the prophet announces the birth of a king, who is designated by a fourfold name, expressing his qualifications for the high functions which he is to discharge—*Wonderful Counsellor, Divine Warrior, Perpetual Father, Prince of Peace.* His destiny is to sit on the throne of David as sovereign, possessing in exceptional measure sagacity and military prowess, and ruling with paternal care and in unbroken tranquillity an extensive dominion.

It is obvious that the oracle depicts a monarch of consummate attributes, but none of the epithets applied to him which on the surface suggest that he is to be of superhuman nature really convey that meaning. The two that appear to do so are the second and third. Of these the former (Heb. *'El Gibbor*) could be rendered by *Mighty God* as well as by *Divine Warrior*, and is actually used of Jehovah in x. 21; but in the light of the phrase which, though translated above by *Wonderful Counsellor*, yet strictly means "a wonder of a counsellor," it seems better to turn it by *Divine Warrior*, literally "a god of a warrior." In Hebrew certain words meaning "God," namely *'El* and its equivalent *'Elōhim*, are not infrequently employed to designate men eminent through the possession of power or authority. In Ezek. xxxi. 11 the heathen king Nebuchadrezzar is styled "the god (*'El*) of the nations," whilst in Ps. xlv. 6 a Jewish king is called "God" and in Ex. xxi. 6, xxii. 8, Ps. lxxxii. 1, 6 "judges" are termed "gods" (*'elōhim*), as being in virtue of their office Jehovah's representatives. These words thus seem to have been used of human beings endowed with god-like qualities or invested with god-like functions, much in the same way as the Latin *deus* occasionally was (cf. Cic. *Att.* IV. 16, 3, *deus ille noster Plato*). The latter of the two epithets under consideration—*Perpetual Father* (Heb. *'abhi 'adh*, literally "father of everlastingness")—still less involves the conclusion that the person so described, though of extraordinary endowments, is more than human. The word *'adh* can be employed of continued existence or activity up to the limits imposed by human nature (see Ps. xxi. 4, xxii. 26, Prov. xii. 19)[1]. Hence "father of everlastingness[2]"

---

[1] The synonymous *'ōlām* can similarly be used to describe not only an indefinite period of long, though not necessarily endless, duration, but even a defined period (Ex. xxi. 6, Dt. xv. 17, and Jer. xxv. 9 compared with *v.* 11).

[2] The alternative rendering "father (i.e. bestower and distributor) of spoil" is incongruous with the general drift of the passage, which stresses the righteous and peaceful character of the promised king's rule.

only means that the king described will be the protector and benefactor of his people (cf. Gen. xlv. 8, Job xxix. 16, Is. xxii. 21) uninterruptedly throughout an extended lifetime, but does not imply that he will be exempt from mortality. The statement that the promised ruler will occupy the throne of David suggests that he will be of Davidic descent and will succeed to the sovereignty by natural right.

It is the existence of this prophecy that inclines the balance of probability in the case of the oracle in vii. 14—16 towards the second of the two explanations considered above, and renders more plausible than would otherwise be the case the interpretation that sees in the predicted *Immanuel* the expected Messiah. If so, it is, of course, obvious that the anticipation expressed in 735 that the Messiah would be born within a few months was disappointed; and it seems, at first sight, unnatural to suppose that Isaiah, after his prediction on that occasion had been falsified, should have committed himself to a repetition of it a generation later. But, as will be seen, successive disillusionments did not prevent successive Hebrew prophets from renewing the predictions of their predecessors, and "projecting upon the shifting future" the figure of an ideal king whom they expected to confirm his countrymen in the ways of God, and in the felicity attendant thereon. Consequently there is nothing strained in the supposition that Isaiah himself in the course of his prophetic ministry foretold on two occasions the near advent of such a king, the non-fulfilment of his earlier prediction not restraining him from repeating it at a later date. And it appears probable that he did not originate the idea of the emergence in Israel of a wonderful Prince but that he took up, and lent his authority to, an anticipation popularly current; and expressly asserted, at different periods separated by a long interval, that the birth of the expected ruler was close at hand.

It is of these two predictions of Isaiah that the prophecy in Mic. v. 2—6 appears to be a re-affirmation. The second of the older prophet's oracles was fulfilled, within the time expected, as little as the first; but the failure of it did not prevent a subsequent prophet from uttering another of similar tenor, which, by the terms in which it is couched, seems to have direct reference to Is. vii. 14. The oracle in question can scarcely be Micah's, but must proceed from a prophet living in the reign of one or other of the last two kings of Judah (see p. 39). The occasion was a time when Jerusalem was beleaguered, probably by the forces of Babylon; and the Judæan king was exposed to the insults (or worse) which in antiquity a cruel foe was wont to inflict upon a defeated enemy. But in the midst of the calamities with which his countrymen were surrounded the prophet alluded to came forward to comfort them with hopes and assurances of a brighter future. In spite of the merited retribution due to national offences, they could still trust Jehovah not to abandon His people finally. To the humiliation of the reigning king, and to the chastisement which the people had yet to endure, there would succeed a time of security, order, and happiness under a subsequent ruler, sprung from the same stock as David himself. The prophet did not intimate clearly whether the relief would come in the near or in a more distant future; but the period of the nation's surrender to its foes would last, at any rate, until the moment was ripe for the mother of the coming king to give him birth. With his advent the fortunes of the people would change. A *David redivivus*, he would draw his strain from Bethlehem. Under him would be re-united the severed branches of the house of Jacob. His government of his subjects would be marked by all the care and tenderness bestowed by a shepherd upon his flock; in the discharge of his duties he would be supported by the plenitude of the Divine favour; and his people would abide undisturbed, since the resources at their king's disposal would render him superior to all possible foes, so that, if hostile forces should renew their inroads upon the land, they would be successfully repelled.

The Messianic character of this prophecy must be judged by its resemblance to the tenor of the two that have just been examined. The import of Is. vii. 14—16 is, as has been seen, ambiguous; but it can scarcely be doubted that *v.* 14 was in the thoughts of the writer of Mic. v. 3, for the words "until the time that she which travaileth hath brought forth" at once recall the announcement "Behold, the damsel shall conceive and bear a son." The two passages, in fact, mutually throw light upon one another; at least, the words of the later prophet shew how he understood the oracle of his predecessor. But there is a conspicuous feature of difference between the outlook of the one and that of the other. By the author of Mic. v. 2—6 the birth of the Messiah, the occurrence of which Isaiah, nearly 150 years previously, expected within a year, is relegated to a future considerably in advance of the prophet's own time, for there lies immediately before the nation an interval during which God's favour will be withdrawn from them.

This Messianic prophecy, included in the book of Micah, appears to date from some year *shortly before* the Exile: the next that calls for notice is one which probably originated *during* the Exile. This is contained in Is. xi. 1—9, and seems to have been delivered after the Fall of the Jewish kingdom, for the opening words "And there shall come forth a shoot from the stock of Jesse, and a scion out of his roots shall bear fruit" point to a time when Judah had ceased to be independent and when the succession of Davidic kings had terminated, though the family from which David himself had sprung was not extinct. The word rendered *stock* by the R.V. really means *stump*, that part of a tree which remains in the earth after the trunk has been felled (Job xiv. 7, 8), and would be inappropriate to the house of Jesse so long as a descendant of it was still on the throne. The promised king, through the presence in him of the spirit of God, will be endowed with the intellectual and practical faculties needed for a consummate judge and ruler. Similar features to these have been noticed in previous portrayals of the Messiah; but a novel element in this prophecy is a predicted transformation of the animal world. The suppression of evil amongst men will be accompanied by a change in the habits of carnivorous beasts, which, abandoning their natural food, will browse like cattle upon herbs and grass. Pictures of peaceful conditions prevailing among mankind enter into other accounts of the Messianic age (see Is. ii. 4 (= Mic. iv. 3), 2 Zech. ix. 10, Ps. lxxii. 7, Hos. ii. 18, Ezek. xxxiv. 25), but here the reign of peace extends to the lower animals, so that the most savage beasts and most deadly reptiles lose their noxious qualities and associate harmlessly with the creatures that have previously formed their prey. The scene of this marvellous change, however, is probably conceived by the prophet to be Judæa or Palestine only (Jehovah's "holy mountain"), not the world at large. Parallel ideal descriptions of past or future felicity occur in various Greek and Latin authors, as is well known: amongst such may be cited Theocritus (*Id.* xxiv. 86, 87), Vergil (*Georg.* i. 125 f., *Ecl.* iv. 18—25, v. 60, 61), and Horace (*Epod.* xvi. 53, 54).

The coming Prince who is the subject of the prophecies just discussed was doubtless regarded by the prophets who spoke of him as being of human origin and nature, though endowed with god-like qualities and intended to be God's agent for ensuring His people's permanent welfare. And probably, if they had been interrogated, they would have admitted that he was mortal like other men, and in the course of nature would die, and be followed on the throne by a successor. But in the intensity of their longing for him, and in the exuberance of the hopes that circled around him, his mortality passed out of view, their thoughts being concentrated solely upon the amelioration which he was to effect in his country's condition and fortunes. And so deep was the impression which they produced upon the minds of their countrymen that the expectation of such a Messiah continued to survive repeated disillusionment, and lasted into the early Christian centuries.

In the course of the Exile, however, the Messianic idea momentarily underwent a strange metamorphosis. When about the year 538 the Elamite Cyrus threatened, and finally destroyed, the power of Babylon, he raised in the hearts of some of the Jewish exiles high hopes that he would not only overthrow the tyrant city but also liberate those whom it detained in captivity. And a contemporary prophet who sought to sustain the spirits of his countrymen with this prospect actually applied to Cyrus the title of *Jehovah's Messiah* (2 Is. xlv. 1) as being God's agent, raised up to fulfil His design of releasing His people from their detention and restoring them to their own land. As the term etymologically only means "Jehovah's anointed, or consecrated, one," it could, of course, be employed in more than one connection (p. cviii); nevertheless the use of it by Deutero-Isaiah to designate a foreign potentate lacks a parallel elsewhere.

When Cyrus, after his overthrow of Babylon, allowed the Jewish exiles confined within his newly-acquired dominions to return to their native soil, a large body availed themselves of the permission. At their head, or at least included among them, was Zerubbabel, variously represented as the son of Shealtiel or of Pedaiah (Ez. iii. 8, 1 Ch. iii. 19), and being presumably the real son of the one, and the legal son of the other (through a Levirate marriage). Both Shealtiel and Pedaiah appear in the O.T. as sons of Jehoiachin; but in Lk. iii. 27 the former (here called Salathiel) is enumerated among the descendants of David through Nathan and not through Solomon, so that he may have been adopted by Jehoiachin. In any case, Zerubbabel drew his lineage from David; and it was natural that on such a happy occasion as the Return from Babylon high hopes should centre in him. The expectations raised found expression in an oracle uttered by the prophet Zechariah (iii. 8, vi. 12), who declared him to be the scion of David's house that had been the subject of Jeremiah's prophecy (p. cxv). But though Zerubbabel rebuilt the temple at Jerusalem which had been destroyed by Nebuchadrezzar, no renewal of Jewish independence was humanly possible under the Persian kings; so that the fulfilment of the Messianic prophecies, which their restoration from exile had led the Jewish people to anticipate, was still deferred.

Nevertheless the confident hope that the Jewish race would again have a king of their own survived the depressing experiences which prevailed for so many years after the Return; and a renewed prediction that this hope would be realized was conveyed to his countrymen by a prophet whose writings have been included in the book of Zechariah (ix. 9, 10), but who appears to have lived at some date subsequent to the destruction of the Persian empire by the Greeks (in 333). The circumstances which were to render possible so desired a consummation would (it was implied) be brought about by God: the king would not achieve independence for himself and his country, but would be vindicated and saved by the Almighty, and would enter his capital not mounted on a war-horse but riding upon an ass, the beast of burden used in times of peace. Under his rule all the agencies of war were to disappear and peacefulness was to pervade his dominions, which would be world-wide (as the world was then known to the Hebrews). The epithet "lowly," which the R.V. employs to represent one of the attributes of the king, and which suggests a meek and submissive disposition, is misleading, for the Hebrew word has reference to *condition*, and describes the Messiah as belonging to a community that had hitherto been held in subjection by some dominant power. This passage from Deutero-Zechariah is all the more noteworthy through the fact that our Lord, on the occasion of His entry into Jerusalem shortly before His arrest and death, deliberately took steps to enact the scene depicted by the prophet.

The only remaining passages in the O.T. which it is desirable to notice here occur in certain psalms. Of these Ps. ii. purports to be written on some occasion when a ruler styled "Jehovah's Messiah" is confronted by a confederacy of rebellious subject-nations. In face of this menace encouragement comes to him, through the psalmist, from Jehovah, Who declares that the king is His Son, and that He will subdue under him the revolting peoples; whereupon the poet admonishes the latter to submit in time, lest they should be overtaken by complete destruction. The date of the psalm has been much disputed, for its origin has been placed as early as the time of Solomon in the tenth century B.C., and as late as that of the Maccabæan sovereigns at the end of the second or the beginning of the first. It probably has in view some historic ruler, and a combination of enemies against him at the beginning of his reign (as suggested by Jehovah's words "*This day* have I begotten thee," i.e. recognized thee as my Son). The privilege of sonship which God is represented as bestowing upon the king is doubtless to be regarded as *official*: each successive Jewish sovereign in virtue of his office embodied and concentrated in himself the filial relationship towards Jehovah which properly belonged to the whole collective people (cf. p. cx). But as the king here addressed fell short, like all his predecessors, either in his qualities, or in his experiences, or in both, of what might be expected of one invested with so great a distinction, the utterance of the poet came later to be applied to the ideal Messiah who was still to come; and in the N.T., *vv.* 1, 2, and 7 are expressly viewed as Messianic in the sense in which this term is commonly used (see Acts iv. 25, 26, xiii. 33, Rom. i. 4, Heb. i. 5, v. 5).

In Ps. lxxxix., obviously written in circumstances of grievous national distress, the writer is deeply moved by the humiliation of his country and its king, in spite of the promises made in the past to David's house. God (through His prophets) had affirmed that He would constitute the king His first-born, the highest of earthly potentates; but notwithstanding this, the contemporary heir of David's sovereignty had been dethroned and covered with dishonour. The date of the psalm is probably shortly before the fall of the Jewish monarchy; and it has been plausibly conjectured that the king whose abasement is deplored is Jehoiachin, who was carried into captivity by Nebuchadrezzar in 597. If so, the poem must have been composed within a few years of the prophetic passage contained in Mic. v. 1—6.

The only other psalm requiring attention is Ps. cx. There the term *Messiah* does not occur, but the psalm is regarded as Messianic in the N.T., and may be included here. In it the poet conveys to one whom he styles his Lord (*'ădhōnai*) a communication from Jehovah to the effect that he has been chosen by God to share His throne; is assured of victory over his enemies; and has been appointed a priest, so that he will unite in himself, like Melchizedek of old (Gen. xiv. 18), the functions of both the kingship and the priesthood[1]. The psalm is, to all appearance, addressed by its author to some historical ruler or national chief; but in the title it is attributed to David, who both by our Lord and by others was assumed to have had in mind the Messiah (see Mk. xii. 36, Acts ii. 34, 35, Heb. i. 13). The person whom the psalmist had in his thoughts was probably Simon Maccabæus (143—135 B.C.). For, in the first place, it can scarcely be an accident that *vv.* 1, 2, 3, and 4 (apart from the prefatory words "The LORD saith unto my lord") each

---

[1] An anticipation of the union in the same person of both royal and sacerdotal functions appears at first sight in Zech. vi. 13; but instead of the words "and he (the "scion" of Jer. xxiii. 5, see p. cxv)...shall sit and rule upon his throne; and he shall be a priest upon his throne; and the counsel of peace shall be between them both," the LXX. has καὶ καθιεῖται καὶ κατάρξει ἐπὶ τοῦ θρόνου αὐτοῦ, καὶ ἔσται ὁ ἱερεὺς (i.e. Joshua) ἐκ δεξιῶν αὐτοῦ, καὶ βουλὴ εἰρηνικὴ ἔσται ἀνὰ μέσον ἀμφοτέρων. This reading, or something like it, alone explains the concluding sentence "and the counsel of peace shall be between them *both*." In the existing Heb. text there is clearly some defect.

begins with one of the letters composing the name *Simon*[1]; and secondly, Simon Maccabæus was made by his countrymen both leader and high priest. The objection urged against this conclusion, that certain of the Maccabees were *first* priests and *then* princes, cannot be considered serious, since the historian of 1 Macc. more than once speaks of Simon as leader and high priest in this order (see xiv. 35, 41). He proved an able ruler; but his achievements did not exhaust his countrymen's ideals; and so after his death a poem, which originally seems to have had him in view, came to be treated by the Jews as prophetic of a still greater personality, and by our Lord's contemporaries was applied to the Messiah (as is presupposed by the argument in Mk. xii. 36).

The survival of the Messianic hope after the Canon of the O.T. was closed is evidenced by the occurrence of it in two Jewish productions emanating, the one from Egypt, the other from Palestine. The first of these was a work based on a collection of oracles passing as *Sibylline*, which was expanded by a Jew (probably of Alexandria) who wrote in Greek during (it is supposed) the last quarter of the 2nd century B.C. The relevant passage is found in III. 652—656, and runs as follows: "And then shall God send from the sun a king, who shall cause the whole world to cease from baleful war, killing some, and with others making trusty compacts. And he will do all these things not through his own counsels, but in obedience to the good ordinances of the great God." This prophecy merely reproduces in very general terms previous predictions of the advent of a king possessing universal sway, enforcing peace, and obeying in all things the Divine will. The second work proceeds not from a Jew of the Dispersion but from a resident or residents in Palestine, probably belonging to the sect of the Pharisees. It is known as the *Psalms of Solomon*, and consists of a collection of poems inferred to have been composed between 70 and 40 B.C. At present the poems are extant in Greek, not in Hebrew; but it is probable that the Greek text is a translation of a Hebrew original. In Ps. xvii., after a lament over the past calamitous experiences of the Jewish people, there occurs a prayer for the speedy advent of a king, who is obviously the Messiah of earlier hopes: "Behold, O Lord, and raise up unto them their king, the son of David, in the time which thou, O God, knowest, that he may reign over Israel thy servant; and gird him with strength that he may break in pieces them that rule unjustly....He shall possess the nations of the heathen to serve him beneath his yoke, and he shall

---

[1] In Heb. *ShiM'oN*.

glorify the Lord in a place to be seen of the whole earth; and he shall purge Jerusalem to make it holy, even as it was in the days of old.... And there shall be no iniquity in his days in their midst; for all shall be holy, and their king is the Lord Messiah." This poet, like the last-mentioned, repeats, for the most part, ideas which occur in various O.T. prophecies, including the descent of the king from David; and the only novel feature calling for remark is the phrase *the Lord Messiah* (Χριστὸς Κύριος). As Κύριος was a title applied by pagans to many of their deities, it is possible that it is here used of the Messiah through the infection of contemporary heathen custom; but it is more probable that the expression is a copyist's mistake for *the Lord's Messiah* (Χριστὸς Κυρίου), since this error actually occurs in the LXX. of Lam. iv. 20, where the Hebrew has *the Anointed of Jehovah*[1] (designating thereby king Zedekiah).

It is unnecessary here to trace further the expectation of a Messiah as it is presented in all the other writings of the 2nd and 1st centuries B.C. It may, however, be observed in passing that in one of these, known as *The Testaments of the Twelve Patriarchs*, the Messiah is represented as springing not from Judah but from Levi, and as combining in his single person both the sovereignty and the priesthood (Test. Reub. vi. 7).

In the passages from the O.T. that have come under review the Messiah is a mundane ruler, wonderfully empowered by God to establish conditions of peace, piety, and prosperity among His own people, and to diffuse a benignant influence over the adjoining nations. But in an Apocalypse comprised in a composite work attributed to the patriarch Enoch, and produced perhaps a quarter of a century before the *Psalms of Solomon*, the title *Messiah* is twice applied to a personality who is not of terrestrial, but of celestial, origin. This heavenly Messiah, who is prevailingly designated in this Apocalypse by the name *Son of man*[2], is described as having the appearance of a man (being like one of the holy angels), as having been present with God ("the Lord of Spirits") before the creation of the luminaries, as being endowed with wisdom and understanding and might (cf. Is. xi. 2), and as being destined to judge the world, to reveal all secrets (bringing hidden good and evil to light), and to support and vindicate the righteous. The title "Son of man" is derived from Dan. vii.[3], where, in a series of visions in which four

---

[1] See Ryle and James, *The Psalms of Solomon*, pp. 137—141.
[2] Other titles applied to him are *The Righteous One* and *The Elect One*.
[3] The probable date of the book of Daniel is between 168 and 165 B.C.

successive heathen empires are symbolized by beasts of prey, there finally appears, coming with the clouds of heaven, a figure "like unto a son of man" (i.e. man-like, instead of beast-like), which represents the Jewish people, who, in contrast to the nations that have preceded them, are to enjoy perpetual dominion. But whereas in Daniel the expression "son of man" is only a *personification* of the collective Jewish race, in Enoch it denotes a *person*. How the transition from the one to the other occurred is a matter of speculation. The circumstance that in Daniel the human figure symbolizing Israel comes with the clouds of heaven is only meant to indicate that the people represented have the sanction and favour of God, as contrasted with the other nations symbolized by beasts, which are depicted as rising from the sea and thereby are marked as worldly powers alien to God. But it would be tolerably easy for prosaic minds to take the representation literally, and to understand the figure "like unto a son of man" to be not a mere symbol, but a heavenly counterpart, of the Jewish people abiding from eternity with God. This would be facilitated by a tendency in post-exilic times for earthly entities to be conceived as subsisting with God in heaven prior to their manifestation upon earth: for instance, in Ex. xxv. 40 the furniture of the Tabernacle is described as being made by Moses after the pattern (obviously supposed to be pre-existent) shewn to him by God in mount Sinai (cf. also Heb. viii. 5, Rev. xxi. 2). And as the historic Jewish people were considered to be represented by, and, in a sense, summed up in, their successive individual rulers, in the series of whom one, of pre-eminent gifts, was expected to rectify finally all the evils committed or sustained by his countrymen, so, when the hope of such an earthly Messiah grew faint, the heavenly counterpart of the collective nation became transmuted into a celestial Messiah who was to descend from heaven as Jehovah's vicegerent in order to bring about the overthrow of the heathen without, and the impious within, Israel, and to avenge the pious people of God who had suffered from both[1]. This development of the Messianic hope, however, was probably peculiar to a narrow circle of thinkers, for the book of Enoch does not seem to have been widely known; and amongst the mass of the people the earlier idea of a terrestrial Messiah, the son of David, held its ground (cf. Lk. i. 32, 33, Acts i. 6).

---

[1] Since, however, *Messiah* merely means "consecrated," and consecration could be used in connection with different functions (p. cviii), the application of the term in Enoch to the celestial "Son of man" may be unconnected with its employment as a title for the terrestrial "Son of David."

From what has been said, it is clear that during that period which is covered by the O.T. Scriptures and for a century later the realization of the Messianic hope ever eluded the prophets and apocalyptists who entertained it. The Anointed king of extraordinary endowments, who was expected to deliver his people both from national sinfulness and from foreign tyranny, and whose near advent was predicted at intervals during seven hundred years, never appeared within that long period; or, if ever for a brief moment some conspicuous figure was identified with him, the impression produced upon his contemporaries speedily faded. It was Jesus of Nazareth who first applied to Himself the titles of *The Christ, The Son of God* (or *The Son*), and *The Son of man*, thereby claiming that in some sense He fulfilled the predictions occurring in the sacred books of His race, and who first succeeded in convincing a number (even though only a small minority) of His countrymen that His claim was well founded. Accordingly it will be worth while to consider very shortly both how (from the standpoint of His humanity) He came to believe Himself to be the Personality designated by these titles, and in what respects the fulfilment, which He contended that the Scriptures received in Him, answered to, or departed from, the original import of the prophecies which He had in mind.

It was merely as a *prophet* that Jesus began His ministry, proclaiming the nearness of the hoped-for kingdom of God[1] and urging repentance as the necessary condition of escaping the judgment which would previously sift those who were worthy to enter the kingdom from those who were unworthy. He was deemed a prophet by the people to whom His first discourses were addressed (Mk. vi. 15); and He applied the same description to Himself (Mk. vi. 4). He claimed to heal the afflicted through His possession of the Holy Spirit (Mt. xii. 28 = Lk. xi. 20); and it was the presence of the spirit of God with men that constituted them prophets (Num. xi. 29, 2 Is. xlviii. 16, 3 Is. lxi. 1, Joel ii. 28; see also 1 Cor. xii. 10, 11)[2].

But at Cæsarea Philippi, not long before He departed from Galilee to

---

[1] Though the idea of Jehovah's sovereignty first over Israel and then eventually over all the earth (1 Sam. viii. 7, xii. 12, Zeph. iii. 15, Ps. xlvii. 2, 7, 2 Zech. xiv. 9) is found in the O.T., the actual phrase *the kingdom of God* or its equivalent *the kingdom of heaven* does not occur there.

[2] Jesus' disciples after His death identified Him with the prophet like Moses who was expected to appear in fulfilment of the prediction in Dt. xviii. 15, 18 (see Acts iii. 22, vii. 37, cf. Joh. i. 21). But this prediction in reality had in view not the emergence from within Israel of a single prophet but of a succession of prophets, who should exercise the influence which amongst heathen people was exercised by diviners (see *vv.* 10—14).

go to Jerusalem, He intimated to His disciples that He really was what they acknowledged they had come to think Him to be—the Christ[1]; and on another occasion (in an utterance recorded in a document which is prior in date to the Gospels of Mt. and Lk. and probably to that of Mk. also, and so is a good authority) He spoke of Himself as "the Son" (i.e. of God) in a pre-eminent and unique sense[2]. Again, when He declared that whosoever should give a cup of water to His disciples because they were Christ's should have his reward, He clearly applied "Christ" to Himself[3]. Once more, when He was questioned about the time of the End, and replied that of the day and hour neither the angels nor the Son had any knowledge, He similarly distinguished Himself by the title "Son" (Mk. xiii. 32). And, finally, when He was being tried before the High Priest, and was asked whether He was the Christ, the Son of the Blessed, He publicly avowed that He was[4]. Yet though it was only near the close of His ministry that He thus openly affirmed Himself to be the Christ, it is plain that (if the earliest report of His life is of any value) He must have been convinced in His own mind, before He began His ministry, that He was in truth all that He afterwards explicitly claimed to be. For the story of the Temptation (an experience that preceded that ministry) obviously depicts in symbolic form certain inward doubts and debates arising in Him, after His baptism by John, about the powers which He, if really the Son of God, was endowed with, and free to use; about the risks He might presume to run in reliance upon God as His Father; and about the kind of career He, as Messiah, was meant by God to embark on. In the last temptation (according to Mt.'s order) there seems to have come before Him the thought of the wordly ambitions which might possibly absorb Him (luring Him to worship Satan, the prince of this world), if He, in pursuance of His Messianic mission, were to seek to bring deliverance and triumph to his countrymen through force of arms and the acquisition of dominion. His repulse of the Tempter must symbolize His final rejection of such aspects of the Messiah's prerogative and rôle as first occurred to Him, and His decision that His duty lay in quite other directions.

Jesus' inward conviction concerning His Sonship, which is pre-supposed in the record of the Temptation, appears to have been first fully reached on the occasion of His Baptism, where it is represented

---

[1] Mk. viii. 27 f.   [2] Mt. xi. 25—27 (=Lk. x. 21, 22) ; cf. also Mk. xii. 6.
[3] Mk. ix. 41.   [4] Mk. xiv. 61, 62.

under sensible imagery and described as a Voice from heaven addressing Him and declaring, "Thou art my Son, the Beloved, in whom I am well pleased"; whilst at the same time the Divine Spirit in the form of a dove descended upon Him. The words ascribed to the voice loosely combine parts of two O.T. passages: (1) Ps. ii. 7, Υἱός μου εἶ σύ, ἐγὼ σήμερον γεγέννηκά σε; (2) 2 Is. xlii. 1, Ἰδού, ὁ παῖς μου, ὃν ᾑρέτισα· ὁ ἀγαπητός μου, ὃν εὐδόκησεν ἡ ψυχή μου[1]. The first refers expressly to the Messiah (p. cxxiv), whereas the second has in view collective Israel; and in these circumstances it seems rather more reasonable to look for the source of the words in Ps. ii. than in 2 Is. xlii., in spite of the slightly greater divergence. However this may be, some of the steps whereby Jesus in His human consciousness attained the momentous conviction which in the Evangelist's narrative is externalized as an utterance from heaven may perhaps with reverence be conjectured. His Davidic descent (Rom. i. 3, 2 Tim. ii. 8) can, indeed, have counted for little or nothing, since there must have been many who could claim the same. But we cannot seriously err, if we include among the grounds of His belief about Himself as the Son of God a profound apprehension of what perfect spiritual Sonship involves, and a singular sense of harmony between His own will and the Father's, pointing to unique relations between them[2]. Such a conclusion concerning Himself and God was presumably not unconnected with the relations believed to subsist between His race and Jehovah: if He was individually the "Son of God," it was because the collective nation was God's Son; and He was its representative in an ideal and pre-eminent degree through knowing Himself to have that full understanding of the Divine requirements and that complete submissiveness to them which were looked for, though vainly, from Israel. And the persuasion that He was endued in full measure with the Spirit of God (cf. Joh. iii. 34) must have become confirmed in Him as soon as He discovered that He possessed in an exceptional degree mysterious psychic faculties enabling Him to produce upon the minds, and through the mind, upon the bodies, of the afflicted marvellous cures. Such cures, whilst related to have been wrought by the prophets of old, had not been performed by John the Baptist, though he was accounted a prophet (Mk. xi. 32); and John had announced that One was appointed to succeed him, who was mightier than he

---

[1] This Greek does not occur in the LXX. of 2 Is. xlii. 1, but comes from a version quoted in Mt. xii. 18.

[2] In Wisd. ii. 13, 18 the righteous man is represented as calling himself the "child (or "servant") of the Lord" (παῖς Κυρίου) and the "son of God" (υἱὸς θεοῦ).

(Mk. i. 7). The relief of physical infirmities was traditionally associated with the Messianic age; and Jesus' consciousness of the presence in Himself of extraordinary powers to effect such relief was calculated to reinforce His conviction that He was the long-anticipated embodiment of the true relationship between Israel and its God[1].

All that now remains to be done here, for the purpose of this sketch, is to compare very succinctly the traditional Messianic expectation with such realization as it obtained in our Saviour. The differences are striking, though the prophetic conception of the Messiah was very far from an ignoble one. The hoped-for king was thought of as one who would be endowed with the Spirit of Jehovah (Is. xi. 2), enabling him to suppress iniquity among his subjects, to terminate their subjection to foreign control, and to promote and maintain universal peace. As being a sovereign, it would be through the authority and the methods of a ruler that he would further the aims of God for the good of his people; and it was expected that, if need required, he would ensure right and justice by an appeal to force (Is. xi. 4). Now the first feature of unlikeness presented by Jesus, the Christ, to the Messiah of popular Jewish anticipation was that of station. Jesus was an artisan; it was amongst the labouring classes, ignorant of the Law, and despised by those who were learned in it, that He principally conducted His ministry; and His emissaries were drawn from such people as fishermen and tax-collectors. A second feature of dissimilarity was the means He used to effect among His countrymen that amendment of life which God demanded. The authoritative tone which marked His utterances (Mk. i. 22) was no more than that of a prophet. His authority was not of an official character, and it was not supported by any compulsion; and though on one occasion Jesus, by the manner in which He entered Jerusalem, recalled to those who were acquainted with the Scriptures the description of the Messianic King contained in the book of Zechariah (p. cxxiv), yet He refrained altogether from participating in political agitation. His humble position in life need not have precluded Him from this, had He been disposed to pursue it; for there must have been numbers of those who afterwards were known as the Zealots who would have followed Him if, as the Messiah, He had summoned them to a war of emancipation from the control of Rome. But the redemption which He sought to bring about was redemption from sin; and so different were His methods from those to which rulers commonly have recourse

---

[1] Cf. McNeile, *N.T. Teaching in the Light of St Paul's*, p. 26.

in dealing with such as oppose them, that He actually directed His followers not to resist those who ill-treated them[1]. And a third divergence from the prophetic conception of the Messiah was even more profound than the other two. Among the attributes of the promised King an earthly life of endless duration (as has been already observed) was probably not included; but if so, the thought of his mortality was naturally kept in the background; and any idea of his undergoing a death by violence in the discharge of the duties committed to him by God is nowhere found. Such an idea, indeed, was wholly repugnant to the current belief concerning him. But Jesus, in the course of His ministry, became convinced that there awaited Him a violent end in consequence of the antagonism which His teaching aroused in the ecclesiastical officials of His nation; and from such a fate He did not shrink. His own conception of the Anointed Son of God, therefore, included the endurance of suffering and death, provided thereby He could promote the purposes of the Father. In order to find in the Scriptures a prediction of such a destiny He put a Messianic construction upon the passage in 2 Is. lii. 13—liii. 12 (see Mk. x. 45), though the Figure whose extinction is there described and whose revival is there foretold appears to have represented in the prophet's thoughts the Jewish people whose national existence had come to a close through exile in Babylon. Thus our Lord, whilst not breaking altogether with the traditional notion that the Messiah must be a King (see Mk. xv. 2), was in the highest degree original and independent in His ideas concerning the way in which the Messianic King was to fulfil God's designs for the salvation of Israel[2]. Born in a humble station, He based His Messianic claims upon a consciousness of Sonship rooted in profound spiritual intuitions and perfect obedience; in pursuing His mission of bringing the people into right relations with God He confined Himself exclusively to instruction and example; and in fulfilling His ministry to the end He submitted patiently to an agonizing death.

It has been already noticed that the title *Messiah* was not only popularly applied to the king of Davidic descent expected by many

---

[1] It was no doubt because of the contrast between His own conception of the Messiah's character and office and that of the populace that He did not publicly disclose, until near the end of His life, His belief about Himself. It was not until His most intimate disciples had become familiar with His ideas and His ideals that He could venture to avow even to them that He was the Messiah. Their faith in His Messiahship, impaired by the Crucifixion, was restored by the Resurrection visions and the gift of the Spirit (Acts ii. 22—36).

[2] Cf. Joh. xviii. 37.

of the O.T. prophets, but is likewise used, though rarely, in the book of
Enoch in connection with the celestial "Son of man" whose office as
Judge of all mankind is described by the Apocalyptist. The designation
"Son of man" was one which (as previously remarked) Jesus sometimes
employed of Himself[1]; and by declaring that He was destined to come
in the glory of His Father (Mk. viii. 38, cf. xiv. 62) He seems to have
identified Himself with the Figure portrayed in Enoch. But here
again Jesus modified the conception of which He made use, for the
Apocalyptic writer nowhere hints that the Being whom he represents as
commissioned in heaven by God to pass final judgment upon men was,
before that, to appear on earth to bring sinners to repentance; whereas
Jesus, though affirming that the same function of judgment was to be
His in the future, yet laboured, during a brief earthly ministry marked
by lowliness, sympathy, and self-surrender even to death, to seek and
to save those who were in danger of being lost[2].

CHAPTER III.

Hebrew Versification.

Inasmuch as some acquaintance with the principles of Hebrew
versification contributes not only to a better appreciation of the
prophetic writings, but also to a clearer understanding of the conditions
which must be taken into account where it is sought to emend suspected
corruptions of the text, it seems expedient to notice the subject here,
though the treatment of it must necessarily be brief[3].

The poetry of national literatures is distinguished from their prose
not in spirit merely but likewise in form; and the formal differences are
of diverse kinds. In Latin and Greek, for instance, verse is marked by
a succession of groups of long and short syllables, so arranged that the

---

[1] In the following passages in the Gospels it is not unlikely that the title has
been substituted by the Evangelists for a different phrase: Mk. ii. 10, 28, Mt. xi. 19
(=Lk. vii. 34), x. 23, xii. 32 (=Lk. xii. 10), xiii. 37, 41, Lk. vi. 22 (contrast Mt. v.
11), xii. 8 (contrast Mt. x. 32): possibly, too, Mt. viii. 20 (=Lk. ix. 58), though
this utterance probably occurred on the way to Jerusalem as Lk. represents. The
title has been arbitrarily inserted in Mt. xvi. 13 (contrast Mk. viii. 27, Lk. ix. 20).

[2] The thought that the "Son of man" should suffer was strange and unintelligible
to Peter and the other Apostles (see Mk. viii. 29—32). In this passage, as in Mk. xiv.
61, 62, the titles "the Christ" and "the Son of man" are treated as equivalent.

[3] Further information will be found in G. B. Gray, *The Forms of Hebrew Poetry*;
and some considerations of importance are emphasized in Sir G. A. Smith's
Jeremiah, p. 30 foll. See also an article by T. H. Robinson in the *Expositor*,
Ap. 1924.

regular recurrence of them in a definite order constitutes a rhythmical system, which is lacking in continuous prose. In modern languages a like rhythmical effect is produced by the recurrence in a series of lines (more or less uniform in length) of words characterized by particular accents or stresses, together with (in most varieties of verse) the rhyming of the terminations of certain of the lines. But in Hebrew, though regularity in respect of accentual beats (as will appear) is a factor in poetic structure, the dominating feature is some measure of correspondence in *meaning*, and not merely in sound, between two or more consecutive clauses or sentences terminated by a pause. It is this *sense-correspondence* between successive lines which is most distinctive of Hebrew verse. Groups of lines related to one another in this way compose a unity in themselves, independent of their immediate context, for through the response which the second of two lines makes to the first (or, in the case of quatrains, the third makes to the first and the fourth to the second[1], or more rarely the fourth to the first and the third to the second[2]), an interruption is caused in the natural sequence of the writer's thought, his train of reflection not being carried forward until the idea contained in one line or pair of lines has been reiterated or otherwise thrown into relief by a second line or pair. The meaning of the two lines or couplets is by no means invariably identical or even similar; but whether the second reproduces more or less closely the sense of the first, or presents a direct contrast to it, there is an unmistakable *symmetry* between them in regard to contents and structure. In many cases the symmetry extends to the number and arrangement of the words, term answering term, though more often it subsists less between individual words than between groups of words. This correspondence in significance and form is designated *parallelism*. The use of it serves more than one end; for not only does the echo of the first line, produced by the purport or the construction of the second, yield an æsthetic gratification to the ear, but it helps to elucidate the thought, either through repeating the same sentiment in other words or through the expression of an opposite idea. By its aid the truth which it is desired to convey can be enforced without the monotony which would result from a mere reiteration of it in identical terms.

As has been already implied, there is a good deal of variety in the quality and the closeness of the parallelism which is so prominent a feature of Hebrew poetry. Not only may the correspondence consist in

---

[1] See Mic. i. 4.   [2] See Mt. vii. 6.

contrast as well as in repetition, but it is often incomplete; the second line of a couplet, if duplicating in some degree the signification of the first, may reproduce only part of it, appending to it some additional notion not present in the other. The nature of parallelism, however, is most clearly apprehended when the correspondence is complete; and some illustrations of *complete parallelism* may with advantage be supplied here. Two main varieties can be discerned. (1) The first has been styled *synonymous* parallelism, in which the tenor of the first line is reproduced by the second in equivalent or proportionate terms. The following are examples wherein, though they are given in English, the various words required to represent a single Hebrew term are united by hyphens, and the order of the original is, as far as possible, observed:—

(*a*) 2 Sam. i. 20^b,
    "Lest-rejoice-should the-daughters-of the-Philistines,
    Lest-triumph-should the-daughters-of the-uncircumcised."

(*b*) Ps. cv. 6,
    "O-seed-of Abraham his-servant,
    O-children-of Jacob his-chosen."

(*c*) Ps. cxlii. 1 (2),
    "With-my-voice to-Jehovah I-cry,
    With-my-voice to-Jehovah I-make-supplication."

In the foregoing instances the arrangement of the words within both lines is the same; but this is not a constant rule: more often the order varies, with the result that the tendency to monotony is further relieved. This occurs in the following:—

(*a*) Ps. lix. 2 (3),
    "Deliver-me from-the-workers-of iniquity,
    And-from-the-men-of blood save-me."

(*b*) Ps. xviii. 14 (15),
    "He-sent-forth his-arrows and-scattered-them,
    And-his-lightnings he-shot-forth and-dispersed-them."

Synonymous parallelism appears not only in couplets but likewise in quatrains, as may be illustrated by the ensuing instance:—

Ps. ciii. 11, 12,
    "As-high-as-is the-heaven above-the-earth,
    So-great-is his-mercy upon-those-that-fear-him;
    As-far-as-is the-east from-the-west,
    So-far-hath-he-removed from-us our-transgressions."

See also Mt. vi. 19, 20, vii. 13^b, 14.

(2) The second variety of parallelism is distinguished as *antithetic,* wherein the sentiment conveyed by the first line is confronted by a contrast in the second. This kind is illustrated by the following examples:—

(*a*) Ps. xviii. 26 (27),
  "With-the-pure thou-wilt-shew-thyself-pure,
   And-with-the-perverse thou-wilt-shew-thyself-froward."

(*b*) Ps. xx. 8 (9),
  "They are-bowed-down and-fallen,
   But-we are-risen and-stand-upright."

By its nature it is particularly adapted for giving expression to the sharp contrasts observable in human dispositions or destinies which proverbial sayings and aphorisms summarize; and instances are abundant in the book of Proverbs. It will be needless to cite here more than one:—

Prov. xi. 3,
  "The-integrity-of the-upright shall-guide-them,
   But-the-crookedness-of the-treacherous shall-destroy-them."

The correspondence, however, of many parallel clauses is by no means as perfect as this; and it is desirable to exemplify *incomplete parallelism* as well as the variety just considered. In couplets which exhibit incomplete parallelism, one line lacks a constituent contained in the other, and the want of this is sometimes made good by an expansion of one of the remaining constituents, though oftener it is left without any compensation. A couplet wherein the verbal correspondence is defective, but symmetry is maintained by the enlargement of one of the terms is found in Jud. v. 4,

  "Jehovah, when-thou-wentest-forth out-of-Seir,
   When-thou-marchedst out-of-the-field-of Edom."

Here the absence, in the second line, of any equivalent for the name *Jehovah* in the first is supplied by the occurrence of the compound expression *the-field-of Edom* in response to *Seir.* On the other hand, in Ps. vi. 1 (2), where the name *Jehovah* similarly appears only in the first line of the couplet, it will be seen that there is no equivalent for it in the second,

  "Jehovah, in-thine-anger rebuke-me-not,
   And-in-thy-displeasure chasten-me-not."

Other examples of incomplete parallelism where some term, present in only one of the lines, is balanced by the expansion, in the second line, of some other of the constituent terms are Ps. xlvi. 1 (2), xlvii. 3 (4), ciii. 7, Prov. v. 1 and ix. 1; whilst instances of incomplete parallelism without such compensation are found in Ps. v. 1 (2), xxv. 4, lxxii. 2, cviii. 3 (4), cxiv. 2, Prov. xi. 9, Is. i. 26ᵃ.

Sense-parallelism, however, in all its varieties is by no means a universal feature of Hebrew poetry, as two or three examples will suffice to shew:—

(a) Ps. xxxix. 13 (14),
   "Look-away from-me that-I-may-brighten-up,
   Before I-go-hence and-be-no-more."

(b) Prov. xxv. 19,
   "A-broken tooth and-a-tottering foot,
   (Such is) confidence in-a-traitor in-a-day-of trouble."

(c) Prov. xxix. 13,
   "A-poor-man and-a-man-of violence meet:
   Jehovah lighteneth the-eyes-of both."

In all these cases the second line of each pair is neither synonymous with, nor antithetic to, the first: it only completes the writer's train of thought and does not repeat it or present a contrast to it. Couplets of this kind were classed by Bp. Lowth under the term *synthetic* or *constructive parallelism*[1]; but the designation is obviously inappropriate, for there is no parallelism of *import* at all[2]. Nevertheless, in spite of the absence of this, a *balance* between the lines is clearly discernible, and this calls for fuller notice.

At first sight this balance or parity between the two halves of each couplet may appear to be secured by the inclusion, in each line, of an equivalent number of words (as is the case with many of the above examples). But it very frequently happens that this numerical equivalence is lacking, and though the inequality is often slight, yet in some instances (both where parallelism of thought is present and also where it is absent) the disproportion in the length of the lines of a couplet, or in the length of both lines as compared with that of the rest of the series in which they are included, is considerable. For example, the couplet in Prov. x. 12 has only three words in the first line, but five in the second; whilst conversely that in Prov. xii. 21 has five in the first but only three in the second. The treatment, however, of these uneven lines in the Massoretic text points to a clue which explains several of the peculiarities of Hebrew versification; for in the case of Prov. x. 12 the first three words

---

[1] See his *Lectures on the Sacred Poetry of the Hebrews* (tr. by Gregory), II. p. 49.
[2] See Gray, *op. cit.* pp. 49, 50.

of the second line, and in the case of Prov. xii. 21 two pairs of words
in the first line, are severally grouped and united together by a sign
called *Makkeph* which has the effect of causing each of these groups to
have the value of only *a single word*, with one rhythmical beat. It will
thus be seen that each line of the two verses cited above has only three
stresses or beats, and so are rhythmically equivalent to one another.
In English the effect may be roughly represented thus:—

(a) Prov. x. 12,

"Hátred stírreth strífes,

(But) over all transgression cóvereth lóve."

(b) Prov. xii. 21,

"There-happeneth not to-the-ríghteous any míschief,

But-the-wicked incur evil."

From this it becomes tolerably clear that in Hebrew poetry the length
of the lines composing a couplet or a series of couplets may be determined
not simply by the number of separate words comprised in them but by
the number of *stresses*; so that in a system of verses the lines may be
equal, if measured by *the stressed words or groups of words* which they
contain, though very unequal if every word in them is counted independently[1].

In the Hebrew text of the poetic books of the O.T. the part played
by *makkeph* in the production of the intended rhythm can easily be
discerned by an attentive reader; but at the same time it is difficult to
avoid the conclusion that by the Hebrew copyists to whom we owe the
present text it has been used carelessly, and that they have on some
occasions inserted it where it is not needed and, more frequently, have
omitted it where the prevailing rhythm of a passage seems to require it.
For example, in Mic. vi. 1—3 the metre obviously consists of a succession of lines of three beats (or trimeters); but they are not perfectly
regular, since here and there in the Massoretic text a *makkeph* is either
lacking or redundant. It is possible, of course, if not probable, that
the Hebrew poets, like others, conceded to themselves some licence;
and numerous passages are found where, though the predominant rhythm
is produced by a series of couplets, severally composed of two trimeters,
yet there occur at intervals couplets of which only the first line contains

---

[1] Further illustrations of the use of *makkeph* occur in Dt. xxxii. *vv.* 1, 13, 22, 41.

three stressed words, or groups of words, the other having but two, these not admitting of being converted into trimeters by the omission of a *makkeph*. Some instances have already come under notice (see p. cxxxvii), and others are afforded by Mic. i. 4ᵃ, Ps. cv. 22, cvii. 29. Occasionally, too, there are interspersed in a system of trimeters couplets of the form 2 : 3 (see Ps. ciii. 18, cvi. 42, cxix. 16); nor are these the only irregularities met with in such a system, for there also occur couplets of the form 4 : 3 (see Ps. cv. 1, 41, 44, cvii. 26) and perhaps 4 : 2 (Ps. cv. 25, cvi. 4). In view of these facts it is likely that the Hebrew writers were not consistently rigorous in their observance of metrical regularity throughout a poem or a poetic passage. Nevertheless, they may have been really stricter than appears on the surface, for it can scarcely be doubted that in some instances the original structure of a verse has been distorted by insertions. This is certainly the case in Mic. iv. 3, for this passage is found also in Is. ii. 4, and there the words for *many* and *afar off*, which disturb the metre in Micah, are absent. See also p. 31.

In attempts to recognize or recover the metrical structure of various poetical passages, which in the present Hebrew text seem irregular, there must be taken into account, besides the possibility of a misuse of *makkeph* by the Hebrew scribes, two other considerations. One is the fact that a series of metrical couplets is often preceded by an introductory, or followed by a concluding, word or phrase which is not comprised within the metre: for example in Joel ii. 28 (= Heb. iii. 1), the words "And it shall come to pass afterward that" are *extra metrum*, the rest of the verse constituting four trimeters. The other is the likelihood that the original text of a passage is sometimes better preserved in the LXX. than in the Hebrew, so that in the former there can be detected the rhythm which in the latter is obscured. Such seems to be the case in Mic. v. 2 (Heb. v. 1), where the symmetry of the opening clauses (tetrameters) is evident in the Greek Version, which begins with καὶ-σὺ, Βηθλέεμ, οἶκος Ἐφράθα (answered by ὀλιγοστὸς-εἶ τοῦ-εἶναι ἐν-χιλιάσιν Ἰούδα), whereas the Heb. has merely *But-thou Bethlehem Ephrathah*. On the other hand, in Mic. i. 3 (where the introductory words *For behold* are not included in the metre) the LXX. does not contain the words *and tread* which occur in the Heb.; and the verb thus translated may be suspected to be an insertion, though the Massoretes have conserved the trimeter rhythm by giving to the words *upon the high places of the earth* (through the use of *makkeph*) a single stress instead of two.

The elevated passages, then, contained in the O.T. Scriptures, and exhibiting poetical structure, are distinguished either by parallelism of thought, or by a series of uniform (or nearly uniform) rhythmic beast or by both these features together[1]. Their writers, like other poets, subjected themselves to rules, though perhaps not very exigent rules, and produced their works under restrictions of form which, whilst limiting in some measure their freedom, gave to what they wrote greater effectiveness. Their words, through being uttered in rhythmical cadence, not only gained in force or sublimity but were more easily remembered and transmitted with accuracy by those who heard them: and it will be recalled that the utterances of the Greek oracles were generally couched in hexameters. It is not necessary to pursue the subject now at any length, as the principal object of the brief treatment of it here is to render intelligible the discussion of some of the textual emendations which will come under notice in the ensuing pages. The contents of the Prophetic books in general, of the book of Psalms, and of the compositions comprised in what is commonly known as "Wisdom" literature (e.g. Proverbs), are largely metrical in the sense explained; so that where corruption of the text is suspected, the attempted correction of it cannot always be independent of metrical considerations; and suggested emendations of many passages suspected to be faulty ought, if they are to commend themselves, to conform to the dominant rhythm of the immediate context. Even in cases where the existing text presents no serious difficulties, the metre of a passage may be a factor in deciding upon the relative merits of two competing readings. For example, if in the Massoretic text a line marked by three rhythmical beats be followed by a parallel line of only two, and if one or more of the Versions should point to the existence of a parallel line having the normal three beats, there is a strong probability that the reading implied by the Versions is original. On the other hand, there must not be overlooked the likelihood that there may have been (as already observed) some laxity in requiring corresponding lines to be in all cases rhythmically equivalent to one another: our knowledge of Hebrew metrical rules is scarcely exact enough to justify disregard of documentary evidence, save in exceptional instances. Accordingly where neither the desired sense nor the evidence of the Versions favours the conclusion that something has been lost from, or added to, the current text, the occurrence, in a verse-system, of a line of irregular length does not appear to afford sufficient ground for emending the line by mere conjecture.

---

[1] Intermingled, of course, with passages having the rhythm of poetry there occur others which are in prose: see, for instance, Jer. vii., where *v.* 29 is metrical, but the verses that follow are not.

The commonest metres used in Hebrew poetic compositions are the dimeter (with two beats) and the trimeter (with three); whilst tetrameters (with four beats) are not rare (see Ps. xxix. 1, 2, lxxxix. 11—16, cxliv. 15, Joel iii. 3, Am. ix. 14, Job iv. 2). After what has been said these do not call for further remark, yet it may be well to subjoin an illustration of all in combination, though some have been exemplified separately already. In many poems there occur rapid transitions from one metrical form to another; and an instance of the three metres just enumerated is found within narrow compass in Is. ix. 2—3 (Heb. 1—2). Here the first verse is in trimeters; the first half of the second is in dimeters; whilst the last half is in tetrameters. In the translation, the English words that represent a single Hebrew term are, as before, joined by hyphens, whilst such insertions as the English idiom requires are placed in brackets:—

2 (1)   "The-péople that-wálked in-dárkness
        Have-séen (a) gréat líght;
        Dwéllers in-a-lánd-of gloóm,
        Líght hath-shóne upon-thém.

3[a] (2)   Thou-hast-múltiplied the-rejoícing[1],
        Thou-hast-incréased the-jóy:

3[b]   They-jóy befóre-thee as-with-the-jóy in-hárvest,
        Líke-as (men) rejóice when-divíding spóil."

Rather more must be said about another metre, in which the lines are not usually arranged in couplets (though see p. 143), so that there is an absence of the *balanced* cadence observable in the varieties previously considered, but every line is commonly divided into two unequal parts, producing the effect of a *falling* cadence. This is generally known by a Hebrew name, *Kinah*, meaning "lamentation" (especially for the dead), see 2 Sam. i. 17, 2 Ch. xxxv. 25, Ezek. xix. 1, Am. v. 1. Whilst, however, the term seems to have denoted specifically the wailing of women employed as professional mourners—"keening" women—(see Jer. ix. 20), and was then extended to songs and poems of a plaintive tone, the rhythm designated by it was also used in other compositions, and particularly in satiric taunt-songs. The metre is marked in general by five accentual beats with a pause after the first three[2], though in

---

[1] This is the rendering of an emendation: the present Hebrew text makes nonsense of the next line and destroys the parallelism.
[2] Instances of isolated couplets exhibiting this rhythm occur in Mic. ii. 2, v. 9, 10, 13, Am. iii. 3, Ps. ii. 11, Is. i. 21[a]. In Mic. vii. 14—21 a series of *Kinah* lines seem spoilt by insertions (see pp. 63, 66).

some instances the pause occurs after the first two (see Mic. vii. 14, Lam. ii. 4[b]), whilst lines are occasionally found where there are only four beats, with the pause similarly after the first two; and still more rarely there are encountered lines of six beats, with the pause after the first four (see Is. xiv. 16[b]). As in the case of other metres, the characteristic rhythm of the *Kinah* is sometimes disguised in the present Heb. text through the absence or intrusion of *makkeph*. In the following illustrative passage from Is. xiv. 4—8, *makkeph* has been inserted in a few places and one or two plausible emendations have been adopted:—

Hów there-is-stílled (the) oppréssor, | stílled (the proud) vaúnting[1]!
Jehóvah hath-bróken the-stáff-of the-wícked, | the-ród-of (the) rúlers,
Which-strúck-at (the) péoples in-ánger | with-stróke unremítted,
Which-rúled (all the) nátions in-fúry | with-rúle[2] unrelénting.
In-péace, in-repóse all-the-eárth! | (They) búrst into-shoúting.
At-thée\e'en-the-fír-trees rejoíce, | the-cédars-of Lébanon:—
"Nów thou-art-próne, there-aríseth | no féller agaínst-us."

The verses quoted exemplify, as far as possible in English, not only the ordinary cadence of the *Kinah*[3] but also one of the rarer rhythms which it sometimes admits. More extensive illustration is afforded by the book of Lamentations; and other instances of poems constructed in this metre will be found, within this volume, on pp. 87, 143. Here exhaustive treatment of it or of other varieties of Hebrew metrical systems is unnecessary for reasons already explained.

---

[1] Here *madhhēbhah* (R. V. *the golden city*) is replaced by *marhēbhah.*
[2] Here *murdāph* (R.V. *persecution*) is replaced by *mirdath.*
[3] An interesting parallel to the *Kinah* is offered in Latin by the Saturnian metre, which was also regulated by accent and not by quantity : each line consisted of two divisions, marked respectively by three accents and two, though certain departures from this norm were permitted. The following is an illustration :
Dábunt málum Metélli | Nǽvio poétæ.

MICAH

CHAPTERS I.—III.

It is generally recognized that these chapters (with the exception of ii. 12—13, see p. 20) consist of genuine utterances of Micah. They are prophecies of a judgment awaiting each of the Hebrew sister-kingdoms; but though the predictions of impending disaster are unqualified by any suggestion that it can be averted by repentance, they were doubtless designed to induce reformation (p. xxiii.); and in the case of Judah, the prophet's purpose was not wholly a failure (p. xxxi.). The cause of the Divine resentment is in ch. i. idol worship, in chs. ii. and iii. social oppression and corruption.

CHAPTER I.

This ch. is an announcement that Jehovah is about to judge His people for their sins of idolatry. Samaria will be demolished; and the enemy that is to bring about its overthrow will sweep onward into Judah, and overwhelm the towns of the Lowland.

I. 1 THE word of the LORD that came to Micah the Morashtite

I. 1. This prefatory verse, in ascribing by implication the whole book to Micah, is shown, by the nature of various sections, to be only partially correct; see pp. xxii. f., 28 f. The resemblance which the verse bears to the opening of the books of Hosea and Isaiah renders it not unlikely that all these prefatory notices are of editorial origin.

The word of the LORD. The original has *The word of Jehovah,* the English substitute for the Divine Name being adopted from the LXX., which has λόγος Κυρίου. From motives of reverence the Jews avoided pronouncing the personal name by which the God of Israel was known. This in historic times was *JAHVEH* (pronounced *Yahweh*), an appellation which, since it coincides with a dialectic form of the ordinary Hebrew for *He will be,* is probably an adaptation (perhaps a popular etymology) of a prehistoric name which is irrecoverable. *JAHVEH* was seemingly interpreted to be an abbreviation of *He will be what He will be* (cf. Ex. iii. 14, 15, mg.), the phrase conveying both a belief in the activity of the national God and an acknowledgment of the inscrutability of His nature and purposes. Fear of infringing the sanctity of this Divine Name caused, in practice, the replacement of its vowels by those of the title *'Adhōnai,* "my Lord" (represented by the Greek Κύριος) whilst the consonants were retained, this modification resulting in the form *JEHOVAH*[1]. Other reverential substitutes were *the Name* (Lev.

---

[1] The *a* and the *e* in the first syllable of *'Adhōnai* and *Jehōvah* respectively are equivalent, the difference being due to the initial consonants of the two, which require dissimilar vowels.

w. 1

in the days of Jotham, Ahaz, and Hezekiah, kings of Judah, which he saw concerning Samaria and Jerusalem.

xxiv. 11), *the Heavens* (Dan. iv. 26), *the Blessed* (Mk. xiv. 61), *the Power* (Mk. xiv. 62). A title like 'Adhōnai or Κύριος had, for the development of religion, a great advantage over a proper name like *Jehovah*, since the latter was only appropriate to a deity who was believed to be one of a large number, whereas the former was not un-suitable for a national divinity when such came to be regarded as the only existing God.

In general, phrases such as *The word of the Lord hath come unto me* (Jer. xxv. 3), *Thus saith the LORD* (*passim*), and the like, only expressed the conviction of the prophet using them that what he said was God's truth; but it is not improbable that they had their origin in the experiences of religious ecstasy. Persons subject to such, in moments of psychic exaltation (sometimes stimulated by music (1 Sam. x. 5—13, cf. 2 Kgs. iii. 15) and doubtless by dancing also), believed that they heard a Voice from heaven addressing them (see Num. xxiv. 3, 4, 15, 16). In the case of men of reflection and insight, the thoughts expressed may well have been long in their minds; but as they were probably subject to strong emotions and at intervals lost their self-control, the ideas that filled them were likely to find utterance without the speakers being conscious of any intermediate step of reasoning or inference, so that the thoughts to which they gave expression would appear to come to them at the moment, and to be received by them directly from God through ecstatic audition[1]. Possibly in the phrase *saith the LORD* (iv. 6, v. 10, vi. 1, etc.) and its equivalents, the present tense should be replaced by the past *said*, alluding to the occasion when the prophet believed that he had heard God addressing him[2].

Micah. In Jer. xxvi. 18 the prophet is called *Micaiah*, which is pro-bably the true form of his name: the LXX. in both places has Μειχαίας.

the Morashtite. I.e. a native of Moresheth-gath, see p. xviii. Similar local designations are appended to the names of Elijah, Elisha, Jonah, Jeremiah, and Nahum (1 Kgs. xvii. 1 (LXX.), xix. 16, 2 Kgs. xiv. 25, Jer. i. 1, Nah. i. 1).

in the days of Jotham, etc. The period covered by the reigns of the kings enumerated may have amounted to forty-six years (738—692); but there is no internal evidence pointing to the conclusion that any part of the book dates from the time of the first-mentioned king. The earliest prediction in it was certainly prior to the destruction of Samaria (i. 6); but the expression *her* (Samaria's) *wounds are incurable* (*v.* 9) suggests that the prophecy was uttered when the fate of the city and kingdom was virtually sealed (i.e. very shortly before 722). It is some-what uncertain who was the contemporary king of Judah (see p. xvi.).

which he saw. The Heb. verb is *hāzah* (see on iii. 7). No visions are recorded in the book as having been seen by Micah; and the word

---

[1] Cf. Joyce, *Inspiration of Prophecy*, p. 74 f.
[2] See T. H. Robinson, *Prophecy and the Prophets in Ancient Israel*, pp. 43—45.

2 Hear, ye peoples, all of you ; hearken, O earth, and all ¹that

¹ Heb. *the fulness thereof*.

saw here used may be conventional (cf. Hab. i. 1) and equivalent to
"received from God." Even in some cases where actual "visions" appear
at first sight to be described (Am. vii. 1, 4, 7, viii. 1, Jer. i. 11—13),
such do not necessarily imply abnormal visual experiences; the object
shewn or *seen* may have been something that happened at the time to
be under the prophet's eyes, and suggested to him thoughts which could
be ascribed to God as their source. The visions related in Zech. i.—vi.,
which are much more complex, are also probably literary devices—
"conscious and artistic allegories¹." On the other hand, those related
to have been witnessed by Isaiah (ch. vi.) and by Ezekiel (ch. i.) can
with more plausibility be explained as seen by the prophets under
conditions of trance². At an early period in Israel's religious history it
was believed that the Deity Himself could be visible to man, since He
had a corporeal form, though the sight of the face of God was fatal to
the beholder (see Ex. xxxiii. 20—23).

concerning Samaria and Jerusalem. The only portion of the book
relating with certainty to Samaria is i. 5—9, though some scholars have
thought vi. 9—16 to have the Northern kingdom in view (p. 53).

2—7. The descent of Jehovah, the universal Judge, from His heavenly
temple to punish the offences of Israel and Judah, and the sentence
pronounced upon Samaria.

2. Jehovah is regarded by the prophet as coming to arraign the
heathen for their sins equally with the two Hebrew kingdoms; but the
only "case" here gone into is that of the latter, at whose trial the other
nations, as being in the like situation, are bidden to attend. There is
no good reason for considering *vv*. 2—5ª to be unoriginal (and supplied
by a subsequent editor) just because in these Jehovah is represented as
judging heathen peoples and it is implied that His temple is in heaven.
The Lord appears as the judge of the heathen in Am. i. 3—ii. 3, Is. iii.
13 (both a little earlier than Micah); and though the passages where
Jehovah's temple is explicitly identified with heaven (Ps. xi. 4, xviii.
6, 9) are certainly or probably later than the 8th century, yet heaven is
the locality from which God descends upon Sinai in Ex. xix. 11ᵇ, 18, 20
(derived from the early source J) and from which His angel calls to
Abraham in Gen. xxii. 11 (from the almost equally early source E). It
is nearly incredible that Micah's prophecy should ever have begun with
so abrupt a question (*v.* 5ᵇ) as *What is the transgression of Jacob?*

The prophet bids the peoples attend to his announcement of Jehovah's
imminent approach. The sentence has been attached quite unintelli-
gently in 1 Kgs. xxii. 28 (Heb.) to an utterance of another Micaiah with
whom the prophet of Moresheth was confused; the addition is absent
from the LXX.

O earth...therein is. In Ezek. xxx. 12 the same words (in the Heb.)

¹ G. A. Smith, *Book of the XII Prophets*, ii. p. 274.
² See Joyce, *Inspiration of Prophecy*, pp. 9 f., 110 f.

therein is: and let the Lord GOD be witness [1]against you, the Lord from his holy temple. 3 For, behold, the LORD cometh forth out of his place, and will come down, and tread upon the high places of the earth. 4 And the mountains shall be molten under him, and the valleys shall be cleft, as wax before the fire,

[1] Or, *among*

are used of a single country (Egypt); but here the reference is to the world at large, and its human inhabitants (LXX. καὶ πάντες οἱ ἐν αὐτῇ).

the Lord GOD. Better, *the Lord JEHOVAH*. As the vowels of *'Adhōnai* were used in the vocalization of Jehovah (p. 1), it became necessary, when *'Adhōnai* (literally, *my Lord*) was prefixed to the latter, to adopt in connection with the consonants JHVH the vowels of *'Elōhim*, "God." Here LXX. B has κύριος Κύριος but in Ob. 1 Κύριος ὁ θεός. Similar to the prefixing of the title *my Lord* to the name *Jehovah* was the employment by the heathen peoples of *Lord* ('Ādhōn) in association with the names of their own divinities—*'Ādhōn 'Eshmun, 'Ādhōn Shalman*, etc. Here, however, the occurrence of the title impairs the rhythm of the *v.*; and it is absent from the Alexandrine codex of the LXX.: there is much evidence that it was frequently inserted by copyists (see Am. i. 8, iv. 2, v. 16, vi. 8, where, though present in the Hebrew, it is absent from the LXX.).

be witness. God is similarly a *witness* against men in Jer. xxix. 23, as being "He that knoweth" their most secret deeds: cf. also Mal. iii. 5.

his holy temple. God's heavenly abode (1 Kgs. viii. 30, Ps. xi. 4), whence He is about to descend to the earth (*v.* 3, cf. Is. xxvi. 21), is similarly called "the sanctuary" (ὁ ναός) in Rev. xvi. 17.

3. *For, behold*, etc. Verses 3 and 4 describe a Theophany, wherein the Divine activity is described through the medium of physical imagery.

and tread. This is absent from the LXX.; and the rhythm of the *v.* is improved by its omission (though see p. cxl.). The verb resembles the preceding word closely enough to be an accidental dittograph; or it may have been inserted by a copyist who recalled Am. iv. 13.

the high places. Better, *the heights* (to avoid the religious associations (see on *v.* 5) attaching to the other phrase). The conception is inspired by the movement, along the mountain tops, of the storm clouds with which the Almighty was believed to screen the brightness of His Presence: cf. Ps. xviii. 10, 11.

4. *And the mountains*, etc. God's descent is thought of as accompanied by a violent thunderstorm (cf. Ex. xix. 18), causing landslides on the hills (like the melting of wax, cf. Ps. xcvii. 5, 3 Is. lxiv. 1, 3) and rifts in the valleys (like the effects of a cataract[1]). Similar descriptions of the results produced on nature by a Theophany occur in Jud. v. 5, Nah. i. 5, Hab. iii. 6.

---

[1] The strict sense of the last clause of *v.* 4 is *the valleys shall be cleft...by the like of waters that are poured down a steep place* : cf. Is. i. 25 (*I will purge away...with the like of lye*).

as waters that are poured down a steep place. 5 For the transgression of Jacob is all this, and for the sins of the house of
Israel. What is the transgression of Jacob? is it not Samaria?
and what are the high places of Judah? are they not Jerusalem?

5. *For the transgression*, etc. I.e. in retribution for the transgression
of Jacob (Northern Israel) and Judah Jehovah's resentment is manifested thus. If the text is sound and the names employed are intended
to be distinct, *Israel* must stand for the Southern kingdom, but this is
natural only in passages written after the destruction of the sister-
kingdom, or where ambiguity is impossible. Here it is too equivocal to
be probable, and it should be replaced by *Judah* (this clause being
assimilated to the next). Although Micah was a Judæan prophet, the
sin and approaching punishment of the kingdom of which Samaria was
the capital were first in his thoughts, since that realm was more exposed
than its neighbour to the assault of an enemy (Assyria) advancing from
the north. For *the sins* the LXX. has *the sin*; which makes the
parallelism closer.

What is the transgression, etc. Strictly, *Who is the transgression?*
i.e. what group of people is the living embodiment of the corruption
infecting the rest of the nation? In each case the answer is, the citizens
of the capital. Amos refers to the idolatry of Samaria (viii. 14), and
Isaiah to the idols of both cities (x. 10).

the high places. The term designates the sites of sacrificial worship
on the summits of hills, positions enabling the smoke of the sacrifices
to disperse easily, and so to convey the savour of the burnt offerings to
the heavenly deities whom it was desired to gratify. In early times in
Hebrew history "high places" were consecrated to the worship of
Jehovah (1 Sam. ix. 12, 1 Kgs. iii. 3, 4, xviii. 20) no less than to that
of other divinities (1 Kgs. xi. 7, Jer. xxxii. 35); and mount Zion, where
the Temple was erected by Solomon, must have been of the nature of
a "high place," one among several others in the land (cf. 1 Kgs. xv. 14,
2 Kgs. xii. 3). Eventually, however, in the 7th century this was constituted the sole locality where sacrifice to Jehovah was permitted
(Dt. xii. 4 f., 2 Kgs. xxiii. 3), the reason for this limitation being
doubtless the pollution of the worship of Israel's God by the licentious
practices associated with the cult of Canaanite deities, which was likewise conducted at "high places." In the present passage the LXX.,
instead of *what are the high places of Judah?* has *what is the sin of the
house of Judah?* which is preferable, since not only does harmony with
the rest of the *v.* require this, but it is difficult to see how "high places"
could exist *in Jerusalem* side by side with the Temple. It has been
suggested that the word for *house-of* (*beyth*) has been corrupted into that
for *high places* (*bāmōth*), since the letters for *y* and *m* in the early Heb.
alphabet were less dissimilar than in the later, and that the word for
sin (*hattath*) has been accidentally lost. (The questions and answers as
here re-constructed seem to form two lines in the *Kinah* metre (p. cxlii.),

6 Therefore I will make Samaria as an heap of the field, *and* as the plantings of a vineyard: and I will pour down the stones thereof into the valley, and I will discover the foundations thereof. 7 And all her graven images shall be beaten to pieces, and all her hires shall be burned with fire, and all her idols will

whereas in the existing Heb. text they appear to constitute four dimeters).

6. *as an heap of the field.* Better, *into a heap* (of stones) *in a field* (cf. the Vulgate, *quasi acervum lapidum in agro*). The Assyrian king Tiglath-Pileser similarly speaks of changing an enemy's territory "into a rubbish mound and fields" (Schrader, *COT.* I. p. 227, II. p. 148). For the rendering *a heap in a field*, where the Hebrew is literally "a heap of a field," cf. the similar use of the objective genitive in Gen. iii. 24, *the way of* (i.e. to) *the tree of life*, Prov. vii. 27, *the way of* (i.e. to) *Sheol*. So in Latin, *abaci vasa* is used for "vessels *on* a sideboard." Many critics propose the omission of the word for *a heap* and would render, *into a field*, so as to bring the statement into harmony with iii. 12; and Wellhausen would substitute (by a slight change) *into a forest of the field* (i.e. a wild forest), comparing Ezek. xx. 46 (xxi. 2 Heb.). But Micah need not be suspected of limiting himself to stereotyped phrases, and the text is supported by the parallel in the second half of the *v.* The predicted demolition of Samaria, which lay on a hill (1 Kgs. xvi. 24, Am. iv. 1, vi. 1), is thought of as causing its stones to be piled in the valley below. For the fulfilment of the prediction, at least so far as the *capture* of Samaria is concerned, see 2 Kgs. xviii. 9—10.

as the plantings, etc. Better, *into the plantings,* etc. The writer's thought is that the foundations of Samaria, after its ruin, will be thoroughly cleared away in order that the good soil needed for vines may be reached.

discover. Better, *uncover* or *expose.*

7. *all her graven images.* The destruction that is to overtake the city will extend to the symbols of the deities to whom it ascribes its blessings (cf. Hos. ii. 5) and renders worship.

beaten to pieces. This implies that the graven images were constructed of stone or marble.

all her hires. This, if the text is sound, must mean the gold and silver given to and for the idol-gods by their votaries (Hos. viii. 4, xiii. 2) in the hope of procuring from them in fuller measure the fruits of the earth and of the flock. But the term *hire* is applied in Hos. ii. 12, ix. 1 to the bounty believed to be given *by* the idol-gods (Israel's lovers) who thereby seduced Israel from the worship of Jehovah; and what is wanted here is a plain designation for objects of idolatry like those on either side, viz. *graven images* and *idols.* J. M. P. Smith and others seek to retain the term thus translated, and to bring it into harmony with the context by assigning it not to the root meaning "to give," "to

I lay desolate: for of the hire of an harlot hath she gathered
them, and unto the hire of an harlot shall they return. 8 For
this will I wail and howl, I will go stripped and naked: I will
make a wailing like the jackals, and a mourning like the ostriches.
9 For her wounds are incurable: for it is come even unto Judah;
it reacheth unto the gate of my people, even to Jerusalem.

hire," but to another (for which support is found in Arabic) signifying
"to resemble," and by supposing that the noun here employed has the
sense of "images." But it is eminently unlikely that there should here
be used for "images" a word identical in form with another occurring
twice in the rest of the *v.* in the sense of "hire": the only resource is
to assume that the text is corrupt. As the objects which the writer had
in mind were such as could be burnt, they must have been of wood, and
Wellhausen conjectures *all her Asherim* (see on v. 14); cf. Dt. xii. 3,
2 Kgs. xxiii. 15. But the noun suggested is fem., whereas the verb is
masc., and a more plausible emendation is *sun-images* (*hammānim*):
cf. Is. xvii. 8, xxvii. 9.

the hire of an harlot. The term *harlot* seems to be used here in
connection with religious prostitution (Dt. xxiii. 17, 18, Hos. iv. 13, 14,
Baruch vi. 43) the proceeds of which were devoted to the adornment
of the idol-gods (cf. Bar. vi. 9—11). The valuables decorating Samaria's
idols are destined to be carried away by her destroyers and used by
them for impure purposes similar to those in connection with which
they were originally procured (cf. Hdt. I. 199).

hath she gathered them. The Syr. and Vulg. have *they were gathered,*
which suits best the parallel *shall they return.*

8—9. Micah's anguish in consequence of the doom foreseen by him,
inasmuch as the fall of Samaria presages that of his own country.

8. *stripped and naked.* Better, *barefoot* (LXX. ἀνυπόδετος) *and
stripped* (i.e. lacking an outer garment, cf. Job xxii. 6, Joh. xxi. 7).
This was a token of mourning; cf. Is. xx. 2—4 (though the word for
barefoot is not the same), 2 Sam. xv. 30.

like the jackals...like the ostriches. Cf. Job xxx. 29. The howling of
the jackal, which is prolonged and mournful, is alluded to in Is. xiii.
22; whilst the Heb. word for *ostrich* in Job xxxix. 13 comes from a root
meaning "to raise a piercing screech"; and the bird's cry has been
described as fearful and affrighting.

9. *her wounds are incurable.* Since the adj. and the verb *come* are in
the sing., and the LXX. has ἡ πληγὴ αὐτῆς, the text should be altered
to *her wound is incurable*: for the last expression cf. Jer. xxx. 15.

it reacheth unto the gate of my people. Perhaps better, *he reacheth,* for
the subject of this verb (which is masc., not fem., so that it cannot, like
the preceding, refer to *wound*) is probably "the enemy." By *the gate of
my people* the prophet designates Jerusalem, which is so called because
it was the principal centre of population, since it was in the gateway of
a town that its inhabitants chiefly assembled for traffic (2 Kgs. vii. 1),

10 Tell it not in Gath, weep not at all : at ¹Beth-le-Aphrah ²have

¹ That is, *A house of dust.*   ² Another reading is, *roll thyself.*

for judicial proceedings (Dt. xxi. 19), or for social converse (Ruth iv. 11, Prov. xxiv. 7). From this point onward Micah's prophecies are exclusively concerned with the destiny of his own country, which he anticipates will be the invader's next victim. If *vv.* 5—9 date from just before 722, the expected approach of the conquerors of Samaria against Jerusalem did not occur till more than 20 years later (701), and then came not from the direction of Samaria (in the N.) but from Lachish in the S.W. (Is. xxxvi. 2). It has been inferred by some that the date of this prophecy must be later than 722 because the tribute paid to Assyria by Ahaz (2 Kgs. xvi. 7, 8) was doubtless continued by Hezekiah during the early part of his reign, so that in 722 there could be no real danger to Judah from Assyria. And as the *city* of Samaria was not destroyed in that year by the overthrow of the kingdom of which it was the capital (Samaria is named as joining in 720 a coalition of Syrian states against Assyria), it has been argued that the present prophecy dates from a later time, when Hezekiah was intriguing with Philistia (as he did in 713—711) or with Egypt (as shortly before 701), occasions when measures may have been taken by the Assyrians to dismantle Samaria. Nevertheless it is difficult to think that Micah could have produced this prophecy, containing a reference to *Jacob* (= Israel) in *v.* 5, *after the Northern kingdom* had come to an end, without a word to intimate that such a catastrophe had occurred; and it seems most likely that this oracle was uttered just before 722, but that the prophet had no clear grasp of the political relations between Judah and Assyria, and expected the impending overthrow of one of the Hebrew states to be but a prelude to that of the other.

10—16. In these verses the prophet visualizes Jerusalem as compassed by a foe who overruns Judah and occupies a number of small towns which were less strongly defended than the capital. Micah apostrophizes these places or their inhabitants in turn, playing upon the etymologies of the names, and using in his addresses to them words that produce assonances, so that their appellations appear prophetic of their fate or else offer a pathetic contrast to it. The effect of the paronomasias in the original may in some measure be illustrated by substituting the names of certain English towns or villages yielding similar assonances :— "Tell it not in Tellisford"; "cry not (see note on *v.* 10) in Crynant"; "at Duston have I rolled myself (or "roll yourselves") in dust"; "pass ye away, O inhabitant of Fairford, in foulness and shame"; "the inhabitant of March hath not marched forth"; "the wailing of Knighton shall take from you the near support thereof"; "the inhabitant of Bitterley waiteth anxiously for fortune's sweets"; "bind the chariot to the horse, O inhabitant of Horsham"; "thou shalt give a parting dowry to Bridekirk"; "the houses of Diss shall be a disappointment to the kings of Israel"; "I will yet bring unto thee, O inhabitant of Herriard, him that shall inherit thee." It may seem surprising that the prophet,

in his state of distress, should thus indulge in puns; but Isaiah, under
like conditions of strong emotion (indignation or grief), made similar
use of paronomasia (v. 7, vii. 9, x. 28—32): cf. also Am. v. 5, Zeph. ii. 4.

10. *Tell it not in Gath.* Hebrew, *Bĕ-Ghath 'al taggīdhu.* The prophet,
borrowing a phrase from David's lament over Saul and Jonathan (2 Sam.
i. 20), deprecates the carrying of news about Jerusalem's perilous
situation to other Palestinian towns where it might be received with
malicious satisfaction. Gath was originally a Philistine city, variously
identified with *Tell el Sâfi* near the *Wâdy es Sunt* (the ancient "valley
of Elah"), some 18 miles from the coast, and with the later Eleuthero-
polis, the modern *Beit-Jibrin,* 8 miles further south, and about 24 miles
from the sea. It had been taken by Uzziah (according to 2 Ch. xxvi. 6);
and as it is not mentioned among other Philistine cities in Am. i. 7, 8,
it may no longer have been in Philistine occupation. Some critics, in
order to obtain mention here of a Judæan, instead of a Philistine, town,
propose *Rejoice not ('al tāghīlu) in Giloh* (Josh. xv. 51), or *in Gilgal*
(Josh. v. 9), the suggested change in the verb having some support in
the Syriac. The LXX. has μὴ μεγαλύνεσθε (i.e. *'al taghdīlu*), *magnify
not yourselves.*

weep not at all. The Heb. is *bācho 'al tibhcu,* which the English of
the R.V. represents. This, if the authentic text (it is supported by Aq.,
Sym. and the Vulg.), must mean "suppress all outward signs of grief
that might betray to unfriendly neighbours your inward distress." But
the circumstance that the exhortation occurs in a context full of word-
plays upon various place-names raises the expectation of a place-name
here, as in the first and third clauses of the verse. The Vatican codex
of the LXX. for *bācho* has οἱ ἐν Ἀκείμ, where the μ may be a dittograph
of the initial of the next word μή. If οἱ ἐν Ἀκεί be the original reading
of the Greek, it points to the conclusion that *bācho* represents *bĕ-'Acco,*
and the translation of this will be, *in Acco weep not* (for the suppression
of the initial letter of *'Acco* cf. (in the Heb.) Josh. xix. 3 (*Balah*)
with Josh. xv. 29 (*Ba'alah*) and the name *Bel* for *Ba'al*). Acco, the
later Ptolemais, is the modern Acre, a city situated at the N. angle of
a bay near mount Carmel. Though included in the tribe of Asher, it
was very imperfectly subjugated by the Israelites at the Conquest, and
remained largely Canaanite (Jud. i. 31). Since the place was not near
enough to Jerusalem for its name to occur readily to a Judean prophet
as a place where, as at Gath, the report of Jerusalem's danger might
soon spread and arouse malicious joy, it was probably chosen because
of the assonance which, when the preposition *bĕ* was prefixed to it, was
afforded with the verb "to weep" (*bāchah*); and (as has been noted) it
retained a native element in the population which was probably not
very friendly to the Hebrews. Some critics, however, thinking the name
of a locality near Jerusalem to be required, replace *bācho* by *bĕ-Bhōchim*
"in Bochim" (Jud. ii. 1), or *be-Bhāchā'* "in Baca" ("Balsam (or Mulberry)
vale") (Ps. lxxxiv. 6 mg., 2 Sam. v. 23 and mg.); and one codex (Q) of the
LXX. has in the margin ἐν Βαχείμ, which favours the first emendation.

Beth-le-Aphrah. This place (the name of which means "House of

I rolled myself in the dust. 11 Pass ye away, O [1]inhabitant of
Shaphir, in nakedness and shame: the [1]inhabitant of Zaanan
is not come forth; the wailing of Beth-ezel shall take from
you the [2]stay thereof. 12 For the [1]inhabitant of Maroth [3]waiteth

[1] Heb. *inhabitress.*　　　　[2] Or, *standing place*　　　　[3] Or, *is in travail*

Dust") is nowhere else mentioned, and as Theodotion has *Ophrah,* some
scholars would substitute *Beth-Ophrah.* There was an Ophrah in Benjamin (Josh. xviii. 23) and another in Manasseh (Jud. vi. 11, 24, viii.
27); whilst a Wâdy called *el Ghufr* seems to point to a third town of
the same name, situated in the Lowland of Judah. The last may be the
one here intended.

　　have I rolled myself. This, the reading of the Heb. text (*hith-
pallashti*), which seems to be intended as a play upon the word for
"Philistine" (*Pĕlishti*), is replaced in the Heb. mg. by an imperative,
roll thyself; whilst the LXX. and Vulg. imply the plural, *roll yourselves,*
which agrees best with the plural imperative in the next verse.

　　in the dust. The Heb. for *dust* (*'āphār*) echoes the sound and significance of *Beth-le-Aphrah* (see above). To roll, or wallow, in dust and
ashes was a habit that marked mourners; see Jer. vi. 26, Ezek. xxvii. 30;
cf. also 2 Sam. xiii. 19 and p. 136.

　　11. *Pass ye away, O inhabitant of Shaphir.* The sing. *inhabitant*
(literally, *inhabitress*) is used collectively, and the Heb. has a pron. in
the masc. plural. *Shaphir* is possibly the same as *Shamir* mentioned as
a town of Judah in Josh. xv. 48, where the Alexandrine MS. of the LXX.
has Σαφείρ. The site has been plausibly identified with *Suâfir,* about
4 miles S.E. of Ashdod, and rather more than that distance N.E. of
Ascalon. There was also a Shamir in Ephraim (Jud. x. 1). The name
Shāphir (? whence the Greek σάπφειρος, "sapphire") means "beauty"
(expressed by the LXX.'s (κατοικοῦσα) καλῶς and the Vulg.'s (*habitatio*)
Pulchra), and so offers a contrast to the miserable plight of its inhabitants, who, on the approach of the enemy, will have to leave it
ignominiously.

　　Zaanan. This is generally identified with the *Zĕnan* (*Tsĕnan*) of
Josh. xv. 37, a town in the Lowland of Judah. The paronomasia here
arises from the occurrence, both in the place-name (Heb. *Tsa'ănān*) and
in the verb *yātsā',* "to come (or "go") forth," of the group of sounds
tsa. The inhabitants of Zaanan will not go forth to succour the fugitives
from other places, lest they themselves should be cut off by the foe.

　　Beth-ezel. This town, the name of which signifies "House of
proximity" (cf. the Vulg. *domus vicina*), and which from its nearness
should be a refuge (cf. mg.) for those flying from their own homes, will
be too panic-stricken to afford relief; and the wail arising from it will
announce, to such as may look to it for help, the failure of their hopes.
Beth-ezel is perhaps the same as the *Azel* of 2 Zech. xiv. 5, its situation
being unknown.

　　12. *For.* The conjunction repeats the *for* in *v.* 9, explaining, like it,
the prophet's distress (*v.* 8).

anxiously for good: because evil is come down from the
LORD unto the gate of Jerusalem. 13 Bind the chariot to the
swift steed, O ¹inhabitant of Lachish: she was the beginning
of sin to the daughter of Zion; for the transgressions of Israel
were found in thee. 14 Therefore shalt thou give a parting gift
to Moresheth-gath: the houses of Achzib shall be ²a deceitful

¹ Heb. *inhabitress.*   ² Heb. *achzab.*

Maroth. The site is unknown, for Ewald's identification of it with
Maarath in the hill country of Judah (Josh. xv. 59) is unlikely. The
meaning of its name, "bitterness" (cf. Sym. ἡ παραπικραίνουσα), affords
a contrast to the good fortune for which its people vainly hope. The
root-meaning of the verb rendered *wait anxiously for* is "writhe," and
can be used of throes of pain, both mental and physical (see mg.).

13. *Bind the chariot,* etc. The people of *Lachish* are bidden to attach
their swiftest steed (Heb. *rechesh*) to their chariot (for the inversion
cf. Gen. xlvi. 29 (literally *made fast his chariot* to the horses)) in order
to escape, if possible, the pursuit of the invader. Lachish was originally
an Amorite city, situated in the Lowland (Josh. xv. 39): it was fortified
by Rehoboam, and to it king Amaziah fled from before a conspiracy
(2 Kgs. xiv. 19). Its site is thought to be *Tell-el-Hesy,* 16 m. E. of
Gaza. Instead of the present Heb. text the LXX. seems to have had
before it *A multitude of chariots and swift steeds* (i.e. of an invader),
O inhabitant of Lachish!—perhaps with reference to the "evil" mentioned in the preceding *v.*

she was the beginning of sin, etc. The most obvious explanation of
this statement is that from Lachish some idolatrous cult had been
introduced into the Jewish capital, though G. A. Smith thinks that,
owing to its situation between Jerusalem and Egypt, it was the first
town to receive the contingents of Egyptian cavalry on which Hezekiah
placed reliance (Is. xxxi. 1). For the parenthetic use of the 3rd pers.,
where the 2nd might be expected, cf. Is. xxii. 16, 17.

the transgressions of Israel. If the *sin* derived from Lachish was some
form of idolatry, *Israel* here probably denotes the Ephraimite kingdom,
where such may have originated (cf. vi. 16); but if the alternative explanation of the sin be accepted, the national name stands for Judah
(as in *v.* 14).

14. *thou.* I.e. Judah.

a parting gift to Moresheth-gath. There is an assonance between the
name *Moresheth* and the Heb. for "a betrothed woman" (*m'oreseth*).
Judah, which is expected to lose the town through the success of an
enemy, is bidden to give a dowry to it, as a parent might do to a
daughter about to marry and pass permanently into the possession of
another (cf. 1 Kgs. ix. 16). The town was Micah's home (*v.* 1).

Achzib. The place here meant (the *Chezib* of Gen. xxxviii. 5) was in
the Lowland (Josh. xv. 44), and is plausibly identified with *Ain Kozbeh,*
a little N. of the valley of Elah.

thing unto the kings of Israel. 15 I will yet bring unto thee, O
¹inhabitant of Mareshah, him that shall possess thee: the glory
of Israel shall come even unto Adullam. 16 Make thee bald, and

¹ Heb. *inhabitress.*

a deceitful thing. Heb. *'achzābh,* a term used in Jer. xv. 18 of a brook
that runs dry, and so disappoints a traveller who has hoped to quench
his thirst at it. The relief anticipated from Achzib is to prove equally
delusive, the town justifying its name (which the Vulg. renders by
domus Mendacii).

the kings of Israel. The plural *kings* should perhaps be replaced by
king, the plur. suffix being a dittograph of the initial of the next word.
Here *Israel* must certainly be a synonym for Judah: cf. 2 Kgs. xviii. 4,
2 Ch. xxviii. 19.

15. *Mareshah.* This also was in the Lowland (Josh. xv. 44), and
among the towns represented in 2 Ch. xi. 5—10 as fortified by Rehoboam. There is a locality still called *Mer'ash,* 2 m. S.W. of Beit-Jibrin.
Between the place-name and the words *him that shall possess thee* (Heb.
yōrēsh, the Assyrian invader being meant) there is a slight assonance.
Normal Heb. syntax would be better preserved by a change of points,
so as to produce (instead of the rendering of the R.V.) the translation
I will bring thee…unto him that shall possess thee (*'ōdh hayyōrēsh 'ābhī
lāch* being replaced by *'adh hayyōrēsh 'ōbhīlēch*). In the English, *yet*
must then be omitted.

the glory of Israel…Adullam. Possibly *the glory of Israel* may
describe the Ark (cf. 1 Sam. iv. 21), which will have to be carried for
safety to Adullam, a town in the Lowland (the modern *Id-'el-mā*),
fortified by Rehoboam, and famous for its caves (Josh. xii. 15, 2 Ch.
xi. 7, 1 Sam. xxii. 1). But the true meaning seems to be that the men
of rank among the Jewish people (for this sense of *glory* see Is. v. 13,
viii. 7, xvii. 3) will be compelled to take refuge there just as David
did. Pusey (with the A.V.) renders *he* (the invader) *shall come unto
Adullam, the glory of Israel*; but there is nothing to account for such
a high estimate of Adullam. An ingenious emendation (*'adh 'Adullām*
being replaced by *'adh 'ōlām*) yields the sense *the glory of Israel shall
go down* (i.e. set, the verb being used in this sense in iii. 6 and elsewhere) *for ever.*

16. *Make thee bald.* Judah is here addressed. To pluck off, or
shave, the hair was a usage practised in antiquity by mourners (Is.
xxii. 12, Jer. vii. 29, Am. viii. 10, Job i. 20, Ez. ix. 3), the custom
perhaps originating with the presentation to the dead of offerings of
hair which were placed on the corpse or laid on the tomb (cf. Hom. *Il.*
XXIII. 135—6, Soph. *El.* 448—451). The custom of making the head
bald in token of grief for the departed survived among several peoples.
Herodotus, for instance, states (IV. 71) that the Scythians, amongst
other ceremonies at the burial of a king, used to shave their hair;
and Suetonius relates (*Vit. Cal.* v.) that on the occasion of the death

poll thee for the children of thy delight: enlarge thy baldness
as the ¹eagle; for they are gone into captivity from thee.

¹ Or, *vulture*

of Germanicus *regulos · barbam posuisse et uxorum capita rasisse ad
indicium maximi luctus.* The practice of the rite in connection with
the cult of the dead was forbidden amongst the Hebrew people—at
any rate by the later codes of the Law; but Judah is here directed to
observe it merely as a token of mourning, since her children are to be
taken from her by her enemies.

as the eagle. Better, *as the vulture.* The Hebrew term is applicable to
both birds; but it is the latter alone that can be meant here since only
certain varieties of *vulture*, notably the griffon vulture (a bird abundant
in Palestine), have the head and neck bare of feathers. The same bird,
which feeds on carrion, must be designated in Job xxxix. 30, Mt. xxiv.
28 (= Lk. xvii. 37).

CHAPTER II. 1—11.

In the first eleven verses of this ch. a return is made from the announcement
of the coming doom of Judah, on account of its wickedness, to an invective
against the perpetrators of the heinous sins calling for retribution. The offences
which the prophet here denounces are anti-social—the seizure of lands and
houses by those who covet them, the practice of highway robbery, and the expulsion of families from their homes; and the prophet declares that the authors
of such spoliation shall themselves be despoiled and deported by a heathen foe.
Unfortunately the text of this ch. is extremely obscure and probably corrupt;
and to render parts of it intelligible recourse has to be made oftener than usual
to emendation.

II. 1 Woe to them that devise iniquity and work evil upon their

II. 1—2. A denunciation of those whose greed leads them to rob their
weaker neighbours of their property in order to augment their own estates.
Like charges of rapacity were brought by Isaiah (v. 8) against wealthy
and grasping landowners, who sought to extend their possessions by ex-
propriating the smaller freeholders (cf. also Hos. v. 10, of Israel). They
possessed the power to do so, and deemed might the equivalent of right.
The methods adopted were seemingly not acts of open violence, but devices which, though violations of morality, could be brought within the
limits of law, for they required to be thought out in the stillness of the
night hours before being put into operation in the day-time. One such
would be the harsh foreclosing of a mortgage before the owner was in a
position to redeem it; for what took place after the Return from the Exile
in the time of Nehemiah (v. 3 f.) is likely to have occurred also in bad
periods prior to the Exile. Another would be the enforcement of false
claims to property through the suborning of unprincipled witnesses and
the bribing of venal judges.

1. *and work evil.* These words have been pronounced to be an insertion

beds! when the morning is light, they practise it, because it
is in the power of their hand. 2 And they covet fields, and
seize them; and houses, and take them away: and they oppress
a man and his house, even a man and his heritage. 3 Therefore
thus saith the LORD: Behold, against this family do I devise an

because upon the "bed" evil could only be planned, not executed; but
in the context they may reasonably be understood to mean the mental
working out of the means for accomplishing the meditated iniquity. For
the use of the verb "to work" in the sense of "to devise" or "to project"
see Ps. lviii. 2 (3); and for *upon their beds* cf. Ps. xxxvi. 4. The phrase
it is in the power of (their) *hand* occurs in Gen. xxxi. 29, Prov. iii. 27.

2. *fields...houses.* The loss of ancestral lands was more deeply felt
in ancient than in modern communities, where manufactures and
commerce offer numerous alternatives to an agricultural life; and the
verb here rendered *seize* is used of tearing away from a man his skin
(iii. 2) and from a woman's bosom her fatherless child (Job xxiv. 9).
The Mosaic Law sought to prevent the permanent alienation of landed
property from its original owners or their kindred by various enact-
ments, such as those which enjoined the restoration of estates (lost by
purchase) every fiftieth year (Lev. xxv. 10), and the right of daughters,
brothers, and uncles to inherit, when a man died without male issue
(Num. xxvii. 1—11, cf. xxxiii. 54). It was assumed that the land, at
its conquest, had been divided by Jehovah between the various tribes
and families which then entered upon its occupation, so that the
retention of patrimonies was tenaciously defended; cf. 1 Kgs. xxi. 4.
In this and some other chapters Micah "speaks as a man of the people,
and reveals to us as no other prophet does, the feelings of the common-
alty towards their oppressors. To the peasantry the nobles seemed to
have no object but plunder." W. R. Smith (*The Prophets of Israel*,
p. 289).

they oppress a man and his house. If the word *house* is taken literally,
then the dwelling is represented as sensible of the oppression to which
the dweller in it is subject: cf. Hab. ii. 11, Job xxxi. 38. But *house* may
be used in the sense of *household*, including wife and servants (as in
Dt. vi. 22, etc.; see *JTS.* vol. xxv. p. 80 f.).

3—5. The retribution destined to fall upon the wrongdoers.

3. *against this family.* I.e. against Israel (= Judah, see i. 5, 15 and
cf. Jer. v. 15) which, out of all the families of the earth, was the one
which Jehovah had admitted to His intimacy (Am. iii. 1, 2). The
application of the term *family* to a *nation* seems to have originated
with the belief that all peoples had descended from the three sons of
Noah and their households (see Gen. x.).

I devise an evil. Jehovah requites the devisers of iniquity by devices
of His own, which aim at their inevitable ruin. The word *evil*, used in
v. 1 of iniquitous conduct, is here employed of retributive punishment:
cf. 2 Is. xlv. 7, Am. iii. 6.

evil, from which ye shall not remove your necks, neither shall
ye walk haughtily; for it is an evil time. 4 In that day shall they
take up a parable against you, and lament ¹with a doleful
lamentation, *and* say, We be utterly spoiled: he changeth the

¹ Or, *with the lamentation, It is done;* and *say &c.*

remove your necks. The evil predicted is compared to a yoke on the
neck of a beast of burden: cf. Dt. xxviii. 48, Jer. xxvii. 12.
  haughtily. Perhaps better, *erect* (LXX. ὀρθοί): under the yoke of a
foreign master they will walk bent, like cattle.
  it is an evil time. The same phrase occurs in Am. v. 13, but whereas
there it refers to the internal corruption of the State, here it has in view
the external calamities menacing the country.
  4. *take up.* I.e. take upon the lips or tongue; cf. Num. xxiii. 7. A
derivative of the verb was employed to denote a prophetic utterance or
oracle, rendered in the English Bible by *burden* (see Is. xiii. 1, Nah. i. 1,
Hab. i. 1, etc.). The similar English word, meaning the refrain of a song,
is of different origin and comes from the Latin *burdo,* the hum of a bee
or the drone of bagpipes.
  a parable. Better here, *a taunt song.* The word used signifies, in
general, any utterance marked by *correspondence* between two things,
whether two objects of thought which are compared or contrasted together, or two sentences which are parallel in form. "Similitude" or
"parable" is, in strictness, its best equivalent (the LXX. has παραβολή),
but according to the character of what is expressed, it acquired the
meaning of "proverb," "by-word," "didactic poem," or "derisive song"
(see Is. xiv. 4, Hab. ii. 6). It is in this last sense that it is used in the
present context, where it describes the character of the lamentation
with which the enemies of the Jewish people travesty their sorrowful
plaint and ridicule their woe.
  doleful. The Heb. term (*nihyah*) thus rendered is taken by some
scholars as part of the verb "to be," and regarded as the beginning of
the lamentation, and the passage has been translated (cf. mg.), "*It is
done*¹" (or "*It has been*²"), one *saith,* "*we be utterly spoiled,*" etc. But
the word in question appears to be due to dittography and should be
omitted; the rendering will then be *and lament with a lamentation* and
say, We, etc. The substantive employed denotes a funeral dirge over
such as are actually dead or such as are about to die (Jer. xxxi. 15,
cf. Ezek. xxxii. 18).
  and say. The verb, if the text is sound, has an indefinite subject—
one *saith,* and (if the previous word (*nihyah*) is retained and translated
It is done, as in the R.V. mg.) must be used like the Latin *inquit.* But
this is not in accord with the Hebrew idiom, and probably a letter has
been lost, the true reading being not *'āmar* but *lĕ'mōr—saying;* the
LXX. has λέγων.

---

¹ Cf. Rev. xvi. 17, Γέγονεν.   ² Cf. *Fuit Ilium.*

portion of my people: how doth he ¹remove *it* from me! to the
rebellious he divideth our fields. 5 Therefore thou shalt have

¹ Or, *depart from*

We be, etc. The words from here to the end of the verse doubtless
compose the parody with which their captors travesty the wailing of
the captives.

he changeth, etc. As the text stands, the subject of the verb is God,
the ultimate Author of Judah's calamity. The procedure which occurred
at the Conquest (it is complained) is reversed: the land which He once
allotted to the Hebrew people is now withdrawn from them, and transferred to, and divided among, those—the heathen—who have been
rebellious in the sense that they have not obeyed His laws, as made
known to them through reason and conscience (cf. Rom. ii. 15). But
the absence of any expressed subject for the verb is strange, and *the
rebellious* (lit. *a rebel,* Heb. *shōbhēbh*), a term suitable enough when
applied to Israel, as in Jer. iii. 14, xxxi. 22, is not very appropriate to
describe the heathen (though it is used of the children of Ammon in
Jer. xlix. 4). A different text is suggested by the LXX. which has
ταλαιπωρίᾳ ἐταλαιπωρήσαμεν· μερὶς λαοῦ μου κατεμετρήθη ἐν σχοινίῳ,
καὶ οὐκ ἦν ὁ καταλύσων αὐτὸν τοῦ ἀποστρέψαι· οἱ ἀγροὶ ἡμῶν διεμερίσθησαν.
The Heb. underlying this has been conjecturally reconstructed in various
ways; and the most plausible emendation, involving a transposition of
the first clause, is, *The portion of my people is measured out by line*
(*yāmīr* being replaced by *yimmadh*, followed by the insertion of *bĕhebhel*)
and there is none to restore it (*'ēych yāmīsh li* being replaced by *vĕ'ēyn
mēshībh*): *to those who lead us captive* (*lĕshōbhēbh* replaced by *lĕshōbhēnu*)
our fields are divided (*yĕhallēch* re-pointed *yĕhullāch*): *we are utterly
spoiled*. This re-construction yields the *Kinah* metre in which taunt-
songs are usually composed (see p. cxlii.).

5. *Therefore*, etc. This is a very difficult verse, and has been diversely translated and interpreted. In view of the singular pronoun
thou, it has been deemed by some to be an indignant reply to Micah
from the classes that he reproaches: they are supposed to declare that
in consequence of his words no representative of his shall participate
in any casting of lots (cf. Josh. xiv. 1, 2) for the division of parcels of
ground (delimited by the measuring line) among the Hebrew community
(Jehovah's congregation). But the pronoun *thou* may denote some
individual representative of the offending classes denounced in *vv.* 1—2,
or else the singular may be an accidental error for the plur. *you* (the
final *m* of the Heb. plural suffix being lost before the initial *m* of the
following word). In any case, the passage is best taken as a continuation
of the sentence pronounced by the prophet upon those who oppress
their social inferiors, the *therefore* of this *v.* resuming the *therefore* of
v. 3. Those who have wronged the weak by robbing them of their
patrimonies will have no posterity (cf. Jer. xxix. 32) to cast the lot
for a share in the apportionment of lands when, after the predicted
chastisement has been undergone, there occurs in Israel a redistribution

none that shall cast the line by lot in the congregation of the
LORD. 6 [1]Prophesy ye not, *thus* they prophesy. They shall not
prophesy [2]to these: reproaches shall not depart. 7 [3]Shall it be

[1] Or, *Prophesy ye not, they are* ever *prophesying,* say they. Heb. *Drop &c.* See
Amos vii. 16.   [2] Or, *of these things: their reproaches never cease*
[3] Or, *O thou that art named the house of Jacob*

of the soil. Some doubt has been thrown upon the authenticity of the
v. through the presence in it of the expression *the congregation* (or
assembly) *of Jehovah,* since elsewhere this is found almost exclusively
in comparatively late writings (like Dt., the Priestly code of the Pentateuch, Neh., and Chron.). Nevertheless the phrase that excites suspicion
occurs in Num. xx. 4 (which may be from JE).

6—7. These verses, admitting various explanations in detail, contain
protests uttered by the classes whom Micah has just denounced, and
the extinction of whose posterity he has predicted. For similar protests
against other prophets see Am. ii. 12, vii. 10 f., Is. xxviii. 9, 10.

6. *Prophesy ye not.* The R.V. appears rightly to consider these
opening words of the *v.* to be addressed by false prophets supporting
the oppressors, or (if the mg. be adopted) by the latter themselves, to
Micah and other true prophets, whom it is sought to hinder from
prophesying woe. The verb here rendered *to prophesy* is literally *to
drop* (see Dt. xxxii. 2, Am. vii. 16, cf. Ezek. xx. 46, xxi. 2), and the
phrase may originally have had reference to the froth and foam which
dripped from the lips of the prophets when they raved in a state of
religious ecstasy. The next clause must be an announcement that
steps will be taken to prevent by force the true prophets from speaking
further—*They shall not prophesy to these* people (Aq. εἰς τούτους), or, as
in the mg., *of these* things (i.e. of impending retribution); and the
concluding words should probably be rendered, *reproaches do not depart* (i.e. never cease), or *shall not reproaches depart?* (i.e. be put an
end to?). Another possible way of translating the first half of the *v.*
(if the Heb. accents are disregarded) is, *Prophesy not: they only shall
prophesy who will not prophesy of these things.* Kirkpatrick[1] distributes
the clauses between the two parties thus:—*Prophesy ye not* is the
utterance of the false prophets, and Micah's rejoinder is, *They* (the
true prophets) *shall prophesy.* To this the others reply, *They shall not*
(at any rate) *prophesy of these* (evils); and Micah's defiant retort is,
Reproaches shall not depart (i.e. shall not be discontinued). But the
text of this last clause is not above suspicion, for whereas the noun is
fem. plur., the verb is in the masc. sing. The word rendered *reproaches*
also means (in the singular) *humiliation* or *ignominy;* and as the Vulg.
has *non comprehendet confusio,* and Aq. renders the verb by οὐ καταλήψῃ,
there is some support for the conjectural emendation *lo' tassigh[2]
cĕlimmah* (for *lo' yissagh[2] cĕlimmōth*), *ignominy shall not overtake us.*

7. *Shall it be said, O house of Jacob.* The R.V., both in the text

[1] See *The Doctrine of the Prophets,* p. 222, note.
[2] These verbs in the Heb. have different sibilants.

said, O house of Jacob, Is the spirit of the LORD [1]straitened?
are these his doings? Do not my words do good to him that
walketh uprightly? 8 But [2]of late my people is risen up as an

[1] Or, *impatient* Heb. *shortened.*   [2] Heb. *yesterday.*

and in the mg., assumes that Micah's opponents in this *v.* address their
fellow-countrymen (*Jacob* standing for *Judah*, cf. iii. 1, 8, 9, v. 7, 8,
Ps. lxxvii. 15), though the rendering of the mg. (for which cf. 2 Is.
xlviii. 1) implies a different vocalization of the consonants of the first
word. But the LXX. and the Vulg. (ὁ λέγων, *dicit*) both regard this
verb as active (not passive); and this has suggested an emendation
giving the translation *Hath the house of Israel said...?* or *Doth the
house of Israel say...?* the enquiry being put by Micah.

Is the spirit of the LORD straitened? The question expresses the incredulity, entertained by those who are denounced by Micah, that
Jehovah can really be angry with them, as represented by the prophet.
The verb rendered *to be straitened* is literally *to be short*; and the
questioners mean, "Is Jehovah's temper short (or impatient; for this
sense cf. Num. xxi. 4, mg., Prov. xiv. 17, Heb.)?"

are these his doings? I.e. does the vengeance with which we are
threatened resemble His usual bearing towards us?

Do not my words, etc. If the text be retained, Jehovah must be
supposed to speak here, correcting the idea, implied in the question
just cited, that He does not resent the deeds of the wicked. But the
LXX. has οὐχ οἱ λόγοι αὐτοῦ, κ.τ.λ., *Do not His words*, etc., the question
being put, like the preceding, by the evil-doers, who are unconscious
that they are otherwise than righteous in their proceedings, and feel
quite assured of Jehovah's favour.

8. *But of late*, etc. This and the following three *vv.* are uttered by
Jehovah speaking through His prophet, and if in the preceding *v.* the
reading of the LXX. be adopted (as is done above), His answer to the
evil-doers begins here. The strong and unscrupulous are charged with
committing robbery by violence, stripping from peaceable wayfarers
their *robe* (an outer mantle enveloping the *garment*, which was worn
next the skin, Ex. xxii. 27, Dt. xxiv. 13). But it is impossible not to
suspect that the text is corrupt. (*a*) There is nothing elsewhere to
indicate that the wickedness complained of is only a very recent
development (the word translated *of late* literally means *yesterday*).
(*b*) The phrase *my people* is here used of those who perpetrate violence,
whereas in *v.* 9 (cf. iii. 3) it is employed, more suitably, of those who
suffer from it. (*c*) The person (or persons) against whom the people
is risen up as an enemy is (or are) left unexplained. (*d*) The preposition
rendered *from off* means *off* (or *in*) *the front of* a person or thing. Of
various proposed emendations one which departs but little from the
existing text whilst yielding a superior sense, is that advocated by
W. R. Smith (*Prophets of Israel*, p. 429), *But ye are to my people* (wĕ-
'attem lĕ 'ammi for wĕ-'ethmûl 'ammi) *as an enemy that rises up* (yāḵūm

enemy: ye strip the robe from off the garment from them that
pass by securely *as men* averse from war. 9 The women of my
people ye cast out from their pleasant houses; from their young
children ye take away my glory for ever. 10 Arise ye, and depart;
for this is not your rest: because of uncleanness [1]that destroyeth, even with a grievous destruction. 11 If a man walking
[2]in wind and falsehood do lie, *saying*, I will prophesy unto thee
of wine and of strong drink; he shall even be the prophet of
this people.

---

[1] The Sept. has, *ye shall be destroyed with &c.*   [2] Or, *in a spirit of falsehood*

for *yĕkōmēm*) *in front of him that is at peace with him* (the LXX.'s
κατέναντι τῆς εἰρήνης points to *shōlĕmōh* for *salmah*): *ye strip the robe
from them that pass by securely, averse from* (i.e. not thinking of) *war*.

9. *The women*, etc. In this *v.* the charge preferred against the upper
classes seems to be the merciless eviction of poor women (probably
widows, cf. Is. x. 2), motived by a boundless desire for extensive estates
(see *v.* 2). The R.V., in rendering the original by *from their pleasant
houses...from their young children*, silently emends the Heb. (which is
ungrammatical) by the LXX.

my glory. This must mean the glory which Jehovah had bestowed;
and probably refers to the fertility of Judah's country, and the beauty
of its capital: cf. Ezek. xvi. 14 (where *my majesty* represents the same
Heb.) and see Dan. viii. 9, xi. 16, Ps. xlviii. 2. This glorious inheritance
the children of the poor, through the exactions of the powerful, have to
abandon. The LXX., however, here has *mountains*; and it may be
suggested that *my glory* should be replaced by *my mountain*, i.e. the
hilly ground constituting the territory of Judah (*hărāri* for *hădhāri*).

10. God's sentence upon the sinners—they are to be treated as they
have treated their victims.

for this is not your rest. The land, though originally given to the
people as their permanent resting-place after the wanderings in the
wilderness (for this sense of *rest* see Num. x. 33, Dt. xii. 9, cf. Josh. i.
13, xxiii. 1), must be forfeited, and they are to depart from it into
captivity because of their moral pollution.

that destroyeth. Instead of the active verb (attached as a relative
clause to *uncleanness*) the LXX. has, preferably, the passive, *ye shall be
destroyed* (the following word *even* being omitted).

11. A description of the kind of prophet acceptable to the people
who would silence Micah. The verse would be more in place after *v.* 6,
conveying the conclusion drawn by Micah from what is there said by
his opponents.

walking in wind and falsehood. The word rendered *wind* also means
spirit, and a preferable translation (the two nouns constituting a hen-
diadys) is *walking in a spirit of falsehood* (cf. 1 Kgs. xxii. 22). For the
construction cf. Prov. vi. 12 (*walketh in frowardness of mouth*). A

prophet who was indifferent to moral truth and was content by his utterances to pander to the sensual cravings of his hearers would stand high in their estimation. For the prevalence of drunken habits in Judah see Is. v. 11, 12, 22; and for intoxication among prophets see Is. xxviii. 7.

CHAPTER II. 12—13.

These two verses are obviously not an immediate continuation of the preceding passage. They declare that those addressed are to be concentrated within some city, whence they are soon to issue forth; but the situation implied has been diversely explained. Some critics (e.g. W. E. Barnes) consider that the section is wholly menacing in tone, and that it predicts that the Jewish people will be herded within their capital, through invasion, and that this will be preliminary to their deportation into exile[1]. But this view is inconsistent with the idea conveyed by the phrase *as a flock in the midst of their pasture*, which suggests care and protection, and by the words *the breaker is gone up before them*, which are less suggestive of an enemy assaulting a besieged city than of a pioneer in an escape from a place of durance. Van Hoonacker, sensible of some of these considerations, seeks to obtain a similar interpretation by changing (*of*) *Bozrah* (*botsrah*) into *in distress* (*batstsārah*) (after the LXX. ἐν θλίψει), by replacing *in the midst of their pasture* (*haddobhĕro*[2]) by *in the midst of plague* (*haddebher*) and by omitting the final clause of *v.* 13, which W. E. Barnes retains but would render *and Jehovah is on high above them* (seated in judgment). Others (including apparently Sellin, *IOT.* p. 176) suppose that the purport of the passage is consolatory in a time of trial prior to the exile, affirming that the remnant of Judah are to be concentrated in Jerusalem for their preservation, when the surrounding country is occupied by an invader; and that they will be enabled to sally forth from it again through his retirement. Both these views leave the verses to Micah. But the situation which the section most clearly presumes is that of a body of Jews detained *in exile*, whence it is announced that they are to be shortly delivered; and if this is correct, the passage probably does not proceed from Micah. It is true that predictions of exile, such as appear in i. 16, ii. 4, 10, are sometimes accompanied by prophecies of a return from it (see Jer. xxxii. 28—44, Ezek. vi., xi. 16—20), yet here the transition from an announcement of deportation into a foreign land to a promise of restoration is exceptionally abrupt; and the writer's language conveys the impression that his fellow-countrymen are actually dispersed in a land of captivity from which he is empowered to predict their return. Moreover the representation that Jehovah will shepherd His flock resembles that of the exilic prophet Deutero-Isaiah (see 2 Is. xl. 11), whilst the reference to the *breaker* and the departure of the people through the gate of their oppressors' capital recalls 2 Is. xlv. 2. It is therefore probable that this small section is an independent oracle of exilic date, addressed to the captives in *Babylonia*, who had been taken thither about 130 years after Micah's time, and who are to be assembled by God preparatory to repatriation.

---

[1] See *JTS.* xxv. p. 81.
[2] This is ungrammatical, so that there must be some error.

12 I will surely assemble, O Jacob, all of thee; I will surely
gather the remnant of Israel; I will put them together as
the sheep of Bozrah: as a flock in the midst of their pasture,
they shall make great noise by reason of *the multitude of* men.
13 The breaker is gone up before them: they have broken forth
and passed on to the gate, and are gone out thereat: and their
king is passed on before them, and the LORD at the head of them.

12. *I will...all of thee.* Perhaps better (as suggested by the LXX.)
I will surely assemble Jacob, all of him. Cf. iv. 6, Is. xi. 12.

the remnant of Israel. The precise phrase occurs only in the relatively
late prophets Jeremiah (xxxi. 7), Ezekiel (ix. 8, xi. 13), and Zephaniah
(iii. 13).

as the sheep of Bozrah. The best known Bozrah was in Edom (1 Ch.
i. 44, Am. i. 12, Is. xxxiv. 6, 3 Is. lxiii. 1, Jer. xlix. 13): and the reason
for alluding to it in connection with flocks of sheep is obscure. There
was, however, also a Bozrah in Moab (see Jer. xlviii. 24), and Moab was
famous as a pastoral country (see 2 Kgs. iii. 4). But a parallel to clause
b, in the midst of their pasture, is desirable, and the Oxford Heb. Lex.
takes *botsrah* here to be a common noun meaning *enclosure* (Sym. and
Th. have ἐν ὀχυρώματι); whilst many scholars conjecture *batstsīrah* for
botsrah, in the sheepfold (the Vulg. has *in ovili*), it being assumed, from
comparison with the Arabic, that there existed in Heb. a word *tsīrah*
meaning "encampment" or "enclosure." For the conception of exiled
Israel as a scattered flock re-assembled by God, their Shepherd, cf.
Ezek. xxxiv. 12 f.

they shall...men. Better (with G. A. Smith), *and they shall hum with
men* (the conjunction *and* being obtained from the suffix ungrammatically
attached to the preceding word). The metaphor of a flock of sheep is,
in this last clause, blended with a reference to the human beings of whom
the sheep are a figure (Ezek. xxxvi. 38). For the promise to the exiled
people of a multiplication of their numbers on their return home cf.
Ezek. xxxvi. 10.

13. *The breaker.* The fences behind which the exiles are confined
will be breached, the *breaker* probably being Jehovah, though the
allusion may possibly be to Jehovah's agent, Cyrus the Elamite, who
captured Babylon and restored the Jews to their own land. The writer
of this passage may, like Deutero-Isaiah, have watched with deep
interest the advance of Cyrus against Babylon.

is gone up. The verb is frequently employed of those who return to
their native soil; cf. Ez. ii. 1, Neh. vii. 6, Hos. i. 11. Jerusalem, in the
thoughts of the exiles, was still their capital.

their king. On the occasion of the Return the representative of
Judah's royal house was Zerubbabel or Sheshbazzar (if these are rightly
identified, cf. Ezra ii. 2 with i. 11). But the parallel clause suggests
that the title *king* designates Jehovah: cf. 1 Sam. xii. 12, Dt. xxxiii. 5,
2 Is. xli. 21, xliii. 15, xliv. 6, lii. 12.

Chapter III.

The contents of this chapter consist of further utterances of Micah, and maintain the denunciatory tone of the foregoing chapters ending with ii. 11. Though the opening words (*Hear, I pray you*, etc.) indicate that it is an address separate from that comprised in ii. 1—11, the general tenor is similar, including both the arraignment of sins committed, and the prediction of calamities that will punish them. But whereas those who are the objects of invective in ch. ii. are the influential and powerful classes without precise definition, those for whom a nemesis is foretold here are specified as the rulers, the prophets, and the priests. The date of the oracle is determined by the reference to it in Jer. xxvi. 18, where it is stated that Micah delivered it in the reign of Hezekiah (727 (or 720)—692 B.C.).

III.   1 And I said, Hear, I pray you, ye heads of Jacob, and rulers of the house of Israel: is it not for you to know judgement? 2 who hate the good, and love the evil; who pluck off their skin from off them, and their flesh from off their bones; 3 who also eat the flesh of my people; and they flay their skin from off them, and break their bones: yea, they chop them in pieces, as for the

1—4. An expostulation and a warning to the governing classes for their rapacious treatment of the governed.

1. *And I said.* These words do not appear to connect the present passage immediately with ii. 11 (no personal pronoun is expressed in the Heb., marking an antithesis between the speaker here and the false but popular prophets referred to there), but they suggest that there once preceded it some account of the circumstances in which the prophet felt constrained to speak.

ye heads of Jacob, and rulers of the house of Israel. The officials of the state were similarly denounced by Isaiah (i. 10). Instead of *ye heads of Jacob* the LXX. has αἱ ἀρχαὶ οἴκου Ἰακώβ, cf. *v.* 9. The names *Jacob* and *Israel* are synonyms for Judah, as in ii. 12.

to know judgement. An essential requirement for those in authority was both a knowledge of the principles of justice and a sense of obligation to administer it to suitors: cf. Am. v. 15.

their skin...their flesh. The pronouns must refer to *my people*, mentioned in the following verse: cf. the similar anticipatory use of the personal pronoun in Is. xiii. 2.

3. *eat the flesh*, etc. For the phraseology cf. Ps. xiv. 4. The people are likened to sheep who are devoured by the shepherds (a figure for the rulers) who should protect them: cf. Ezek. xxxiv. 2—4.

break their bones. The verb seems to mean literally "to cause to break forth"; so perhaps the rendering should be, *lay bare* (to sight) *their bones.*

chop them in pieces. The verb appears to be another form of a commoner word meaning "to divide for distribution"; cf. 3 Is. lviii. 7 (and see next note): LXX. ἐμέλισαν.

pot, and as flesh within the caldron. 4 Then shall they cry unto the LORD, but he will not answer them : yea, he will hide his face from them at that time, according as they have wrought evil in their doings. 5 Thus saith the LORD concerning the prophets that make my people to err; that bite with their teeth and cry, Peace; and whoso putteth not into their mouths, they

as for the pot. The rendering *for* is unnatural. The Vulg. rightly has *in lebete,* whilst the LXX. has ὡς σάρκας εἰς λέβητα; and a rearrangement of the consonants of the word translated *as* gives the reading (which the LXX. supports and the parallelism demands) *they deal them out like meat in the pot.* For the last word cf. 1 Sam. ii. 14. The prophet's complaint against the rulers seems to be that they subordinate equity to the promotion of their own interest, or that of their class, the weak and helpless being brought under the operation of oppressive ordinances, designed to extract from them their money or other possessions, in order to swell the fortunes, or minister to the enjoyment, of those who should be their protectors.

4. *Then shall they cry,* etc. To the oppressors there will come a time of retribution; and then they who have been deaf to entreaties will find their own prayers to Jehovah disregarded: cf. Job xxvii. 9.

he will hide his face. To do this was to manifest displeasure; see Dt. xxxi. 17, Ps. xiii. 1, xxx. 7, xliv. 24, and cf. Is. i. 15. Conversely, Divine satisfaction was indicated when God turned, or lifted, upon His servants the light of His countenance; see Ps. iv. 6, xxxi. 16, lxvii. 1, lxxx. 3, etc. To "see the face" of a king was a privilege which might be granted or refused to a subject (2 Sam. xiv. 24, 2 Kgs. xxv. 19); and to "see the face" of God figuratively, through happy experiences, was a still higher privilege. The words *at that time* spoil the balance of the clauses, and should probably be omitted.

according as. The LXX. has ἀνθ᾽ ὧν, *because* (a meaning which the Heb. admits: cf. 1 Sam. xxviii. 18, 2 Kgs. xvii. 26 (end)).

5—8. Here transition is made to the false prophets who, indifferent to moral and religious truth, make the favourable or unfavourable purport of their utterances to depend upon what they can exact from those who consult them. For such conduct requital will come through the withdrawal, in the hour of their need, of all Divine illumination.

5. *that make my people to err.* Contemporary prophets are similarly charged with being deceivers in Is. ix. 15, Jer. v. 31, xiv. 14, xxiii. 13, Ezek. xiii. 9.

that bite with their teeth and cry, Peace. The verb *bite* is commonly employed in connection with venomous serpents (Gen. xlix. 17, Num. xxi. 6, 9, Am. v. 19, Eccles. x. 8, 11) or used figuratively of the effects of wine (Prov. xxiii. 32); but here it must refer to the satisfaction, by the prophets, of their bodily needs. The second clause is conditional on the first; and the meaning is—only when their appetites are gratified by enquirers consulting them do they utter favourable oracles (cf.

even [1]prepare war against him : 6 Therefore it shall be night unto
you, that ye shall have no vision; and it shall be dark unto you,
that ye shall not divine; and the sun shall go down upon the
prophets, and the day shall be black over them. 7 And the seers

[1] Heb. *sanctify*.

Jer. vi. 13, 14): if they fail to get what they want, their utterances
become menacing.

prepare war against him. The words are not to be taken in a literal
sense. What the false prophets did was to pronounce anyone, who
would not feed and support them, to be an enemy of God and the
state, and so, by exposing him to suspicion and persecution, to accomplish his ruin. *To prepare war* is literally "to consecrate (or, as
in the mg., "sanctify") war" (cf. Jer. vi. 4, Joel iii. 9); and soldiers
were *consecrated* men (Is. xiii. 3, cf. Jer. xxii. 7). In primitive times
among Semitic peoples war was not a struggle merely between human
antagonists but between the gods of the combatant nations (cf. p. cx.),
and so had a religious aspect: the two sides, before the campaign
opened, offered sacrifices to their respective deities and sought and
received their directions for the conduct of it; and after it, if successful, they devoted to them the lives and possessions of the defeated
enemy: see for the Hebrews 1 Sam. vii. 9, xiii. 9, 2 Sam. v. 19, Josh.
vi. 17; and for the Moabites the inscription of Mesha[1] (where the
king relates how Chemosh, the Moabite deity, bade him go and take
Nebo, and when he had captured it, he devoted it to his god). How
completely in the early history of Israel the cause of the nation was
deemed the cause of its Deity appears from the fact that the Israelites'
wars were called "the wars of Jehovah" (Num. xxi. 14), that His Ark
accompanied their armies (Num. x. 35, 36), and that the prophetess
Deborah, when the city of Meroz held aloof from Israel's revolt against
the Canaanites, cursed it because it came not *to the help of Jehovah.*

6. *Therefore,* etc. The false prophets, whose predictions have been
dictated by their self-interest, will be deprived of all their pretended
faculties of insight and prevision when God's judgment is executed (cf.
Ezek. xiii. 2 f., Is. xxix. 10, 11). Their ostensible ability to counsel or
console will disappear just when most needed, and in place of basking
in the sunlight of prosperity, as hitherto, they will be plunged in the
gloom of calamity. For the figures of speech cf. Am. v. 18, viii. 9.
Instead of the verb *it shall be dark* the LXX. and Vulg. have nouns
(σκοτία, *tenebræ*), which preserve the parallelism better.

7. *the seers.* It would seem that the individuals who were denoted
by the term *seer* (which is used to translate two Hebrew synonyms, *rō'eh*
and *hōzeh*) actually were, or were believed to be, endowed by God with
a faculty of clairvoyance or second-sight, which caused them to be

---

[1] See Hastings, *DB.* iii. pp. 404—408.

shall be ashamed, and the diviners confounded; yea, they shall
all cover their lips: for there is no answer of God. 8 But I truly

consulted by persons in perplexity. A narrative throwing light upon
the reputation which they enjoyed in early times for abnormal powers
of mental vision, upon the nature of the enquiries put to them, and
upon the remuneration which was offered to them is contained in 1 Sam.
ix. 1—x. 16. In this account it is explained that the term (*rō'eh*), there
applied to Samuel (cf. 1 Ch. ix. 22), was an ancient one, afterwards
supplanted by the term "prophet" (*nābhi'*) which, if derived from the
root *nābha'*, "to bubble up," denoted one who was thought to exhibit the
influence of God within him not through clairvoyance but through
outbursts of ecstatic speech[1]. But though "prophet" became the prevailing title, yet *seer* was retained in use: see 2 Sam. xv. 27, 2 Ch.
xvi. 7, Is. xxx. 10 (instances of *rō'eh*) and 2 Kgs. xvii. 13, 2 Ch. ix. 29,
xix. 2, Am. vii. 12 (instances of *hōzeh*).

ashamed. I.e. overwhelmed with disappointment at the failure of
their hopes and predictions. The combination of the verb with *confounded* recurs in Jer. xv. 9, Ps. xxxv. 26, xl. 14, etc.

diviners. These were a class of persons whose presence in Israel was
probably due to foreign influence, for they are associated with the
Philistines (1 Sam. vi. 2), Canaanites (Dt. xviii. 14, 1 Sam. xxviii. 8),
Ammonites (Ezek. xxi. 29 (34)), and Babylonians (2 Is. xliv. 25). They
were perhaps addicted to necromancy and magic arts, for which, in
Israel, the intellectual and spiritual illumination marking the true
prophets of Jehovah was (according to Dt. xviii. 10) to be the substitute.

shall all cover their lips. This was a sign of distress displayed especially
by mourners for the dead (Ezek. xxiv. 17, 22). The word rendered *lips*
is literally "moustache" (the LXX. in 2 Sam. xix. 25 translates it by
μύσταξ, from which the English term is derived); and the practice of
covering the hair of the chin and upper lip on occasions of mourning
was perhaps a substitute for the removal of it. This custom of removing
or concealing the hair of the lips, on the part of the relatives of a dead
person, may have been originally designed to alter the appearance of
the face, and so prevent recognition by the ghost of the deceased, who
might otherwise haunt them. (The adoption, by mourners, of a special
garb, dissimilar to that worn at other times, may have the same explanation.) Eventually, the covering of the lips became a mere conventional token of wretchedness, for the practice was observed by lepers
(Lev. xiii. 45).

8. *But I truly,* etc. Micah, in distinction from the prophets just
described by him (*v.* 5), claims to be divinely enabled to denounce with
courage the sins prevalent in the nation. By *power* is meant the exceptional capacity conferred upon him for the discharge of his mission;

---

[1] Another derivation connects *nābhi'* with Arabic and Assyrian words meaning
to "announce," "proclaim," which would imply that the prophet got his Heb.
name because he was regarded as God's spokesman.

am full of power ¹by the spirit of the LORD, and of judgement, and of might, to declare unto Jacob his transgression, and to Israel his sin. 9 Hear this, I pray you, ye heads of the house of Jacob, and rulers of the house of Israel, that abhor judgement, and pervert all equity. 10 They build up Zion with blood, and

¹ Or, *even the spirit*

judgment stands for the decisions he has to pronounce; whilst *might* describes the resolution and fortitude with which he will face opposition in the discharge of his duty.

by the spirit of the LORD. To the spirit of God was ascribed the origin of any extraordinary force, physical or psychical, by which a man felt himself to be empowered beyond the normal limits of human ability (cf. Acts i. 8), or which carried him away on some irresistible tide of emotion. This sense, which the prophets had, of being subject to some influence constraining them to act, against their inclination, in a certain way finds expression in vivid metaphors: see 1 Kgs. xviii. 12 (cf. 2 Kgs. ii. 16), Jer. xx. 7—9, Ezek. ii. 2, iii. 12, 14, xi. 1. The feeling of external compulsion exerted by the spirit caused it sometimes to be described as "Jehovah's hand" (1 Kgs. xviii. 46, Ezek. viii. 1). The Heb. of the phrase *by the spirit of the LORD* is peculiar, though the meaning *by* given to the preposition here used may perhaps be defended by Gen. iv. 1, xlix. 25 (but see Driver, *ad loc.*). The phrase, however, seriously disturbs the rhythm of the *v.*, and it is probably the correct but unnecessary comment of a copyist or reader, which has become inserted in the text.

declare...transgression. Cf. 3 Is. lviii. 1.

9—11. In these *vv.* there is a resumption of the arraignment of the civil magistrates contained in *vv.* 1—4; but on this occasion the priests are joined with them, and both classes are charged with venality in connection with their decisions upon civil and religious matters.

9. *this.* I.e. the announcement of merited doom (*v.* 12).

10. *They build.* Better (continuing the preceding sentence), *building*: the Heb. has the sing., which requires correction to the plur., after the LXX. οἱ οἰκοδομοῦντες, Vulg. *qui ædificatis.* The prophet's meaning seems to be that the wealth which enabled the ruling classes to erect imposing mansions and so to enlarge and beautify the capital was amassed through judicial murders (the property of innocent victims being confiscated (cf. Is. i. 15, Hab. ii. 12)), or through a system of forced labour (whereby they compelled the poor to work for them without remuneration (Jer. xxii. 13—19)).

Zion. This, in primitive times, was only part of the larger area afterwards included in Jerusalem. It was the name belonging to the Jebusite fortress (2 Sam. v. 7) which was captured by David and made the capital of his kingdom. The later Jerusalem occupied two adjacent hills separated from the adjoining country on the east and west respectively

Jerusalem with iniquity. 11 The heads thereof judge for reward, and the priests thereof teach for hire, and the prophets thereof divine for money: yet will they lean upon the LORD, and say,

by the valley of the Kidron[1] and the valley of the son of Hinnom[2], and divided from one another by a shallow depression[3]; and the Jebusite fortress was in all probability situated on the eastern hill. Though the name *Zion* came to be given later to the western hill, which is the more extensive and the more commanding of the two heights, yet the eastern must have been the one occupied by the Jebusite community, since it alone has a water supply (in the Kidron valley). The southern end of this hill was known as *the Ophel* (cf. iv. 8), and was the original site of *Zion*: the northern extremity, which was of higher elevation, was the site of the Temple, this being, at first, outside of Zion (1 Kgs. viii. 1).

11. *judge for reward.* For other allusions to judicial corruption in Judah see vii. 3, Is. i. 23, Ezek. xxii. 12. Warnings against it occur in the Law (Ex. xxiii. 1, Dt. xvi. 19).

the priests. The misconduct of the sacerdotal order is dwelt upon by other prophetic writers (see Is. xxviii. 7, Hos. iv. 6, v. 1, Jer. ii. 26, v. 31, etc.). The accusation against them here is that in expounding the Divine Law (which was one of their functions (see Lev. x. 11, Dt. xvii. 8—13, Mal. ii. 7)) when application was made to them for the solution of perplexing questions of conduct, wherever the codes included in the Pentateuch (so far as they were in existence at this time) did not afford guidance, they delivered as decisions of Jehovah such answers as the enquirers made it worth their while to furnish.

the prophets. These, as well as the priests, were channels of Divine instruction; and were intended to occupy in Israel the place of the augurs, sorcerers, wizards, and necromancers to whom the heathen resorted (Dt. xviii. 10 f.): cf. p. 25.

divine. Though the verb and the corresponding noun (*divination*) are generally used in connection with methods of ascertaining the will of heaven practised by heathen peoples and forbidden in Israel (cf. Ezek. xxi. 21, 1 Sam. xv. 23 (where *witchcraft* is properly *divination*)), and commonly carried with them associations of falsehood and lying (see Jer. xiv. 14, Ezek. xiii. 6, 9, xxii. 28, 2 Zech. x. 2), yet the substantive is employed in a good sense in Prov. xvi. 10 (mg.).

yet will they lean upon the LORD. The magistrates, priests, and prophets, whom Micah condemns were worshippers of Jehovah, as the national divinity, but were so little sensible of His moral character that, whilst committing all kinds of iniquity, they reposed serene confidence in His protection, not recognizing that this was conditional upon their right-dealing (cf. Am. v. 14). The source of their confidence was the

---

[1] Now called *Wâdy Sittna Mariam* (Valley of our Lady Mary).
[2] Now *Wâdy er Rabâbi*.
[3] Formerly known as the *Tyropœon* (Valley of the cheese-makers), but now as *El Wâd* (the Valley).

Is not the LORD in the midst of us? no evil shall come upon us.
12 Therefore shall Zion for your sake be plowed as a field, and
Jerusalem shall become heaps, and the mountain of the house
as the high places of a forest.

bond thought by Semitic peoples to subsist between a god and the nation
which offered to him the sacrifices and ceremonial homage that he was
believed to value. They reflected that in Jerusalem was Jehovah's
Temple (cf. Jer. vii. 4), and within the Temple was the Ark (cf. Jer.
iii. 16), with which His presence and glory were peculiarly associated
(see Num. xiv. 42, 44, 1 Sam. iv. 3, 21, Ps. lxxviii. 61). In the time of
our Lord similar trust was placed by the Pharisees and Sadducees in
their descent from Abraham (Mt. iii. 9).

    12. *Therefore*, etc. The prediction contained in this *v.* was not ful-
filled for more than a century; and a subsequent generation recognized
that the fulfilment had been deferred in consequence of the repentance
of the king and his people (Jer. xxvi. 19). But the religious and moral
collapse that occurred under later kings brought at last the judgment
foretold; and in 587 Jerusalem was captured by the Babylonians, its
walls dismantled, and its principal citizens deported.

    for your sake. I.e. in consequence of your misconduct: cf. Dt. i. 37.

    heaps. I.e. heaps of ruins (as in i. 6).

    the mountain of the house. I.e. mount Zion, the site of the Temple
(p. 27).

    the high places of a forest. The LXX., Sym. and Th. all represent
high places by a singular (ἄλσος, ὕψος and βουνός respectively). The
notion here conveyed is that of a clearing (like the Latin *lucus*) on the
summit of a wooded hill. To such a bare and lonely condition would
the city, with its splendid fane, be reduced: cf. Lam. v. 18.

CHAPTERS IV., V.

    With ch. iii. there ends all of the book that can with confidence be assigned
to Micah (prophesying in the 8th century), though there are two other passages
which may also proceed from him (see pp. 52, 56). The rest of it would seem
to be of later origin. These two chapters, in particular, consist of several
oracles—some very short—apparently having in view diverse situations, and
probably composed by various writers living at separate periods of Hebrew
history, but all subsequent to the 8th century.

CHAPTER IV. 1—5.

    In this section the tone of menace towards Jerusalem marking chs. i.—iii
gives place to an utterance of different spirit, predicting for mount Zion pre-
eminence over other heights, and the dignity of becoming a centre for the
diffusion of a knowledge of Jehovah's requirements among the nations of
the world, who will resort thither for instruction, and will submit their disputes
to Jehovah's arbitrament. Its contents, when compared with those of the

preceding ch., suggest for it quite other authorship (cf. p. xxiii. f.). Thus (1) the assumption made in it that the Temple at Jerusalem is the sole seat of the worship of Jehovah would be impossible in Micah's time, and presupposes the abolition of the country sanctuaries by Josiah (2 Kgs. xxiii.), *circ.* 620 B.C. (2) There is a complete lack of connection between it and its immediate context (ii. 12—13 is remote), for the initial assertion that Jerusalem will become the seat of religious instruction for the heathen world involves a situation which is unexplained, since nothing is said to account for the circumstance that after the city has been doomed to destruction (iii. 12), and its populace, by implication, slaughtered or enslaved, it is once more the home of Jews and the site of Jehovah's house: contrast Jer. iii. 6—25. (3) The idea that the heathen will spontaneously make pilgrimages to Jerusalem to obtain there some knowledge of Jehovah presupposes a wonderful intervention by Him in the fortunes of the Jews, attracting attention to their God; but no light is here thrown on the nature of the occurrence: contrast vii. 15—16, Ezek. xx. 41, xxviii. 25, xxxvii. 21—28, 2 Is. xlv. 1—6, 14, 22—24, xlix. 7. These features in combination render it tolerably certain that the passage does not proceed from Micah. The greater part of the section occurs also in Is. ii. 2—4; and the reasons that cause Micah's authorship to be questioned are likewise obstacles in the way of believing it to be a genuine prophecy of Isaiah, or to be derived by both prophets from an earlier source. The character of the passage points to its being of post-exilic origin, and inserted in both of the books wherein it is now included. The passage in Is. xi. 10 which is sometimes cited as a pre-exilic parallel is probably itself post-exilic[1]. Certain small variations are discernible in the two versions when compared; and that in Micah contains a verse that is absent from Isaiah. This will be apparent if they are placed side by side in a translation a little more exact than that of the R.V.

Isaiah ii.	*Micah iv.*
2 And it shall come to pass in the sequel of days that established shall be the mountain of Jehovah's house on the top of the mountains, and shall be lifted up above the hills, and unto it shall all the nations stream.	1 And it shall come to pass in the sequel of days that the mountain of Jehovah's house shall be established on the top of the mountains and it shall be lifted up above the hills, and on to it shall peoples stream.
3 And many peoples shall go and say, Come ye, and let us go up to the mountain of Jehovah, to the house of the God of Jacob, that He may teach us out of His ways, and that we may walk in His paths, for out of Zion shall go forth instruction, and the word of Jehovah from Jerusalem.	2 And many nations shall go and say, Come ye, and let us go up to the mountain of Jehovah, and to the house of the God of Jacob, that He may teach us out of His ways, and that we may walk in His paths, for out of Zion shall go forth instruction, and the word of Jehovah from Jerusalem.

---

[1] See the commentary on Isaiah in this series, p. 86, or Gray, *Isaiah*, p. 223 (I.C.C.).

Isaiah ii.	*Micah iv.*
4 And He shall judge between the nations and shall give decisions for great peoples; and they shall beat the swords of them into coulters and their spears into pruning hooks; nation shall not lift up sword against nation, neither shall they any more learn war.	3 And He shall judge between great peoples and shall give decisions for strong nations afar off; and they shall beat their swords into coulters and their spears into pruning hooks; nation shall not lift up sword against nation, neither shall they any more learn war.
	4 But they shall sit every man under his vine and under his fig tree, none making them afraid; for the mouth of JEHOVAH of hosts hath spoken it.

IV. 1 ¹But in the latter days it shall come to pass, that the mountain of the LORD'S house shall be established ²in the top of

¹ See Is. ii. 2—4.   ² Or, *at the head*

1. *in the latter days.* Better, *in the sequel*¹ *of days*, an expression which denotes a future period varying in connotation with the outlook of the successive speakers or writers who employ it. It is generally used in connection with predictions of good fortune, and "designates the period when the hopes, whatever they are, that relieve a dissatisfying present will be fulfilled." In Gen. xlix. 1 the range of the prospect signified by it does not extend beyond the conquest of Canaan; in Num. xxiv. 14 it is the time of the monarchy and the mastery by Israel of the surrounding countries of Moab and Edom; in Hos. iii. 5 (end) and Dt. iv. 30 it is the restoration of Israel from conditions of tribulation and distress; whilst in Dan. ii. 28 it is the emergence of the kingdoms destined to succeed to the empire of the Babylonians under Nebuchadrezzar. In the present passage it denotes an ideal age subsequent to the restoration of Israel to its own land. The N.T. equivalents are ἐπ' ἐσχάτου τῶν χρόνων (1 Pet. i. 20), ἐπ' ἐσχάτου τοῦ χρόνου (Jude 18), and ἐπ' ἐσχάτου τῶν ἡμερῶν τούτων (Heb. i. 2).

the mountain, etc. I.e. the Temple hill (see on p. 27), which, at the point where the Temple was built, reaches an altitude of 2400 ft. above the sea.

established in the top. Better, *established on the top* (cf. Ex. xxiv. 17, Ps. lxxii. 16). The writer conceives mount Zion not merely as being at the head of all other heights (as in the mg.), but as elevated upon them, this not only marking its superior rank as the site of Jehovah's sanctuary, but also enabling it to be descried from a distance by those who

---

¹ The term rendered *sequel* sometimes means the end of a period as distinguished from its beginning (2 Is. xlvi. 10), or the end of an individual life, or of a phase in a nation's career (Prov. v. 4, Jer. xxxi. 17).

the mountains, and it shall be exalted above the hills; and peoples shall flow unto it. 2 And many nations shall go and say, Come ye, and let us go up to the mountain of the LORD, and to the house of the God of Jacob; and he will teach us of his ways, and we will walk in his paths: for out of Zion shall go forth [1]the law, and the word of the LORD from Jerusalem. 3 And he shall judge [2]between [3]many peoples, and shall [4]reprove strong nations afar off; and they shall beat their swords into plowshares,

[1] Or, *instruction*   [2] Or, *among*   [3] Or, *great*
[4] Or, *decide concerning*

wish to reach it. In the parallel passage in Isaiah the order of the words has been disturbed, and the metre impaired.

it. The pronoun is here expressed in the Heb., preserving the rhythm: in Is. it is absent.

peoples. Is. has *all the nations.*

flow. Or *stream*: cf. Jer. xxxi. 12, li. 44.

2. *And many nations shall,* etc. Cf. Zech. viii. 21, 22.

the God of Jacob. The name *Jacob* here describes the people of Judah only, as in iii. 1, 8.

teach us of his ways. Literally, *teach us out of his ways,* i.e. impart from His unlimited store of spiritual illumination such amount as is essential and sufficient for the course of life He requires from men.

the law. Better (as in the mg.), *instruction*: the noun corresponds to the verb *teach* in the previous clause. In the N.T. a counterpart of the statement here made may be found in Lk. xxiv. 47: cf. also 1 Cor. xiv. 24, 25.

3. *And he shall judge,* etc. The utterance of the nations ceases with the end of *v.* 2, and the speaker here is the prophet.

many peoples. Better (as in the mg.), *great peoples* (parallel with *strong nations,* cf. Dt. iv. 38). The clause, however, is too long to be in keeping with the prevailing rhythm, and Is., where there is no adj. with *peoples,* has preserved the better text.

reprove. Better, *give decisions for* (note mg.); cf. Is. xi. 4. Where Jehovah is universally accepted as arbitrator in international disputes, there will be no more occasion for appeals to the sword.

afar off. This is in all probability an interpolation: it is absent from Isaiah and spoils the balance of the clauses.

plowshares. Perhaps better, *coulters* (the blade fixed in front of the ploughshare), into which swords could be more easily converted. Sym., however (on 1 Sam. xiii. 20), gives as its equivalent the Greek σκαφεῖον, "a spade" or "mattock." The abolition of military weapons from among both houses of Israel, and the proclamation of universal peace amongst the surrounding nations, is predicted for the Messianic Age in 2 Zech. ix. 10, Ps. xlvi. 9, Is. xi. 9.

and their spears into pruninghooks: nation shall not lift up
sword against nation, neither shall they learn war any more.
4 But they shall sit every man under his vine and under his fig
tree; and none shall make them afraid: for the mouth of the
LORD of hosts hath spoken it. 5 For all the peoples ¹will walk
every one in the name of his god, and we will walk in the name
of the LORD our God for ever and ever.

¹ Or, *walk*

pruninghooks. Compare Martial's epigram (*Falx ex ense*): *Pax
me certa ducis placidos curvavit in usus; Agricolæ nunc sum, militis
ante fui* (xiv. 34).
4. This *v.* is not contained in Is., and is probably an expansion in
prose of the preceding oracle. Vines and fig trees were characteristic
products of Palestine (Dt. viii. 8, Hos. ii. 12). Similar descriptions of
peace and plenty are found in 1 Kgs. iv. 25, 2 Kgs. xviii. 31, Zech. iii.
10: for the second clause cf. Is. xvii. 2, Jer. xxx. 10, xlvi. 27, etc.
the LORD of hosts. It has been debated whether, in the phrases
JEHOVAH of hosts and *God of hosts* (Am. iii. 13, v. 27), the hosts are
terrestrial, or celestial, armies. If the former, the forces of Israel
(called *the hosts of JEHOVAH* in Ex. vii. 4, cf. 1 Sam. xvii. 36) must be
meant; but probably the term really has reference to armies of angels;
cf. Dt. xxxiii. 2, Joel iii. 11¹.
5. *For all the peoples,* etc. Better, *Though all the peoples walk* (cf. mg.)
*each in the name of his god, yet we will walk in the name of JEHOVAH,
our God, for ever and ever.* For the translation *though* (or *although*)
cf. Ps. xlix. 18 (19), Ex. xiii. 17, Dt. xxix. 19 (18), Josh. xvii. 18.
This *v.* places in contrast to the ideal future depicted in the foregoing
vv. the contemporary condition of the surrounding world, wherein
idolatry still prevails; but the writer, notwithstanding, voices his own
and his countrymen's resolve to be unfalteringly loyal to Jehovah. *To
walk in the name of Jehovah* probably means to behave according to the
revelation of Himself which God has granted. Though *the name of
Jehovah* is occasionally used to denote a Theophany (Is. xxx. 27), it
more commonly expresses a disclosure of His character; so that
Jerusalem, with its temple, which was the locality where God's moral
and spiritual nature was pre-eminently revealed through the Mosaic
Law and Prophetic instruction, was styled the place where Jehovah
had put His name (see Dt. xii. 11, and cf. 1 Kgs. viii. 20, 29).

---

¹ See further, *The Book of Isaiah* (in this series), pp. 12, 13.

CHAPTER IV. 6—8.

That these three verses originated at a time distinct from that which witnessed the composition of the previous five is suggested by the different situation of the Jewish people. Whereas in *vv.* 1—5 it is assumed that the people are already restored to their own land, and the predictive element relates to the future dignity which they are to enjoy, *here* it is presupposed that, having undergone rejection by Jehovah, they are still in exile, and the prediction which the passage contains foretells their return to their former homes, and the restoration to them of the dominion which was once theirs. The most natural conclusion to which the interna evidence points is that this oracle is neither by Micah nor by the author of the preceding section, but (like that in ii. 12—13) proceeds from a prophet living in exilic times amongst the captives in Babylon, and was designed to console and encourage them with a near prospect of deliverance. (Note the occurrence of the verbs *I will assemble* and *I will gather* in both ii. 12 and iv. 6.) A pre-exilic date, however, becomes possible if these verses and verses 9—10 are transposed, as suggested by J. M. P. Smith, though the century in which they were written must have been not the 8th (when Micah lived) but the 6th, or not earlier than the very end of the 7th; see p. 35.

6 In that day, saith the LORD, will I assemble her that halteth, and I will gather her that is driven away, and her that I have afflicted; 7 and I will make her that halted a remnant, and her that was cast far off a strong nation: and the LORD shall reign

6. *In that day.* I.e. the coming Day of Jehovah, which, in the mind of the pre-exilic prophets, was generally conceived to be a time of judgment and disaster for the sinful people, but which during and after the Exile was increasingly regarded as an occasion fraught with redemption for those who had already undergone retribution for their offences; see Is. xi. 11, xii. 1, Am. ix. 11, and contrast Am. v. 18.

her that halteth. A figure for an afflicted community: cf. Zeph. iii. 19.

and her that I have afflicted. The presence of this clause disturbs the parallelism between the rest of the *v.* and 7ᵃ; it is probably a prosaic explanation of the preceding metaphorical term.

7. *a remnant.* In this context the word must signify a germ from which the nation can be renewed: cf. v. 7. For the promise cf. 3 Is. lx. 22.

her that was cast off. The Vulg. has *eam quæ laboraverat* (i.e. "her that was distressed"), apparently reading *hannilā'ah* for *hannahălā'ah.*

the LORD shall reign over them. In prophetic descriptions of the happy future in store for Jehovah's people sometimes the sovereign who is to rule them is a king of human descent, endowed with Divine qualities (Is. viii. 8, ix. 6 f.); at other times he is Jehovah Himself (Is. xxiv. 23, Ob. 21): see p. cxiv.

w.

over them in mount Zion from henceforth even for ever. 8 And
thou, O tower of ¹the flock, ²the hill of the daughter of Zion,
unto thee shall it come; yea, the former dominion shall come,
the kingdom of the daughter of Jerusalem.

¹ Or, *Eder* See Gen. xxxv. 21. ² Heb. *Ophel*.

from henceforth. Better, *from thenceforth.*

8. *O tower of the flock.* The term likens Jerusalem to a solitary
watch-tower, such as might be constructed by shepherds to protect
them, whilst guarding their sheep on lonely pasture grounds, from
marauders or beasts of prey (cf. 2 Ch. xxvi. 10, 2 Kgs. xvii. 9); and
consequently it implies that the city apostrophized by the prophet is
situated amid solitude and desolation, its surviving buildings being no
better than temporary shelters. The Heb. for the phrase is *Migdal
'Edher*, identical with the name of a place (according to Jerome, a mile
from Bethlehem) mentioned in the history of the patriarch Jacob (Gen.
xxxv. 21); but here the term is only symbolical.

the hill. Heb. *the 'Ophel*, a word meaning "a swelling" (cf. the Latin
tumulus) and so applicable to several heights. There was an *ophel*
within the territory of the Northern Kingdom (2 Kgs. v. 24), and the
Moabite king Mesha mentions in his inscription "the wall of the Ophel"
in connection with a place variously vocalized as *Korhah* or *Kĕrēhoh*:
but the term was used especially of the southern extremity of the Temple
hill (see 2 Ch. xxvii. 3, xxxiii. 14, Neh. iii. 26, 27), as here.

shall it come...shall come, etc. The text has probably undergone some
slight dislocation: one of the verbs lacks a subject, one of the nouns
(*the kingdom*) wants a verb, and the rhythm is faulty. A plausible rearrangement is, *unto thee shall come the former dominion, and there shall
arrive* (the verb here differs from the preceding) *the kingdom of the
daughter of Jerusalem.* The verb rendered *come* (*'āthah*) is one which
appears comparatively late in Hebrew literature, and seems to be used
first in Deuteronomy (seven times), unless Is. xxi. 12, 14 are earlier
instances, so that its occurrence here favours for this section a date
later than Micah's age. By *the former dominion* is meant the extensive
authority which was possessed by David, Solomon, and their more
powerful successors on the throne of Judah (such as Uzziah). In the
second clause the LXX. has βασιλεία ἐκ Βαβυλῶνος τῇ θυγατρὶ Ἰερουσαλήμ,
the name of Babylon being probably an insertion suggested by *v.* 10.

CHAPTERS IV. 9—V. 15.

This large section is by some critics treated as a single whole: whether it
can reasonably be regarded as a unity can best be determined after the several
divisions into which it naturally falls have been surveyed in detail. If a plausible
conclusion as to origin can be reached in regard to the first group of verses
(*vv.* 9—10), it can be reconsidered whether the contents of the succeeding groups,
prima facie rather discrepant, allow them to be viewed as emanating from the
same period.

These two verses appear to be distinct from the preceding context. They imply that Jerusalem, at a time when it still had a king, was in a desperate plight, its citizens being penned within it by a hostile army at its gates, and exile being in prospect for some or all of them. The mention of Babylon in *v.* 10 as the destined place of exile precludes the reign of Hezekiah as the date of the oracle unless the words *even unto Babylon* be omitted as a mistaken gloss. The hypothesis which best suits the situation is that the prophecy was uttered near the close of the reign of Zedekiah. The armies of Babylon had beleaguered Jerusalem for nearly 18 months (2 Kgs. xxv. 1—3, Jer. lii. 1—6). At the termination of that period a breach in the fortifications was made by the enemy; and Zedekiah, with his chief officers, fled by night, leaving the kingdom and its capital without a head. This will explain the question asked mockingly by the prophet in *v.* 9. The city was soon captured and the king taken, and both he and the flower of his people were carried to Babylon.

9 Now why dost thou cry out aloud? Is there no king in thee, is thy counsellor perished, that pangs have taken hold of thee as of a woman in travail? 10 Be in pain, and labour to bring forth, O daughter of Zion, like a woman in travail: for now shalt thou go forth out of the city, and shalt dwell in the field,

9. *Now why dost thou cry*, etc. If this passage could be referred to Micah as its author, the situation which the prophet had in mind would be the advance upon Jerusalem of Sennacherib's forces, as described in 2 Kgs. xviii. 17, and the *king* and *counsellor* might be taken to be Jehovah (the question, *Is there no king in thee?* implying that the people need not despair as though God had altogether forsaken them—He was not finally estranged). But this view is rendered impossible by *v.* 10 unless it is emended; and the occasion must be the flight of Zedekiah during the siege of Jerusalem by the Babylonians. It may be assumed that tidings have just spread among the populace that the king and his nobles have deserted them; and the prophet tauntingly asks the terrified citizens (who for the most part had supported the senseless revolt against Babylon) whether they have not a ruler or counsellor to direct them in the defence of the city.

as of a woman, etc. The same simile to express acute suffering occurs frequently (cf. Jer. vi. 24, xxii. 23, etc.).

10. *Be in pain*, etc. The prophet here drops his taunting tone, and declares that there is real cause for anguish: the population of Jerusalem must leave their homes, and be carried captive to Babylon; and only after exile there will deliverance come.

labour to bring forth. Literally, *thrust forth*, though this sense is rare (cf. Ps. lxxi. 6ª).

shalt thou...the city. I.e. thou must surrender and evacuate it: cf. 2 Kgs. xxiv. 12.

shalt dwell in the field. Outside the city walls the captives would be

and shalt come even unto Babylon; there shalt thou be rescued;
there shall the LORD redeem thee from the hand of thine enemies.

herded together by the conquerors in preparation for removal to Babylon,
more than 500 miles away as the crow flies.

even unto Babylon. If this section is assigned to an occasion just
before the Fall of Jerusalem in 587, the mention of Babylon as the
destined place of exile is perfectly natural (cf. Jer. xx. 4 f., xxii. 25,
xxvii. 12), but in the time of Micah *Assyria* was Judah's most menacing
enemy, and Babylon was merely one of Assyria's subject states[1]; so
that if Micah's authorship of the section be defended, these words must
be omitted as an interpolation (for 2 Kgs. xvii. 24 is not a real parallel),
due to a misunderstanding as to the scene of the promised rescue, which
in Micah's thoughts was *the field* (i.e. the open country outside Jerusalem, where the invading Assyrians would meet with disaster), but
was taken by a post-captivity reader to be Babylon, and an explanation
inserted in the mg., whence it was introduced into the text. But the
view adopted above, that the prediction really has in view the Babylonian captivity seems more plausible. It was not until the overthrow
of the Assyrian empire by the Medes and the capture of Nineveh in
607 (later investigations point to 612 as the correct date) that Babylon
attained independence under Nabopolassar, who aided the Medes in
their assault upon Nineveh. The predominance in W. Asia previously
enjoyed by Assyria was grasped at by Egypt; but the Egyptian forces
were defeated at Carchemish (on the Euphrates) in 605 by Nebuchadrezzar, son of Nabopolassar; and in consequence the Babylonian
king had Palestine at his mercy, and proceeded to overrun Judah and
to besiege Jerusalem.

CHAPTER IV. 11–13.

In these verses Jerusalem, after its rescue from Babylon, is again thought of
as surrounded by enemies bent on its overthrow. Their hostile efforts, however,
are not destined to result in the city's destruction: on the contrary, Jehovah
designs the assailants to be slaughtered by those whom they attack, and their
spoil to be devoted to Him. There is here no allusion to any particular enemy,
such as the Assyrians or the Babylonians, but to a multitude of hostile nations,
such as are represented in Ezekiel xxxviii., xxxix. as mustering to fight against
Jerusalem, and there is a striking contrast between the predictions of the
overthrow of the city in iii. 12 and in iv. 10 and the present announcement of
its inviolability and of the annihilation of its foes. The latter anticipation occurs
in various post-exilic writers, but as it is also found in Ezekiel, whose ministry
began a few years before the Fall of Jerusalem, the presence of the same idea
here does not altogether preclude for this prophecy an origin just preceding
the Exile, though a confident opinion about its date is impossible.

---

[1] On Is. xxxix. 6 see the commentary on Isaiah in this series, p. 246.

11 And now many nations are assembled against thee, that say, Let her be defiled, and let our eye [1]see *its desire* upon Zion. 12 But they know not the thoughts of the LORD, neither understand they his counsel: for he hath gathered them as the sheaves to the threshing-floor. 13 Arise and thresh, O daughter of Zion: for I will make thine horn iron, and I will make thy hoofs brass: and thou shalt beat in pieces many peoples: and

[1] Or, *gaze upon*

11. *And now.* This appears to indicate an occasion distinct from the *now* of *v.* 9.

many nations, etc. Though Isaiah in the 8th century could speak of many nations as assailing Jerusalem (xvii. 12, 13, xxix. 7, cf. xxii. 6), the various subject nationalities included in the Assyrian hosts being in his mind[1], yet in various passages of his prophecies he names the enemy that in his day imperilled the Jewish capital; and he looked for the defeat of that enemy to be effected not through the Jewish people themselves but through the direct interposition of Jehovah (Is. xxxvii. 21—35). Here the writer's conception more nearly resembles that in 2 Zech. xii. 2 f.

Let her be defiled. I.e. let her be desecrated. The prophet makes the enemy speak from the standpoint of an inhabitant of Jehovah's land, who would regard its occupation by a heathen foe as a pollution: cf. Joel iii. 17.

let our eye see, etc. The phrase in the original is merely *let our eyes look* (or *gaze*) *upon Zion*; but when the object looked upon was an enemy, it carried with it the implication of satisfaction at the sight, and so became equivalent to "gloating over": cf. (though the verb used is different) Ezek. xxviii. 17, Ob. 12, 13, Ps. xxii. 17.

12. *they know not,* etc. The foe, in pursuit of their own purposes, unconsciously fulfil Jehovah's: the mustering of their forces to assail Zion only paves the way for their own wholesale destruction.

13. *Arise and thresh.* For the metaphor cf. 2 Kgs. xiii. 7, Am. i. 3, Hab. iii. 12, Jer. li. 33, Is. xxi. 10, 2 Is. xli. 15. The processes of threshing adopted by the Hebrews with different kinds of cereals and pulse are described in Is. xxviii. 27, 28 mg.

thine horn...thy hoofs. Oxen were used to separate the grain from the husk by treading upon it (Dt. xxv. 4, Hos. x. 11, 1 Cor. ix. 9), so that the mention of *the hoofs* is appropriate; but the reference to the *horn* seems to introduce the alien idea of goring and tossing an adversary (1 Kgs. xxii. 11, Dt. xxxiii. 17[b]). Hebrew writers were specially prone to mix their metaphors (see, for example, Is. xiv. 29, xxviii. 18[b], xxx. 28); but possibly here the figure is merely meant to suggest power and strength.

[1] Cf. also Is. viii. 9, where the reference is to the allied forces of Syria and Northern Israel.

¹thou shalt devote their gain unto the LORD, and their substance
unto the Lord of the whole earth.

¹ So the ancient versions. The Hebrew text as pointed reads, *I will devote.*

thou shalt devote their gain, etc. Though the Heb. text has a form
which is the regular one for the *first* person (*I will devote*), the Versions
(as the mg. notes) have the second person (e.g. LXX. ἀναθήσεις) and are
followed by the R.V. The verb rendered *devote* means to "seclude" or
"withdraw" something from common use (the root being the same as
that of *harem*). Such separation, in the case of enemy persons or
possessions previously associated with the worship of alien gods, was
designed to prevent the infection of a foreign cult from spreading
amongst those whose loyalty to their own God it was desired to safeguard. Human beings who were thus devoted were destroyed, and total
destruction was sometimes extended to cattle and other kinds of booty
(hence the Vulg. here has *interficies*); whilst if they were spared, they
were dedicated to the service of the national sanctuary; see Dt. ii. 34,
35, Josh. vi. 17—19, 1 Sam. xv. 3. The custom was not peculiar to the
Hebrews, but was practised by the Moabites likewise (see p. 24). By
gain is meant acquisitions obtained by violence: the Vulg. has *rapinas.*

the Lord of the whole earth. When the word *Lord* is not printed in
capitals, it is a title, *'Ādhōn* (cf. p. 4), and does not represent the
personal name JEHOVAH (see p. 1): cf. Josh. iii. 11, Zech. iv. 14, vi. 5,
Ps. xcvii. 5.

CHAPTER V. 1—9.

This section, when compared with the preceding, manifestly has in view
quite another situation. In iv. 11—13, Jerusalem, though attacked by numerous
foes, is enabled by Jehovah to destroy them. But here, in the first place,
Jerusalem is depicted as besieged and its ruler insulted; and next, it is
announced that, after a period of national humiliation, there will emerge from
David's birthplace, Bethlehem, a ruler who will be invested with world-wide
dominion, and under whom the land will be safe from hostile invasion; and the
remnant of the people surviving the period of depression will become as
formidable to their enemies as a lion is to sheep. If all these nine verses are
grouped together, the *data* for settling the time of their origin are, on the
surface, conflicting. Verse 1 points to the time of the monarchy, for *the judge
of Israel* must signify the king; but the only occasions when the Judean king
was exposed to personal indignity at the hands of foreign enemies occurred
towards the close of the monarchical period, first when Jehoahaz was taken
prisoner by the Egyptian Necho, and next when Jehoiachin and Zedekiah
were successively captured and deported by the Babylonian Nebuchadrezzar
in the first quarter of the 6th century. It accords with this that the appearance
of the great ruler who is to be his people's permanent safeguard is placed
after a period of national subjection to foreign foes, a condition which is most
intelligible if explained by the Babylonian captivity. On the other hand, the

enemy from whom the promised ruler is to secure his people is called *the Assyrian*, this people being the dominant power in the second half of the 8th century, but losing its imperial position at the end of the 7th century. There is evidence, however, that the name *Assyria* was applied to the various peoples who succeeded in turn to the empire of the Assyrians, viz. the Babylonians (Lam. v. 6), the Persians (Ez. vi. 22, Is. xxvii. 13?), the Greeks of Alexander's Age (2 Zech. x. 10, note the mention of *Greece* in ix. 13), and perhaps the Syrians of Maccabæan times (Ps. lxxxiii. 8?); so that there is nothing unreasonable in taking *Assyria* in *v.* 6 to designate Babylonia. The prophet from whom the oracle proceeds may (unlike Deutero-Isaiah) have expected his countrymen to be restored to independence and greatness otherwise than through the total destruction of the Babylonian empire, and to need protection against renewed assaults by the same power. Accordingly the simplest solution of the problem of date seems to be the assignment of the section to some period within the last 20 (or preferably the last 10) years prior to the Fall of Jerusalem in 587.

These nine verses are here treated as a single oracle; but several critics (e.g. J. M. P. Smith) deny their unity and consider that *v.* 1 stands in isolation from the verses that follow; and that *vv.* 5, 6 are distinct from the context on either side of them; and it must be allowed that of the problem presented no solution is very satisfying.

V. 1 Now shalt thou gather thyself in troops, O daughter of

1. *Now shalt thou...troops*, etc. Better, *Now shalt thou gather thyself for a foray, O daughter of forays*. The time here indicated by *now* seems to be the same as that of iv. 9, 10. The word (*gĕdhŭdh*), rendered *troops* by the R.V., is generally used of bands of marauders (1 Sam. xxx. 8, 2 Kgs. v. 2, xxiv. 2, Hos. vi. 9, vii. 1), though occasionally of regular divisions of the Israelite armies (2 Ch. xxvi. 11), as well as of the hosts of God (Job xxv. 3). It seems not improbable that the prophet, in calling Jerusalem *daughter of forays*, has in mind highway robberies, like those alluded to by Micah (ii. 8) as rife in his time. Such disorders, if frequent in the 8th century under Hezekiah, are not likely to have been less common in the 7th and 6th under such rulers as Manasseh, Jehoiakim, Jehoiachin, or Zedekiah; and the term *gĕdhŭdh* in the plural occurs in Hos. vi. 9 in reference to troops of robbers who seemingly raided unprotected homesteads outside Samaria. If so, then the address, *Now shalt thou gather thyself for a foray* may be a sarcastic command to the lawless population of Jerusalem, penned in by a powerful enemy, to act under such circumstances as they had previously been wont to do when at large. The verb employed (*gādhadh*) is that occurring in Ps. xciv. 21 (of those who combine against the righteous) and in Jer. v. 7 (of the throngs of profligates who in that prophet's time gathered at the houses of loose women). In the phrase *daughter of forays* (the Heb. has the sing.) the gen. is descriptive (cf. Num. xvii. 10, *sons of rebellion*). The Vulg. has *filia latronis*. In the LXX. the opening sentence is Νῦν ἐμφραχθήσεται θυγάτηρ ἐμφραγμῷ, im-

troops: he hath laid siege against us: they shall smite the judge
of Israel with a rod upon the cheek.

2 But thou, Beth-lehem Ephrathah, which art little to be

plying the noun *gādhēr* and the verb *gādhar*; and if the 2 pers. imper.
be substituted for the 3 pers. fut., the rendering will be *Now fence
thyself, daughter of fences* (i.e. defences), and the command can be
understood as an ironical exhortation to Jerusalem to put in order her
fortifications, if she contemplates defiance of Babylon, as happened in
the reigns of both Jehoiachin and Zedekiah (2 Kgs. xxiv. 10—12, 20).
This reading seems preferable to that of the present Heb. text, though
the particular form of the verb implied does not occur elsewhere.
Wellhausen, followed by many scholars, corrects the text to *Now cut
thyself severely* (one meaning of *gādhadh*), the command being a mocking
direction to the people of Jerusalem to gash themselves after the
manner of the heathen, for this was a practice customary in appeals
to their divinities for help (1 Kgs. xviii. 28).

the judge of Israel. The word *judge* appears to be used in place of
king (cf. Am. ii. 3) for the sake of an assonance with the word *rod*
(*shōphēt* and *shēbhet*).

2. *But thou, Beth-lehem Ephrathah.* The prophet relieves the gloom
of the distressful present by placing before his beleaguered and humiliated countrymen the prospect of a happier time to follow, when from
Bethlehem there will come forth a ruler who will repeat on a grander
scale the services rendered to his people by David. The representation
that the promised ruler is to arise from *Bethlehem* possibly implies
that he is not to be a descendant of David though he is to spring from
Jesse's family: the prophet may have anticipated the extinction of
the seed royal of Davidic origin; cf. Jer. xxii. 28—30. But more
probably the expression is chosen in order to suggest that the destined
sovereign will be a second David.

Ephrathah. This appears to have been the name of the district in
which the Bethlehem here intended was situated (see Ruth iv. 11 and
cf. i. 2, 1 Sam. xvii. 12), for there was another Bethlehem in the
territory of Zebulun (Josh. xix. 15), from which it was sometimes
distinguished as *Bethlehem Judah* (Jud. xvii. 7). The *Ephrath* where
Rachel died (Gen. xxxv. 19, xlviii. 7) was near Bethel (in Benjamin,
not Judah, 1 Sam. x. 2), and its identification with Bethlehem (in
Gen. *l. c.*) seems to be an erroneous gloss. The *Ephrathah* of Ps. cxxxii. 6
is probably the same as that here mentioned, for *Kiriath-Jearim*, with
which it is associated by the Psalmist, is placed by Eusebius 9 or 10
miles W. of Jerusalem, and so may have been included in the same
district as Bethlehem. Van Hoonacker thinks that the name is here
introduced because of the assonance with the root *pārāh*, "to produce,"
with allusion to Bethlehem as the birthplace of the Messianic prince.
The LXX. has Βηθλέεμ οἶκος Ἐφράθα, which probably points to the
true text of the Heb. original (p. cxl.).

among the [1]thousands of Judah, out of thee shall one come
forth unto me that is to be ruler in Israel; whose goings forth
are from of old, [2]from everlasting. 3 Therefore will he give them

[1] Or, *families* See Judg. vi. 15.　　　　　[2] Or, *from ancient days*

little to be among. I.e. barely populous enough to be included
among. Bethlehem does not figure among the cities of Judah enumerated in Josh. xv. 20—63; and it is called a village in Joh. vii. 42.
It is situated 6 miles south by west of Jerusalem.

the thousands of Judah. The term *thousand* was applied to a division
of an army (Ex. xviii. 21, Num. xxxi. 14), a division of a tribe (Jud.
vi. 15, mg., 1 Sam. x. 19), and apparently an area within the territory
of a tribe.

unto me. The speaker is Jehovah, whose purposes the predicted
ruler will carry out.

This *v.*, down to *Israel*, is quoted in Mt. ii. 6, where the numerous
divergences from the LXX. (which appear when the passages are
placed side by side) point to the employment by the Evangelist of an
independent translation made from a Heb. text not exactly the same
as ours, and included in a collection of O.T. passages "regarded as
prophecies of events in the life of the Messiah[1]."

LXX.	Mt.
καὶ σύ, Βηθλέεμ, οἶκος 'Εφράθα, ὀλι- γοστὸς εἶ τοῦ εἶναι ἐν χιλιάσιν 'Ιούδα· ἐξ οὗ μοι ἐξελεύσεται τοῦ εἶναι εἰς ἄρχοντα τοῦ 'Ισραήλ.	καὶ σύ, Βηθλέεμ, γῆ 'Ιούδα, οὐδαμῶς ἐλαχίστη εἶ ἐν τοῖς ἡγεμόσιν 'Ιούδα· ἐκ σοῦ γὰρ ἐξελεύσεται ἡγούμενος ὅστις ποιμανεῖ τὸν λαόν μου τὸν 'Ισραήλ[2].

whose goings forth, etc. Some take the expression *goings forth* to
refer to the origin of the Messianic king in the eternal purposes of God.
But more probably it is an allusion to the promised ruler's lineage,
which was of great antiquity, his line of descent reaching back to the
distant past. If the oracle dates from near the end of the monarchy
(*circ.* 587), something like 400 years must have elapsed since the time
of David the son of Jesse the Bethlehemite.

from everlasting. Better (as in the mg.), *from ancient days*; cf. vii.
14, 20, Mal. iii. 4, 3 Is. lxiii. 11, Am. ix. 11.

3. *Therefore will he give them up, until,* etc. This seems to imply that
Judah is to be surrendered by God to its foes for no more than a limited
period. Since a David *redivivus* is destined to appear, the surrender
will last *only* until the mother of the promised ruler gives birth to him
(cf. Is. vii. 14, a passage which the prophet probably had in mind).
The words *she which travaileth* have been taken by some to refer to the
collective nation. By certain scholars the whole *v.* is regarded as a later
insertion; but this is a needless supposition, since Jeremiah, with whom

[1] Box, *St Matt.* p. 76 (C.B.).　　　　　[2] Cf. 2 Sam. v. 2.

up, until the time that she which travaileth hath brought forth:
then the residue of his brethren shall return ¹unto the children
of Israel. 4 And he shall stand, and shall feed *his flock* in the
strength of the LORD, in the majesty of the name of the LORD
his God: and they shall abide ; for now shall he be great unto
the ends of the earth. 5 And this *man* shall be *our* peace : when
the Assyrian shall come into our land, and when he shall tread

---

¹ Or, *with*

---

the writer of the present passage was probably contemporary, anticipated
for his countrymen a period of subjection under a foreign power, to be
followed by subsequent deliverance.

the residue of his brethren. It is not clear whether the allusion is to
the exiles of Judah, or to those of the Northern Kingdom: probably
the latter, *Israel* standing for Judah (representing the true Israel).
The re-union of both branches of the Hebrew people is a feature of
many prophecies: see Hos. iii. 5, Is. xi. 12, Jer. iii. 18, Ezek. xxxvii.
16 f.

4. *shall feed* his flock. The relation of a ruler to his subjects is
likened to that of a shepherd to his flock hardly less frequently in the
O.T. than in the poems of Homer (who regularly styles the Greek chiefs
shepherds of their people); see 2 Sam. v. 2, Jer. iii. 15, Ezek. xxxiv.
23, xxxvii. 24.

in the strength of the LORD. Cf. the endowments of the sovereign
whose advent is foretold in Is. xi. 2.

in the majesty of the name. The *name* of Jehovah was a summary
expression for the disclosure of His character (p. 32), and by this the
future ruler would be enlightened and supported in his task.

they shall abide. I.e. shall continue in security; cf. iv. 4.

for now. Better, *for then*: cf. vii. 4.

great unto the ends of the earth. Cf. the description of the king in
Ps. ii. 8, lxxii. 8; also Lk. i. 32.

5. *And this* man *shall be* our *peace,* etc. If *this* is rightly taken (as
by the Vulg., *iste*) to mean "this man" (cf. Gen. v. 29 Heb.), *peace* must
stand for "peacemaker" (cf. Eph. ii. 14, which was perhaps suggested
to St Paul by this passage, and the title *Jehovah-Shalom* in Jud. vi. 24),
or possibly "protector" (cf. Zech. viii. 10, where *peace* stands for
"protection"). This function of the Messiah is emphasized in Is. ix. 6
(cf. Lk. ii. 14). Nevertheless the Heb., which is literally *And this shall
be peace* (cf. the LXX. ἔσται αὕτη εἰρήνη), admits of a different and
perhaps preferable interpretation—"And in this way (as explained in
the rest of the *v.*) will peace be ensured." For the pronoun in this kind
of connection cf. Gen. xx. 13.

the Assyrian. If the prophecy has been correctly dated (see p. 38),
the Babylonians must be designated by this term.

in our palaces, then shall we raise against him seven shepherds,
and eight ¹principal men. 6 And they shall ²waste the land of
Assyria with the sword, and the land of Nimrod in the entrances
thereof: and he shall deliver us from the Assyrian, when he

¹ Or, *princes among men*　　　　² Or, *eat up* Or, *be shepherds over*

in our palaces. The LXX. has ἐπὶ τὴν χώραν ἡμῶν; and as the entry
of the foe into Judah's palaces would mean their presence in the heart
of the country, the text should probably be emended to *on our soil*:
cf. *v.* 6.

then shall we raise, etc. At first sight, this *v.* seems to represent the
security of the land as being ensured by a plurality of defenders rather
than by the single ruler and shepherd described in *vv.* 2—4; and some
critics (e.g. Van Hoonacker) have concluded that this *v.*, together with
6ᵃ, is too little in accord with its context to be of the same origin. But
the *seven shepherds and eight principal* (literally *anointed*, cf. Josh. xiii.
21, Ezek. xxxii. 30 Heb.) *men* may denote the subordinates of the Ruler,
who, like David of old, will have his chieftains and officers for the execution of his plans of defence. The combination *seven and eight* where
we should say "seven *or* eight" (the use in Heb. of *and* as equivalent
to *or* may be illustrated by Lev. xxii. 23, Job xxxi. 26)¹ merely expresses a considerable but indefinite number; cf. Am. i. 3, Eccles. xi. 2,
Job v. 19, Ecclus. xxv. 7.

6. *waste.* Literally, *pasture on*, and so consume: see Jer. vi. 3, and
cf. Num. xxii. 4.

the land of Nimrod. The kingdom of Nimrod, as described in Heb.
legend, was at first the land of Shinar, i.e. Babylonia; but was subsequently extended so as to include Assyria (Gen. x. 9—11). The figure
of Nimrod himself is usually identified with the *Gilgamesh* mentioned
in the cuneiform inscriptions, who, though differing from Nimrod in
name, is depicted, like him, as a great hunter, and as having saved the
city of Erech, one of the places included in Nimrod's dominions (Gen. *l.c.*).

in the entrances thereof. The word *entrances* is more suitable to a
city (Is. iii. 26) than to a country (though cf. Nah. iii. 13, *the gates of
thy land* (of Nineveh), and the pass through the Taurus mountains,
called the *Cilician gates*); and the parallelism suggests that the true
reading and rendering is *with drawn* (literally *opened*) blade (*biphthihah*
for *biphthāhehā*); cf. Ps. lv. 21 (22). Reference here to a weapon is
favoured by Aq.'s ἐν ζιβύναις ("spears" or "pikes") and the Vulg.'s *in
lanceis eius* (though the particular weapon meant must have been mis-
understood). The verb "to open" (*pāthah*) is used of drawing swords
in Ezek. xxi. 28 (33), Ps. xxxvii. 14.

he shall deliver us. Strictly *he shall effect deliverance*, there being no
us in the Heb. The pronoun *he* refers to the promised ruler. Some

¹ Cf. the Greek τρὶς καὶ τετράκις and the Latin *ter quaterque.*

cometh into our land, and when he treadeth within our border.
7 And the remnant of Jacob shall be in the midst of many peoples
as dew from the LORD, as showers upon the grass; that tarrieth
not for man, nor waiteth for the sons of men. 8 And the remnant
of Jacob shall be among the nations, in the midst of many
peoples, as a lion among the beasts of the forest, as a young lion
among the flocks of sheep: who, if he go through, treadeth down
and teareth in pieces, and there is none to deliver. 9 Let thine
hand be lifted up above thine adversaries, and let all thine enemies
be cut off.

critics, who think that *vv.* 5, 6 together contain an oracle distinct from
that in *vv.* 2—4, change the sing. into the plur.,—*they shall deliver us.*
 7. *And the remnant of Jacob.* Cf. ii. 12 (*the remnant of Israel*). The
title *Jacob* is used of Judah, as in ii. 12, iii. 9.
 as dew...as showers. At first sight the point of the comparison would
seem to be the numbers of the dewdrops and raindrops (cf. Ps. lx. 3),
but the verbs *tarrieth* and *waiteth* are in the singular and must belong
to *the grass*, to which the relative *that* in the next clause refers. Consequently the increase which Israel is to experience must be likened to
the innumerable blades of the herbage, watered by the dew and rain
(cf. Dt. xxxii. 2), and thus owing their multiplication to God and not
to man: cf. Job v. 25, Ps. lxxii. 16. The writer here thinks of the remnant of the Jews not as exercising a gentle and beneficent influence
amongst mankind but as possessing, through augmented numbers,
great powers of offence.
 8. *as a lion...as a young lion.* Israel by reason of its increase through
Divine help will prevail over, and annihilate, its enemies; it will be
comparable to a lion among other wild animals or among still more
defenceless sheep, able to destroy them without resistance.
 the beasts of the forest must here include the weaker beasts of prey
(Dt. xxviii. 26, Is. xviii. 6), though the word rendered *beasts* usually
means "cattle."
 9. *Let thine hand,* etc. In the Heb. this verse appears to be a prayer
to Jehovah (cf. Is. xxvi. 11) to promote the triumph of the remnant
over its foes, the prophet assuming that Israel's enemies are God's
enemies. But the LXX. and Vulg. have future tenses instead of jussives,
and presumably consider Israel to be addressed: cf. 3 Is. lx. 12.
 The three verses 7—9 by certain scholars are assigned to some date
in the Persian period, on the ground that they imply a widespread
dispersion of the Jews throughout the world, such as did not obtain in
the 6th century.

CHAPTER V. 10—15.

These verses consist of an announcement of Jehovah's decision to remove from the nation both the material resources and the superstitious symbols and practices in which trust had been placed instead of in Himself. The passage has been very widely attributed to the 8th century, with Micah as its author; but its contents are equally suitable to a later period. It is true that reliance upon chariots and horses obtained from Egypt was a feature in the state-policy of Judah during the reign of Hezekiah, which was denounced by Isaiah (xxx. 16, xxxi. 1); and the worship of graven images, of Asherim, and of pillars, and the practice of soothsaying prevailed amongst the people (Is. ii. 6, 8, x. 10, xvii. 8, xxx. 22, xxxi. 7). Nevertheless reference to all or almost all the objects and usages here mentioned as sources of confidence occurs in writings of, or relating to, the 7th century—see Dt. xvii. 16 (horses), xviii. 10, Jer. xxvii. 9 (sorcerers and soothsayers), Dt. vii. 5, Jer. viii. 19 (graven images), 2 Kgs. xxiii. 14 (pillars and Asherim); so that there is nothing to prevent the section from dating from the end of that century or from the beginning of the next. A post-exilic origin for the section is discountenanced by the allusions to military forces and (fortified) cities: the Jews were then for several centuries in a position of subjection to one or other foreign power.

From a review of the several groups of verses (iv. 9—v. 15) that have just been considered, it becomes apparent that, as the references to contemporary conditions in each of them point to, or are compatible with, a date just before the close of the 7th century or early in the 6th, save for the mention of *the Assyrian* in v. 5, whilst this name admits of being understood of the Babylonians, there is no insuperable obstacle preventing all these oracles from being regarded as proceeding, if not from a single prophet writing during the reign of Zedekiah, at least from prophets of that period, though in the ideas or the spirit of certain passages (especially iv. 11—13) there is a suggestion of the atmosphere of post-exilic times.

10 And it shall come to pass in that day, saith the LORD, that I will cut off thy horses out of the midst of thee, and will destroy thy chariots: 11 and I will cut off the cities of thy land, and will

10. *thy horses.* These, in war, were employed for drawing chariots. In the reign of Solomon they were procured from Muzri (south of the Taurus mountains) and Cuë (Cilicia, north of the same chain)[1], but at a later date were obtained from Egypt. In the future here contemplated the people will no longer trust for security to military defences but to the protection of Jehovah.

11. *the cities of thy land.* I.e. fortresses, which might foster in the nation feelings of self-sufficiency: the overthrow of such strongholds is predicted in Is. ii. 15, Hos. viii. 14, Jer. iv. 7, ix. 11, Ezek. vi. 6. In lieu of such defences, Israel, though dwelling in the open country, will have her safety ensured by God: cf. Zech. ii. 4, 5.

---

[1] See Burney, *Heb. Text of Kings*, p. 151.

throw down all thy strong holds: 12 and I will cut off witchcrafts out of thine hand; and thou shalt have no *more* soothsayers : 13 and I will cut off thy graven images and thy ¹pillars out of the midst of thee; and thou shalt no more worship the work of thine hands. 14 And I will pluck up thine ²Asherim out of the

¹ Or, *obelisks*   ² See Ex. xxxiv. 13.

12. *witchcrafts.* Perhaps better, *sorceries* (the rendering of the R.V. in 2 Is. xlvii. 9). The verb (*cut off…out of thine hand*) suggests that the sorcerers employed something material, such as drugs or herbs (cf. LXX. φάρμακα, Vulg. *maleficia*), to cause the magical effects which they professed ability to produce.

soothsayers. These were prevalent in Judah during Isaiah's time (see Is. ii. 6). The Heb. term which in the R.V. is sometimes translated *one that practiseth augury*, and was formerly thought to be connected with a Heb. root meaning "a cloud," is now considered to refer to the humming or crooning noise which marked the utterances of such diviners. The LXX. here renders it by ἀποφθεγγόμενοι.

13. *pillars.* These were upright stones or obelisks (cf. mg.) which, being probably at first unhewn boulders (the Celtic *meini hirion*), were regarded as the abodes of deities in consequence of some noteworthy occurrence that had happened in proximity to them. They were wont to be smeared with fat or oil, in order that such offerings might be thereby conveyed to the spirits thought to dwell in them, or to be connected with them (cf. Gen. xxxv. 14, 15). Subsequently artificial columns were erected near altars, or in front of temples, probably as symbols of the divinity to whom worship was offered. Such pillars must at one time have been associated with JEHOVAH (as the story of Jacob at Bethel implies, cf. also Is. xix. 19) as well as with other gods (2 Kgs. iii. 2, x. 26, 27, cf. Dt. vii. 5, xii. 3), and the two columns reared in front of the Temple (1 Kgs. vii. 15) were presumably of similar significance. As the religion of Israel became more spiritual under the influence of the prophets, the erection of pillars was discountenanced by them; and in the legislation of Deuteronomy they were directed to be destroyed.

the work of thine hands. Cf. Is. ii. 8, Jer. xxv. 6, 7, 2 Kgs. xxii. 17.

14. *Asherim.* The singular is *Ashērah*, and in addition to *Ashērim* there is a rarer plur. *Ashēroth* (2 Ch. xix. 3, xxxiii. 3). The objects denoted by the name were tree-trunks or wooden poles (Jud. vi. 26), which could be plucked up, cut down, or burnt (Ex. xxxiv. 13, 2 Kgs. xviii. 4, xxiii. 15, 2 Ch. xiv. 3); and, like the pillars, were raised beside altars, both of Jehovah (as implied by the prohibition in Dt. xvi. 21, cf. Jer. xvii. 2) and of the Baalim (Dt. vii. 5, xii. 3). They were probably survivals of tree worship; for trees in primitive times were thought to be animated by spirits, whose activities were manifested in the movements and rustle of the leaves (cf. Is. i. 29, lvii. 5, Ezek. vi. 13). There is, however, some evidence (derived from inscriptions) that

midst of thee: and I will destroy thy [1]cities. 15 And I will execute vengeance in anger and fury upon the nations [2]which hearkened not.

[1] Or, *enemies*   [2] Or, *such as they have not heard*

Asherah was also the name of an Amorite and Babylonian goddess; and this is confirmed by passages in the O.T. which speak of the prophets of the Baal and of the Asherah (1 Kgs. xviii. 19), of a graven image of the Asherah (2 Kgs. xxi. 7), and of houses (shrines) of the Asherah (2 Kgs. xxiii. 7, mg.). If the name were originally a divine appellation, the deity so designated was perhaps a deity of "good fortune" (*'āshar* is the root whence come the Heb. words for "happiness"), like the masculine *Gad* (see 3 Is. lxv. 11, mg.). Of such a goddess the pole which the word usually denotes must have been a symbol[1].

cities. This word, *'ārim*, as a parallel here to the Asherim, is inappropriate, if rendered as usual by *cities*; and still more so, if translated *adversaries* (cf. 1 Sam. xxviii. 16, Ps. cxxxix. 20), or replaced by *tsārim, enemies*; for the rest of the objects mentioned are sources of Judah's self-confidence. Some other term meaning "images" is wanted, and an emendation with this signification, approved by many, is *'ătsabbim* (coupled with *'Asherim* in 2 Ch. xxiv. 18), whilst Van Hoonacker proposes the substitution of *'ētsim, trees,* comparing Dt. xvi. 21. But it may be suggested that a correction closer to the existing text would be *tsīrim,* a word occurring with the required sense of *idols* in 2 Is. xlv. 16.

15. *And I will execute,* etc. This *v.* seems to be an announcement of vengeance upon the heathen guilty of idolatry. The connection, however, with the preceding *v.* is obscure; and this has possibly been added by someone who could not suppose that idols were to be abolished in Israel, without any reference to their extinction among foreign nations, or to the punishment that would overtake those who should retain them.

which hearkened not. I.e. which shall not have hearkened to the Divine command to abandon idolatry. (For the perf. in the sense of a future perf. cf., in the Heb., Gen. xlviii. 6.) The LXX. has *because* (for this sense of *'āsher* cf. Num. xx. 13) *they hearkened not.* The relative pronoun, however, may be taken, as in the mg., to refer to the Divine vengeance, and the rendering will then be, *such as they have not* previously *heard of,* i.e. unprecedented.

CHAPTERS VI.—VII.

These two chapters are clearly marked off by their contents from those that precede; but there are sufficient differences between various parts of them to render it desirable to examine each of these parts separately, with a view to collecting the evidence throwing light upon the circumstances of its origin, as this will decide whether all are assignable or not to a single period or author.

---

[1] See Burney, *Judges,* p. 195 f.

CHAPTER VI. 1–8.

This section is not a continuation of any in the preceding chapter. It conveys an address from Jehovah to Israel, explaining to His people (who feel that He is estranged from them, but are at a loss to know how to satisfy Him) the nature of the service which He really requires. Presumably some disappointing experience had caused them to infer that God was angry with them; and in order to propitiate Him, they had had recourse to more numerous or more costly sacrifices than the ordinary, but with no satisfactory result. Accordingly, the prophet, commissioned to be God's spokesman, enters into argument with his countrymen and seeks to disabuse them of certain mistaken ideas about what God desires. The general drift of his contention—that God values in man justice and mercy towards fellow-men and a humble bearing towards Himself, and not material oblations—resembles that of several other prophetic writers (see p. 52); but there is a calmness and tenderness in this expostulation which is distinctive; and the concluding definition of the Divine requirements is as profound as it is concise. The tone of the passage is unlike that which marks the parts of the book most confidently assignable to Micah; but there is not much evidence to enable the date of its origin to be determined with anything like precision. The sacrifice of children is mentioned in connection with the reigns both of Ahaz (2 Kgs. xvi. 3) and of Manasseh (2 Kgs. xxi. 6 f., cf. Jer. vii. 31, xix. 5, Ezek. xx. 26). The presence in it, however, of phrases (*v.* 4) characteristic of the book of Deuteronomy points to the conclusion that it is not earlier than the probable date of that work, viz. the reign of Manasseh, 692—638 (see Driver, *Dt.* p. xliv f.). On the other hand, the allusion to *burnt offerings* (*v.* 6) as the sacrifices thought to be needed for expiating offences against God suggests that the passage is earlier than the time of Ezekiel or the Exile, for then *sin-offerings*, specifically so designated, were ordained (Ezek. xliii. 19, xlv. 17). Hence the time of composition may be the age of Jeremiah (second half of the 7th century). With this agrees the individualizing address, *O man* (*v.* 8), for it was in this age that a sense of the importance of the individual, independently of the family or the community, began to make itself felt.

VI. 1 Hear ye now what the LORD saith : Arise, contend thou before the mountains, and let the hills hear thy voice. 2 Hear, O ye mountains, the LORD's controversy, and ye endur-

1. *Hear...saith.* The prophet declares the commission he has received from JEHOVAH (*Arise, contend thou*, etc.) to act as His advocate in the controversy between Him and Israel.

contend thou before the mountains. The physical world, the abiding scene and witness of human history, is to hear the pleadings (as in Is. i. 2, Jer. ii. 12, Ps. l. 1, 4, Dt. xxxii. 1). In connection with the verb here employed the preposition *'eth* commonly signifies *with* (i.e. against), see Num. xx. 13, Jud. viii. 1, 2 Is. l. 8; but it has the meaning *before* (i.e. in the presence of) in Gen. xx. 16 end (mg.), Is. xxx. 8.

2. *ye enduring foundations of the earth.* The order of the Heb. which

ing foundations of the earth: for the LORD hath a controversy
with his people, and he will plead with Israel. 3 O my people,
what have I done unto thee? and wherein have I wearied thee?
testify against me. 4 For I brought thee up out of the land of
Egypt, and redeemed thee out of the house of bondage; and I
sent before thee Moses, Aaron, and Miriam. 5 O my people, remember now what Balak king of Moab consulted, and what
Balaam the son of Beor answered him; *remember* from Shittim

is thus rendered is irregular, and many critics favour the conjectural
emendation, *Give ear, ye foundations of the earth* (the same verb being
used as a parallel to *hear* in Joel i. 2, Dt. xxxii. 1, Is. i. 2).

Israel. Judah must be meant, as in v. 1.

3. *what have I done unto thee?* Jehovah, instead of proceeding with
His charge against Israel, leaves it to the latter to state their complaint
against Him: cf. Jer. ii. 5.

wherein have I wearied thee? I.e. in what respects have My demands
been so onerous as to palliate thy misconduct towards Me? Cf. 2 Is. xliii.
23, Mal. i. 13.

4. *For I brought thee up,* etc. Jehovah forestalls any complaint from
Israel that He was exacting in His requirements by referring to His care
for them, from their sojourn in Egypt to their arrival in Canaan (*v.* 5).

redeemed...bondage. The phrases *to redeem* (in connection with the
deliverance from Egypt) and *the house of bondage* (literally, *of bondmen*)
recur frequently in Dt. (vii. 8, xiii. 5, xxiv. 18), but are rare elsewhere
(see Driver, *Dt.* pp. lxxix, lxxxii).

and Miriam. This association of Miriam with Moses and Aaron in
a prominent capacity on the occasion of the Exodus finds no parallel
elsewhere, though she is represented as leading the women's triumph
song (Ex. xv. 20, 21) and as *claiming* (in conjunction with Aaron) to
be an agent of Divine communications equal to Moses (Num. xii. 2 f.),
her self-assertion being punished with leprosy.

5. *consulted.* Better, *planned,* see Num. xxii. 4—6. Balak, in desiring
Balaam to curse Israel, believed that an imprecation, once uttered, fulfilled itself automatically (cf. Zech. v. 3, 4). The Moabite king's design
was foiled through Balaam's substitution (by Jehovah's direction) of a
blessing, which was similarly thought to be irreversible (cf. Gen. xxvii. 33,
Mt. x. 13 = Lk. x. 6[1]). Maurer compares Hom. *Il.* ix. 453—457, and Hor.
Epod. v. 89—90, *Diris agam vos: dira detestatio nulla expiatur victima.*

Balaam. For his replies to Balak see Num. xxii. 8, 13, 18, xxiii. 11 f.
Though he was used by Jehovah as a channel of revelation, he was not
an Israelite by race, but is variously represented as living either in
Pethor (Mesopotamia) near the Euphrates, or amongst the Ammonites
(see Num. xxii. 5 Vulg., Dt. xxiii. 4).

from Shittim unto Gilgal. Before these words there seems to have been

---

[1] Here *your peace* means "your blessing" (or "salutation").

unto Gilgal, that ye may know the righteous acts of the LORD.
6 Wherewith shall I come before the LORD, and bow myself before
the high God? shall I come before him with burnt offerings, with
calves of a year old? 7 Will the LORD be pleased with thousands
of rams, *or* with ten thousands of rivers of oil? shall I give my

lost some expression like *and the passage*, the allusion being to the
crossing of the Jordan (subsequent to the incident in which Balak and
Balaam figured); for *Shittim* was the site of the camp on the E. bank,
whence the Israelites started for the river, and *Gilgal* was the spot
where they first encamped on the W. bank after the crossing: see Josh.
iii. 1, iv. 19, v. 9.

the righteous acts. Literally, *the righteousnesses*; cf. Jud. v. 11, 1 Sam.
xii. 7, Ps. ciii. 6. The word in these passages has the special connotation
of actions wrought by God in vindication of His people (cf. vii. 9, Ps.
xxxvi. 10, li. 14), such being demonstrations of His faithfulness to His
covenant with Israel.

6. *Wherewith*, etc. The speaker (a representative Israelite) assumes
that Jehovah can be appeased, like other divinities, by material offerings,
if these are sufficiently valuable; but is in doubt as to what will content
Him.

the high God. I.e. the God who dwells on high: cf. Is. xxxiii. 5, 3 Is.
lvii. 15.

with burnt offerings. For the expiation of sin by offerings see 1 Sam.
xxvi. 19. Animal sacrifices, specifically designated *burnt offerings*, were
wholly consumed by fire, the victims being (it was thought) thereby
conveyed (through the smoke and savour) to the Deity in their entirety;
but in *peace offerings* only portions of the victims were burnt, the rest
being consumed partly by the offerer and his household and partly by
the priests, the idea being that they were feasts of *communion* between
the worshipper and the Deity, whose representatives the priests were.

calves of a year old. According to the Law, this age was a requirement in the case of the Passover sacrifice (Ex. xii. 5) and of certain
offerings enjoined in Lev. ix. 3, Num. xv. 27.

7. *thousands of rams...rivers of oil.* Both expressions are highly
rhetorical; similar rhetoric occurs in Job xx. 17, xxix. 6. The word
rendered *rivers* is literally *torrents*, answering to the modern *wâdies*,
channels that are dry in summer, but swollen with rain in the winter.
Oil in small quantities was an accompaniment of several sacrifices
prescribed in the Mosaic Law; but in primitive times it may have been
offered independently of other things (cf. Gen. xxviii. 18). In a pastoral
stage of civilization it was probably the melted fat of animals, since
vegetable oil could only come into use after an agricultural phase of life
was reached. The Vulg. instead of *ten thousands of rivers of oil* has
many thousands of fat goats (*multis millibus hircorum pinguium*), a
rendering which may be either a deliberate substitution for the sake of
improving the parallelism, or an attempt to make sense of a depraved

firstborn for my transgression, the fruit of my body for the sin

reading, χειμάρρων ("winter streams") having been corrupted into χιμάρων ("goats"). LXX. B has χειμάρρων πιόνων[1], but codex A replaces the noun by ἀρνῶν.

my firstborn. Human sacrifices were practised in Israel during the monarchy by kings who imitated the barbarous usages of their neighbours (see 2 Kgs. xxi. 6 f., Jer. vii. 31, xix. 5, xxxii. 35, 3 Is. lvii. 5; and cf. 2 Kgs. iii. 27), but it is clear from the instance of Jephthah that in still earlier times they were not regarded by religious minds as repugnant to Jehovah, if occasion appeared to call for them; and the execution of captives and others "before Jehovah" must have been survivals of such sacrifices (1 Sam. xv. 33, 2 Sam. xxi. 9). The story of Abraham's offering of Isaac, for whom a ram was substituted before the sacrifice was completed (just as in one form of the Greek legend of Iphigenia, the maiden, when about to be sacrificed to Artemis, was replaced by a hind, Eur. *I. A.* 1578—1589), probably reflects the transition from human sacrifices in honour of Jehovah to a less repulsive rite (Jephthah's offering of his daughter at a later period being accounted for by the circumstances of his vow). It is, however, unlikely that, in the age when the present passage was written, such were still thought by any but the most unethical characters to be compatible with the worship of Jehovah; the expression is an hyperbole, the sacrifice of the firstborn son being the costliest conceivable. The idea behind the kind of sacrifice here imagined is plainly that atonement for sin could be made by the sinner through some self-inflicted mortification or loss; but this is not the only principle that can be traced in the piacular sacrifices of the Hebrews. There are two others: (1) the satisfaction imparted by a gift, which (it was thought) would dispose the offended deity to overlook the sinner's offence (cf. 1 Sam. xxvi. 19); (2) the substitution, for the offender's forfeited life, of the life of another, though innocent (see 2 Sam. xxi. 1—14, xxiv. 10, 17, 2 Is. liii. 5, 6, 10, 4 Macc. vi. 29). A contrast to these beliefs was presented by the ethical principle, asserted by most of the Hebrew prophets, that reconciliation with God (at-one-ment) could only be effected by the repentance of the sinner, followed by his reformation. Nevertheless, for bringing about such repentance and reformation the suffering or death of a person or persons other than the sinner has often proved a most potent agency. Such a result may ensue (*a*) from the knowledge of a better ideal of conduct, which the relatively righteous, through involuntary misfortune patiently borne, may become the means of diffusing among the unrighteous (as exemplified by the Jews, who, through their dispersion among the Gentiles, acquainted the latter with a monotheistic faith[2]); (*b*) from the appeal which the *voluntary self-sacrifice* of the righteous on behalf of the unrighteous is calculated to make to the latter (as illus-

---

[1] Aq. has χειμάρρων ἐλαίου.
[2] This seems to have been in the mind of the writer of 2 Is. lii. 13—liii. 12.

of my soul? 8 He hath shewed thee, O man, what is good; and
what doth the LORD require of thee, but to do justly, and to love
mercy, and to walk humbly with thy God?

trated by our Lord's surrender of Himself to death for the redemption
of "many" (Mk. x. 45)).

8. *He hath shewed.* The subject of the verb, if the latter is correctly
vocalized, is JEHOVAH, but the Vulg. has *indicabo* and the LXX. the
passive—ἀνηγγέλη.

what doth the LORD, etc. Contrary to the popular belief that God
could be placated or conciliated in one or other of the ways explained
above, it is here affirmed that the Divine favour could only be gained
or regained by the discharge of moral obligations to fellow-men, and by
a right attitude of heart towards the Almighty. That the requirements
of God from man consist not in ceremonial worship and material offerings
(though these may be *aids* to spiritual religion) but in the practice of
the social duties of justice and mercy and in the religious virtue of
humility is asserted in various terms by other prophets (see Is. i. 11, 19,
Am. v. 21—24, Hos. vi. 6, Jer. vii. 4—7, 21—23, Zech. vii. 9, 10) and
by several of the psalmists and other O.T. writers (Ps. xl. 6, 7, l. 7—15,
li. 16—17, Dt. x. 12 f., Prov. xv. 8, xxi. 3, 27, 1 Sam. xv. 22); and is
re-affirmed in the N.T. (Mk. ii. 23—28, iii. 1—6, xii. 33, 34, Mt. ix. 13,
xii. 7, xviii. 4, xxiii. 23 (= Lk. xi. 42), Lk. xiv. 1—6, James i. 27, ii. 13,
iv. 10, 1 Pet. v. 6).

to walk humbly. The word represented by *humbly* only occurs elsewhere in Prov. xi. 2, where the LXX. for the corresponding adjective
uses ταπεινός. Jehovah's demands for justice and mercy had been
affirmed before (see above); but the third requirement is stressed for
the first time here (though both Amos and Hosea condemned the pride
of Israel (Am. vi. 8 mg., Hos. v. 5, vii. 10)). To bear oneself humbly
with God involves not merely submission to His will, as indicated in the
circumstances and events of life, but also a spirit of teachableness,
responsive to intimations of His wishes conveyed through ideas and
ideals—whether originating from within or imparted from without. This
quality of docility, indeed, is a more essential part of true humility than
resignation, for adverse circumstances may be designed by God for men,
not to induce a spirit of submissiveness, but to stimulate intelligent
efforts to ameliorate them.

CHAPTER VI. 9—16.

This section, by its contents and spirit, is quite unlike that just considered,
and more nearly resembles the passages ii. 1—11, iii. 1 f. Both here and in
vi. 1—8 Jehovah addresses His people, but whereas the preceding section is
marked by a pleading and appealing tone, this breathes a spirit of stern
indignation against the inhabitants of Jerusalem for the practice of dishonesty
in trade, the perpetration of violence, and the general prevalence of falsehood
and insincerity; and pronounces the punishment which is to be inflicted upon

such a guilty people. Fraud, force, and falsehood have, of course, been peculiar
to no age in Hebrew or any other history; but the allusions to *Omri* and
Ahab (*v.* 16) are most natural in a composition written before rather than
after the complete disappearance from among the Jews of a national government; and if, as this suggests, the present passage is pre-exilic, it may originate
with Micah in the reign of Hezekiah, or with a later prophet living under
Manasseh or the corrupt successors of Josiah. In the references to the
retribution impending over the city, there is one (*v.* 13) which, if the Heb.
text be retained (see note), seems to imply that it has in some measure
occurred already; but even this would be quite consistent with a date in the
reign of Hezekiah (when Judah was invaded by Sennacherib) or in the reign
of Jehoiakim (see 2 Kgs. xxiv. 2). The complaint in *v.* 16 that the people
whom the prophet addresses follow the evil precedents of Omri and Ahab,
who were rulers of Northern Israel, need not involve the conclusion (favoured
by Van Hoonacker) that *Samaria* is the object of the prophet's denunciation,
for the kings of Judah from Ahaziah onwards were descendants, on the female
side, of Omri through Athaliah; and it is made a charge against Ahaziah that
he walked in the way of the house of Ahab (see 2 Kgs. viii. 26, 27, and cf.
xvii. 19).

9 The voice of the LORD crieth unto the city, and *the man of*
wisdom will [1]see thy name: hear ye the rod, and who hath

[1] Some ancient versions read, *fear.*

9. *The voice of,* etc. or *Hark! JEHOVAH crieth.* The prophet directs
the attention of the denizens of the city (Jerusalem) to Jehovah's complaints against them.

and the man of *wisdom*, etc. This sentence as it stands in the Heb.
is very difficult. The verb is in the masc., though the term rendered
wisdom is fem.; and to get sense out of the construction, it must be
assumed that *wisdom* is equivalent to "man of wisdom" (cf. Prov. xiii.
6 mg., where *sin* stands for "man of sin," and Prov. xvii. 4, where
falsehood is used for "a liar"). Moreover, though the verb *to see* can
denote other sense-perceptions besides vision (cf. Ex. xx. 18, Jer. ii. 31)[1],
yet the phrase *to see thy name* is unusual; and there is probably some
corruption. In Heb. the verbs "to see" and "to fear" are in some of
their forms very similar; and since the LXX. has σώσει φοβουμένους
τὸ ὄνομα αὐτοῦ, a very slight alteration of one word (*yir'āh*[2] for *yir'eh*)
will yield the unexceptionable sense, *and it is wisdom to fear Thy
name* (cf. Job xxviii. 28, Prov. ix. 10, xv. 33, Ecclus. i. 14)—a parenthetic reflection that Jehovah's complaints cannot be trifled with. The
word rendered *wisdom* is found, for the most part, in the books of
Proverbs and Job, though it also occurs in Is. xxviii. 29; and the
aphorism, coming between two clauses that balance one another, is
suspected, not without reason, to be a moralizing insertion.

hear ye the rod, etc. This, if the text be sound, can only mean, "Be

[1] Cf. Mt. xiv. 30, Rev. i. 12.   [2] For the form cf. Ps. lxxxvi. 11.

appointed it. 10 Are there yet the treasures of wickedness in the house of the wicked, and the scant ¹measure that is abominable? 11 Shall I be pure with wicked balances, and with a bag of deceitful weights? 12 For the rich men thereof are full of

¹ Heb. *ephah.*

warned by the instrument of the present chastisement (see *v.* 13) and by Him who has appointed it (cf. Jer. xlvii. 7) for its task (in order that the punishment may not be prolonged)"; and the reference is probably to a foreign invader, who, if the section proceeds from Micah, will be the Assyrian (styled by God His "club" and "rod" in Is. x. 5). But there are serious difficulties of grammar involved in this translation; for beside the facts that the Heb. has merely *rod* (not *the rod*) and that the pronoun rendered *it* is fem., whereas *rod* is elsewhere masc., the word rendered *who* is not equivalent to *him who*, but is an interrogative. Instead of *rod* the LXX. (φυλή), Syr. and Vulg. imply "tribe" (another signification of the same word, *matteh*), treating it as a vocative; whilst the LXX. includes in this sentence the word '*ōdh* (*yet*), which in the Heb. stands at the beginning of the next (in an unnatural position before the interrogative (though cf. (in the Heb.) Gen. xix. 12)), but reads it as '*īr* (*city*); and Wellhausen, guided by this, has proposed the ingenious emendation, *Hear, O tribe* (i.e. Judah, distinguished from its capital) *and assembly of the city* (i.e. Jerusalem), replacing *ūmī yĕʾādhah 'ōdh* by *ūmōʿēdh hāʾir*. This agrees with the mention of the city in the preceding clause.

10. *Are there...?* The form of the word (*ha-'ish* instead of *hă-yēsh*) thus rendered is irregular (though cf. 2 Sam. xiv. 19); and it has been proposed by Wellhausen to add a letter and so produce a verb (*hăʾeshsheh*), meaning *shall I condone...?* (the Vulg. has *numquid iustificabo?*): cf. the question in the following *v.* The word rendered *yet* is doubtless due to textual corruption (see above) and is wrongly included in this *v.*

the scant measure. Literally, *the lean ephah*, an *ephah* being a "dry" measure containing approximately a bushel.

11. *Shall I be pure with*, etc. The speaker may be God, asking Himself whether He will be free from complicity if He overlooks such dishonesty; or it may be the prophet (representing his countrymen) parleying with his conscience. The LXX. has εἰ δικαιωθήσεται ἐν, etc., *shall* a man *be held pure* (or *innocent*) before God *with*, etc.; but better than either the LXX. or the present Heb. text is the proposal to retain the 1st pers. of the latter, but to change the points—*shall I* (God) *hold* a man *pure in spite of wicked balances?* For this sense of the preposition (*bĕ*) cf. 2 Is. xlvii. 9.

a bag. This, for containing portable weights, was carried by traders or hawkers; see Dt. xxv. 13, Prov. xvi. 11.

weights. Literally, *stones.* Early inscribed stone weights have been found both in Babylonia and in Palestine; see Hastings, *DB.* iv.

violence, and the inhabitants thereof have spoken lies, and their
tongue is deceitful in their mouth. 13 Therefore I also have
smitten thee with a grievous wound; I have made thee desolate
because of thy sins. 14 Thou shalt eat, but not be satisfied; and
thy [1]humiliation shall be in the midst of thee: and thou shalt
remove, but shalt not carry away safe; and that which thou
carriest away will I give up to the sword. 15 Thou shalt sow, but
shalt not reap: thou shalt tread the olives, but shalt not anoint

[1] Or, *emptiness*

pp. 902, 904. The prevalence of the kind of dishonesty here denounced
is attested by Hos. xii. 7, Am. viii. 5 (prophets in Northern Israel),
and by the prohibitions in Dt. xxv. 13—15 (a Judæan document),
Ezek. xlv. 10, Lev. xix. 35, 36 (post-exilic).

12. *For the rich men thereof.* The translation *for* (or *because*) is
justified by Num. xx. 13, Josh. iv. 7; so that there is no need to
render *of which* (the pronoun referring to the city in *v.* 9) *the rich men*,
etc. and to transpose (as some scholars suggest) *vv.* 11 and 12.

13. *I also have smitten...wound.* Literally, *I also have made grievous
the smiting of thee.* This suggests that the chastisement is already severe
(cf. *v.* 9, note): but the LXX. (which has the verb ἄρχεσθαι), and Aq.
(καὶ ἐγὼ ἠρξάμην τοῦ πατάξαι) imply *I also have begun to smite thee.*
The correction (involving merely a change of points) admits of being
construed with the following verb as easily as does the existing text.
The pronoun *thee*, being masc., must refer to the citizens viewed
collectively. In the light of the next *v.* the chastisement must be
supposed to be ravage and siege at the hands of an enemy.

14. *not be satisfied.* I.e. there will be a shortage of food in consequence of a hostile blockade: compare the language of Hos. iv. 10,
Lev. xxvi. 26.

thy humiliation. This rendering follows the Vulg., but a preferable
translation (see mg.) is *thy emptiness* (in a physical sense). The Heb.
word only occurs here.

thou shalt remove...sword. Of these two clauses the first apparently
refers to goods (cf. Is. v. 29), the second (as shewn by mention of the
sword) to persons.

15. *Thou shalt sow,* etc. The offenders will lose not only their dishonest gains, but the fruit of their industry. This *v.*, implying the
ravage of the land by the enemy and resultant scarcity in the city,
would certainly be more appropriately placed immediately after *v.* 14[a],
which it explains; and some critics accordingly transpose it. For the
tenor of the *v.* cf. Lev. xxvi. 16, Dt. xxviii. 30, 33, 38—40, 67, Am. v. 11.

tread the olives. Allusions to the treading of olives in presses occur
in Dt. xxxiii. 24, Jud. ix. 27, Job xxiv. 11, Is. xvi. 10, 3 Is. lxiii. 2, Joel ii.
24; but the berries were also crushed by being beaten (as implied in
Ex. xxvii. 20).

thee with oil; and the vintage, but shalt not drink the wine.
16 For the statutes of Omri are kept, and all the works of the
house of Ahab, and ye walk in their counsels: that I should make
thee ¹a desolation, and the inhabitants thereof an hissing; and
ye shall bear the reproach of my people.

¹ Or, *an astonishment*

the vintage. The Heb. word is the same as that generally translated
new wine (see Joel i. 10, Prov. iii. 10), and denotes for the most part
the unfermented juice of the grape (3 Is. lxv. 8); but here must mean
"the grapes": cf. Is. xxiv. 7.

16. *the statutes of Omri are kept.* The verb is inappropriate in both
form (reflexive) and number (sing.), and the LXX. and some other
Versions have *thou hast kept the statutes of Omri*, which is preferable.
The historian of Kgs., though describing Omri as exceeding his predecessors in wickedness, only explains that, like Jeroboam, he worshipped
Jehovah under the figure of a calf or young bull. But after an enu-
meration of offences like those in *vv.* 10—12, *the statutes of Omri* are
probably to be interpreted by *the works of the house of Ahab*, which
may be illustrated by the judicial murder of Naboth and the confiscation
of his estate (1 Kgs. xxi.); and it may perhaps be inferred that Omri's
government (like his son's) was oppressive to the poorer classes among
his subjects. Politically, he was one of the most powerful sovereigns
of Northern Israel, the territory of which the Assyrians called after his
name.

that I should make thee, etc. According to Heb. idiom, the penalty
consequent upon a crime can be represented as a purpose, as though
the criminal designed his own retribution. The law that sin brings
chastisement is assumed to be known, so that he who plans the one
plans the other. There is considerable confusion among the genders
and numbers of the pronouns in this verse (*ye...thee* (masc. sing.)...
thereof (fem. sing.)), reference being made sometimes to the people
(either distributively in the plural or collectively in the singular) and
sometimes to the city; but probably *thee* should be replaced by *it* (i.e.
the city, *v.* 9, which is fem.).

an hissing. I.e. an object of derision (cf. Jer. xix. 8, xxv. 9, 18,
xxix. 18).

of my people. There is clearly a textual error here: what the sense
requires is *of the peoples* as read by the LXX.: cf. Ezek. xxxvi. 15.

Chapter VII. 1—6.

These six verses depict conditions of disorder, corruption, and strife,
resembling those presented in the previous section (vi. 9—16), though they
lack any specific allusions pointing to a particular period as the date of their
origin. In form they consist of a complaint from the prophet concerning the
prevalence of violence among the people, the failure of justice, and the existence

of feuds dividing friends and families. Most of these evils were features in Hebrew history that often recurred, and are consistent equally with the age of Micah (see i.—iii.), and with the age after the Return in 537 (see 3 Is. lix.). But in the absence of any criteria decisive for one period rather than another, there is no cogent reason for separating these verses from those in vi. 9—16 (see p. 52).

VII. 1 Woe is me! for I am as when they have gathered the summer fruits, as the grape gleanings of the vintage: there is no cluster to eat; [1]my soul desireth the firstripe fig. 2 The godly man is perished out of the earth, and there is none upright among men: they all lie in wait for blood; they hunt every man his brother with a net. 3 [2]Their hands are upon that

[1] Or, *nor firstripe fig which my soul desired*
[2] Or, *Both hands are put forth for evil to do it &c.*

1. *I am as when they have gathered*, etc. Literally, *I am as the gatherings of* (Heb. *'ospē*). The LXX., however, has ἐγενήθην ὡς συνάγων (*'ōsēph*), and the original text was probably *I am as the gathering of* (*'ōseph*, etc.). The abstract noun is coupled with the following concrete term *gleanings* just as a similar abstract is combined with the latter term in Is. xvii. 6, xxiv. 13. The concise comparison requires in English to be expanded (see below).

my soul desireth, etc. Better (cf. mg.), *there is no firstripe fig which my soul desireth* (the negative expressed in the preceding clause being supplied in this). The first figs of the season, for which Heb. has a special term, ripen at the end of May or the beginning of June, and in early times were highly appreciated (Is. xxviii. 4, Jer. xxiv. 2, Hos. ix. 10; cf. Mk. xi. 13). The speaker means "I am as one who, at the end of the vintage or the fig harvest, looks for fruit in vain," the "fruit" being a figure for the godly and the upright.

2. *The godly man.* The writer proceeds to explain the significance of the preceding metaphors. The adjective here employed describes one who displays both kindness to his fellow-men and love to God. Its primary meaning appears to be *kind*; but since kindness, especially at times when the higher ranks of society ill-treated their inferiors, was a mark of the God-fearing, it acquired the secondary sense of *pious*, or *godly*[1].

out of the earth. Better, *out of the land.* The like complaint finds expression in 3 Is. lvii. 1, Ps. xii. 1.

blood. Properly, *deeds of blood*, the Heb. plural being similarly used in 2 Sam. xvi. 8, Is. i. 15, iv. 4, etc.

they hunt...net. An expressive figure for the efforts made by the designing and malicious to entrap their neighbours. For the use of nets in hunting see 2 Is. li. 20, and for the figure of speech cf. Ps. xxxv. 7, lvii. 6.

3. *Their hands*, etc. The literal sense of the Hebrew seems to be

[1] See Driver, *Parallel Psalter*, pp. 443—4.

which is evil to do it diligently; the prince asketh, and the judge *is ready* for a reward; and the great man, he uttereth the mischief of his soul: thus they weave it together. 4 The best of them is as a brier: ¹the most upright is *worse* than a thorn hedge: the day of thy watchmen, even thy visitation, is come;

¹ Or, *the straightest is* as it were taken *from &c.*

Upon the evil (are) *both hands* (or *palms*) *skilfully* (or *thoroughly*) *to do it*; but the real meaning is perhaps *As regards that which is evil, their two hands are ready to do it skilfully* (or *thoroughly*). For the rendering of the preposition by *as regards* or *concerning* cf. Lev. vi. 7 (Heb. v. 26). Nevertheless the sentence is awkward, and since the LXX. has ἐπὶ τὸ κακὸν τὰς χεῖρας αὐτῶν ἑτοιμάζουσιν, many critics emend the text so as to yield the sense *To do evil they make skilful* (or *ready*) *their hands.*

the prince. The title here seems to signify no more than *the magistrate*; cf. Ex. ii. 14, xviii. 21 (where the word *rulers* translates the same Heb. term), Is. i. 23, etc.

asketh. The object, supplied in thought, is "a reward" (i.e. a bribe), as in the next clause.

the judge is ready *for a reward.* The Heb., if sound, should perhaps be rendered *the judge* doeth it (the request of a suitor) *for a reward.* But possibly (as Nowack has suggested) a verb, *judgeth*, has been lost through haplography. The acceptance of bribes is expressly prohibited in the Law (see Dt. xvi. 19).

the great man. The person here described is the influential suitor who seeks to obtain a decision in his favour by corrupt means from a venal magistrate.

the mischief. Better, *the* evil *desire* (for so the same word is rendered in Prov. x. 3). Sym. has τὴν ἐπιθυμίαν, the Vulg. *desiderium.*

thus they weave it together. The Heb. verb does not occur elsewhere (it seems to mean "to twist" or "intertwine"), and possibly there has occurred the loss of a word or words. The sentence presumably describes some arrangement between a litigant and an official for the deliverance of an unjust decision.

4. *as a brier.* I.e. they are dangerous to have to do with.

is worse *than a thorn hedge.* I.e. is more crooked and harmful than such a hedge. For this explanation of the Heb. text (in which there is absent an adjective or a verb equivalent to "(is) worse") cf. the construction in Is. x. 10. But Sym. has ὡς ἐξ ἐμφραγμοῦ, and the true reading may be *cimsūchah* instead of *mimmĕsūchah—is like a thorn hedge.*

the day of...is come. The prophet here addresses the people. The verb is fem., agreeing with *thy visitation*, and possibly *the day of thy watchmen* is a note inserted by a copyist, identifying the "visitation" with the "day" of nemesis which the prophets, the city's "watchmen" (cf. Is. xxi. 6, Jer. vi. 17, Ezek. iii. 17, xxxiii. 7, Hab. ii. 1), anticipated. As the poss. pron. attached to *perplexity* at the end of the v. is in the 3rd pers. plur., *thy visitation* should probably be replaced by *their visitation.*

now shall be their perplexity. 5 Trust ye not in a friend, put ye not confidence in a ¹guide: keep the doors of thy mouth from her that lieth in thy bosom. 6 For the son dishonoureth the father, the daughter riseth up against her mother, the daughter in law against her mother in law; a man's enemies are the men of his own house.

       ¹ Or, *familiar friend*

now. Better, *then*; cf. v. 4.

perplexity. I.e. the bewilderment created by the coming of unexpected retribution (cf. Is. xxii. 5).

5. *a guide.* Better, *an intimate,* or (as in the mg.) *a familiar friend.*

6. *dishonoureth.* Cf. LXX. ἀτιμάζει. The Heb. literally is *treats as a fool:* the same word occurs in Nah. iii. 6, Dt. xxxii. 15, Jer. xiv. 21; and in the R.V. is rendered by various equivalents.

the men of his own house. I.e. his domestic servants (Gen. xvii. 23, etc.). Amongst the Hebrews parental authority was supreme over the children, who could be sold as slaves (Ex. xxi. 7, 2 Kgs. iv. 1, Neh. v. 5), or even offered in sacrifice (Jud. xi. 29—40, 2 Kgs. xxi. 6). In the case of daughters marriage only transferred them from the despotic authority of the father to that of the husband; and amongst the Romans the position of women was similar (cf. Livy xxxiv. 2, *Maiores nostri feminas voluerunt in manu esse parentium, fratrum, virorum*). So far as parents are concerned, it is the power of the father rather than of the mother that generally comes under notice in the O.T. writings, yet the utmost respect towards both parents was enjoined in the Law and elsewhere (Ex. xx. 12, Lev. xix. 3, Dt. xxvii. 16, Prov. xxiii. 22, etc.); and it was directed that anyone guilty of striking or cursing either father or mother should be put to death (Ex. xxi. 15, Lev. xx. 9). Hence the conditions here depicted would be more shocking to Eastern even than to Western sentiment. Over servants and slaves the rights of a Hebrew were likewise extensive, and included the infliction of physical chastisement; so that it was deemed necessary to limit them by imposing punishment on the owner of a slave, if the latter died under his master's blows, and to require that a slave should gain his liberty as compensation, if he sustained severe bodily injury from his master (Ex. xxi. 20 f.). But the relations between master and servant were sometimes very intimate (Gen. xxiv. 2); and the latter, if the former had no son, might, as a member of the household, become his heir (Gen. xv. 2).

This *v.* suggested the words used by our Lord to describe the divisions that would be occasioned even within family circles by the welcome given to His teaching by some members, and the antagonism roused by it in others (Mt. x. 35, 36 = Lk. xii. 51—53). Maurer compares Ov. *Met.* I. 444 f., *Non hospes ab hospite tutus, Non socer a genero; fratrum quoque gratia rara est. Imminet exitio vir coniugis, illa mariti. Lurida terribiles miscent aconita novercæ;* and there may be added Seneca, *Thyestes,* 40—43, *Fratrem expavescat frater et natum parens, Natusque patrem...immineat viro Infesta coniux.*

CHAPTER VII. 7—20.

This group of verses, as a whole, offers a marked contrast to what has gone before. In the preceding group there is an indignant lament over the prevalence of dishonesty and crime amongst the people, and there is placed before them the prospect of impending retribution. But here the retribution for the national offences has come to pass, and the people are in a situation of adversity and abasement, though not bereft of hope. Obviously a considerable interval must separate *v.* 7 from the foregoing *v.* 6. It is not, however, clear at the first glance that all these 14 verses date from one period. The extremely plaintive tone of *vv.* 7—10 implies that the humiliation of the people is extreme, and suggests that they are still in exile, and that the passage dates from the period 587—537. But the next three *vv.*, announcing that the walls of Jerusalem are to be rebuilt, appear to proceed from a time when the Jews were once again in their own land, i.e. after the Return in 537 but before the refortification of Jerusalem by Nehemiah in 444 (p. 61). Even then, however, there was present in the Jewish community an acute sense of depression and disappointment: neighbours were insolent and malicious; the territory reoccupied was very restricted, and numbers of their fellow-countrymen were still in foreign countries, so that the chastisement due for past sins appeared unexhausted by the 50 years' exile, and the people were despondent on account of their straitened and defenceless position. In the light of this, the first impression produced by *vv.* 8—10 calls for re-consideration, since in the middle of the 5th century (as well as in the 6th) there was not lacking occasion for a confession like that contained in these *vv.*, for an announcement like that in *v.* 12, and for an attitude of prayerfulness and expectancy such as is manifested in the concluding *vv.* 14—20 (p. 63). On the whole, therefore, the simplest conclusion is that this whole section is a unity, and was composed in the 5th century after the Return, about 450. Sellin suggests as a reason for its inclusion in the expanded book of Micah that it was added in order that the book should once more close on a note of promise.

7 But as for me, [1]I will look unto the LORD; I will wait for the God of my salvation: my God will hear me. 8 Rejoice not against me, O [2]mine enemy: when I fall, I shall arise; when I

[1] Or, *in the* LORD *will I keep watch*   [2] See ver. 10.

7—10. An acknowledgment, on the part of the personified community, deeply penitent, of sin against Jehovah; a resolve to bear patiently the retribution that has been merited; and an assertion of confidence in the Divine mercy.

7. *I will look unto.* Better, *I will look out for* (or *watch for*): for the sense cf. Ps. v. 3 (4).

wait for. The same verb is translated *hope in* (God) by the R.V. in Ps. xxxviii. 16 (15), xlii. 5 (6), xliii. 5.

the God of my salvation. Better (in this connection), *the God of my deliverance*; cf. Is. xvii. 10, Ps. xviii. 46, xxvii. 9, Hab. iii. 18.

8. *O mine enemy.* The original is a fem. sing., and represents a per-

sit in darkness, the LORD shall be a light unto me. 9 I will bear
the indignation of the LORD, because I have sinned against him;
until he plead my cause, and execute judgement for me: he will
bring me forth to the light, *and* I shall behold his righteousness.
10 Then mine enemy shall see it, and shame shall cover her; which
said unto me, Where is the LORD thy God? Mine eyes shall behold
her; now shall she be trodden down as the mire of the streets.

sonified collective, either Babylon (cf. 2 Is. xlvii. 1 f., Jer. l. 9, 10), or
Edom (Ob. 12), or the ill-disposed neighbours of the Jews about the
time of Nehemiah, such as the Samaritans and the Ammonites with
their allies (Neh. ii. 19, iv. 1—3), according to the conclusion reached
concerning the date of these four *vv.* (p. 60).

when I fall...when I sit.   Better, *though I have fallen...though I sit.*
For these verbs used in connection with a city or people cf. Am. v. 2,
Lam. i. 1.

darkness.   I.e. the gloom of adversity in contrast to the light of
prosperity (cf. Is. ix. 2, 3 Is. lviii. 10).

9. *the indignation of the LORD.*   Jehovah had employed, as the in-
struments of His wrath, the heathen (cf. Is. x. 5), who had destroyed
Judah's independence.

plead my cause.   The sense would be better expressed by *strive in my
quarrel* or (more literally) *contend in my contention*: cf. Ps. xliii. 1,
cxix. 154, etc.

his righteousness.   I.e. His faithfulness, as manifested by Judah's
ultimate vindication (cf. 3 Is. lvi. 1[b] and lix. 9).

10. *shame.*   I.e. confusion and disappointment (cf. Ob. 10).

Where...thy God?   The same derisive question occurs in Joel ii. 17,
Ps. lxxix. 10, cxv. 2, cf. Num. xiv. 15, 16, Dt. ix. 28: the humiliation of
a people was thought to prove the inferiority of its national divinity to
that of the triumphant enemy.

shall behold her.   I.e. shall view with satisfaction the degradation of
her who had fancied that Jehovah, the God of the Jews, was impotent.

now.   Better, *then*, as in v. 4, vii. 4.

CHAPTER VII. 11—13.

This short passage conveys an assurance from Jehovah, through the prophet,
that the walls of Jerusalem are to be built and those of her people who are
still in exile are to return to her.

The date of these verses can scarcely be any but shortly before the period
of Nehemiah, who arrived at Jerusalem from Persia in 445, and, with the
sanction of the Persian king, proceeded to restore the city's walls, the re-
building of which was completed in 444. The decision reached about the
occasion when these *vv.* originated should probably be allowed to dominate
the discussion concerning the origin of the whole section *vv.* 7—20 (p. 60);
and if there is no interruption between the four *vv.* 7—10 and the present
three, these contain Jehovah's response to the prayer in the former.

11 [1]A day for building thy walls! in that day shall [2]the [3]decree be far removed. 12 In that day shall they come unto thee, from Assyria and the cities of [4]Egypt, and from [4]Egypt even to the River, and from sea to sea, and *from* mountain to mountain.

[1] Or, *In the day that thy walls are to be built*   [2] See Zeph. ii. 2.
[3] Or, *boundary*   [4] Heb. *Mazor*.

11. *A day...thy walls!* The prophet addresses Jerusalem (personified as a woman). The word here used for *walls* strictly signifies *fences* (cf. Sym. τοὺς φραγμούς σου) separating a vineyard from the road or from waste ground (Is. v. 5, Ps. lxxx. 12, Num. xxii. 24, Prov. xxiv. 31), but it is applied to the wall of Jerusalem in Ezra ix. 9.

the decree. If this rendering be retained (cf. LXX. νόμιμα, Sym. ἐπιταγή, Th. πρόσταγμα), the meaning is that the Persian decree restricting the liberties of the Jews will be cancelled (cf. Ezra iv. 21). But the verb employed favours the translation *the limit* or *the boundary* (see mg. and cf. Prov. viii. 29, Jer. v. 22, and for the same verb in a similar connection see Is. xxvi. 15), the writer having in his thoughts the confined area prescribed for the Jews by the Persian authorities when the exiles were allowed to settle once more on their native soil.

be far removed. Better (to suit the translation advocated above), *be extended*, i.e. for the accommodation of the additional numbers whose return is predicted in the next *v.* The circumscribed boundaries of the district occupied by the Jews in the time of Nehemiah may be inferred from the names of the towns whose inhabitants alone took part in the re-building of the walls (see Neh. iii.). It has been calculated that the localities enumerated were included within an area of 20 miles square[1].

12. *shall they come unto thee.* The reference is probably not to heathen peoples hasting to join themselves to Israel (iv. 2, 2 Is. xlv. 14, lv. 5, Zech. viii. 20—23) but to Jewish exiles returning to their native land (Is. xi. 11, xxvii. 13, Hos. xi. 11, 2 Is. xliii. 5, 6, xlix. 12).

Assyria. In the time of Nehemiah Assyria as an empire had perished, but its name was retained to designate one or other of the empires that had displaced it (p. 39). Here it seems to stand for *Persia*.

and the cities of Egypt. A parallel to the clauses in the rest of the *v.* is wanted, and a very slight emendation of the text gives *even unto Egypt* (va'ădhē for vĕ'ārē), which meets the requirements. The term here used for *Egypt* is not that commonly employed (*Mizraim*) but that occurring in 2 Kgs. xix. 24, Is. xix. 6, xxxvii. 25 (*Mazor*). Assyria and Egypt are similarly used to mark the north-eastern and south-western confines of the Jewish Dispersion in Is. xi. 15, xxvii. 13, Hos. xi. 11, 2 Zech. x. 10.

the River. I.e. the Euphrates (Gen. xxxi. 21, Ex. xxiii. 31, etc.).

from sea to sea, and from *mountain to mountain.* This is a rendering of the LXX. rather than of the Heb., which, through some accident,

[1] See Kent, *Hist. of the Jewish People*, p. 159.

13 Yet shall the land be desolate because of them that dwell therein, for the fruit of their doings.

has become disarranged and defective. The expression is probably merely rhetorical (cf. Ps. lxxii. 8); but if the limits are to be defined, the seas may be the Mediterranean and the Persian Gulf, and the mountains those of Abyssinia and Armenia.

13. *Yet shall the land*, etc. This rendering implies a reminder that the predicted redemption must be preceded by a judgment. For the adversative sense given to the conjunction see iv. 4, Is. x. 20, 1 Kgs. x. 7. The translation, however, should perhaps be, *And the earth shall*, etc. (the *earth* being contrasted with Jewish territory as *man* is contrasted with *Israel* in Jer. xxxii. 20). The mercy granted to the Jews is to be accompanied by vengeance wreaked on the heathen world that has oppressed them beyond what God desired (cf. 2 Is. xlvii. 6, Zech. i. 15).

for the fruit. I.e. because of the issue (or outcome); cf. Hos. x. 13, Is. iii. 10, Prov. i. 31.

CHAPTER VII. 14—20.

A prayer to God from the prophet on behalf of the people, entreating Him to do for them wonders as of old, and voicing a conviction that He will shew them compassion and forgiveness.

To the date of this passage (in which, as contrasted with *vv.* 7—13, God is addressed directly in the 2nd person) the only clue is contained in *v.* 14, which reflects the conditions of a period when the Jewish people were a small and depressed body, conscious of a guilty past, surrounded by aliens, and longing for a renewal of the happier times long ago when they enjoyed a more ample territory. This situation is most intelligible on the hypothesis that the passage was composed in the post-exilic age, perhaps within the 5th century B.C.; and probably the section is continuous with the preceding *vv.* 11 (or 7)—13, but, unlike those verses, is written in the *Kinah* rhythm, though this, in places, has been disturbed.

14 ¹Feed thy people with thy rod, the flock of thine heritage,

¹ Or, *Rule*

14. *Feed thy people*, etc. Jehovah is likened to a shepherd (cf. Gen. xlix. 24, Ps. xxiii. 1, lxxx. 1), carrying a club with which to protect his sheep from fierce animals (Ps. xxiii. 4).

the flock of thine heritage. This particular combination of terms does not appear elsewhere (though cf. Ps. xxviii. 9). Israel, however, is frequently styled Jehovah's *heritage* (Dt. iv. 20, ix. 26, Joel ii. 17, etc.), the expression being apparently transferred from the land of Canaan (*the mountain of Jehovah's inheritance*, Ex. xv. 17, cf. 1 Sam. xxvi. 19) to the people whom Jehovah planted in it. Land could not be alienated in perpetuity (Lev. xxv.), and so the description of Israel as Jehovah's heritage emphasizes the permanence of the relation believed to subsist between them and God.

which dwell solitarily, in the forest in the midst of Carmel: let
them feed in Bashan and Gilead, as in the days of old. 15 As in
the days of thy coming forth out of the land of Egypt will I shew

solitarily. In some passages the expression describes the seclusion
of Israel under God's peculiar care (Num. xxiii. 9, Dt. xxxiii. 28), but
here it seems to have reference to the isolation (cf. Lam. i. 1) of the
small Jewish post-exilic community closely encompassed by unfriendly
and jealous neighbours.

in the forest...Carmel. Carmel is the sole headland that breaks the
straight coast of Palestine between Sidon and Egypt, and constitutes
the seaward extremity of a limestone ridge 12 or 13 miles long, and
(at the promontory) 500 ft. high. If the name is here understood of
this ridge, the phrase *in the forest...Carmel* must be construed with
the verb *feed*, with reference to the woods clothing it (Is. xxxiii. 9,
Am. i. 2), regarded as affording shelter (cf. Ezek. xxxiv. 25), and to
the fertile glades intersecting them. But the Hebrew word is also
a common noun, meaning a garden-like district (cf. Is. xvi. 10, Jer.
ii. 7), and a preferable rendering is, *in a forest in the midst of a garden-
land.* The area of unproductive soil to which (either through restrictions
imposed on the Jews by their over-lords, or in consequence of the few-
ness of their numbers) they were at first confined, and which was
surrounded by more fruitful regions in the possession of others, is
likened to a sterile forest in the middle of a fertile and beautiful
country.

let them...Gilead. Compare 2 Zech. x. 10. The districts named,
which were once in the occupation of united Israel, were pasture lands
(cf. Jer. l. 19). Bashan, stretching (for some 30 miles) eastwards of the
Sea of Galilee and the Waters of Merom, and reaching from the Yarmuk
northwards in the direction of Hermon, was famous for its horned
cattle (Dt. xxxii. 14, Am. iv. 1, Ps. xxii. 12); whilst Gilead, on the
E. of the Jordan, extending from the north end of the Dead Sea to
the south extremity of the Sea of Galilee, was also adapted for pasturage,
and was in consequence desired, at the time of the Conquest, by the
tribes of Reuben and Gad that were rich in flocks and herds (Num.
xxxii.).

as in the days of old. The reference to the re-occupation of Gilead
by the prophet's countrymen is not easily reconcilable with Micah's
authorship of this section, for in his time it was either actually in the
possession, if not, indeed, of Judah, at any rate of the sister-kingdom
of Northern Israel, or had only recently been lost (2 Kgs. xv. 29).

15. *thy coming forth...will I shew.* Probably Jehovah speaks here
(to the end of *v.* 17), declaring, in answer to the petition in *v.* 14, that
He will do as much for Israel in the immediate future as He did for
them on the occasion of the Exodus. But some critics consider that
the prophet and people are the speakers (as in the preceding *v.* and
apparently in *v.* 17), and propose to replace the future *will I shew*

unto him marvellous things. 16 The nations shall see and be ashamed of all their might : they shall lay their hand upon their mouth, their ears shall be deaf. 17 They shall lick the dust like a serpent; like crawling things of the earth they shall come trembling out of their close places : they shall come with fear unto the LORD our God, and shall be afraid because of thee. 18 Who is a God like unto thee, that pardoneth iniquity, and passeth by the transgression of the remnant of his heritage? he

unto him by the imperative *shew unto us*; in which case *thy coming forth* must refer to Jehovah as having accompanied Israel in their departure from Egypt. But this alteration is superfluous, if *v.* 17 be emended. The only correction required here is the omission of *land* (*of*), which impairs the rhythm and is absent from the LXX.

marvellous things. The expression is similarly used in relation to the Exodus in Ex. xv. 11, Ps. lxxviii. 11.

16. *ashamed of all their might.* I.e. abashed because of their proved inferiority to Israel supported by Jehovah: cf. 2 Is. xlv. 14.

lay their hand upon their mouth, etc. Their confusion will deprive them temporarily of speech (Jud. xviii. 19, Job xxi. 5, Prov. xxx. 32) and hearing. Cf. Ps. xxxviii. 13—14.

17. *lick the dust.* A figure for utter abasement; cf. Ps. lxxii. 9, 2 Is. xlix. 23.

like crawling things of the earth. These words should be connected with the preceding clause, and a full stop should be placed at *earth.*

they shall come trembling, etc. This clause should go with the following (see below) and begin with a capital letter.

their close places. I.e. their fortresses, in which they had previously felt secure: cf. Ps. xviii. 45.

they shall come with fear. Literally, *they shall fear.*

unto the LORD our God. These words harmonize badly with the natural impression that in *vv.* 15—17 God is the speaker, and have with some reason been suspected to be interpolated, for they destroy the rhythm. Without them, *v.* 17 consists of two *Kinah* lines, of which the second is, *They shall come trembling out of their close places : they shall fear and be afraid because of thee* (Israel).

18. *Who is a God like unto thee.* This and the following *vv.* are a response to Jehovah's assurances in *vv.* 15—17. The opening question finds summary expression in the name *Micah* (see p. xviii).

that pardoneth iniquity. Compare the description of the Divine character in Ex. xxxiv. 6, 7, Ps. ciii. 8, Jer. iii. 12. The next clause would afford a better balance to this, if it were reduced to *and passeth by transgression*: the additional words may have been suggested to a reader by Jer. l. 20. The Divine forgivingness, here expressed absolutely, is really conditional, though upon the sincerity of human repentance, not upon the sum of human deserts.

retaineth not his anger for ever, because he delighteth in mercy.
19 He will turn again and have compassion upon us; he will
¹tread our iniquities under foot: and thou wilt cast all their sins
into the depths of the sea. 20 ²Thou wilt ³perform the truth to
Jacob, *and* the mercy to Abraham, which thou hast sworn unto
our fathers from the days of old.

¹ Or, *subdue our iniquities*   ² Or, *Thou wilt shew* thy *faithfulness &c.*
³ Heb. *give.*

he retaineth not, etc. This latter part of *v.* 18 and the first half of
v. 19 (down to *foot*), both of which are marked by the 3rd pers. (contrast the 2nd pers. in 18ª, 19ᵇ) are suspected of being insertions:
certainly the rhythm changes.

19. *he will tread...sea.* These are strong metaphors for the complete
removal of Israel's offences from the Divine memory; put out of sight,
they will be out of mind: cf. the similar figures of speech in Is. xxxviii.
17. Instead of *all their sins* the LXX. and Vulg. have preferably *all
our sins.* With the second half of the *v.* (*and thou*, etc.) there is a return to the *Kinah* metre.

20. *wilt perform the truth to.* I.e. wilt deal faithfully with: cf. Neh.
ix. 33. God's changelessness (which is implied in the description of
Him as the God of truth, Ps. xxxi. 5) makes it certain that the
graciousness once shown to Israel's ancestors will not be wanting to
their descendants.

Jacob...Abraham. The names of the patriarchs here stand for their
posterity.

hast sworn. See Gen. xxii. 16, and cf. Lk. i. 73.

OBADIAH

1 THE vision of Obadiah.

Thus saith the Lord GOD [1]concerning Edom: We have heard tidings from the LORD, and an ambassador is sent among the

[1] See Jer. xlix. 7—22.

1. *vision.* The term, which strictly refers to impressions of a visual character actually or ostensibly experienced in prophetic ecstasy (see Dan. viii. 1, 2, 15, ix. 21, cf. Ezek. xiii. 16)[1], is here used to designate the contents of a prophetic book, conveying Divine revelations received through the intellectual and spiritual faculties (not through the senses); cf. Is. i. 1, Nah. i. 1, Hab. ii. 2. The LXX. has ὅρασις, but Aq. ἔκστασις.

Obadiah. For the significance of the name see p. xxxii. Besides occurring frequently in the O.T., it has also been found on a seal bearing, in the early Hebrew script, the words '*Obhadhyāhu ʽebhed hammelech, "Obadiah* servant of the king" (Benzinger, *Heb. Arch.* p. 258). Proper names parallel in formation to *Obadiah* or *Abdiah* are *Ebed-Ashtoreth, Ebed-eshmun, Ebed-baal.*

Thus...Edom. These words are a necessary introduction to what follows in order to render clear what people are meant by the pronouns *her* and *thee,* and accordingly are not likely to be a later addition, as Ewald and others have thought, but must have been attached to the oracle from the first.

We have heard tidings from the LORD. If the Heb. text is correct, the speakers must be people in general, who had heard a report about a confederation being organized against Edom, the words *and an ambassador is sent,* etc. being equivalent to *that an ambassador is sent,* etc.: cf. Gen. xxx. 27 (where "I have divined that the LORD hath blessed me" is literally "I have divined and JEHOVAH hath blessed me"). But the expression coming from Jehovah must imply a Divine oracle, which would be imparted directly not to a multitude of people but to a prophet. And the LXX. here and the Heb. of the parallel passage Jer. xlix. 14 have the 1st pers. sing. instead of the 1st pers. plur.; and if, as is probable, this is the authentic text, the translation should be *I* (i.e. the prophet) *have heard a communication* (the same word as that which is used of an oracle and rendered *message* in Is. xxviii. 9, 19) *from JEHOVAH.* This announcement is prefatory to the actual oracle, which begins with *v.* 2.

and an ambassador is sent. If in the preceding clause the reading of the LXX. be adopted, in this the word rendered *is sent* should be pointed

[1] Cf. Thouless, *Int. to the Psychology of Religion,* p. 73 f.

nations, *saying*, Arise ye, and let us rise up against her in battle.
2 Behold, I have made thee small among the nations: thou art
greatly despised. 3 The pride of thine heart hath deceived thee,

as in Jer. xlix. 14 (which, instead of *shullah*, has *shāluah*) and the
translation should be, *whilst a messenger is being sent*, the clause implying that the revelation from Jehovah to the prophet coincides with
the despatch of an envoy to a group of nations (probably neighbouring
Arabian tribes) to concert against Edom a combined attack which will
prove the agency destined to fulfil the oracle which the prophet proceeds
to disclose. For the Heb. *tsīr* in the sense of *messenger* cf. Prov. xiii.
17, xxv. 13. Ewald takes the messenger to be an angel, charged by
God to rouse the nations to battle against Edom: compare Jud. v. 23.
The rhythm of this introductory line is either 4 : 3 or 3 : 3, according
as the text is retained as it stands or a *makkeph* is inserted between
mē'ēth and *Yĕhōvah*, cf. p. cxxxix.

Arise ye, etc. The words are those of the ambassador addressing (in
the name of the people taking the lead in promoting a confederacy
against Edom) the nations to whom he is sent. The rhythm here is
2 : 2. The introductory "saying" is absent, as in Mic. ii. 11, Is. iii. 6,
Ps. lii. 6. The fem. pronoun *her* refers to the *land* of Edom (cf. Ezek.
xxxvi. 5 Heb.), though the masculine (representing the population) is
employed subsequently. The Vulg. substitutes the masc. here, and
Wellhausen, followed by Nowack, would alter the Heb. text accordingly.
Jer. xlix. 14 has, *Gather yourselves and come against her*, which is
probably nearer the language of the original prophecy, since the sentence
constitutes an unexceptionable pentameter, whereas Ob.'s version is
metrically irregular.

2. *Behold, I have made thee small.* The speaker here is Jehovah. The
perfect tense introduces a prediction (cf. 2 Is. xli. 15 Heb.), the purpose
of God being regarded as already virtually accomplished. The agency
about to be employed for the reduction of Edom to powerlessness is the
confederacy alluded to in *v.* 1. The oracle (*vv.* 2—5) is probably composed in the *Kinah* rhythm. The introductory *Behold* (Jer. *For behold*)
is outside the metre.

thou art greatly despised. The parallel passage, Jer. xlix. 15, has *and
despised among men* (the words depending upon *I have made thee*). In
Ob. the pronoun *thou* (art) conveys an unnecessary emphasis; and since
Jer.'s reading forms an excellent pentameter, of which Ob.'s is easily
explicable as a corruption, the original source probably had the line in
the form in which it appears in Jer.

3. *The pride of thine heart.* The phraseology resembles that of
1 Sam. xvii. 28. The source of Edom's arrogance was the fancied
security ensured by its precipitous cliffs (see p. xlv).

hath deceived thee. The LXX. has ἐπῆρέ σε, mistaking *nāshā'* for *nāsā'*;
and in the same version a similar error occurs in *v.* 7. The parallel
in Jer. xlix. 16 is *Thy terribleness, the pride of thine heart hath deceived*

O thou that dwellest in the clefts of ¹the rock, whose habitation
is high; that saith in his heart, Who shall bring me down to the
ground?　4 Though thou mount on high as the eagle, and though

¹ Or, *Sela* See 2 Kings xiv. 7.

thee, and a slight emendation, yielding the translation *Thy terribleness
hath deceived thee, the pride of thine heart,* probably reproduces the
original, of which Ob. retains only a part.

O thou that dwellest in the clefts of the rock. The word rendered *clefts*
occurs elsewhere only in the parallel Jer. xlix. 16 and in Cant. ii. 14
(where it is used of the abode of the dove). The term *the rock (selaʿ)*
may either refer (as in Is. xvi. 1, 2 Is. xlii. 11) to the rocky surface of
Edom generally (as *the mount of Esau* in *vv.* 8, 19 does to its hilly
character), or convey (see mg.) an allusion to the Edomite capital Sela
(2 Kgs. xiv. 7), the later *Petra.* The city is very difficult of approach,
for it lies in a quadrangular plain bounded by cliffs of great height
(cf. Pliny, *H.N.* vi. 32, *oppidum...circumdatum montibus inaccessis*),
which are penetrated by passes defensible by a mere handful of men.
The almost vertical sides of the crags are covered with columns and
pediments carved out of the solid rock and forming the entrances to
tombs and temples excavated in the cliff walls.

whose habitation is high. The Heb. literally translated is *the height of
his habitation,* and it is possible to connect the words with the foregoing
participle *thou that dwellest* by supplying a preposition from the preceding clause (as is done in Is. xxviii. 6, 2 Is. xlviii. 14). A second
participle, however, is preserved in Jer. xlix. 16, which has *that holdest
the height of the hill,* and probably the participle was included in the
text of the original oracle which, if a poem in the *Kinah* metre, perhaps
here had, *O dweller in the clefts of the rock, holder of the height* (to which
Jer.'s addition *of the hill* is a needless supplement). The LXX. here has
ὑψῶν κατοικίαν αὐτοῦ, which implies (instead of the substantive *height*)
a participle from the same root, *raising on high his habitation*; and this,
which is supported by the Syr., Old Latin, and Vulgate, has been widely
adopted by modern editors. For the insertion of a description in the
3rd person into an address couched in the 2nd pers. cf. Mic. i. 13.

that saith...to the ground. This secret defiance does not occur in
Jer. xlix. 16; and since, in addition, it is not cast in the normal *Kinah*
metre (though the rhythm (2 : 3) here occurring is permissible), it is
probably no part of the original oracle, but has been added to illustrate
how far Edom's self-confidence could carry her. In Heb. *to say in* one's
heart means "to think" (cf. Ps. liii. 1, Is. xiv. 13), for the heart was
regarded by the Hebrews as the seat of intelligence (*men of understanding* in Job xxxiv. 10 is literally *men of heart*; cf. Job xxxvi. 5,
Prov. xv. 32). The Latin *bene cordatus* and *excors* similarly mean
"intelligent" and "unintelligent" respectively.

4.　*Though thou mount on high.* LXX. ἐὰν μετεωρισθῇς. This rendering
suggests lofty *flight* (an admissible interpretation of the Heb. verb, see

thy nest be set among the stars, I will bring thee down from thence,
saith the LORD. 5 If thieves came to thee, if robbers by night,
(how art thou cut off!) would they not steal till they had enough?
if grapegatherers came to thee, would they not leave some

Job xxxix. 27); but the allusion must really be to the situation of the
Edomite *dwellings*, and in the original oracle the verb was connected
with the substantive *nest* (see Jer. xlix. 16), so that a preferable translation is, *If thou makest on high* thy nest (the noun being supplied from
the following clause). For the metaphor cf. Num. xxiv. 21, Hab. ii. 9.
as the eagle. Or *as the vulture*; see on Mic. i. 16.

and though thy nest be set...stars. This translation assumes an exceptional construction in the Heb.—*'im* with the passive participle
(the latter here is unusual in form, though cf. Num. xxiv. 21); but the
LXX. has καὶ ἐὰν ἀνὰ μέσον τῶν ἄστρων θῇς νεοσσιάν σου, which supports
Nowack's emendation *tāsīm* for *sīm*, yielding the rendering *and though
thou settest thy nest among the stars*. For the hyperbole cf. Is. xiv. 13,
Ps. lxxiii. 9, Jer. li. 53, Job xx. 6, Am. ix. 2; Mart. VIII. 36, 11, *Domus
quæ vertice sidera pulsat*; Hor. *Od.* I. 1, 36, *Sublimi feriam sidera
vertice*; Shakespeare, *Hamlet*, III. 3, *Then trip him up that his heels may
kick at heaven.*

I will bring thee down. Compare Mt. xi. 23[a]. For this *v.* Jer. xlix.
16[b] offers a different text, *Though thou makest on high as a vulture thy
nest, from thence I will bring thee down, saith Jehovah.* The concluding
phrase of the *v.* (*saith Jehovah*) is absent from the LXX., and if this is
regarded as outside the metre, the reading of Jer. is a normal *Kinah*
line, and probably represents the wording of the original source;
whereas Ob.'s text is unmetrical and has presumably arisen through
expansion.

5. *If thieves*, etc. Better, *If* merely *thieves*, etc. (the restrictive
merely, or *only*, being supplied mentally, as in Is. v. 10, Am. vi. 9). To
accentuate the completeness of the spoliation threatening Edom, it is
contrasted with the less thorough clearance made when thieves rifle a
house or vintagers strip a vineyard: in both of these cases something
is generally left, but the despoilers of Edom will take all.

if robbers by night. This clause does not occur in the parallel passage
Jer. xlix. 9, though the words *by night* are there included in the preceding sentence, which runs, *If thieves by night*, etc.

(*how art thou cut off !*). Literally, *how art thou made to cease!* (cf.
Is. xv. 1, Jer. xlvii. 5, Zeph. i. 11). This abrupt exclamation is a comment elicited from Obadiah by the fulfilment of the oracle in his own
days: cf. *v.* 6. The LXX. has read the verb *dāmah* as *rāmah*, "to
throw," "cast," and rendered it by ἀπερρίφης; and the Vulg. has confused it with *dāmam*, "to be brought to silence."

grapegatherers. Vines were grown in Edom (cf. Num. xx. 17); and
travellers in the country have observed on the rocky hill-sides vestiges
of terraces designed as sites for vineyards.

gleaning grapes? 6 How are ¹*the things of* Esau searched out!
how are his hidden treasures sought up! 7 All the men of thy
confederacy have ²brought thee on thy way, even to the border:

¹ Or, the men   ² Or, *driven thee out*

some gleaning grapes. The Heb. has a single word, *gleanings*, which
is restricted in usage to the remains of the grape or olive harvest (cf.
Is. xxiv. 13, Mic. vii. 1), except where it is employed metaphorically
(as in Jud. viii. 2). In Jer. xlix. the corresponding *v.* is shorter and
differently arranged, constituting two pentameters (if a *makkeph* be
inserted in one place and removed in another); and probably reproduces
the original oracle, which had, *If grapegatherers come to thee, they
will not leave any gleanings. If thieves by night, they will destroy till
they have enough.* Here the terms *grapegatherers* and *thieves* are used
figuratively for hostile invaders (cf. Jer. vi. 9), who will make a clean
sweep of everything. The original has been modified by Ob., who has
taken the metaphors literally and converted an affirmative sentence
into an interrogation.

6. *How are,* etc. In this verse and the following the writer, who
has hitherto quoted from an earlier prophecy, views its prediction in
the light of what has since happened to Edom, where the unsparing
spoliation foretold has now been realized. The two verses 6 and 7
were probably written (like the preceding) in the *Kinah* metre (the
opening exclamation *How...!* is common in dirges, Mic. ii. 4, Jer. ix.
19) but have undergone some corruption.

the things of Esau. The literal rendering of the Hebrew is, *How are
they searched out,* even *Esau,* the subject being differently explained
in the text and mg. of the R.V. The personal name *Esau* is a synonym
for Edom, as in Gen. xxxvi. 1, 8, 19.

his hidden treasures. The Heb. word only occurs here. The insecure
conditions of Oriental life, and the absence, in early times, of anything
like the modern banking system, led to the secreting of accumulated
wealth.

sought up. This rather curious phrase was presumably suggested to
the translators by the root-meaning of the Heb. verb (*bāʻāh*) here used,
which primarily signifies "to swell up" (Is. xxx. 13), and secondarily
"to seek" with "swelling" eagerness (Is. xxi. 12).
Of similar tenor to this *v.* is Jer. xlix. 10, *But I have made Esau
bare, I have uncovered his secret places.*

7. *All the men of thy confederacy.* Literally, *All the men of thy
covenant* (for the phrase cf. the similar expression in Jer. xxxvii.
22 mg.). The people meant are perhaps some neighbouring tribes,
who, without actually participating in the open attack upon Edom
made by others (as described in the next clause), did not respond to
the obligations which a compact with Edom imposed upon them.

have brought thee...even to the border. A more literal translation is
have sent thee as far as the border; but the meaning is obscure. The

the men that were at peace with thee have deceived thee, and
prevailed against thee; [1]*they that eat* thy bread lay a [2]snare under

¹ Or, *thy bread they make &c.*   ² Or, *wound*

most plausible way of interpreting the verb is to give it the sense of
"dismiss" or "escort back," as in 2 Sam. iii. 21, Gen. xii. 20; and
then two explanations are possible : (1) *have escorted as far as the
border* thy envoys, with their appeal for help refused; (2) *have escorted
as far as the border* thy fugitives, who had crossed it in flight and who
have now been turned back and thereby exposed to the savagery of the
pursuing foe. The R.V. mg. *have driven thee out even to the border* (i.e.
have expelled thy people from their native soil) is improbable; for
though the verb (*shālah*) can signify "to drive out" (cf. Gen. iii. 23,
Ex. vi. 1, 2 Sam. xiii. 16, 1 Kgs. ix. 7), the preposition *as far as* (*'adh*)
is not very suitable in this connection; *from* (*min*) or *across* (*'el 'ēbher*)
would be more appropriate.

the men that were at peace, etc. Literally, *the men of thy peace;* cf.
Ps. xli. 9, Jer. xx. 10, xxxviii. 22 (where the R.V. has *thy familiar
friends*). The people referred to are clearly those who, in time of peace,
had made an unexpected attack upon Edom; and they have been
plausibly identified with the Nabatæans (see p. xli).

they that eat thy bread lay a snare under thee. If the Heb. text is
to be retained as it stands, the only admissible translation is that of
the R.V. mg., *thy bread they make a snare under thee.* This, which
seems to be the explanation adopted by Aq., who has ἄρτον σου θήσουσιν
ἐπίδεσιν, means "they ("the men of thy peace") recompense by
treachery the hospitality which thou hast shown to them." Some
scholars think that the word *men* can be extended from the preceding
clause to this (*the men of thy bread* meaning "thy dependants"); but
such extension is difficult to parallel. As these interpretations of the
existing text are unsatisfactory, there is probably some defect or
corruption in it. The simplest correction is to change the pointing of
the word rendered "bread" (*lehem*), and by converting it into the
participle of *lāham*, "to war," get the translation *they that war against
thee lay a snare under thee.* But the verb *lāham*, "to war," is rare in the
form here proposed (though see Ps. xxxv. 1 (Heb.), lvi. 2 (3)), and the
clause would have four beats instead of the three required by a normal
Kinah line. Hitzig and Grätz assume the loss, before the word *bread,*
of a participle (*'ōchĕlē*, "eaters," cf. Sym. οἱ συνεσθίοντές σοι, Vulg. *qui
comedunt tecum*), and render (like the R.V. text) *they that eat thy
bread lay a snare under thee.* This, however, also destroys the rhythm,
though emendation of the text is to be sought in this direction. The
letters LHMCh may be an accidental dittograph of part of the
preceding ShLMCh (for the LXX. ignores the word), and the phrase
the eaters of thy bread (*'ōchĕlē lahmĕchā*) may be disguised in part of
the previous clause translated (*have*) *prevailed against thee* (*yāchĕlu
lĕchā*): if so, the whole v., rendered literally and with the order of the
Heb. retained, will run: *As far as the border did send thee* | *all the*

thee: there is none understanding ¹in him. 8 Shall I not in that
day, saith the LORD, destroy the wise men out of Edom, and understanding out of the mount of Esau? 9 And thy mighty men,
O Teman, shall be dismayed, to the end that every one may be cut

¹ Or, of it

*men of thy covenant: Deceived thee the eaters of thy bread, | the men of
thy peace: Place they a snare underneath thee; | no sense is there in him.*
This reconstruction preserves the *Kinah* metre satisfactorily¹. The
eating of bread together involved obligations of friendship and mutual
protection (cf. Ps. xli. 9), which Edom's neighbours had violated. The
meaning of the word (*māzōr*) rendered *snare* is doubtful. Elsewhere
(Hos. v. 13 and perhaps Jer. xxx. 13) it has the signification of *wound*,
as given in the mg. here; but this is unsuitable to the present context.
The meaning *cord* or *snare* has been deduced from a root signifying
to "twist" or "weave," and Th. has δεσμόν; but a very slight emendation (*mātsōdh*) proposed by Van Hoonacker furnishes a term, signifying
net, which occurs in Job xix. 6, Prov. xii. 12. The LXX. has ἔνεδρα,
Sym. ἀλλοτρίωσιν, and the Vulgate *insidias*. Another emendation,
which disregards the evidence of the Greek and Latin renderings, is
Marti's *mādhōr*, "dwelling" (Dan. iv. 25 (22), 32 (29)); this produces
the translation *they that eat thy bread make their dwelling in thy place*
(for in Heb. "under" a person is often equivalent to "instead of" that
person).

there is none understanding in him. LXX. οὐκ ἔστιν σύνεσις αὐτοῖς. The
words probably describe not so much the lack of foresight which caused
the Edomites to fall victims to treachery as the bewilderment consequent upon such an experience: they do not know what to do. For
the phraseology cf. Dt. xxxii. 28.

8—9. The transition in these *vv.* (cf. Jer. xlix. 7) to the future tense
suggests that here the earlier oracle may be drawn upon, though the
Kinah rhythm is not maintained. The vengeance which, in *v.* 7, is
represented as having already befallen is once more regarded as still to
come (as in *v.* 4).

8. *Shall I not,* etc. The counsellors of Edom will fail to avert from
their nation an imminent disaster, or to extricate it from one already
present; and this failure will be occasioned by Jehovah, whose *day* is
coming (see *v.* 15).

understanding. I.e. men of understanding: cf. p. 53.

the mount of Esau. I.e. the mountain land of Edom: see Ezek.
xxxv. 2 and cf. Josh. xx. 7 (where *the hill country of Naphtali* is
literally *the mount of Naphtali*).

9. *Teman.* This, though strictly a district at one extremity of
Edom (*qua vergit ad australem partem*, St Jerome), just as Dedan

---

¹ See *JTS.* xvii. pp. 405—6 (T. H. Robinson, who, however, prefers a slightly
different order of the wording).

off from the mount of Esau by slaughter. 10 For the violence done
to thy brother Jacob shame shall cover thee, and thou shalt be
cut off for ever. 11 In the day that thou stoodest ¹on the other
side, in the day that strangers carried away his ²substance, and

¹ Or, *aloof*   ² Or, *forces*

was at the other (see Ezek. xxv. 13), is here a synonym for Edom in
general (as in Jer. xlix. 7, Am. i. 11, 12). The Temanites had a reputation for wisdom; see Baruch iii. 23.

by slaughter. If this expression is retained within *v.* 9, the preposition
is correctly translated. But the balance of the clauses is best kept by
the transfer of the word to the next *v.* (where the Versions place it, see
below), in which case the preposition must be otherwise rendered.

10. *For the violence,* etc. I.e. by reason of the violence, etc. The
LXX., Syr., and Vulg. begin this *v.* with *For the slaughter and for the
violence,* i.e. because of the outrages inflicted by the Edomites on the
Jews; and this arrangement of the text is preferable to that of the
present Hebrew. There is, however, no conjunction between the two
nouns in the original; and since in Joel iii. 19, which seems to have
this passage of Ob. in view, the expression *For the slaughter* does not
appear, it should probably be rejected here as an interpolation: it may
have been inserted (as Nowack suggests) in order to paint in more
lurid colours Edom's guilt, to which the term *violence* by itself did less
than justice. The Heb. word translated *slaughter* occurs within the
O.T. nowhere but here; and the corresponding verb is found only in
late writings (Ps. cxxxix. 19, Job xiii. 15, xxiv. 14), but is frequent in
Aramaic. It can scarcely be a *gloss* on the word rendered *violence*
(*hāmās*), for this is quite a common term, and would not require an
explanatory addition.

thy brother Jacob. The name *Jacob* is expressly used (in place of
Israel or *Judah*) in order to recall the relationship between the nations.
In Deut. xxiii. 7 the claims of kinship between the two peoples are
urged upon Israel; but Edom had shown no reciprocal sense of the
brotherly relationship.

shame shall cover, etc. Although this *v.* has future tenses, it seems
to proceed not from the early oracle quoted in *vv.* 1—5 (to the metrical
scheme of which it cannot be easily adjusted) but from the writer
(Obadiah) who incorporated the latter. Obadiah, for the moment,
adopts the predictive tone of the prophet from whom he has previously
borrowed.

thou shalt be cut off for ever. The expression is an hyperbole: the
Edomites, though dispossessed by the Nabatæans, long remained
a thorn in the side of their Jewish neighbours; and eventually an
Edomite, in the person of Herod, became king of Judæa (p. l).

11. *on the other side.* The phrase can be used both of mere aloofness
(cf. mg. and see 2 Kgs. ii. 7, Ps. xxxviii. 11 (12), and the verb in Lk.
x. 31, 32 (ἀντιπαρῆλθεν)), and also of a hostile attitude (2 Sam. xviii. 13

foreigners entered into his gates, and cast lots upon Jerusalem,
even thou wast as one of them.　12 But look not thou on the day

and (with a different preposition) Dan. x. 13). Probably the latter
sense is meant here: Vulg. *adversus eum.*

strangers...foreigners. I.e. the Babylonians (p. xxxix): cf. Lam. v. 2.
Against these foreign foes the ties of kindred should have led Edom
to side with Judah.

carried away his substance. Though the verb rendered *carry away*
commonly means to "transport" captives, it is used in connection with
spoil (not prisoners) in 2 Ch. xxi. 17; and the substantive with which
it is here employed is, in view of its use in *v.* 13 (cf. Is. viii. 4, Jer.
xv. 13), rightly rendered by *substance* rather than by *forces* (as in the
mg.), though the LXX. has δύναμιν and the Vulg. *exercitum.*

his gates. This is the reading of the Heb. mg., and is supported by
the LXX. and Vulg.: the Heb. text has *his gate,* which is confirmed
by *v.* 13. Mention of the entry into the city *after* the looting is in
strictness illogical (contrast *v.* 13); but the second clause really marks
the *occasion* which afforded opportunity for looting: cf. Verg. *A.* ii. 353,
Moriamur et in media arma ruamus.

cast lots upon Jerusalem. The previous mention of the removal of
the *substance* of the Jewish people is in favour of understanding this
phrase of the apportionment of the *persons* of the vanquished as slaves
(cf. Joel iii. 3 (iv. 3)), the name of the city representing its inhabitants,
as in 2 Is. xl. 1, 2. For the practice of casting lots to settle claims cf.
Num. xxxiv. 13, Ps. xxii. 18, Mk. xv. 24, and see p. 16.

even thou wast as one of them. Though the Ammonites, Moabites,
and Philistines also exulted like the Edomites over the fall of Jerusalem (Ezek. xxv.), the close relationship between Israel and Edom
aggravated the offence of the last-named people, when they shared in
the despoiling of a kindred race.

12—14. These verses appear to be written in the *Kinah* metre
(p. cxliii), though not with perfect regularity. The imperatives which
they contain are merely rhetorical, the writer really having in mind
past events and not future contingencies. He is carried back in thought
to incidents in the sack of Jerusalem; and as though present on the
occasion, he cautions the Edomites against committing the offences of
which he knows them to have been guilty, and which subsequently
brought vengeance upon them.

12. *But look not thou on,* etc. I.e. gaze not with satisfaction upon,
etc.; for the phrase see p. 37. The occurrence of the conjunction
before the imperative here and the absence of one before *v.* 13, together
with the tautology of 12[a] and 13[b], have led Wellhausen to place *v.* 13
next to *v.* 11 and to reject *v.* 12 as a later insertion. But the three
verses 12—14 seem to have in view successive proceedings on the part
of the Edomites, against which they are dramatically warned. In *v.* 12
they are still outside the doomed city, and are bidden not to gloat over
its fall; in *v.* 13 they are about to enter it, and are admonished not to

of thy brother in ¹the day of his disaster, and rejoice not over the
children of Judah in the day of their destruction; neither speak
proudly in the day of distress. 13 Enter not into the gate of my
people in the day of their calamity; yea, look not thou on their

¹ Or, *the day that he was made a stranger*

do so, or to witness, or participate in, the looting; whilst in *v.* 14 they
have withdrawn from it in order to cut off the fugitives, and are urged
to spare them. The conjunction (*vav*) at the beginning of *v.* 12 may be
explained by its use "to introduce an impassioned speech, without
anything *expressed* previously, to which it can be attached" (Driver,
*Heb. Tenses*³, p. 168, note).

the day of thy brother. I.e. the occasion of thy brother's reverse; cf.
Ps. xxxvii. 13, Is. xiii. 22, Job xviii. 20. The expression *day* is often
thus used to denote the occurrence of either good or bad fortune in
connection with some place or person; cf. Ps. cxxxvii. 7 (*the day of
Jerusalem*), Is. ix. 4 (*the day of Midian*), Hos. i. 11 (ii. 2) (*the day of
Jezreel,* i.e. of Israel), 2 Macc. xv. 36 (*the day of Mordecai*). But in
view of the fact that *day* is repeated immediately afterwards, the word
here may be an unerased scribal error, and the true reading be (as
Winckler suggests), *Look not thou on thy brother.*

in the day of his disaster. The precise sense of the word (*nōcher*)
rendered *disaster,* and found only here, is rather doubtful. Since it is
etymologically connected with the term usually rendered "stranger" or
"foreigner," the phrase in this connection may mean "the day of his
becoming a stranger" (cf. the mg.) in the eyes of God, and being deprived of all claim to His consideration; and this interpretation is
supported by Aq.'s ἀποξενώσεως αὐτοῦ (cf. the use of the cognate verb
in Jer. xix. 4). But the signification *disaster* seems warranted by the
occurrence of the similar form *necher* in Job xxxi. 3 (where it is parallel
to "calamity"), and may be illustrated by the Latin *aliena fortuna.*

neither speak proudly. The literal translation is, *and enlarge not thy
mouth,* an expression which does not recur in the O.T., though the
similar phrases *make wide,* and *open wide, the mouth* are found in 3 Is.
lvii. 4, Ps. xxxv. 21, Lam. ii. 16; cf. also 1 Sam. ii. 1. Possibly it has
reference to indulgence in unrestrained and insulting *laughter.* The
rendering of the R.V. seems to follow the LXX. μὴ μεγαλορημονῇς, but
this corresponds to a different Heb. phrase ("make large *with* thy
mouth") occurring in Ezek. xxxv. 13.

13. *the gate of my people.* I.e. Jerusalem, cf. Mic. i. 9. The LXX.
has *gates,* cf. *v.* 11.

in the day of their calamity. In place of the threefold recurrence of
the same word *calamity* (*'ēdh*) in this verse the LXX. has distinct terms,
πόνων, ὀλέθρου, and ἀπωλίας. The true reading cannot be restored with
certainty; but *běyōm 'ămālām, in the day of their trouble,* would be
suitable here, and the LXX. renders *'āmāl* by πόνος in Gen. xli. 51,

affliction in the day of their calamity, neither lay ye *hands* on their
substance in the day of their calamity. 14 And stand thou not in
the crossway, to cut off those of his that escape; and deliver not
up those of his that remain in the day of distress. 15 For the day

Job v. 6. The reference is to the destruction of Jerusalem by the
Babylonians, which is described in similar terms in Ezek. xxxv. 5.

neither lay ye hands. The Heb. text has suffered some corruption
(the 2nd pers. fem. plur. appearing where the masc. sing. is wanted) but
Bewer's proposal to replace *'al tishlahnah* by *'al tishlah nā'* (for the
position of *nā'* after the verb instead of after the negative cf. Jud. xix.
23) is all that is needed to restore the required form of the verb: the insertion, in the Heb., of "hand" seems unnecessary in view of 2 Sam. vi. 6.

their calamity. Here, where the Hebrew has *calamity* for the third
time within a single verse, the LXX. has ἀπωλίας αὐτῶν, which in *v.* 12 is
its rendering of *'obhădhām, their destruction,* so that probably this word
should be substituted for the present Heb. text *'ēdhām* (which may be
due to a scribal error).

14. *the crossway.* The Heb. word (*perek*) thus translated is of doubtful meaning here. In Nah. iii. 1, the only place where it recurs, it must
be equivalent to "rapine" (the root signifying "to rend"): but in the
present passage it must mean either a *breach* in the city's walls (usually
expressed by *perets*), a *parting* (or *fork*) of the roads, or (as Marti
suggests) a mountain *pass* or *ravine* (cf. the cognate verb in 1 Kgs. xix.
11). The LXX. has τὰς διεκβολάς, the Vulg. *exitibus.*

15—21. The tenor of the contents of the book here undergoes a
change. The remainder is concerned not with a past judgment that has
already overtaken Edom exclusively, but a future judgment awaiting
the heathen world in general, including, but not confined to, the
Edomites. Here destruction from Jehovah is impending over all the
nations, who are doomed to drain the cup of His fury and to perish;
whereas of the Israelites who have already drunk of it a remnant will
survive, and will recover from their spoilers the possessions of which
they have been robbed. Here, too, there is a change in the people
addressed by the writer, and in the manner of the address. Previously
Edom has been apostrophized in the 2nd pers. sing., and Israel has been
referred to in the 3rd pers.; but in *v.* 16 it is the Israelites who are
addressed (in the 2nd pers. plural). The coincidence of these features
points to the conclusion that there begins in *v.* 15 the work of a different
prophet. In the second half of *v.* 15, however, there is a brief recurrence
to the earlier subject-matter and mode of speech; so that within the
verse the utterances of the two prophets have been dovetailed, and 15[b],
which is the sequel of *v.* 14, should logically change places with 15[a],
which connects with *v.* 16 f.

15[a]. *For,* etc. The section (beginning with this clause) which is here
added to the earlier part of the book is of an Apocalyptic character,
see p. xlii.

of the LORD is near upon all the nations: as thou hast done, it
shall be done unto thee; thy ¹dealing shall return upon thine

¹ Or, *recompence*

the day of the LORD. This term denotes a signal manifestation (in
the nearer or remoter future) of Jehovah's activity which the populace
and the prophets of Israel alike looked for, but to which they attached
a different significance. By the populace, inasmuch as Israel was
Jehovah's people, it was uniformly expected to bring destruction upon
their oppressors and relief to Israel itself (Am. v. 18); but in the view
of the prophets its coming was fraught with overthrow for everything
(whether within Israel or in the outside world) that was morally evil.
Yet whilst the prophets anticipated that on the Day of Jehovah their
countrymen would have to sustain a judgment from God no less than
other nations, so far as they had ignored His ethical and spiritual requirements, they were not oblivious of the covenant believed to subsist
between Him and His chosen people. Consequently even among the
prophets *the day of Jehovah* had a varying import, according as contemporary conditions rendered admonition or consolation the more
urgent duty. Prior to the Exile they made the former task their principal
aim, and sought to convince the people that in consequence of their sins
they had more to fear than to hope from some exceptional intervention
of Jehovah in human affairs (see Am. v. 18—20, Is. ii. 12 f.). But in
post-exilic times, when their country's offences seemed to have been
expiated, and their chastisement to have been intensified, by the agents
who inflicted it, beyond what was deserved, they encouraged their
countrymen to await from Jehovah the speedy occurrence of vindication
for Israel and of punishment for its enemies.

is near. The same assertion appears in Joel i. 15, iii. 14.

all the nations. The fact that the Jewish people, even when they had
reached a monotheistic stage of belief, nevertheless continued to draw
such a line of cleavage between themselves and the rest of the world as
is implied in this and similar passages can be accounted for partly by
the retention of the name of the national deity, *Jehovah,* to denote the
God of all the earth, and partly by the circumstance that after the
Exile their religion was all that remained of their nationality, and
consequently perpetuated in some measure the limitations of the latter.

15ᵇ. *as thou hast done,* etc. This half of the *v.* is a continuation of
the direct denunciation of Edom in *vv.* 2—14 (that nation being
addressed here, as there, in the 2nd pers. sing.); and it would be more
in place if it preceded the first half. It may proceed from the prophetical
writer who composed the earlier part of the book (exclusive of the verses
borrowed from a still earlier prophet), but has been transposed; or else
it is a connecting link introduced by the author of *vv.* 15ᵃ, 16—21.
For the sentiment expressed cf. Is. iii. 11, Jer. l. 15, 29, Hab. ii. 8,
Lam. iii. 64, Ezek. xxxv. 15, Rev. xviii. 6. The word rendered *dealing,*
though it has the sense of *recompense* (as given in the mg.), is here used

own head. 16 For as ye have drunk upon my holy mountain, so
shall all the nations drink continually, yea, they shall drink, and
¹swallow down, and shall be as though they had not been. 17 But
in mount Zion there shall be those that escape, and it shall

¹ Or, *talk foolishly*

of the initial offence provoking retribution; see Joel iii. 4, 7 and cf.
Prov. xii. 14. For the phrase *return upon thine own head* cf. Ps. vii. 16.

16. *For as ye have drunk...so shall all the nations drink.* It seems
absolutely necessary to put upon the verb *drink* the same sense in both
clauses; and since in the second it can only be reasonably interpreted,
in a metaphorical sense, of draining the cup of suffering and woe (as in
2 Is. li. 17, 22, Jer. xxv. 15, xlix. 12, Lam. iv. 21, Ezek. xxiii. 32—34,
Ps. lx. 3, lxxv. 8, Hab. ii. 16, Mk. x. 38, xiv. 36, Joh. xviii. 11, Rev. xiv.
10, etc.), it must have the same signification in the first. Under these
circumstances the words must be addressed to the prophet's countrymen, who are meant to understand that the Divine chastisement which
they had experienced will now be undergone by the heathen peoples,
cf. Jer. xlix. 12. Some scholars, however, suppose that the prophet's
utterance is directed to the Edomites, and König (*ap.* Van Hoonacker)
gives to the verb *drink* in both clauses a literal meaning—"as ye
Edomites have drunk in revelry upon the mountains of Judah on the
occasion of the overthrow of Jerusalem, so shall all the nations drink
upon the mountains of Edom in continuous triumph"; and some codices
of the LXX. actually insert οἶνον as the object of the verb πίονται (see
below). But this explanation is contradicted by the concluding clause
of the *v.*, which predicts for the nations not triumph but destruction.

my holy mountain. I.e. the Temple hill (as in Is. xxvii. 13, 3 Is. lvi. 7,
Zeph. iii. 11, Joel ii. 2, iii. 17, etc.).

shall...drink continually. The nations, unlike Israel whose chastisement was only temporary, are to undergo retribution uninterruptedly
until their extermination is accomplished. The principal MSS. of the
LXX. have nothing corresponding to *continually* (*tāmīdh*), but some (as
has been said above) have, instead, the word οἶνον; and several modern
scholars, in consequence, would replace *tāmīdh* by *hēmer* (*wine*); cf.
Dt. xxxii. 14.

swallow down. This rendering is very uncertain, for the Heb. verb
elsewhere means *to talk wildly, rave* (see mg.; and cf. Job vi. 3, Prov.
xx. 25). Wellhausen and Nowack propose to replace this verb, *lā'u,* by
nā'u, stagger (cf. Is. xxiv. 20, xxix. 9); whilst Bewer suggests the
passive (pual) of *bāla', be swallowed up* (cf. Job xxxvii. 20, Is. ix. 16 mg.).

as though they had not been. Cf. Job x. 19, Wisd. ii. 2 (ὡς οὐχ
ὑπάρξαντες).

17. *But in mount Zion...escape.* The name *mount Zion* (for the
strict denotation of which see p. 26) here designates Jerusalem as a
whole. There the survivors of Israel will be secure from the annihilation
in store for the nations. The survival of a remnant of Jehovah's people,

be holy; and the house of Jacob shall possess their possessions. 18 And the house of Jacob shall be a fire, and the house of Joseph a flame, and the house of Esau for stubble, and they shall burn among them, and devour them: and there shall not be any remaining to the house of Esau; for the LORD hath spoken

purified by chastisement, is predicted by other prophets also; see for pre-exilic times Is. iv. 2, x. 20, xxxvii. 31, 32, and for the post-exilic age Zech. viii. 12, Joel ii. 32 (which seems to be a quotation from the present passage). The word rendered *those that escape* is an abstract (like "captivity" for "a body of captives," Jer. xxxiii. 7).

and it shall be holy. The Hebrew may also be rendered, *and there shall be holiness*, or *and there shall be a sanctuary* (i.e. an inviolable retreat). The clause, if retained, assures to Zion immunity from a repetition of the outrages previously sustained at the hands of the heathen nations (*v.* 16). But since it seems to impair the balance of the *v.* (which consists of two tetrameters), it is most likely an insertion from Joel iii. 17, where it forms part of a longer description, and where it is more appropriate to the context. If it is really an interpolation from Joel, the gender of the verb has been adjusted to its present surroundings.

the house of Jacob. The phrase is here equivalent to *Judah* (cf. *v.* 18).

shall possess their possessions. I.e. shall repossess their own former territories: for *possess* in this sense cf. Dt. xxx. 5, Jer. xxx. 3. The LXX. (followed by the Vulg.) has *shall possess those that dispossessed them* (τοὺς κατακληρονομήσαντας αὐτούς), involving a different pointing. The passage implies the return of Jewish exiles to their own land, predictions of which occur in Is. xi. 11 f., xiv. 2, 2 Is. xliii. 5, xlix. 22, 3 Is. lx. 4, Jer. xxx. 10, xlvi. 27, Mic. vii. 12.

18. *Jacob...Joseph.* These stand respectively for the two branches (or erstwhile kingdoms) of the Israelite people (cf. Ps. lxxvii. 15), whose reunion is anticipated by the writer as by other prophets (Is. xi. 13, Jer. iii. 18, xxx. 3, xxxi. 5, 6, 27, Ezek. xxxvii. 16, Hos. i. 11, iii. 5, 2 Zech. x. 6).

a fire...for stubble. Similar imagery occurs in Is. v. 24, x. 17, 2 Is. xlvii. 14, 2 Zech. xii. 6, Mal. iv. 1. For parallel predictions of Israel's participation in the execution of judgment upon its former oppressors see Is. xi. 14, 2 Is. xli. 15, 16, Mic. iv. 11—13.

there shall not...remaining. Compare Jer. xlii. 17. The Alexandrine codex of the LXX. has οὐκ ἔσται πυρφόρος (of which the πυροφόρος of the Vatican codex is a corruption), and the Old Latin version has *ignifer*. The term πυρφόρος denoted a priest who, in a Spartan army, had charge of the sacred fire taken from the altar of Zeus, which was always kept alight to consume the sacrifices offered for the army; and since his person, by Greek international usage, was held inviolable (Hesychius being quoted as explaining the word to mean ὁ πῦρ φέρων καὶ ὁ μόνος διασωθεὶς ἐν πολέμῳ), there arose the proverb (descriptive of complete

it. **19 And they of the South shall possess the mount of Esau;**

annihilation) οὐδὲ πυρφόρος ἐλείφθη (cf. Hdt. VIII. 6). The prediction in the present passage obtained fulfilment in some degree during the Maccabæan period of Jewish history (see p. l).

19. This verse predicts the expansion of the Jewish community in all directions beyond the narrow boundaries encompassing it in post-exilic times (see Mic. vii. 11 and cf. 3 Is. lxi. 7); but the precise meaning of the passage is obscure, and the text has probably undergone much corruption. The literal rendering of the Hebrew is, *And the South shall possess the mountain of Esau and the Lowland the Philistines and they shall possess the field of Ephraim and the field of Samaria and Benjamin Gilead.* The *South* and the *Lowland* were physical divisions of the territory of Judah (which alone the writer in this *v.* seems to have in view); and as the passage stands, it declares that the in-habitants of the first are to occupy Edom, and those of the second are to seize in the W. the land of the Philistines (cf. Is. xi. 14) and to spread in the N. over the former territory of Ephraim and Samaria, including Benjamin (lying between Ephraim and Judah); whilst the Benjamites, in lieu of their prior possessions (thus lost), are to cross the Jordan, and appropriate the district of Gilead. But it is difficult to think that the passage in its present form is complete. The extension of the population of the South towards Edom and of the denizens of the Lowland towards Philistia is natural enough; but it is not equally natural that the dwellers in the Lowland should be destined to occupy Ephraim also. Hence there is probably some defect in the text, the real subject of the second verb *shall possess* being lost. The LXX. instead of *the field of Ephraim* has τὸ ὄρος 'Εφράιμ, and though at first sight τὸ ὄρος looks like an accus., it may really be a nominative, implying in the Heb. *hā-hār 'eth 'Ephraim* (instead of *'eth sĕdhēh 'Ephraim*, as the present text has it). If this is the original form of the passage, as supposed by Ewald and G. A. Smith, the translation of the second half of the verse will be *and they of the hill country* (of Judah) *shall possess Ephraim and the field of Samaria, and they of Benjamin Gilead.* This supplies the defect under which the Hebrew, as we now have it, labours, and brings the passage into harmony with Jer. xxxii. 44, xxxiii. 13.

the South. In Heb. *the Neghebh.* This was the district, originally within Judah (Josh. xv. 21), lying south of Hebron and extending towards the border of Edom as far as the plateau of *Jebel es Magrah.* It consists of a succession of rolling hills, the ridges running east and west; its surface is treeless and waterless (except when the wâdies which cut it are filled by the winter rains); and its present aspect is one of barrenness and desolation. There are reasons, however, for thinking that at various times it has been cultivated and has main-tained a considerable population.

shall possess...Esau. The occupation of Edom by Judah is predicted in Am. ix. 11, 12, Is. xi. 14; cf. Num. xxiv. 18.

and they of the lowland the Philistines: and they shall possess

the lowland. In Heb. *the Shephēlah*; Aq. ἡ πεδινή. This was a region lying between the hill country of Judah (see below) and the maritime plain. It thus bordered on Philistia, but was of rather uncertain delimitation, though cities within it were certainly included in Judah, according to Josh. xv. 33—36. It consists of a mass of low hills which, when viewed from the maritime plain, appear "buttressing the central range" of Judah, but which are really separated from the latter by a series of valleys[1].

the Philistines. I.e. the land of the Philistines. There has been much speculation as to the origin of this people. The association of *Philistines* and *Pelēthites* (perhaps another form of the same national title) with *Cherēthites* in Ezek. xxv. 16, Zeph. ii. 5, 2 Sam. viii. 18, xv. 18, xx. 7 has suggested that they were Cretans[2]; and the conclusion that they were a non-Semitic race is supported by the fact that they did not practise circumcision, a usage prevailing among the majority of the Semitic peoples inhabiting Palestine. It is perhaps also significant that the LXX. frequently represents their name by ἀλλόφυλοι. In Gen. x. 14 they are connected with the *Casluhim*; but in Am. ix. 7 their home, prior to their settlement in Palestine, is said to have been *Caphtor* (cf. Jer. xlvii. 4), a name plausibly identified with *Keftiu*, which in the Egyptian inscriptions denotes a locality from which articles resembling the products of Crete were brought to Egypt in the reign of Thutmose III (first half of the 15th century B.C.)[3]. Crete, however, does not appear to have been their native soil: at least, they differed in their military equipment from the Minoan inhabitants of that island; and it has been thought that they crossed to Crete from Caria[4]. In the Egyptian inscriptions there are allusions to a people called *Pulasati*; and if the identification of the Philistines with these is correct, the occasion of their establishing themselves in Canaan was their failure in an attempt, made in conjunction with a number of allied tribes, to over-run Egypt in the 12th century B.C.: being foiled in this enterprise by Rameses III, they settled on the seaboard that trends from the Delta northward. Their immigration into the country (Palestine) which came to be named after them probably took place later than the conquest of Canaan by the Israelites, but not later than the period of the Judges (see Jud. xiii. 1); and their occupation of the coast affords a reasonable explanation of the movements of the Danites recorded in Jud. xviii. If this synchronism is approximately correct, the mention of Philistines in Canaan in the age of Abraham (Gen. xxvi. 1), or even at the date of the Exodus (Ex. xiii. 17), must be anachronistic[5]. The relations between them and Israel were generally

---

[1] G. A. Smith, *HGHL.* p. 203.
[2] The LXX. in Ezek. and Zeph. represent the *Cherethites* by Κρῆτες.
[3] Macalister, *The Philistines*, etc. pp. 9—10.
[4] See *Cambridge Ancient History*, II. pp. 286—7.
[5] Cf. Sayce, *Early History of the Hebrews*, p. 64.

the field of Ephraim, and the field of Samaria: and Benjamin

unfriendly. They were conquered by David (2 Sam. v. 17—25), but continued to be troublesome long after his time (2 Kgs. xviii. 8, 2 Ch. xxviii. 18, Ps. lxxxiii. 7); and the subjugation of them by the Jews is often the subject of prophetic predictions (see Is. xi. 14, Jer. xxv. 20, Ezek. xxv. 15—17).

and they shall possess...Samaria. If, as is argued on p. 81, the reading of the LXX. καὶ κατακληρονομήσουσι τὸ ὄρος Ἐφράιμ καὶ τὸ πεδίον Σαμαρείας should be adopted here, the subject of the verb will be *they of the hill country* (τὸ ὄρος representing hā-hār, which, followed by the particle *'eth*, must be substituted for *'eth sĕdhēh* in the present Heb. text). Part of the territory assigned to Judah at the Conquest (according to Josh. xv.) was distinguished as *the Mountain*, in contrast to *the South, the Lowland,* and *the Wilderness.* The sense, then, of this passage will be that whilst the inhabitants of the South are to possess Edom, and those of the Lowland are to acquire Philistia, the occupants of the Mountain (or hill country) are to expand northward and possess the territory of the former tribe of Ephraim (extending from Bethel and Bethhoron on the south to the brook of Kanah (near Shechem) on the north). The words *and the field of Samaria* are perhaps a gloss, the conjunction being explanatory and equivalent to *even* (cf. 1 Sam. xvii. 40): the omission of them would improve the symmetry of the clauses in the *v.* The term *field* has the signification of "region" or "territory," as in Gen. xiv. 7, Num. xxi. 20, etc.; and can be applied to a hilly district as well as to level ground (see Gen. xxxii. 3).

and Benjamin shall possess *Gilead.* If the inhabitants of the hill country of Judah are thought of as destined to spread into the former territory of Ephraim, they would inevitably absorb that of Benjamin (lying between Judah and Ephraim); and the Benjamites are accordingly to be compensated with Gilead. The LXX. has καὶ Βενιαμεὶν καὶ τὴν Γαλααδεῖτιν, apparently regarding both words as acc. after the foregoing κατακληρονομήσουσιν, and supposing that a section of the *Judeans* are to occupy Gilead in addition to the territories of Benjamin and Ephraim; but Sym. and Th. have καὶ Βενιαμὶν δὲ τὴν Γαλαάδ, taking Βενιαμίν as the subject of the verb supplied; whilst the Vulg. has explicitly *et Benjamin possidebit Galaad.* Bewer thinks that the whole verse contains various explanatory glosses, and considers that it originally ran, *And they shall possess the South and the Lowland, and they shall possess mount Ephraim* (adopting the LXX.'s τὸ ὄρος Ἐφράιμ and treating the phrase as object), *and the Ammonites* (replacing binyāmīn by bĕnē 'ammōn). After the local names there were then inserted definitions (marked by the prefixed particle *'eth*) as in Ezek. iv. 1, xxxvi. 12, *the South* being explained by *the mount of Esau, the Lowland* by *the Philistines, mount Ephraim* by *the field of Samaria,* and *the Ammonites* by *Gilead* (the insertions being designed to identify the localities in the writer's own time). But this interpretation does not

shall possess Gilead. 20 And the captivity of this [1] host of the

[1] Or, *fortress*

account for the conjunction in *and the field of Samaria,* supposed to be a gloss on *mount Ephraim* (for there is no conjunction before the other hypothetical glosses); whilst *Gilead* should be glossed by *the Ammonites* (not the reverse).

20. The authentic text of this *v.* is so uncertain that any explanation of it is bound to be precarious. The original rendered literally is *And the captivity of this fortress* (or *host*) *of the children of Israel who* (or *which*) *the Canaanites even unto Zarephath and the captivity of Jerusalem which is in Sepharad shall possess the cities of the South*; but this is clearly defective, and has been supplemented in various ways:

(1) The R.V. text supplies before *the Canaanites* the preposition "among" (*bĕ*) and after it the verb "possess," which may be got from the concluding clause of either this *v.* or the preceding. By *the captivity of this host* (if such be the right rendering) *of the children of Israel* must be meant members of some Hebrew provincial community (in contrast to members of the Jewish capital), held prisoners among *the Canaanites* (or Phœnicians): these when released are to have possessions extending *even unto Zarephath.* But this explanation leaves unexpressed the object of the verb "possess" which is supplied in the first half of the *v.* and needs before *the Canaanites* the word *dwell* (as well as *among*).

(2) The R.V. second mg. avoids one difficulty by regarding *the cities of the South* (at the end of the *v.*) as the destined possessions of *both* groups of captives, defining the first as those *which are* among *the Canaanites even unto Zarephath.* But to take the words *even unto Zarephath* as marking the extent of the dispersal of captive Hebrews among the Phœnicians still requires the insertion, after the relative *which,* of a verb like *dwell.*

(3) The R.V. first mg. supplies the verb "shall possess" *before,* not after, the relative pronoun (which it treats as neuter) and supplies before *the Canaanites* not the preposition "among" but the preposition "to" (*lĕ*); and the resultant translation of the first half of the verse is *And the captivity of this host of the children of Israel shall possess that which* belongeth to *the Canaanites, even unto Zarephath.* This rendering not only furnishes an object to the verb "shall possess," but also affords a natural connection for the words *even unto Zarephath.* But before the word *Canaanites* there might be expected the preposition commonly employed to mark possession, *lĕ* or *la(c).*

(4) The LXX. has γῆ before τῶν Χαναναίων, suggesting that the Greek translators had before them the reading *'eth 'erets* instead of the relative pronoun *'ăsher* of the present Hebrew text. The adoption of this, and of the rendering of *hēl* by *fortress* instead of by *host,* yields the translation, *And the captivity of this fortress of the children of Israel shall possess the land of the Canaanites even unto Zarephath*; and such seems the best solution of the difficulties presented by the passage. The words *this fortress* possibly designate Samaria (since it is contrasted

children of Israel, [1]which are *among* the Canaanites, *shall possess*
even unto Zarephath; and the captivity of Jerusalem, which is in

[1] Or, shall possess *that which* belongeth to *the Canaanites, even &c.* Or, *which
are* among *the Canaanites, even unto Zarephath, and &c.*

with *Jerusalem*); if so, *the captivity* (i.e. the captives) *of this fortress*
must signify Samaria's deported inhabitants, whom the prophet ex-
pects to return and take possession, not of their former abode (for this
is to be occupied by the inhabitants of the hill country of Judah, see
on *v.* 19), but part of Phœnicia as far as Zarephath. The word *hēl*
which the translation *host*, adopted by the R.V. text, assumes to be
equivalent to *hayil* (cf. Sym. and Th. τῆς δυνάμεως ταύτης and Vulg.
exercitus huius) probably here has the meaning which it bears in
Lam. ii. 8, Nah. iii. 8—namely, *rampart* or *fortification*; and the
writer, by attaching to it the pronoun *this*, seems to imply that he
dwelt near the fortress designated. Ewald proposed to replace the
term by *hōl*, "sand," interpreted in the sense of *coast*, and took it to
refer to the Israelite tribes north of Ephraim, flanking the Mediterranean. *Zarephath* (mentioned in 1 Kgs. xvii. 9) is represented in the
LXX. by *Sarepta* (cf. Lk. iv. 26): it was situated between Tyre and
Zidon, about 8 miles S. of the latter. There still survive ruins of it
along the shore in front of the Arabic village of *Sarafend*.

Bewer, who takes (like the supporters of the interpretation given
above) *the children of Israel* to mean descendants of the northern
Israelites, whose independence was destroyed by Sargon, considers
that in *ha-hēl* there is disguised (through textual corruption) the
locality *Halah*, to which, among other places, the captives of Samaria
were deported (2 Kgs. xvii. 6); and he reconstructs the text so as to
obtain the translation *And the captivity of the children of Israel that
are in Halah shall possess the Canaanites* (i.e. Phœnicia) *as far as
Zarephath.*

the captivity of Jerusalem. I.e. bodies of Judean captives deported
from Jerusalem, first by the Babylonian Nebuchadrezzar, and later
possibly by various Persian rulers.

Sepharad. The locality intended is quite uncertain. East of Palestine
a *Saparda* in S.W. Media is named in an inscription of Sargon
(721—705), and another, situated N.E. of Nineveh, is mentioned in
an inscription of Esar-haddon (681—668); and if either of these was
an Assyrian possession, it may, on the overthrow of Assyria, have fallen
to Babylon and become the abode of Jewish captives. In the west there
was a Çparda (Sparda) situated in Asia Minor, near Bithynia and
Galatia, which was conquered by Cyrus, the Persian, and again by
Darius Hystaspis (Sayce, *HCM.* p. 483); and Jews are related to
have been transported into Asia Minor by Artaxerxes Ochus (358—
337). The fact that Çparda is mentioned in connection with the *Iauná*,
i.e. the Ionians (Schrader, *COT.* I. p. 446) has suggested its identification with Sardis. The LXX. has ἕως Ἐφράθα which (it has been

Sepharad, shall possess the cities of the South. 21 And saviours
shall come up on mount Zion to judge the mount of Esau; and
the kingdom shall be the LORD's.

conjectured) is a scribal error for ἕως Σεφράθα. The Vulg. represents
in Sepharad by *in Bosporo* (which may possibly preserve a tradition
that associated Sepharad with Bithynia). By later Jewish interpreters
the locality was identified with Spain, and the Spanish Jews are still
known as the Sephardim.

the cities of the South. At the time when the author of this passage
wrote, the South of Judah may have been occupied by a hostile
people—probably Edomites, who even in the 2nd century B.C. were
in possession of Hebron (1 Macc. v. 65). In any case the Jews dwelling
there, by pushing into Edom (*v.* 19), would leave room for the returning
exiles here spoken of.

21. *And saviours...Zion.* The meaning seems to be that deliverers
(cf. Jud. iii. 9, 15, 2 Kgs. xiii. 5, Neh. ix. 27) will come to mount Zion
to ensure the safety of the Jews gathered there, and to inflict the
destined retribution on Edom (cf. *v.* 18); and these thoughts may have
been inspired by the visit to Jerusalem of Nehemiah, who fortified the
city. The construction *come up on* (instead of *come up to,* or *on to*)
mount Zion is rather unusual (*bĕ* instead of *'el* or *'al*), but seems
sufficiently defended by 2 Sam. ii. 1, 1 Ch. xiv. 11. The LXX., however, has καὶ ἀναβήσονται ἀνασωζόμενοι ἐξ ὄρους Σειών, *And those who are
saved* (see *v.* 17) *shall go up* (i.e. on an expedition, cf. Jer. xlix. 29,
l. 9) *from mount Zion* (using other vowels and a different preposition).

to judge, etc. I.e. to execute judgment (cf. 1 Sam. iii. 13) on the
mountain land of Edom.

and the kingdom...the LORD's. The rule of Jehovah over the whole
world, which could be questioned so long as the wrongs inflicted on
His people were unredressed, would be vindicated as soon as retribution
overtook the wrongdoers: cf. Ex. xv. 18, Ps. xxii. 28, xlvii. 8, xciii. 1,
2 Zech. xiv. 9, Rev. xix. 6. Although the context here involves
a narrow racial conception of Jehovah's kingdom, which is viewed as
established through the supremacy of Israel over other peoples, the
prediction has found, and is finding, a more universalist and spiritual
fulfilment through the extension of Christianity, which, though originating in the midst of Judaism, has become detached from it, and with
such detachment has shed the idea of Jewish sovereignty over the
Gentiles.

APPENDIX

THE ORACLE QUOTED IN COMMON BY OBADIAH AND JEREMIAH.

The likeness between the two passages Ob. 1—5 and Jer. xlix. 14—16, 9 cannot be satisfactorily accounted for except on the supposition that they have a common origin in an earlier oracle which has been incorporated by both prophetic writers. This oracle was metrical in structure; but it is not at once clear in what metre it was composed, since, where the two texts are in conflict, the underlying source can be reconstructed in more than one way. Certain lines obviously are marked by the *Kinah* (or Pentameter) rhythm, but several of the alternate lines admit of being regarded as either hexameters or pentameters, according to the deductions drawn from the available data. If the poem be reconstructed so as to present a series of alternating hexameter (or double trimeter) and pentameter lines, we get a system of verses resembling the Elegiac poems occurring in Greek and Latin literature. It would probably, however, be difficult to find a parallel for such an arrangement elsewhere in the O.T.; and general considerations are in favour of the conclusion that the oracle consisted of a succession of pentameters, with the exception of the first line, which must be an hexameter (or two trimeters).

The discrepant texts of Ob. and Jer. have been compared in the commentary in some detail. From this comparison the original form of the oracle can be recovered with some confidence; and a plausible reconstruction of it is as follows:—

Loquitur propheta ignotus.
" A communication have I heard from Jehovah, | while a messenger
    among the nations is being sent:—

[*Nuntii iussum.*]
' Assemble yourselves, and come against her, | and rise up for war.'

[*Jehovae Oraculum.*]
' Small I make thee among the nations, | despised among men.
Thy terribleness hath deceived thee, | the pride of thine heart.
O dweller in the clefts of the rock, | holder of the height,
Though thou makest on high, as a vulture, thy nest, |
                        [from thence will I bring thee down.
If vintagers come to thee | they will not leave gleanings,
If thieves by night, | they will destroy till satisfied.'"

JOEL

This section of the book describes the disastrous effects of the plague of locusts, explains the need of repentance on the part of the people for the sins occasioning the Divine wrath, and voices the prophet's demand for an appeal to God to spare the sufferers.

I. 1 THE word of the LORD that came to Joel the son of Pethuel.

2 Hear this, ye old men, and give ear, all ye inhabitants of the land. Hath this been in your days, or in the days of your fathers? 3 Tell ye your children of it, and *let* your children *tell*

1. This *v.* constitutes the title of the book, and in form resembles Hos. i. 1, Mic. i. 1, Zeph. i. 1, Hag. i. 1. The phrase *The word of the LORD* (or *JEHOVAH*, see p. 1) *came to...* is frequent in connection with Divine revelations, see Gen. xv. 1, 1 Sam. xv. 10, 2 Sam. vii. 4, xxiv. 11, 1 Kgs. xvi. 1, Is. xxxviii. 4, Jer. i. 2, 11, Ezek. iii. 16, etc.

Joel. On the meaning of the name see p. li.

Pethuel. This appellation occurs only here. The Heb. form is followed by the Vulg. (*Phatuel*), but the LXX., Old Latin, and Syr. have *Bethuel* or *Bathuel*, identical with the name of Rebekah's father (Gen. xxii. 22). Both names are difficult to interpret. *Pethuel*, if connected with the Heb. *pāthah*, presumably means " Persuaded of God[1]." The first element of *Bethuel* cannot be explained from any Heb. verb: in the Oxford Heb. Lex. it is suggested that it is equivalent to *Methuel*, "man of God."

2—7. Attention is called to the unprecedented character of the recent calamity, and its consequences.

2. *Hear...give ear.* The same parallelism occurs in Gen. iv. 23, Jud. v. 3, Is. i. 2, Hos. v. 1, Ps. xlix. 1.

ye old men. This (cf. *v.* 14, ii. 16) is a better rendering than *ye elders* (the official heads of the community) since appeal is made to length of experience (cf. Dt. xxxii. 7).

the land. I.e. Judah (as appears from the mention of the Temple in *vv.* 9, 13, etc.).

this. I.e. the like of what is explained in *v.* 4: the Old Latin has *talia.*

3. *Tell ye...generation.* To adapt this *v.* to the metre of the surrounding context (where trimeters are employed) Nowack proposes, by the omission of the middle portion, to reduce it to *Tell ye your children*

---

[1] Cf. *Jeruel*, "Founded of God."

their children, and their children another generation. 4 That
which ¹the palmerworm hath left hath ¹the locust eaten; and
that which the locust hath left hath ¹the cankerworm eaten;
and that which the cankerworm hath left hath ¹the caterpiller
eaten. 5 Awake, ye drunkards, and weep; and howl, all ye
drinkers of wine, because of the sweet wine; for it is cut off from
your mouth. 6 For a nation is come up upon my land, strong,

¹ Probably, different kinds of locusts, or locusts in different stages of growth.

of it and let *your children* tell *another* (i.e. the next, cf. Ps. cix. 13)
generation.

4. The four names used in this *v.* to denote various sorts of locusts
might etymologically be represented by *the shearer, the swarmer, the
lapper* (i.e. one that laps, or licks up, herbage), and *the finisher.* The
variety of names, however, seems to be employed, not for the purpose
of distinguishing with precision different species (for only one of the
names which in Lev. xi. 22 are used to denote *kinds* occurs here), still
less to denote distinct stages of growth in the same insect (for the same
terms appear in a different *order* in ii. 25, and the mature locust would
not consume what in an earlier stage of development it had left un-
devoured, but would move on to fresh ground), but to suggest the
interminable succession of the swarms. For allusions in the O.T. to
the locusts' incalculable numbers cf. Jud. vi. 5, vii. 12, Jer. xlvi. 23,
Nah. iii. 15, Ps. cv. 34¹.

5. *Awake, ye drunkards.* The sleep induced by intoxication must
cease, since the means of further indulgence in potations has been
destroyed. For the injury caused by locusts to vines cf. Theoc. v. 108,
ἀκρίδες ... μή μευ λωβασεῖσθε τὰς ἀμπέλος.

the sweet wine. The Heb. word ('*āsīs*), thus rendered, denotes juice
"pressed" (cf. the verb in Mal. iv. 3 (iii. 21)) not only from grapes but
also from other fruits: it recurs in Am. ix. 13 (= Joel iii. 18), 2 Is.
xlix. 26, Cant. viii. 2. In such raw juice the process of fermentation
had started but was not completed: cf. the effects attributed to γλεῦκος
in Acts ii. 13. The LXX. in iii. 18 renders it by γλυκασμός, but in Is.
and Cant. by οἶνος νέος and νᾶμα respectively.

for it is cut off from your mouth. The LXX. has *because there have
been cut off from your mouth joy and gladness* (a pentameter instead of
a trimeter).

6. *a nation.* This expression, here applied to locusts, is paralleled
by the use of *people* in connection with the same insects in ii. 2, and
with ants and coneys in Prov. xxx. 25, 26. So Homer employs ἔθνεα of
geese, cranes, flies, bees, and swine (*Il.* ii. 87, 458, 469, *Od.* xiv. 93);
and Maurer quotes Verg. *G.* iii. 73, *gentis* (of horses), and Columella,
ix. 13, *duo populi* (of bees).

¹ Agatharchides (quoted by Henderson) speaks of ἀκρίδων πλῆθος ἀμύθητον.

and without number; his teeth are the teeth of a lion, and he hath the jaw teeth of a great lion. 7 He hath laid my vine waste, and ¹barked my fig tree: he hath made it clean bare, and cast it ²away; the branches thereof are made white. 8 Lament like

¹ Or, *broken* ² Or, *down*

is come up. The verb is regularly used of hostile incursions, cf. 1 Kgs. xiv. 25, 2 Kgs. xviii. 13, and see p. 86.

my land. The prophet, here and in *v.* 7, speaks as the representative of his countrymen.

strong. I.e. in virtue of their irresistible numbers. The adjective is sometimes merely a synonym for "many" (Am. v. 12, Ps. xxxv. 18, Prov. vii. 26, 2 Is. liii. 12).

the jaw teeth. The Heb. word only occurs in late writings (Prov. xxx. 14, Job xxix. 17). The LXX. has αἱ μύλαι αὐτοῦ, and the Latin versions *molares eius,* so that if these versions are followed, perhaps a more expressive rendering would be *the grinders.* Sym. has καὶ αἱ μύλαι ὡς λέοντος and the Latin versions recognize ὡς, so that Sievers, followed by Marti, may be right in proposing to read in the last clause *and his grinders* are *as* the teeth *of a great lion.* The import of the comparison consists in the locusts' destructiveness, though their mandibles are actually both strong and sharp, and are described by one traveller as "saw-like."

a great lion. The term (*lābhi'*) here used is rendered by the R.V. in Gen. xlix. 9, Num. xxiv. 9, Dt. xxxiii. 20, and other places by *lioness,* but in Is. v. 29 by *lion.* The LXX. has σκύμνου, the Vulgate *catuli leonis.*

7. *He hath...fig tree.* Literally, *he hath made my vine a desolation, and my fig tree chips.* The word rendered *chips* only occurs here; but a very similar one is found in Hos. x. 7 (see mg.). Locusts are known to devour the bark and young twigs of trees; and Pliny, *HN.* xi. 29, describes them as *omnia morsu erodentes, et fores quoque tectorum.* The vine and the fig tree are mentioned together as being characteristic of Palestine (see on Mic. iv. 4).

made it clean bare, and cast it away. The first verb has in view the consumption by the locusts of the edible portions of the trees, the second the rejection of those parts which they have gnawed but found uneatable, and so dropped (cf. mg.).

8. *Lament.* An exhortation to mourning addressed to the land, or to its collective people, personified as a woman: cf. Is. iii. 26, Am. v. 2, Jer. xiv. 17. The verb in this sense occurs only here.

girded with sackcloth. The wearing of sackcloth was an accompaniment of sorrow in general, whether for the dead (2 Sam. iii. 31), for private or public calamities (Am. viii. 10, Jer. vi. 26, Job xvi. 15, Esth. iv. 3), or for sin (1 Kgs. xxi. 27, Neh. ix. 1). The expression implies the wearing of a loin cloth woven of dark hair (cf. 2 Is. l. 3, Rev. vi. 12), probably of the goat (cf. μελαναιγίς) or of the camel. The Old

a virgin girded with sackcloth for the husband of her youth.
9 The meal offering and the drink offering is cut off from the
house of the LORD; the priests, the LORD'S ministers, mourn.
10 The field is wasted, the land mourneth; for the corn is wasted,

Latin version here has *praecinctam cilicium*. To the use, in connection
with mourning and penitence, of this, the scantiest and cheapest of
garments, more than one motive probably contributed. On the one
hand, the prevalent physical conception of "uncleanness" attaching to
the dead (cf. Num. xix. 13—19) and of its infectious character (Hag.
ii. 13) would lead to the employment of something that could be dis-
carded without much loss, to save valuable attire from becoming con-
taminated and useless. On the other hand, since sackcloth was the
garb of slaves and captives (1 Kgs. xx. 31, 32), the use of it would be
a mark of humility, calculated to propitiate an offended deity, whose
anger had been manifested by the death of the person mourned. For
another possible explanation of mourning apparel see p. 25.

the husband of her youth. For the combination cf. *a wife of youth*
(Prov. v. 18, 2 Is. liv. 6, Mal. ii. 14, 15). In view of the word *virgin*
(LXX. νύμφη), the term here rendered *husband* (literally *owner*, Gen.
xx. 3, Ex. xxi. 3, 22) must refer to one to whom the maid was only
betrothed and not yet wedded (though the same law applied to her as
to the wedded wife, Dt. xxii. 22—24, Mt. i. 19).

9—13. A renewed description of the devastation caused by the
locusts, and the consequent interruption of the Temple offerings.

9. *The meal offering.* The Heb. term (*minhah*) thus translated was
in early times applied to offerings of all kinds (see Gen. iv. 3, 4, 1 Sam.
ii. 12—17), and the LXX. here has θυσία, the Old Latin *hostia*, and the
Vulg. *sacrificium*. Later, however, it came to denote specifically a cereal
offering (Lev. ii. 1—3, 1 Kgs. viii. 64, 1 Ch. xxi. 23), this, together with
a drink offering (of wine), being the usual accompaniment of a flesh
offering (Num. xv. 1—10). Such accessories illustrate the close analogy
subsisting between sacrifices and feasts in early religious usage (cf. Bel
and the Dragon, 3). The suspension of the meal and drink offering is
here viewed as one of the greatest calamities resulting from the plague
of locusts, a fact suggesting that what the writer has particularly in
mind is the daily burnt sacrifice, accompanied by offerings of fine flour,
oil, and wine, prescribed in Ex. xxix. 38—42, Num. xxviii. 3—8 (cf.
Neh. x. 33, 39).

the LORD'S ministers. The LXX. implies the reading *the ministers
of the altar*, as in *v.* 13.

10. The cessation of the Temple offerings is caused by the destruction
of the agricultural products that provided them.

the land mourneth. The "pathetic fallacy" whereby inanimate nature
is represented as sentient by those who, from a desire for sympathy,
transfer to their environment their own moods is aided in some circumstances by the actual appearance of natural objects, according as

the new wine is ¹dried up, the oil languisheth. 11 ²Be ashamed,
O ye husbandmen, howl, O ye vinedressers, for the wheat and for
the barley; for the harvest of the field is perished. 12 The vine
is ¹withered, and the fig tree languisheth: the pomegranate tree,
the palm tree also, and the apple tree, even all the trees of the

¹ Or, *ashamed*   ² Or, *The husbandmen are ashamed, the vinedressers howl*

they flourish or fade under favourable or unfavourable conditions: cf.
Am. i. 2, Jer. xii. 4, Is. xxxiii. 9, Ps. lxv. 13.

the new wine. From the passages in which this term (*tirōsh*) is used
(if they are interpreted strictly) it would appear that it was applied to
the juice of the grape both before fermentation (ii. 24, 3 Is. lxv. 8) and
after it (Hos. iv. 11, Jud. ix. 13)¹. The LXX. generally represents it by
οἶνος, but sometimes by μέθυσμα.

is dried up. Or, *is abashed* (cf. mg.), see *v.* 11 (where it is applied to
the husbandmen). The new wine, failing through the destruction of the
vines, is represented as conscious that it has not answered expectations:
cf. Jer. xiv. 3, 4. Corn, wine, and (olive) oil constituted the three main
products of Palestine (Dt. vii. 13, xi. 14, xii. 17, Hos. ii. 8, Jer. xxxi.
12). The last was used as an unguent (Ex. xxx. 24, 25, Dt. xxviii. 40,
Am. vi. 6, Mic. vi. 15), as an illuminant (Ex. xxvii. 20), as an in-
gredient in food (1 Kgs. xvii. 12, Ezek. xvi. 13) and religious offerings
(Num. xxviii. 5, Lev. ii. 1), and as a remedy for wounds (Is. i. 6, Lk.
x. 34).

11. *Be ashamed...howl.* The commands are equivalent to a description. But the LXX. for the former has a past tense, whilst Sym. has
κατῃσχύνθησαν, and this is followed in the R.V. mg.

ye vinedressers. The word is here used of fruitgrowers in general:
cf. *v.* 12.

for the wheat, etc. The writer here has in mind the husbandmen
only; the reason for the vinedressers' grief is deferred till *v.* 12 (where
trees are mentioned).

the harvest. The LXX. has τρυγητός, perhaps reading *bātsīr* for *kātsīr.*

12. *the pomegranate tree.* This, *Punica granatum,* grows to a height
of 20 ft., has lancet-shaped leaves, and bears large red blossoms and a
fruit of the size and colour of an orange, though rather redder and with
a harder rind, enclosing numerous red pips. Its juice was converted
into a beverage (Cant. viii. 2).

the palm tree. This, *Phœnix dactylifera,* though abundant only in
the warmest parts of Palestine, such as the neighbourhood of Jericho in
the Jordan valley (Dt. xxxiv. 3, Jud. i. 16), and of Engedi by the
margin of the Dead Sea (Ecclus. xxiv. 14), was sufficiently common to
be associated particularly with Judæa. Pliny (*HN.* XIII. 6 (4)) writes,
Judæa vero inclita est vel magis palmis; and the coins by which
Vespasian commemorated the Fall of Jerusalem in A.D. 70 represent the

¹ See Driver, *Joel and Amos,* p. 79.

field are withered: for joy is [1]withered away from the sons of men. 13 Gird yourselves *with sackcloth*, and lament, ye priests; howl, ye ministers of the altar; come, lie all night in sackcloth, ye ministers of my God: for the meal offering and the drink offering is withholden from the house of your God. 14 Sanctify

[1] Or, *ashamed*

city, personified as a weeping woman, seated under a palm tree (Madden, *Coins of the Jews*, p. 209).

the apple tree. The Heb. term only occurs in late compositions (Prov. xxv. 11, Cant. ii. 3, 5, vii. 8, viii. 5). On the strength of Prov. *l.c. apples of gold in baskets* (or *filigree work*) *of silver*, it has been argued that the word means the citron, the orange, or the apricot, rather than the apple; but the bitter taste of the citron (contrast Cant. ii. 3) and the lack of scent in the apricot (contrast Cant. vii. 8) are against its identification with either of these; whilst the orange is said not to have been introduced into Palestine until the Middle Ages. By some scholars it is denied that Prov. xxv. 11 can refer to any natural fruit[1]: if so, the evidence of Cant. favours the apple.

for joy is withered, etc. Perhaps better, *for joy is abashed from* (i.e. avoids in shame) the presence of *the sons of men*. The causal particle *for* introduces the reason, not for the statement immediately preceding, but for the exhortation to howl and lament, in *vv.* 5, 8, 11. In an agricultural country like Palestine prosperity was so closely dependent upon the fruits of the earth that the joy of harvest became proverbial for extreme gladness (Is. ix. 3, cf. xvi. 10, Ps. iv. 7).

13. *Gird yourselves* with sackcloth. The verb here is used elliptically as in Is. xxxii. 11; contrast Jer. iv. 8, vi. 26.

lament. The use of this Heb. word in Is. xxxii. 12 suggests that, like the Greek κόπτομαι and the Latin *plango*, it originally implied the beating of the breast, though it came to mean no more than the utterance of doleful cries (Jer. iv. 8, 2 Zech. xii. 10).

ye ministers of the altar. Cf. Ezek. xlv. 4 (*the ministers of the sanctuary*), xlvi. 24 (*the ministers of the house*).

lie all night. Their intercession is not to be suspended through need for repose.

ye ministers of my God. The LXX. has *ye ministers of God*, which, in view of *your God* at the end of the *v.*, is preferable.

14—20. An exhortation urging an appeal to God to relieve the distress occasioned by the locust-plague and an accompanying drought.

14. *Sanctify a fast.* The command is addressed to the priests. The verb *to sanctify*, used in connection with fasts, gatherings of the people (ii. 16), and war (iii. 9), implies that with all these things there was associated the idea of consecration (see p. 24), though the verb, in such contexts, practically means "to institute, set on foot." Fasting was

[1] See Toy, *Prov.* p. 462.

a fast, call a solemn assembly, gather the ¹old men *and* all the inhabitants of the land unto the house of the LORD your God, and cry unto the LORD. 15 Alas for the day! for the day of the LORD is at hand, and as destruction from ²the Almighty shall it

¹ Or, *elders*　　　　　　² Heb. *Shaddai*.

probably at first a *means* of sanctification, whereby religious devotees prepared themselves for the reception of sacred food (such as the flesh of a totem animal). At a more developed stage of belief it was a natural expression of penitential humiliation; and as the Jewish religious system became increasingly organized, it passed into a formal act of self-mortification. Fasting on the part of individuals as a manifestation of humility and penitence is mentioned in 2 Sam. xii. 16, 1 Kgs. xxi. 27, Ez. x. 6, Neh. i. 4, and Dan. ix. 3; and general fasts are described in Jud. xx. 26, 1 Sam. vii. 6, 2 Ch. xx. 3, Ez. viii. 21, Jer. xxxvi. 9, etc. The anniversaries of national calamities were marked by fasts in post-exilic times (Zech. vii. 5); and the fasting enjoined on the Day of Atonement (Lev. xvi. 29) led to its being styled pre-eminently "the Fast" (Acts xxvii. 9).

a solemn assembly. The term ('ătsārah), though it could be applied to any gathering (Jer. ix. 2), usually denoted an assemblage for some religious purpose, such as might be held in connection with the worship not only of Jehovah (Is. i. 13) but also of other gods (2 Kgs. x. 20). It was specifically employed to designate gatherings of pilgrims on the concluding days of the feasts of Unleavened Bread (Dt. xvi. 8) and of Tabernacles (Lev. xxiii. 36, Num. xxix. 35; cf. Neh. viii. 18).

the house of the LORD your God. The LXX. lacks the name *Jehovah*, and *the house of your God* alone suits the metre (dimeters).

15. *the day of the LORD is at hand.* Cf. ii. 1, iii. 14. The same phrase occurs in several other prophecies; Is. xiii. 6, Ezek. xxx. 3, Ob. 15, Zeph. i. 7. See p. 78.

as destruction from the Almighty. Better (since there is an assonance in the original), *as destruction from the Destroyer* (Heb. *Shaddai*): cf. Is. xiii. 6. If there is any etymological connection between the Divine title *Shaddai* here used and the Heb. root *shādhadh*, "to destroy," the former eventually lost its sinister significance and came to mean *the Mighty* (Job xv. 25), whose power was employed for beneficent as well as for harmful purposes (Ps. xci. 1, Job xxii. 25, xxix. 5). In some passages in the O.T. it is attached as an adjective to *El* (God), as in Gen. xvii. 1, xliii. 14, xlviii. 3, etc.; and in other passages it is used alone as a personal name for the Deity (Num. xxiv. 4, 16, Ps. lxviii. 14, Job v. 17, etc.). It is also an element in the theophoric names *Zurishaddai* and *Ammishaddai* (Num. i. 6, 12). By the writer of the Priestly narrative (P), forming one of the strands of the Pentateuch, *El Shaddai* was regarded as the sole name for God known in pre-Mosaic times (Ex. vi. 3); and it was probably from the same point of view that it was used by the writer of Job (where it occurs thirty-one times). In

come. 16 Is not the meat cut off before our eyes, *yea*, joy and gladness from the house of our God? 17 The seeds ¹rot under their clods; the garners are laid desolate, the barns are broken

¹ Or, *shrivel*

addition to the derivation from *shādhadh*, which this passage suggests, other etymologies have been proposed: (1) the word *shēdh*, which in the O.T. means "demon" (Dt. xxxii. 17, Ps. cvi. 37), but which may once have meant "lord"; (2) the Assyrian *shadu*, "mountain," a title applied in the cuneiform inscriptions to the gods Bel and Asshur, and perhaps transferred by the Hebrews to Jehovah (cf. the use of "my rock," in Ps. xviii. 2, xxxi. 3, lxii. 6); (3) the Hebrew *shadh*, meaning "breast," but this, in spite of the name *Thaddæus*, seems highly improbable.

16. *the meat.* Better, *the food*, i.e. the materials for the Temple sacrifices (*vv.* 9, 13).

joy...of our God. The Hebrew feasts were originally agricultural festivals, the feast of Unleavened Bread marking the beginning of the harvest, that of Weeks the completion of the same, and that of In-gathering the close of the vintage, so that all were seasons of plenty and mirth. The early aspect of them became modified in later times, but was not obliterated.

17. *The seeds rot under their clods.* Perhaps better, *The grains* (of corn) *shrivel under their clods.* It seems to be implied that the locust-plague was accompanied by a severe drought (see *v.* 20), but this clause is of very uncertain meaning, for three of the four Heb. words only occur here. The last word, in particular (*meghrĕphōthēhem*), presents great difficulties; for it seems to be derived from *gāraph*, "to sweep or scrape away," and so should mean an implement like a broom, besom, or shovel; but the translation *the grains shrivel under their* (the hus-bandmen's) *shovels* yields a very indifferent sense. It is best to assume that there has been some textual corruption, and to substitute (with Sievers) *righbhēhem*, the term used for *clods* in Job xxi. 33, xxxviii. 38, translating as above. The LXX. has ἐσκίρτησαν δαμάλεις ἐπὶ ταῖς φάτναις αὐτῶν, which has been explained to mean *the calves stamp* (impatiently) *at their* (empty) *stalls.* The Greek δαμάλεις certainly represents *paroth* (in place of *pĕrudhoth*), and ταῖς φάτναις probably implies *riphthehem* (cf. Hab. iii. 17). But if ἐσκίρτησαν stands for *pāshu* (instead of *'ābhĕshu*), this means "frisk light-heartedly" (Mal. iv. 2 (Heb. iii. 20)), and the sense given to the prepos. is unusual; whilst the mention of the cattle here is premature (see *v.* 18). The Vulg. has *computuerunt iumenta* (*pĕrādhoth* for *pĕrudhoth*) *in stercore suo.*

the garners. The Heb. word ordinarily means *treasures*, but is some-times used as a compact expression for *treasure-houses* and must here have the transferred sense of *store-houses* (for grain): cf. 1 Ch. xxvii. 25, Neh. xiii. 12.

the barns. The Heb. word (*mammĕghuroth*) only occurs here, and is perhaps an accidental error for the plural of one which is found in Hag. ii. 19 (*meghurah*). The LXX. has ληνοί, but the Vulg. *apothecæ.*

down; for the corn is ¹withered. 18 How do the beasts groan!
the herds of cattle are perplexed, because they have no pasture;
yea, the flocks of sheep ²are made desolate. 19 O LORD, to thee do
I cry: for the fire hath devoured the ³pastures of the wilderness,
and the flame hath burned all the trees of the field. 20 Yea, the
beasts of the field pant unto thee: for the water brooks are dried
up, and the fire hath devoured the ³pastures of the wilderness.

¹ Or, *ashamed*   ² Or, *suffer punishment*   ³ Or, *folds*

are broken down. I.e. have become dilapidated through neglect (cf.
Prov. xxiv. 31), since there has been no grain requiring storage.

is withered. Or, *is abashed.* The LXX. has ἐξηράνθη; but the Vulgate,
confusum est.

18. *How do the beasts groan!* The LXX., translating from a slightly
different text, has τί ἀποθήσομεν ἑαυτοῖς—in the sense of *what shall we
put into them* (the stalls)?; and Bewer thinks this text preferable.

are perplexed. Perhaps better, *are at a loss.* The verb is used in Ex.
xiv. 3 of the confused movements of the Israelites in their escape from
Egypt; and here means that the cattle do not know where to turn for
pasturage. But the LXX. has ἔκλαυσαν, implying *bāchu* for *nābhōchu.*

yea, the flocks. Less pasture would suffice for sheep than would be
needed for cattle, but even the flocks cannot find enough.

are made desolate. Literally, *are made guilty* (*ne'shāmu*), which must
be understood to signify (as in the mg.), *suffer punishment.* But the
LXX. has ἠφανίσθησαν, and the Vulg. *disperierunt*, which probably
represent the ordinary term for *are made desolate* (*nāshammu*), i.e. are
famished (cf. Lam. iv. 5); and Wellhausen and others would substitute
this for the present Heb. text.

19. *to thee do I cry.* Only Jehovah, who sent the destruction (*v.* 15),
could avert it. Instead of the 1st pers. sing. Sievers, followed by
Bewer, would read the 3rd pers. plur., *they* (the beasts) *cry*: cf. *v.* 20.

the fire. The locusts and drought together had produced the same
effects as fire would have caused; cf. ii. 3.

the pastures of the wilderness. The word which the R.V. renders by
wilderness denotes uncultivated ground, suitable for the feeding of sheep.

20. *the beasts of the field.* I.e. the wild animals. Some of these,
though not dependent for food upon the vegetation destroyed by the
locusts, would require water, which the drought had exhausted.

pant unto thee. For the verb here used cf. Ps. xlii. 1: for the thought
cf. Job xxxviii. 41, Ps. cxlvii. 9.

the water brooks. The Heb. word, though applicable to natural
watercourses (see Ps. xlii. 1), seems strictly to denote artificial con-
duits (*runnels*), being most frequently employed by Ezekiel, who lived
in Babylonia.

and the fire, etc. These concluding words of *v.* 20 repeat part of
v. 19, and it has been proposed by Marti and others to omit them as
an accidental repetition: certainly without them there is more symmetry between this *v.* and the preceding.

Chapter II. 1—17.

II. 1 Blow ye the trumpet in Zion, and sound an alarm in my holy mountain; let all the inhabitants of the land tremble: for the day of the LORD cometh, for it is nigh at hand; 2 a day of darkness and gloominess, a day of clouds and thick darkness, as the dawn spread upon the mountains; a great people and a strong,

1—17. A summons addressed to the collective people to attend a service of intercession at the Temple, in the hope that Jehovah, in response to the prayers of His people, may refrain from punishing them further.

The opening *v.* is a command from Jehovah communicated through the prophet to the officials of the community; but the explanation of the need for it passes into a second description of the locust-plague, couched in even more alarming terms; so that the injunction of *v.* 1 is repeated in *v.* 15.

1. *the trumpet.* Strictly, *the horn* or *cornet.* Rams' horns, though employed to give martial signals (Jud. iii. 27, 2 Sam. ii. 28, xx. 1), were also used, especially in later times, in connection with religious functions, such as the Day of Atonement (Lev. xxv. 9): cf. Ps. xlvii. 5, lxxxi. 3, 2 Ch. xv. 14.

sound an alarm. The verb is commonly used of uttering martial, distressful, or joyful, *shouts* (Jud. vii. 21, 1 Sam. xvii. 52, Is. xv. 4, Mic. iv. 9, 1 Sam. iv. 5, Ps. xlvii. 1 (2)); but here means to "sound a blast" with a horn (as in Hos. v. 8), rousing the people to a sense of their situation.

my holy mountain. I.e. Zion (*v.* 15): cf. iii. 17, Is. xxvii. 13, 3 Is. lxv. 11, Ezek. xx. 40.

cometh. The tense in the original is a prophetic perfect: though *the day of Jehovah* has not yet fully come, the locusts are regarded as God's agents in initiating His judgment (*v.* 11).

for it is nigh at hand. The break between *v.* 1 and *v.* 2 should be neglected, and the text should run—*for nigh at hand is a day,* etc. The words *a day of darkness...thick darkness* are quoted from Zeph. i. 15 [b], and the clause here prefixed to them seems to be *extra metrum.* Though flights of locusts darken the sky (cf. Pliny, *HN.* xi. 29, *solem obumbrant*), the gloom here meant is not so much physical as mental, and implies conditions of alarm as great as that which an abnormal darkening of the sky might occasion (cf. Is. v. 30, viii. 22, Jer. xiii. 16, Am. v. 18).

2. *as the dawn,* etc. These words should be linked with the following (not with the preceding) sentence, for the quotation from Zephaniah ends at *thick darkness;* and the rendering should be, *As the dawn there is spread upon the mountains a great people and a strong* (cf. the LXX., ὡς ὄρθρος χυθήσεται ἐπὶ τὰ ὄρη λαὸς πολὺς καὶ ἰσχυρός). The dawn is usually a simile for relief from gloom or distress (Is. viii. 20,

there hath not been ever the like, neither shall be any more after them, even to the years of many generations. 3 A fire devoureth before them; and behind them a flame burneth: the land is as the garden of Eden before them, and behind them a desolate wilderness; yea, and none hath escaped them. 4 The appearance of them is as the appearance of horses; and as ¹horsemen, so do

¹ Or, *war-horses*

3 Is. lviii. 8); but here the comparison has in view the dimness (*diluculum*) produced on the horizon by the enormous numbers of approaching locusts. An American lady, in an article published in the *Times* of Sept. 15, 1916, writes of swarms observed at Beirut in Syria, "the steady sub-tropical sunlight was changed into a fluttering, uncertain, wavering half-dimness."

there hath not...the like. Similar rhetorical phrases occur in Ex. x. 6, 14, xi. 6, 2 Kgs. xviii. 5, xxiii. 25.

3. *A fire.* That locusts, by devouring the herbage, create all the appearance of a prairie fire is attested by many travellers. One, writing of experiences in Formosa, says, "Bamboo groves have been stripped of their leaves and left standing like saplings after a rapid bush fire.... And grass has been devoured, so that the bare ground appeared as if burned" (quoted by Driver from the *Standard*, Dec. 25, 1896).

the garden of Eden. This is a compressed phrase for *the garden of Jehovah* (or *of God*) *in Eden* (see Gen. ii. 8, and cf. Gen. xiii. 10, 2 Is. li. 3, Ezek. xxxi. 8, 9). The converse of the transformation here described is contemplated in Ezek. xxxvi. 35. Eden was seemingly the alluvial plain (Assyrian, *edinu*) watered by the Tigris and Euphrates, wherein the legendary garden of Jehovah was believed to be situated. But the LXX., here as in some other places, connects it with a word meaning "delight," and renders *the garden of Eden* by παράδεισος τρυφῆς.

none hath escaped them. The strict sense (in view of 2 Sam. xv. 14) must be *nothing of it* (the land, regarded as masc., cf. Gen. xiii. 6) *hath escaped.* The Heb. expression, which is commonly used in connection with human beings (ii. 32 (Heb. iii. 5), Ob. 17, Is. iv. 2), is here applied to vegetation, as in Ex. x. 5. The American lady previously quoted says of the young broods of locusts, "They do not fly, but like armies of large black ants, they marched across the sandy plain until they reached the first field. There they stopped to eat, and never moved until every plant had been stripped. Herbs, bushes, and trees were left naked, robbed even of the bark."

4. *as the appearance of horses.* Compare Rev. ix. 7. The resemblance between the head of a locust and that of a horse is confirmed by other observers, and is reflected in the Italian word *cavallette* and the German name for a grasshopper, *Heupferd.*

as horsemen. Better (as in the mg.), *as war-horses.* The Heb. term is ambiguous, but the parallelism and the converse comparison in Job xxxix. 20 favour the mg., though the LXX. has ὡς ἱππεῖς.

they run. 5 Like the noise of chariots on the tops of the mountains do they leap, like the noise of a flame of fire that devoureth
the stubble, as a strong people set in battle array. 6 At their
presence the peoples are in anguish: all faces are waxed pale.
7 They run like mighty men; they climb the wall like men of
war; and they march every one on his ways, and they break not

5. *Like the noise of chariots.* Better, *As with the noise of chariots*;
cf. Rev. ix. 9. The noise caused by flights of locusts is widely attested.
Pliny, for example (*HN.* x. 29), states, *tanto volant pennarum stridore
ut aliæ alites credantur*; and the sound has been compared to the
dashing of water occasioned by a mill-wheel, to the roar of a cataract,
to the noise of wind blowing through trees, and to the tramp of armed
hosts.

leap. The verb in Heb. ordinarily means "to dance" (Job xxi. 11),
but is also used of the "jumping" of chariots, when rapidly driven
(Nah. iii. 2).

like the noise of a flame, etc. This comparison has been thought to
illustrate the sound of the locusts' mandibles in the process of eating:
an American entomologist (quoted by Driver) likens the sound to "the
crackling of a prairie fire."

as a strong people. The LXX. has ὡς λαὸς πολὺς καὶ ἰσχυρός (as in
v. 2), and the additional adjective makes this clause agree metrically
with the preceding clauses, which are pentameters.

6. *the peoples are in anguish.* This is explicable from the prospect
of the scarcity of food that so frequently attends the ravages of locusts.

are waxed pale. Literally, *gather* (or *collect*) *colour*; but it is doubtful
whether this means "to contract" (or "withdraw") colour, and so "to
grow pale"; or "to accumulate" colour, and so "to flush" (with excite-
ment). Perhaps the latter is the more probable (cf. Is. xiii. 8), for
a different verb (*'āsaph*, not *kibbets*) is used for "to withdraw": see
v. 10, iii. 15.

7. *They run like mighty men.* Thomson, *The Land and the Book*,
p. 297, describes locusts as coming on "like a disciplined army"; and
Morier (quoted by Henderson) says, "They moved in one body, which
had the appearance of being organized by a leader."

they climb the wall. Morier (*sup.*) writes, "They entered the inmost
recesses of the houses, were found in every corner, stuck to our clothes,
and infested our food."

they break not their ranks. The sense of the Hebrew seems to be
they do not entangle their tracks, each keeps his own course; but the
verb elsewhere signifies "to take, or lend, on pledge," and from this
the meaning required here is not easily obtained. If the text is to be
kept, probably a different root must be assumed. But the LXX. has
οὐ μὴ ἐκκλίνωσιν τὰς τρίβους αὐτῶν, and conjectural emendations based
on this are, *they do not make crooked,* or *they do not turn aside, their
tracks* (of which the first seems the better).

their ranks. 8 Neither doth one thrust another; they march every one in his path: and [1]they burst through the weapons, and [2]break not off *their course.* 9 They leap upon the city; they run upon the wall; they climb up into the houses; they enter in at the windows like a thief. 10 The earth quaketh before them; the

[1] Or, *when they fall around the weapons, they &c.*
[2] Or, *are not wounded*

8. *every one in his path.* Literally, *each on his highway,* as if he had a road defined for himself alone. Jerome (quoted by Henderson), referring to the order maintained by the locusts even in their flight, writes "tanto ordine...volitant ut instar tesserularum, quæ in pavimentis artificis figuntur manu, suum locum teneant, et ne puncto quidem, ut ita dicam, ungueve transverso declinent ad alterum."

they burst through the weapons. This rendering, in view of the context, is preferable to that of the mg. (where *fall around* seems to mean "alight among"). The verb employed can be used of violent assaults, "fall upon" (see Is. xvi. 9); and here implies that the locusts fling themselves through (or between) the weapons with which men vainly try to oppose their march. The Heb. noun for weapon (*shelah*), here used collectively, strictly means a missile, and occurs only in late writings like Job (xxxiii. 18), Chronicles (2 Ch. xxxii. 5), and Nehemiah (iv. 17 (11)). In 2 Ch. xxiii. 10 it replaces the more ordinary term for weapon (*cĕlī*) employed in the parallel passage 2 Kgs. xi. 11. Even modern measures for staying the progress of locusts are very often ineffectual. The lady whose description has already been drawn upon writes: "Hedges of thorn and bramble were built round the fields....At the thorny barricade they (the locusts) immediately began to climb and creep through. Then the owners of the field, when the whole hedge was filled with young locusts, set fire to it. Millions of insects were destroyed in that way, but myriads were moving on behind, creeping over the smouldering branches and bodies, burning up themselves, leaving room for the next. New thorn branches were thrown down and burnt up again, but the brambles gave out long before the locusts did." Recently in South Africa arsenic has been used in attempts to destroy them.

9. *They leap upon the city.* The Heb. verb in strictness means that the locusts swarm round about the city (Jerusalem), eagerly seeking ingress: the same word (*shākak*) describes the "ranging" bear in Prov. xxviii. 15.

enter in at the windows. Cf. Ex. x. 6. The writer has in mind latticed, unglazed, windows. It is said that in 1869 many inhabitants of Nazareth had to abandon their houses in consequence of the locusts.

10. *The earth quaketh,* etc. The language, like that of *v.* 2, is not to be understood literally, but describes conventionally how the plague of locusts occasioned all the terror associated with earthquake or eclipse; see p. lx.

heavens tremble: the sun and the moon are darkened, and the stars withdraw their shining: 11 and the LORD uttereth his voice before his army; for his camp is very great; for he is strong that executeth his word: for the day of the LORD is great and very terrible; and who can abide it? 12 Yet even now, saith the LORD, turn ye unto me with all your heart, and with fasting, and with weeping, and with mourning: 13 and rend your heart, and not your garments, and turn unto the LORD your God: for he is gracious and full of compassion, slow to anger, and plenteous in

the heavens tremble. The sky is regarded as a solid vault: cf. 2 Sam. xxii. 8 (= Ps. xviii. 7), Is. xiii. 13.

the sun and the moon, etc. Cf. Is. xiii. 10, Ezek. xxxii. 7, Mt. xxiv. 29, Rev. vi. 12.

11. *uttereth his voice.* I.e. thunders (Ps. xviii. 13). Thunder is generally a feature in O.T. descriptions of awe-inspiring scenes; see Ex. xix. 16.

his army. The locusts are viewed as Jehovah's agents of vengeance.

his camp. The Heb. for *camp* can be used of an army on the march; see Josh. viii. 13, x. 5, Jud. iv. 15, 2 Kgs. iii. 9.

for the day, etc. See *v.* 21 and Mal. iv. 5. Instead of *very terrible* the LXX. has ἐπιφανὴς σφόδρα and the Old Latin *manifestus nimium,* implying *nōdha'* for *nōrā'.* But Sym. has ἐπίφοβος.

who can abide it? The passage shows the influence of Mal. iii. 2: cf. Jer. x. 10.

12. *Yet even now.* I.e. in spite of the dreadful prospect, there yet may be a possibility, through a change in the people's disposition and conduct, of prevailing upon Jehovah to withhold the worst. *Yet* is literally *and* : cf. p. 63.

with all your heart. I.e. resolutely (cf. 1 Sam. vii. 3, 1 Kgs. viii. 48), the *heart* amongst the Hebrews being regarded as the seat of the will as well as of the intelligence (p. 69): cf. Ex. xxxv. 5, *of a willing* (literally, *free*) *heart.*

fasting...weeping...mourning. The same combination occurs in Esth. iv. 3.

13. *and rend your heart,* etc. This exhortation shows that the prophet, whilst enjoining the outward tokens of contrition, had no defective sense of the need of inward penitence: cf. Jer. iv. 4.

and not your garments. I.e. not your garments only. Tearing the apparel (Gen. xxxvii. 29, 34, Josh. vii. 6, 1 Sam. iv. 12, 1 Kgs. xxi. 27), like tearing the hair and beard (Ez. ix. 3), was, no doubt, originally an uncontrollable act, giving relief to intense emotion; but eventually came to be a conventional expression of humiliation and self-abasement.

gracious and full of compassion. This order of the Heb. words is commonest in late writings (2 Ch. xxx. 9, Neh. ix. 17, 31, Ps. cxi. 4, cxii. 4,

mercy, and repenteth him of the evil. 14 Who knoweth whether he will not turn and repent, and leave a blessing behind him, even a meal offering and a drink offering unto the LORD your God?

15 Blow the trumpet in Zion, sanctify a fast, call a solemn assembly; 16 gather the people, sanctify the congregation, assemble the ¹old men, gather the children, and those that suck the breasts: let the bridegroom go forth of his chamber, and the bride out of her closet. 17 Let the priests, the ministers of the LORD, weep between the porch and the altar, and let them say, Spare thy

¹ Or, *elders*

cxlv. 8). The reverse order occurs in the early passage Ex. xxxiv. 6 (JE), and is preserved in Ps. lxxxvi. 15, ciii. 8.

and repenteth him. Better, *and repentant*, for, like the preceding phrase, this describes a permanent feature of character¹.

14. *and repent.* God relents when man repents: cf. Jonah iii. 9.

leave a blessing. I.e. leave some surviving portion of the products of the soil, now exposed to complete destruction. For *blessing* in a concrete sense cf. Gen. xxxiii. 11, Josh. xv. 19, Jud. i. 15, etc.

15. *Blow*, etc. The command of *v.* 1 is here resumed and expanded. *a solemn assembly.* See on i. 14. The Heb. word etymologically seems to mean a concourse *confined* within a limited space.

16. *sanctify the congregation.* The sanctification of the people, as a preliminary to their approaching near to the Deity or to sacred things, consisted during early times in ablutions, in a change of apparel, and in abstention from conjugal relations; see Gen. xxxv. 2, Ex. xix. 10, 15, 2 Kgs. x. 20—22, 1 Sam. xxi. 4, 5. The word *congregation*, though used to denote an assemblage in general, was specially employed to designate the community of Israel, which was Jehovah's assembly (Mic. ii. 5, Num. xvi. 3); the LXX. here renders it by ἐκκλησία.

the old men. This is preferable to *the elders* of the mg.: see on i. 2.

the bridegroom. The exemption from public duties ordinarily granted to newly married persons (Dt. xx. 5) was on this occasion to be suspended.

chamber...closet. These words must here be synonyms for the bridal pavilion (Ps. xix. 5, 2 Sam. xvi. 22).

17. *the porch.* The existence of this in connection with the first Temple is specifically mentioned (1 Kgs. vi. 3, vii. 19); and it was probably reproduced in the second Temple, particulars of which are largely wanting. The position of the porch was at the east end of the main structure.

the altar. I.e. the altar of burnt offering in the open forecourt extending eastwards in front of the Temple buildings.

---

¹ Joel ii. 13 forms one of the introductory sentences prefixed in the Prayer Book to the Order for Morning and Evening Prayer.

people, O LORD, and give not thine heritage to reproach, that the nations should ¹rule over them: wherefore should they say among the peoples, Where is their God?

¹ Or, *use a byword against them*

give not thine heritage to reproach. The phrase *to give to reproach* recurs only in Jer. xxiv. 9, xxix. 18, Ezek. v. 14. For the conception of Israel as Jehovah's heritage see p. 63: Israel is similarly described as Jehovah's peculiar treasure (Ex. xix. 5, Dt. vii. 6, Ps. cxxxv. 4).

rule over them. Better (as in the mg.), *use a byword against them.* The verb (*māshal*) is of ambiguous meaning, and, when employed elsewhere with the preposition here used, uniformly signifies *to rule over* (cf. Gen. iii. 16, iv. 7, xxiv. 2, etc.); and such is the sense given to it in this passage by the LXX. (τοῦ κατάρξαι αὐτῶν ἔθνη) and the Vulg. (*ut dominentur eis nationes*). This, however, is incompatible with the context, which contemplates not the rule but the railing of foreigners, and requires the other sense—*to make proverbs* (or *bywords*) *concerning*; though with this signification the verb ordinarily takes not the preposition that appears here (*bĕ*) but others (see Ezek. xvii. 2, xviii. 2).

wherefore should they say, etc. The attention of Jehovah is called to the possibility of His power being disparaged by the heathen (cf. Mic. vii. 10) through the misfortunes of His people, in order that He may thereby be induced to vindicate both Himself and them ¹.

CHAPTER II. 18—27.

This section, constituting the second of the three parts of the book, represents Jehovah's response to the prayer of His penitent people. He promises to remove the locusts, to end the drought, and to renew the vegetation that has been destroyed. It is left to be understood that the exhortation in ii. 12—17 had been acted upon, and that the people's repentance was sincere, influencing Jehovah to stay the further execution of His judgment upon them, and to restore fertility to the wasted land.

18 Then was the LORD jealous for his land, and had pity on his

18—20. These *vv.* describe a change in Jehovah's attitude consequent upon His people's penitence, and convey assurances that He will undo the evil that He has inflicted.

18. *jealous.* The Heb. word is used in two connections, where (1) *jealous* and (2) *zealous* seem to be respectively the best equivalents. The emotions implied are represented as roused in Jehovah (1) by Israel's offences against Himself, especially their worship of other gods; (2) by their sufferings at the hands of their enemies: see for (1) Ex. xx. 5, xxxiv. 14, Josh. xxiv. 19, and for (2) Is. ix. 7, xxxvii. 32, Ezek.

---

¹ In the Prayer Book Joel ii. 12—17 forms the Epistle for Ash Wednesday.

people. 19 And the LORD answered and said unto his people, Behold, I will send you corn, and wine, and oil, and ye shall be satisfied therewith: and I will no more make you a reproach among the nations: 20 but I will remove far off from you the northern *army*, and will drive him into a land barren and desolate, ¹his forepart ²into the eastern sea, and his hinder part

¹ Or, *with his forepart*   ² Or, *toward*

xxxvi. 5, Zech. i. 14, viii. 2. Pusey regards the tenses in this and the next *v.* as futures (*will...be jealous..., (will) pity,...will answer and say*); but the Heb. construction continues the perfect tenses in *vv.* 10, 11. The LXX. rightly has ἐζήλωσεν...ἐφείσατο...ἀπεκρίθη...εἶπεν.

19. *make you a reproach.* The phrase differs slightly from that employed in *v.* 17, and recurs in Ezek. xxii. 4, Ps. lxxviii. 66.

20. *the northern* army. Literally, *the northerner* (LXX. τὸν ἀπὸ βορρᾶ, Vulg. *eum qui ab Aquilone est*). Since locusts usually enter Palestine from the S.E., this expression has embarrassed the interpretation of Joel. It must, however (as the rest of the *v.* shews), refer to the locusts; and instances have occurred of their presence in Syria, whence a north wind would carry them into Palestine. But the epithet cannot imply such an accidental association with the north as this; and as a standing attributive, if understood to mean that their home and breeding-ground was north of Palestine, it would be false (p. liv). Hence the use of it here must be explained differently, namely, through associations that had gathered round *the day of Jehovah.* It had been predicted by Jeremiah that evil would come to Judah from the north (i. 14, x. 22), and Babylon, which proved to be the agent of Jehovah's judgment, is represented by both Jeremiah (xvi. 15, xxiii. 8) and Zechariah (ii. 6, 7) as in the *north*, though really it was situated as regards Palestine almost due E. Similarly Ezekiel represents Gog, whose invading hordes comprise several nations lying to the south or south-west of the Holy Land (such as Ethiopia and Libya), as destined to advance against Judah from the uttermost parts of the *north* (xxxix. 1, 2). Thus that quarter would naturally come to be regarded as the direction whence the executors of Divine judgments were generally to be looked for; and eventually, by a usage common to all languages, the word *northerner* could discard its etymological sense and be employed to denote any agency bringing danger or calamity, whether it came from the geographical north or not. Accordingly, the word here, as applied to the locusts, has not a local but a symbolical significance. It is probable that the original reason why the north came to be regarded by the Jews as the quarter whence evil would issue is to be found in the situation, relative to Judah, of its great oppressor (in the 8th cent.) Assyria, which, though in strictness N.E. of Palestine, could be loosely considered to lie to the N. of it (cf. Is. xiv. 31, Zeph. ii. 13).

and desolate. The rhythm would be improved by the omission of this adjective, which is absent from the LXX.; but as the latter begins the

¹into the western sea; and his stink shall come up, and his ill savour shall come up, because he hath done great things. 21 Fear not, O land, be glad and rejoice; for the LORD hath done great things. 22 Be not afraid, ye beasts of the field; for the pastures of the wilderness do spring, for the tree beareth her fruit, the fig

¹ Or, *toward*

next clause with a verb (καὶ ἀφανιῶ), probably (as Bewer suggests) it had virtually the same Hebrew, but read it differently.

his forepart, etc. The swarm of locusts is assumed to be stretched across the country, so that whilst the central body was to be driven into the southern desert (whence presumably they had really come), the extremities would be cast into the Dead Sea and the Mediterranean. The eastern flank of the swarm is called the *forepart* and the western *the hinder part* because the front and back of anything were, in the view of the Hebrews, the sides which severally faced, or extended towards, the east and west.

the eastern sea...the western sea. Literally, *the front sea* (Ezek. xlvii. 18) and *the hinder sea* (Dt. xi. 24, xxxiv. 2).

his stink...his ill savour. The tautology of these two clauses and a syntactical irregularity, if the second is rendered *and his ill savour shall come up*¹, favour the conclusion that the word translated *stink* (which is an ordinary term) is a gloss on the rare word (*tsahănah*) rendered *ill savour*, which only recurs in the Hebrew fragments of Ecclus. (xi. 12). The second half of the verse will then be reduced to *that his ill savour may come up*, which is what the syntax demands.

because he...great things. These words, if authentic, must be equivalent to "because he hath acted overweeningly" (or "hath magnified himself"; cf. Lam. i. 9, Ps. xxxv. 26). The representation of the locusts as acting (like human beings) arrogantly is not impossible in a context which describes them after the manner of a host of men; but the resemblance of the expression to that used of *Jehovah* immediately afterwards (*v.* 21, cf. Ps. cxxvi. 2, 3) makes it difficult to think it genuine here: it looks like an accidental dittograph, which should be omitted. The offensive exhalations arising from immense quantities of drowned locusts have been noticed by historians and travellers both ancient and modern.

21—24. These *vv.*, which assume that the promises of *vv.* 19 and 20 have been fulfilled, constitute a short ode, in which the prophet exhorts the people to be grateful to the God who has given them relief.

21. *O land.* Better, *O ground* (the Heb. being not *'erets* but *'ădhāmah*).

22. *of the wilderness.* Better, *of the prairie* (cf. p. 96).

do spring. Better, *put forth grass*; cf. Gen. i. 11.

for the tree, etc. Here the writer seems to pass from the beasts that

¹ See Driver, *Heb. Tenses*, § 175 obs.; Davidson, *Heb. Syntax*, § 64, Rem. 6.

tree and the vine do yield their strength. 23 Be glad then, ye
children of Zion, and rejoice in the LORD your God: for he giveth
you the former rain ¹in just measure, and he causeth to come
down for you the rain, the former rain and the latter rain, ²in

¹ Or, *in* (or *for*) *righteousness*   ² Or, *at the first*

graze in the pastures to men, who make more use of the fruits of trees
than do most animals.

their strength. I.e. all that they are capable of producing: cf. Gen.
iv. 12.

23. *the former rain.* This term (*hammōreh*, cf. Ps. lxxxiv. 6 (7))
denotes the rain that falls at the beginning of the agricultural year in
November; but a general rather than a specific term would be most
appropriate here. Possibly there is some textual corruption: if so, it
may be suggested that the expression should be replaced by *copiousness*
of water (*hā-rĕvāyah*). The LXX. has τὰ βρώματα, and Vollers, in consequence, has proposed *habbiryah*, "food," which the LXX. translates
by βρῶμα in 2 Sam. xiii. 5, 7, 10; but mention of food in this place
seems premature, for the crops have still to grow. Sym. has τὸν
ὑποδεικνύοντα (cf. the Vulg. quoted in the next note).

in just measure. Better, *faithfully*, since a literal translation is
according to (Jehovah's) *righteousness*, i.e. His faithfulness to His
promises: cf. Dt. xxviii. 11, 12. For this sense of the Heb. word cf.
2 Is. xlii. 6, xlv. 13, Zech. viii. 8. But it is also possible to render (with
the mg.) *for* (i.e. as a token of) *righteousness*; the irrigation of the
springing crops and the promise of abundance would be evidence to the
world that the people were no longer counted offenders by their God.
The Heb. rendered in the R.V. by *the former rain in just measure* is
translated in the Vulg. (against the context) by *doctorem iustitiæ*, the
word *moreh* having the signification of *teacher* in Prov. v. 13, Is. xxx. 20,
Hab. ii. 18, and the prepos. *lĕ* being taken to express the gen.

the rain. The term (*geshem*) here used has a comprehensive sense, as
in Lev. xxvi. 4, Ezek. xxxiv. 26, Am. iv. 7.

the former rain. See above. This and the following word are perhaps
explanatory insertions: their omission would improve the rhythm of the *v.*

the latter rain. This term (Heb. *malkōsh*) denotes the spring rain in
March and April, which falls shortly before harvest, when its value is
very great (see Job xxix. 23, Prov. xvi. 15).

in the first month. This rendering of the Heb. (*bārī'shōn*) can be
justified by Gen. viii. 13, Num. ix. 5, Ezek. xxix. 17, xlv. 18; but if
the text is sound, it must refer to the season of the *latter rain* only,
for the first month (of the ecclesiastical year) was Nisan, corresponding
to our March—April when the late (or spring) rain fell. The LXX.,
however, has καθὼς ἔμπροσθεν and the Vulgate *sicut in principio* (implying
cārī'shōnah)—*as at the first* (cf. Dt. ix. 18, Dan. xi. 29), i.e. the previous
happier conditions are to be restored. Another variant (*bārī'shōnah*) is
implied by the R.V. mg., *at the first* (better, *first of all*, cf. 1 Kgs.

the first *month*. 24 And the floors shall be full of wheat, and the fats shall overflow with wine and oil. 25 And I will restore to you the years that [1] the locust hath eaten, the cankerworm, and the caterpiller, and the palmerworm, my great army which I sent among you. 26 And ye shall eat in plenty and be satisfied, and shall praise the name of the LORD your God, that hath dealt wondrously with you: and my people shall never be ashamed. 27 And ye shall know that I am in the midst of Israel, and that I am the LORD your God, and there is none else: and my people shall never be ashamed.

[1] See ch. i. 4.

xvii. 13), i.e. the material blessings promised in *vv.* 19—27 will precede the gift of the spirit mentioned in *v.* 28.

24. *the floors.* These, used in threshing, consisted of a space of ground, beaten hard, upon which the ears of corn (for the length of stalk cut was very short) were spread in a layer. One method of threshing was to drag over the ears a heavy sledge (i.e. a board, roughened on the under-side with pieces of sharp stone), which pressed out the grain and chopped the straw into chaff, the latter being afterwards winnowed away[1]. For another process see p. 37.

fats. An archaism for *vats.* The vat (*yekebh*) was a small but relatively deep trough hewn in the rock (Is. v. 2 mg.) at a lower level than the wider but shallower winepress (*gath*), and was designed to receive the juice flowing from the grapes trodden in the press. The LXX. distinguishes them as ὑπολήνιον and ληνός respectively. The word rendered *vat* is sometimes used irregularly for the winepress (Job xxiv. 11, Is. xvi. 10), and the LXX. here has οἱ ληνοί.

with...oil. Presses and vats were also used in the extraction of oil from olives (see Mic. vi. 15), a circumstance of which the name *Gethsemane* (oil-press) is a reminder.

25. *And I*, etc. The utterance of Jehovah, interrupted at *v.* 21, is here continued.

the years...eaten. I.e. the equivalent of the produce destroyed in the past years.

26. *praise.* The verb here used is characteristic of the Psalms (lxxiv. 21, cxlviii. 5), and seems to be one peculiarly associated with the Temple worship.

27. *that I am...Israel.* The changed condition of the land would be an effectual reply to the mocking challenge in *v.* 17. Israel here stands for Judah: see iii. 2, 16, and cf. Mic. vi. 2.

I am the LORD your God. Better, *I am JEHOVAH your God.* The phrase occurs in Ezek. xx. 5, 7, 19, etc., and is exceedingly frequent in the Priestly code of the Pentateuch (Ex. vi. 7, xvi. 12, Lev. xviii. 2, etc.).

[1] See Driver, *Joel and Amos*, p. 227.

there is none else. The thought, expressed in more than one form, is characteristic of, though not confined to, Deutero-Isaiah (see 2 Is. xlv. 5, 6, 14, etc., xlvi. 9); and its occurrence here is perhaps due to the influence of that prophet's writings.

and my people...ashamed. This sentence repeats the conclusion of *v.* 26, and as its presence here weakens the emphasis which the preceding clause in this *v.* requires, it should probably be omitted as an accidental duplicate. Wellhausen and others, on the contrary, propose the omission of the final clause in *v.* 26.

CHAPTERS II. 28—III. 21.

With ii. 28 begins the third section of the book, extending to the end. This has in view a sequel to the predictions (in ii. 19—27) of the material blessings which are about to be conferred on God's people; for the return of plenty is to be followed by the bestowal of spiritual gifts also, whilst ensuing upon this will occur the advent of Jehovah's day of judgment. Of that Day the devastation of the land by the locusts had previously been regarded as a preliminary phase, presaging a fuller outbreak of Divine resentment upon the Jews in the near future; but from the terrors of it they, in consequence of the moral change in them, will be delivered, and the Divine judgment will be confined to the heathen for their malice towards the Jews. In the Hebrew the section ii. 28—32 constitutes ch. iii.

28 And it shall come to pass afterward, that I will pour out my spirit upon all flesh; and your sons and your daughters

28—32. A prediction of the descent upon all ages and classes amongst the Jewish people of God's spirit, followed by signs of Jehovah's Day, when destruction, from which the true worshippers of Jehovah will escape, is to overwhelm the heathen.

28. *afterward.* This, rendered in Acts ii. 17 by ἐν ταῖς ἐσχάταις ἡμέραις, is virtually equivalent to *in the latter* (or *the sequel of*) *days* (Mic. iv. 1): cf. Jer. xlviii. 47 with xlix. 6.

I will pour out. The same verb is used in connection with the Divine Spirit in Ezek. xxxix. 29, 2 Zech. xii. 10; and the like physical metaphor is employed of the manifestation of such impalpable realities as anger (Hos. v. 10, Ezek. xiv. 19) and contempt (Job xii. 21). So in Greek Homer uses χέω in connection with ὕπνος and even κάλλος (*Od.* II. 395, XXIII. 156).

my spirit. God's Spirit is represented alike as the origin of all life (Job xxxiii. 4, Ps. civ. 30), as the cause of the transformation of nature (Is. xxxii. 15) and of the reformation of man (Ezek. xxxvi. 27), and as the source of all exceptional human faculties, whether physical (Jud. xiv. 6), artistic (Ex. xxxv. 31), intellectual, or moral (Mic. iii. 8, Is. xi. 2), but especially of prophetic ecstasy (Num. xi. 25 f., 1 Sam. x. 6, 10). Here it is promised that the psychical endowments and emotional out-

shall prophesy, your old men shall dream dreams, your young
men shall see visions: 29 and also upon the servants and
upon the handmaids in those days will I pour out my spirit.
30 And I will shew wonders in the heavens and in the earth,
blood, and fire, and pillars of smoke. 31 The sun shall be turned
into darkness, and the moon into blood, before the great and

bursts, hitherto confined to a few individuals, constituting them seers
and prophets, will be extended to all classes, even the humblest. Cf.
Num. xi. 29, 3 Is. lix. 21.

all flesh. The expression, which is sometimes inclusive of all living
creatures (Gen. vi. 17, Lev. xvii. 14, Num. xviii. 15) and sometimes
limited to mankind (Gen. vi. 12, 13, Num. xvi. 22, Dt. v. 26, 2 Is.
xlix. 26), is here confined to Jews only (as the words *your sons and your
daughters* shew): cf. Ezek. xxxix. 29.

prophesy. The term here probably has in view the utterance of fervid
and rapturous language under the influence of powerful religious emotion, as illustrated by the narratives in Num. xi. 25—27, 1 Sam. x. 5,
6, 10, xix. 24.

dreams...visions. These were usual, but not the sole, channels whereby
God was believed to communicate with His prophets and others (Num.
xii. 6; cf. 1 Sam. xxviii. 6, 15, Dt. xiii. 3, Jer. xxiii. 25—28, 2 Zech.
xiii. 4, Dan. vii. 1).

young men. I.e. men of military age, actual or potential warriors
(Jud. xiv. 10, Is. ix. 17, 2 Kgs. viii. 12).

29. *the servants.* The LXX. has τοὺς δούλους μου.

30. *wonders.* Perhaps better, *portents*, extraordinary occurrences
suggestive of Divine action, or of the nearness of the Divine presence:
cf. Ex. vii. 3, xi. 9, Dt. vi. 22, Ps. cv. 5. By such the Day of Jehovah
is to be ushered in.

blood...fire...smoke. It is not quite clear whether the portents here
mentioned are celestial or terrestrial. They may be blood-red, fiery, and
lurid appearances in the sky and atmosphere (the *pillars of smoke* being
suggested by the columns of dust and sand raised by whirlwinds), or
they may be accompaniments of war—carnage, the firing of towns, and
the columns of smoke rising from the conflagrations. In the latter case
the parallelism with the first half of the *v.* is inverted, see p. cxxxv.

31. *The sun shall be turned,* etc. Cf. Is. xiii. 10. The language is
taken from the phenomena of eclipses, but it is not so much the
phenomena themselves as the alarm attending them that the writer
wishes to call before the mind: cf. p. lx. The passage has influenced
Rev. vi. 12. Cf. Lucan, *Phars.* I. 539—542, *Iam Phœbe...subita per-
cussa expalluit umbra. Ipse caput medio Titan cum ferret Olympo,
Condidit ardentes atra caligine currus Involvitque orbem tenebris.*

before the great...come. The phraseology is identical with that of
Mal. iv. 5 (iii. 23). For *terrible* the LXX. has ἐπιφανῆ: cf. ii. 11.

terrible day of the LORD come. 32 And it shall come to pass, that
whosoever shall call on the name of the LORD shall be delivered:

32. *whosoever shall call on the name*, etc. Strictly, the Heb. means
whoso shall call with the name of Jehovah: the same phrase occurs in
Gen. iv. 26, xii. 8, Jer. x. 25, Zeph. iii. 9. The invocation of a deity by
his name was believed to exert an influence upon him, so that it was
often deemed expedient to keep the name from the knowledge of those
who might use it to the detriment of his true worshippers. It was for
this reason that the name of the tutelary deity of Rome is alleged to
have been wrapped in mystery, lest, through its becoming known to an
enemy, the safety of the city should be imperilled[1]. The persons
designated by the phrase here employed are the Jews collectively; but
in Rom. x. 13 St Paul, quoting from the LXX., adduces the words πᾶς
ὃς ἂν ἐπικαλέσηται τὸ ὄνομα Κυρίου σωθήσεται in support of his contention
that God is merciful to all who call upon Him, whether Jews or Gentiles.

Verses 28—32ᵃ were quoted by St Peter at Pentecost (Acts ii. 17—21).
The Apostle (or his reporter) used a Greek version, but the quotation
deviates in some respects from the LXX. The differences are as follows:

Joel (LXX.).	Acts.
(a) μετὰ ταῦτα καὶ	(a) ἐν ταῖς ἐσχάταις ἡμέραις
(b) οἱ πρεσβύτεροι ὑμῶν ἐνύπνια ἐν-υπνιασθήσονται καὶ οἱ νεανίσκοι ὑμῶν ὁράσεις ὄψονται.	(b) οἱ νεανίσκοι ὑμῶν ὁράσεις ὄψονται καὶ οἱ πρεσβύτεροι ὑμῶν ἐνυπνίοις ἐν-υπνιασθήσονται.
(c) καὶ	(c) καί γε
(d) τὰς δούλας	(d) τὰς δούλας μου
(e) ἐκχεῶ ἀπὸ τοῦ πνεύματός μου	(e) ἐκχεῶ ἀπὸ τοῦ πνεύματός μου καὶ προφητεύσουσι
(f) ἐν τῷ οὐρανῷ	(f) ἐν τῷ οὐρανῷ ἄνω
(g) καὶ ἐπὶ τῆς γῆς.	(g) καὶ σημεῖα ἐπὶ τῆς γῆς κάτω.

The speaking with tongues at Pentecost, in which St Peter saw
a fulfilment of this prediction of Joel, was doubtless akin in nature to
the prophesying which is here in view (see on *v.* 28). Various passages
in the O.T. imply that in many cases "prophesying" meant wild and
uncontrolled speech resulting from religious rapture or enthusiasm, so
that a prophet was sometimes derided as a madman (see Hos. ix. 7,
Jer. xxix. 26, 2 Kgs. ix. 11); and that the utterances of the Christian
believers assembled at Pentecost were of a fervid and excited character
is suggested by the contemptuous observations made by some of those
that heard them (Acts ii. 13), whilst the comments passed by St Paul
upon the similar phenomena at Corinth point in the same direction
(1 Cor. xiv. 23). Probably the disciples, under the influence of religious
emotion, broke out into ecstatic speeches and exclamations, which were
only partially intelligible to many who were present. Into such utterances there might enter phrases, or even long passages, couched in

---

[1] The divinity in question is said to have been called *Valentia*, probably a
translation of the Greek Ῥώμη.

for in mount Zion and in Jerusalem there shall be those that
escape, as the LORD hath said, and ¹among the remnant those
whom the LORD doth call.

¹ Or, *in the remnant whom &c.*

languages or dialects not normally used by the speakers, their memory
and speech-centres being so stimulated by the stress of emotional feeling
as to recall and to repeat what had once been heard but had become
forgotten. Various parallels from the experience of religious revivals
in later times have been collected by A. Wright, *Some N.T. Problems*,
p. 297 f., and K. Lake, *The Earlier Epistles of St Paul*, p. 241 f. The
occurrence, in what was uttered, of some foreign words or expressions
would account for the impression produced on the multitude at Pentecost that the speakers were acquainted with foreign languages (Acts ii.
5—11), as well as for the need of an interpreter on other occasions
(such as St Paul alludes to, 1 Cor. xiv. 27). The feature in the incident
at Pentecost which led St Peter to see in it a fulfilment of the prophecy
of Joel was the *diffusion*, amongst the whole body of disciples, of such
a gift of "prophecy" as was ordinarily confined to a few chosen individuals; and the bestowal of this gift, in the light of the promise
made by Jesus (as reported in Lk. xxiv. 49), was regarded as proof of
His Messiahship (Acts ii. 33—36). But the most cogent evidence that
the early Christian believers were taken possession of by the Holy
Spirit was afforded not by any temporary outbursts of religious ecstasy
but by the permanent change that occurred in their characters, and by
their manifestation of the fruits of the Spirit, such as are enumerated
by St Paul in Gal. v. 22, 23.

for in mount Zion, etc. Jerusalem is to be the only place of safety
from the terrors of the Day of Jehovah. The phrase seems to be borrowed
from Ob. 17 (to which the words *as the LORD hath said* probably allude).

and among the remnant, etc. Better, *and among the remnant* (or
among the survivors) *there shall be those whom Jehovah doth call*. By
these are meant the Jews of the Dispersion, who will be summoned
from among the heathen to share the preservation ensured to their
fellow-countrymen who dwell in Zion. For the gathering of dispersed
Jews cf. Is. xi. 11, xxvii. 13, 2 Zech. x. 10, Jer. xxiii. 3, Ecclus. xxxvi.
11—14, 2 Macc. ii. 18. The heathen, in contrast to the Jews, are
reserved for vengeance (iii. 2). The final clause of this *v.* was in
St Peter's mind when he spoke at Pentecost (Acts ii. 39).

CHAPTER III.

III. 1 For, behold, in those days, and in that time, when

1—3. These *vv.* explain the nature of the crisis from which the
Jews are to be preserved (as promised in ii. 32) and introduce the
account, continued in *v.* 9 f., of the mustering of all the heathen in
one spot, where, in retribution for the evil done by them to Israel,
they are doomed to extermination. In the Heb. this ch. constitutes ch. iv.

I shall bring again the captivity of Judah and Jerusalem,
2 I will gather all nations, and will bring them down into
¹the valley of Jehoshaphat; and I will plead with them there
for my people and for my heritage Israel, whom they have
scattered among the nations, and parted my land. 3 And they
have cast lots for my people: and have given a boy for an harlot,

¹ See ver. 12.

1. *bring again the captivity.* This rendering is supported by the
LXX. (ἐπιστρέφω τὴν αἰχμαλωσίαν); but perhaps a better translation
is, *retrieve the fortune* (literally *retrieve the retrieval*), for this is the
only admissible rendering of the phrase in Job xlii. 10 and Ezek.
xvi. 53, and is the most suitable in some other passages. Even after
the Return in the time of Zerubbabel the situation of the Jews for
a long while was very depressed, and a happy turn in their fortunes
(including the restoration of such Jews as were yet in heathen lands)
was still an object of earnest desire (cf. p. 60).

2. *I will gather all nations*, etc. The assembling, by Jehovah, of all
the heathen for annihilation is similarly predicted in 3 Is. lxvi. 16—18,
Mic. iv. 12, Zeph. iii. 8.

the valley of Jehoshaphat. The name is here chosen for its symbolic
meaning (" Jehovah judges "), as appears from *v.* 14, and Th. has τὴν
χώραν τῆς κρίσεως; but whether it was taken from some spot actually
called after king Jehoshaphat is unknown. The writer cannot have in
mind the locality which (according to 2 Ch. xx. 1—30) was the scene
of an overthrow sustained by a confederation of Moabites, Ammonites,
Edomites, and Meunim (*id.* xxvi. 7), who attacked Israel in the time
of Jehoshaphat, for this was near Tekoa. The place in the prophet's
thoughts is clearly near Jerusalem (see *v.* 16), and the name he gives
to it has been traditionally associated since the 4th cent. A.D. with
the gorge of the Kidron, E. of Jerusalem. The Kidron, however, is
a torrent-valley (*nahal*) and not a vale (*'ēmek*), the word used here¹.
The situation which answers the writer's imaginative conception least
inadequately is the valley of Hinnom, W. of Jerusalem, or the extension
of it (after its junction with the Kidron) S. of the city. This is usually
described as a *valley* (*gai*'), but is called a *vale* in Jer. xxxi. 40.

I will plead with them. Better, *I will join issue with them* (cf. the
LXX. διακριθήσομαι πρὸς αὐτούς, Vulgate *disceptabo cum eis*). The Heb.
has a form (here used in a reciprocal sense) of the verb *shāphat*, which
enters into the composition of the name *Jehoshaphat.*

whom they have scattered. The occasion alluded to is probably the
capture of Jerusalem and the deportation of its citizens in 587.

3. *cast lots.* For this way of disposing of captives, see Ob. 11, Nah.
iii. 10.

given...for an harlot. I.e. given as the price of a harlot: cf. Aq.

¹ Cf. G. A. Smith, *HGHL.* pp. 384, 654.

and sold a girl for wine, that they might drink. 4 Yea, and what
are ye to me, O Tyre, and Zidon, and all the regions of Philistia?
[1]will ye render me a recompence? and if ye recompense me, swiftly
and speedily will I return your [2]recompence upon your own head.
5 Forasmuch as ye have taken my silver and my gold, and have

---

[1] Or, *will ye repay a deed of mine, or will ye do aught unto me? swiftly &c.*
[2] Or, *deed*

ἐδίδουν κοράσιον ἀντὶ πόρνης. The offence of selling members of Jehovah's community into slavery was aggravated by the sensuality to
which the proceeds of the sale were devoted.

that they might drink. Better, *and drank it.* But the symmetry of
the parallelism and the rhythm of the *v.* (for both this and the foregoing appear to consist of trimeters) are improved by the omission of
the clause (as suggested by Schwally) as a needless expansion of what
precedes.

4—8. For the reasons that render it probable that these *vv.* are an
insertion and not part of the book in its original form, and for
a suggestion as to the date of their composition see p. 114. They are
written in prose and express the complaint which Jehovah has against
the people of Phœnicia and Philistia for pillaging the possessions, and
enslaving the persons, of His people; and they go on to announce the
nemesis which is to befall them.

4. *Yea, and what...to me.* Better, *And ye, too, what will ye do
to me?* In the Heb. there is no verb, but the phrase must be understood
as in Hos. vi. 4 (where the verb *do* is expressed).

all the regions of Philistia. Literally, *all the circuits of Philistia.*
The word (*gālīl*) rendered *regions* means anything that can roll or
turn (and is applicable to rings and folding doors), but could be used
to describe a circuit or area of ground (see Is. ix. 1 mg., Ezek. xlvii. 8
(*region*), Josh. xxii. 10, 11). Here it is employed to denote the districts,
probably each under separate authority, which constituted the Philistine
Pentapolis (1 Sam. vi. 4, Josh. xiii. 2, 1 Macc. v. 15).

will ye render me, etc. The whole *v.* is better translated (cf. mg.)
a deed of mine will such as ye repay? or will such as ye (unprovoked)
*do aught to me? Swiftly and speedily will I return your deed upon your
head.* The pronoun *ye* is emphatic in the Heb. and the use of it is
intended to accentuate the disproportion between the adversaries.
The word *gĕmūl* in the last clause, which in the R.V. text is rendered
by *recompence,* is rarely used of good or evil done *spontaneously,* but
must here mean some gratuitous act of aggression (as in 2 Ch. xx. 11).

5. *taken.* Probably they had purchased what had been pillaged by
others.

my silver...my gold. The reference may be either to the nation's
possessions in general (for these, in a sense, were Jehovah's, cf. Hos.
ii. 8, 1 Ch. xxix. 14), or to the treasures of the Temple in particular.
The occasion may be the plundering of the capital by the Babylonians

carried into your temples my goodly pleasant things; 6 the children
also of Judah and the children of Jerusalem have ye sold unto
the sons of the Grecians, that ye might remove them far from
their border: 7 behold, I will stir them up out of the place
whither ye have sold them, and will return your ¹recompence
upon your own head; 8 and I will sell your sons and your
daughters into the hand of the children of Judah, and they shall
sell them to the men of Sheba, to a nation far off: for the LORD
hath spoken it.

¹ Or, *deed*

in 587; but if the passage (*vv.* 4—8) is an insertion, it is likely to be
some much later act of spoliation, such as occurred when punishment
was inflicted on the Jews by Artaxerxes Ochus, about the middle of the
4th cent. B.C.

carried into your temples. Compare the action ascribed to Nebuchadrezzar in Dan. i. 2. A similar proceeding is recorded of David in
2 Sam. viii. 11.

6. *the children also of Judah,* etc. The Phœnicians were known not
only as slave-dealers (Ezek. xxvii. 13, Am. i. 9, 1 Macc. iii. 41) but
also as kidnappers (Hdt. I. 1, II. 54). It will be recalled that *Syrus* was
a common slave-name among the Greeks and the Romans; and the
appellation would doubtless be applied to Jews as well as to other
captives from Palestine.

the sons of the Grecians. Cf. the Homeric phrase υἷες Ἀχαιῶν.
The name used by the Hebrews for Greece and the Greeks—*Javan*—
was derived from the Ionians, i.e. the Ionian colonies in Asia Minor.
The expression here employed (*the sons of the Grecians*) where *the sons
of Greece* might be expected (cf. *the sons of Ammon*), is parallel to the
use, in 2 Chron. xx. 19, of *the sons of the Korahites* instead of *the sons
of Korah* (Ps. xlii. title, and elsewhere). Allusions to the Greeks occur
in Gen. x. 2, 4 (P), Ezek. xxvii. 13, 3 Is. lxvi. 19, Dan. viii. 21, xi. 2
(all passages later than the Exile).

7. *I will stir them up.* I.e. I will incite and aid them to depart.

your recompence. Better, *your* (unprovoked) *deed*: see p. 113.

8. *I will sell.* The verb *sell*, which is used in the literal sense in
the next clause, is here employed figuratively in the sense of "I will
deliver up" (cf. Jud. ii. 14, iii. 8). So far as the prediction in these *vv.*
was realized, it found fulfilment, after Joel's time, in the enslavement
of numbers of the people of Tyre and Gaza by Alexander in 333 B.C.
Many of those who were then reduced to slavery were doubtless bought
by the Jews in order to sell again.

the men of Sheba. These were a people of South Arabia, variously
represented as Semites (Gen. x. 28, xxv. 3 (JE)) and Hamites (Gen. x. 7
(P)), and well known as traders (cf. Ezek. xxvii. 22). Their country was
famous for its spices (1 Kgs. x. 10), and was regarded by Jewish writers

9 Proclaim ye this among the nations; ¹prepare war: stir up the mighty men; let all the men of war draw near, let them come up. 10 Beat your plowshares into swords, and your pruninghooks into spears: let the weak say, I am strong. 11 ²Haste ye, and come, all ye nations round about, and gather

¹ Heb. *sanctify*.   ² Or, *Assemble yourselves*

as a distant and wealthy land (Ps. lxxii. 10); its situation was some 200 miles N. of Aden, and it could be reached by caravans.

to a nation far off. Perhaps better (as there is a change in the preposition), *for a nation far off*, who would purchase the slaves from the men of Sheba.

9—17. Here the declaration of what Jehovah is about to do to the heathen nations (begun in *vv.* 1—3) is continued. They are bidden to arm themselves for a conflict with Jehovah and His celestial hosts, but are destined to be annihilated by Him, with whom His own people will find security.

9. *Proclaim ye this.* Jehovah charges His messengers to convey a challenge to the nations (*v.* 2): cf. the challenge in Is. viii. 9, 10.

prepare war. Literally (as in the mg.), *sanctify* (or *consecrate*) *war*: see p. 24.

draw near. The expression is used of warlike collisions (Jud. xx. 23, 2 Sam. x. 13, etc.).

10. *Beat your plowshares*, etc. The heathen are bidden to take care that there is no deficiency in their equipment for so critical a contest. Classical parallels for the conversion of tools into weapons, here contemplated, occur in Ovid, *F.* I. 699, *Sarcula cessabant versique in pila ligones*, Vergil, *G.* I. 508, *Curvæ rigidum falces conflantur in ensem.* The precise agricultural implement intended by the word rendered *plowshare* is uncertain; perhaps *coulters* is the best equivalent (see p. 31).

spears. The word (*rĕmāhim*) here used differs from that employed in the converse passage Mic. iv. 3 (= Is. ii. 4), and is confined to late, or comparatively late, compositions such as Jeremiah, the Priestly narrative of the Pentateuch, Nehemiah, and Chronicles, with the exception of two passages, Jud. v. 8 (the Song of Deborah) and 1 Kgs. xviii. 28 (the history of Elijah), both of which appear to be of Ephraimite origin. Some dialectic features of the northern tribes seem to have survived in later Hebrew.

let the weak, etc. Cf. 2 Zech. xii. 8. In such a crisis there must be universal service.

11. *Haste ye.* This Heb. verb ('*ūsh*) occurs only here, and is of doubtful meaning. The LXX. and Syr. render it (as in the mg.) *Assemble yourselves*; but, according to Driver, there is no philological basis for this translation. The R.V. assumes that it is equivalent to the common word for *haste* (*hūsh*).

gather yourselves together. The Heb. really has *and they shall gather*

yourselves together: thither cause thy mighty ones to come down,
O LORD. 12 Let the nations bestir themselves, and come up to the
valley of [1] Jehoshaphat: for there will I sit to judge all the nations
round about. 13 Put ye in the sickle, for the [2] harvest is ripe:
come, [3] tread ye; for the winepress is full, the fats overflow; for
their wickedness is great. 14 Multitudes, multitudes in the valley

[1] That is, *The LORD judgeth.* [2] Or, *vintage*
[3] Or, *get you down*

themselves together; but this disturbs the sequence of imperatives, and
the R.V. has silently adopted the reading of the LXX. συνάχθητε.
Metrical considerations are in favour of the omission of the verb
altogether.

thither. I.e. to the vale of Jehoshaphat.

cause thy mighty ones, etc. Jehovah was believed to have at His disposal a host of supernatural warriors (see 2 Kgs. vi. 17, Ps. lxxviii. 25,
ciii. 20, and cf. Josh. v. 13—15, 2 Th. i. 7), whom He is urged by the
prophet to bring from heaven. But the LXX. has ὁ πραὺς ἔστω μαχητής,
let the soft (or *faint*)-*hearted become a mighty one* (or *warrior*); cf. *v.* 10
(end).

12. *come up.* The vale of Jehoshaphat is assumed to be near Jerusalem, the Jewish capital, so that this verb is used where, at first sight,
descend would seem to be more appropriate (cf. p. 86).

will I sit to judge. The clause reproduces the significance of the
name *Jehoshaphat* (p. 112), but Jehovah is here conceived as presiding
at the annihilation, not the trial, of the nations.

13. *Put ye in*, etc. The command is addressed by Jehovah to His
attendant angels. Cf. Mt. xiii. 39—41.

the harvest. Better (as in the mg.), *the vintage.* The slaughter of the
heathen is represented under the figure of the treading of grapes (cf.
3 Is. lxiii. 3, Lam. i. 15, Rev. xiv. 19, 20, xix. 15); and the Heb. word
here employed, though it properly means "harvest," is applied to the
vintage, as in Is. xvi. 9, xviii. 4, 5. The LXX. has τρυγητός.

is ripe. The verb elsewhere signifies *to be boiled* (Ezek. xxiv. 5), and
the transition of meaning may be illustrated by the use of the Latin
coquo; see Cic. *de Sen.* § 71, *Poma...si matura et cocta decidunt,* Verg.
G. II. 522, *Mitis in apricis coquitur vindemia saxis.*

tread ye. This rendering, which assumes that the imperative comes
from *rādhah,* is supported by the LXX. (πατεῖτε), but the mg. *get you
down* (i.e. into the winepress, p. 107), which takes the verb to be *yāradh,*
has the Vulg. in its favour (*descendite*).

the fats overflow. The previous exhortation to tread the grapes in the
press would be uncalled for if the vats were already full and running
over; and as the LXX. has ὑπερεκχεῖτε τὰ ὑπολήνια, Bewer with reason
suggests a change of points in the verb (imperat. for indic.), and gives
it a causal sense, *make the vats overflow.*

of decision! for the day of the LORD is near in the valley of
decision. 15 The sun and the moon are darkened, and the stars
withdraw their shining. 16 And the LORD shall roar from Zion,
and utter his voice from Jerusalem; and the heavens and the
earth shall shake: but the LORD will be a refuge unto his people,
and a strong hold to the children of Israel. 17 So shall ye know
that I am the LORD your God, dwelling in Zion my holy mountain: then shall Jerusalem be holy, and there shall no strangers
pass through her any more. 18 And it shall come to pass in that

their wickedness. The figure of speech in the early part of the *v.* is
here abandoned, the pronoun *their* referring to the nations symbolized
by the grapes.

14. *Multitudes, multitudes,* etc. The speaker, in this and the next
two *vv.,* is the prophet. The duplication of the word *multitudes* serves,
according to Hebrew idiom, to heighten the sense of the numbers: cf.
Jud. v. 22, Ex. viii. 14 (Heb. 10, literally *heaps, heaps*).

of decision. Literally *of sharp* (or *strict*) *decision.*

15. *The sun and the moon,* etc. Probably the writer only wishes to
illustrate the terrifying character of the crisis by recalling to the mind
the consternation occasioned by eclipses (see p. lx); but it is possible
that the darkening of the luminaries (cf. Is. xiii. 10, xxxiv. 4) is meant
to imply the suppression, before Jehovah's might, of the heavenly bodies,
regarded as the abodes of celestial powers antagonistic to Him (cf. Is.
xxiv. 21), for the host of heaven at some periods of Heb. history were
the objects of idolatrous worship (2 Kgs. xxiii. 5, 11).

16. *And the LORD shall roar,* etc. The words occur also in Am. i. 2,
the coincidence pointing to borrowing on the part of one writer or the
other (see p. lxix). Jehovah is expressly likened to a lion, whose lair is
Jerusalem, in Ps. lxxvi. 2, mg.; cf. Hos. xi. 10.

a refuge unto his people, etc. Jehovah is described in similar terms
in Ps. xiv. 6, xlvi. 1.

17. *dwelling in Zion.* Jehovah is represented by Ezekiel (xi. 23) as
having abandoned Zion (in consequence of its wickedness) to the on-
slaught of the Babylonians; but on the restoration of its people to their
country, He had returned with them (cf. Mic. ii. 13, 2 Is. xl. 10, 11),
and His continuous presence in Jerusalem would thenceforward secure
the city from further molestation.

shall...be holy. I.e. shall be undefiled by the entry into it of heathen
foemen: cf. Ob. 17, 2 Zech. ix. 8, 2 Is. lii. 1, Nah. i. 15. A more ethical
conception of holiness is attached to the New Jerusalem in Rev. xxi. 27,
xxii. 14, 15.

18—21. A description of the fruitfulness which, after the crisis just
described, is to mark the land of Judah (cf. Is. iv. 2), in contrast to the
doom of barrenness which is to be the fate of Egypt and Edom for the
crimes committed by them.

day, that the mountains shall drop down sweet wine, and the hills
shall flow with milk, and all the brooks of Judah shall flow with
waters; and a fountain shall come forth of the house of the LORD,
and shall water ¹the valley of Shittim. 19 Egypt shall be a deso-

¹ That is, *the valley of acacias.*

18. *the mountains...milk.* The passage is substantially identical with
Am. ix. 13ᵇ (save for the concluding words); and represents hyper-
bolically the exceptional fertility of the vineyards on the hillsides
(cf. p. 70), and the richness of the upland pastures. Parallels among
Latin writers occur in Ov. *Met.* I. 111, *Flumina iam lactis, iam flumina
nectaris ibant, Flavaque de viridi stillabant ilice mella*; Verg. *G.* I. 132,
Passim rivis currentia vina.

all the brooks, etc. Literally, *all the channels* (Is. viii. 7). In a land
like Palestine, where so many of the wâdies run dry in summer (cf. i. 20
and note), an ample supply of water is one of the most desired of
blessings: cf. Is. xxx. 25, Jud. i. 15.

a fountain shall come forth, etc. The conception is derived from
Ezekiel xlviii. 1 f. (p. lxviii) and recurs in 2 Zech. xiv. 8. The idea of a
fountain issuing from the house of Jehovah was probably suggested by
the Gihon spring (the *Ain Sitti Mariam*), which gushed from below the
hill upon which the Temple stood, and flowed down the Kidron gorge.
This is presumably the *fons perennis aquæ* mentioned by Tacitus,
Hist. v. 12.

the valley of Shittim. Literally " the torrent-valley of the acacias."
Even this, conspicuous for its dryness (since the acacia, which is
a thorny tree (Sym. has τὴν κοιλάδα τῶν ἀκανθῶν), producing pods and
having heavy and very hard wood, flourishes in a dry soil, and " is the
characteristic tree of the desert wâdies")¹, will be irrigated like the rest
of the land. No ravine bearing the name here mentioned is alluded to
elsewhere in the O.T. (though there was an " Acacia meadow " (*Abel
Shittim*) on the east side of the Jordan seven or eight miles from the
N. extremity of the Dead Sea (Num. xxv. 1, Josh. ii. 1, Mic. vi. 5));
but since in the passage in Ezekiel, upon which the writer of Joel has
drawn, the irrigating waters flow from the east of the Temple, the
" torrent-valley of the acacias " was probably the name of some arid
wâdy lying between Jerusalem and the Jordan. The present passage
has contributed to influence Rev. xxii. 1.

19. *Egypt shall be,* etc. The occasion of the wrongs inflicted by
Egypt which the writer has in mind was probably the invasion of Judah
by Pharaoh Necho at some date between 610 and 594 (2 Kgs. xxiii.
29—35, 2 Ch. xxxv. 20—24). This reference is not excluded by the
fact that the bloodshed at Megiddo, where Necho defeated Josiah, took
place in war, for the second half of the *v.* may relate to Edom only.
Bewer suggests that the passage alludes to the incursion into Palestine

---

¹ Hastings, *DB.* IV. p. 507.

lation, and Edom shall be a desolate wilderness, for the violence done to the children of Judah, because they have shed innocent blood in their land. 20 But Judah shall [1]abide for ever, and Jerusalem from generation to generation. 21 And I will [2]cleanse their blood that I have not cleansed: for the LORD dwelleth in Zion.

> [1] Or, *be inhabited*   [2] Or, *hold as innocent*

of Ptolemy Lagi in 320 B.C. The prediction of Egypt's *desolation* can hardly be said to have been fulfilled; but the country at least lost its independence when it became included first within the Macedonian, and next within the Roman, empire. Prophecies of parallel import occur in Is. xix., xx., Jer. xlvi., Ezek. xxix.—xxxii. The occasion when Edom earned, most of all, the bitter hatred of the Jews, such as is evinced here, was the capture of Jerusalem by the Babylonians in 587 (see p. xlix).

for the violence, etc. The expression is perhaps derived from Ob. 10 (with some modification): cf. p. 74.

in their land. If the occasions of Egyptian and Edomite malevolence have been correctly identified, this must mean, in the land of the children of Judah. But Driver and others think that the reference is to the lands of Egypt and Edom, where Jews who were dwelling there peaceably may have been treacherously massacred.

20. *shall abide.* I.e. shall continue unmolested: cf. Mic. v. 4 (3). The mg. *shall be inhabited* (cf. LXX. κατοικηθήσεται) finds support in Is. xiii. 20, Ezek. xxvi. 20, 2 Zech. ix. 5: and the same ambiguity as is present here occurs in Jer. xvii. 25.

21. *I will cleanse their blood*, etc. This, if the text is sound, must mean, "I will cleanse (through the infliction of retribution upon the blood-guilty) their (i.e. the victims') blood that I have hitherto (by sparing those who spilt it) left uncleansed." But the Heb. verb rendered "cleanse" elsewhere means "to clear," or "treat as innocent" (cf. mg.), and has as its object *persons* (Jer. xxx. 11, Job ix. 28). The LXX. has καὶ ἐκζητήσω (or ἐκδικήσω) τὸ αἷμα αὐτῶν, καὶ οὐ μὴ ἀθῳώσω, *I will avenge their blood and I will not hold innocent* the guilty (cf. Ex. xxxiv. 7, Num. xiv. 18, Nah. i. 3). This implies in the first clause the reading *vĕ-nikkamti* for *vĕ-nikkēthi* and seemingly treats *lo' nikkēthi* (in the second clause) as a prophetic perfect (equivalent to a future). But a prophetic perfect is here unnatural, and the passage is brought into closer accord with Hebrew usage by substituting (with Nowack) the verb *nikkēm* for *nikkah* in *both* clauses, and so obtaining the translation, *I will avenge their blood* which *I have not* (hitherto) *avenged*.

for the LORD dwelleth in Zion. Literally, *and Jehovah dwelleth in Zion*, which is tantamount to "as surely as Jehovah dwelleth in Zion." For this use of the conjunction *and* cf. 2 Is. li. 15 (where *For I am Jehovah thy God* is literally *And I am Jehovah thy God*).

JONAH

Chapter I.

I.   1 Now the word of the LORD came unto Jonah the son of

1—3. Jonah's commission to declare to Nineveh its doom, and his attempt to evade his duty.

1. *Now.* Strictly, *And.* Since the writer casts his censure of his countrymen's attitude towards the Gentiles into the form of an historical narrative, he begins in the way usual with Hebrew historians (see the opening words of Exodus, Leviticus, Numbers, Joshua, Judges, Ruth, Samuel, Kings, Ezra and Esther): the conjunction attaches the book (as it were) to other and earlier narratives. The prophetic book of Ezekiel begins similarly.

the word of the LORD came. See p. 88.

Jonah. What is known about the prophet is related on p. lxxviii. Various places are pointed out in local traditions as his tomb, there being one near Nazareth, a second close to Hebron, and a third hard by the ruins of Nineveh (p. 122). The name means "a dove." Many Hebrew personal names were those of animals; and though it is possible that they may have been of the nature of individual nicknames, due to some fancied resemblance in feature or disposition between the animals and the human personalities designated, it is perhaps more probable that they go back to a totemistic stage of thought, and were originally *tribal* names, though they were afterwards transferred to individuals. A totem is customarily some species of animal or plant from which a particular tribe or clan believes that its life is derived, and upon which its welfare depends. The members of the community are called after its name; and they ordinarily abstain from injuring it (as being akin to themselves) except when, in order to assimilate its virtues, or to place themselves more fully under its protection, they sacramentally eat it or (if it is an animal) dress themselves in its hide. The animal or plant in question is thus practically regarded as a god from whom the tribe is descended, the explanation of such an attitude of mind being presumably that primitive races were deeply impressed by the difference between themselves and the life around them, and were prone to look upon many objects of the lower creation as super-human rather than as sub-human. This system of belief prevails widely among savage races in Africa, America, and Australia at the present day; and it has been inferred that it once existed among the Semitic nations, including the Hebrews, for the following reasons. (*a*) Many of these regarded themselves as being the offspring of, or filially related to, the deities whom they worshipped (cf. Num. xxi. 29, Dt. xiv. 1, Hos. xi. 1, Mal. ii. 11). (*b*) Numerous Semitic gods were thought to

Amittai, saying, 2 Arise, go to Nineveh, that great city, and

have animal shapes: there was a heifer Baal (Tob. i. 5); Jehovah in
early times was represented as a calf or young bull (Ex. xxxii. 4 mg.,
1 Kgs. xii. 28), and perhaps also as a *sărăph* or winged serpent (Num.
xxi. 8, 9, 2 Kgs. xviii. 4); at Eryx, in Sicily, Ashtoreth had the form
of a dove; whilst other divinities were worshipped under the figures
of a lion, a horse, or a vulture. (In Greece, too, certain deities were
associated with animals; e.g. Artemis was connected with the bear,
and Dionysus (ταυροκέρως θεός) with the bull; whilst the epithets
Λυκαῖος and Σμινθεύς, attached to Apollo, suggest some primal link
between that god and the wolf (λύκος) and the mouse (Cretan σμίνθος).)
(*c*) A considerable number of both tribal and individual appellations
among the Semites were those of animals. Nahash, an Ammonite king
(1 Sam. xi. 1), bore the name of "snake." Epher, the name of a Midianite
clan (Gen. xxv. 4), means a stag or mountain goat; the Midianite chiefs
Oreb and Zeeb (Jud. vii. 25) and the Midianitess Zipporah (Ex. ii. 21)
had names signifying "raven," "wolf," and "sparrow"; and the
Israelites Caleb, Shaphan, Achbor, Laish, Hezir, and the women Eglah
and Deborah, were designated after the dog, coney, mouse, lion, swine,
calf, and bee respectively. (*d*) Names of this type occur very frequently in narratives relating to early times, but rarely after the Exile.
(*e*) Several of the animals just mentioned were for the Hebrews
"unclean" (Lev. xi.); and this, with some probability, may be taken
to mean that they were once taboo, and too holy to be used as food
under ordinary circumstances, but might be eaten at a religious feast;
and some of the creatures enumerated were thus eaten by degenerate
Jews in post-exilic times (3 Is. lxv. 4, lxvi. 3). The evidence here sum-
marized is confessedly inconclusive, but certainly favours the view that
has been indicated above[1].

Amittai. The name, which only occurs here and in 2 Kgs. xiv. 25, is
a derivative of *'emeth*, "truth," and means "man of truth": cf. *Bar-
zillai*, "man of iron." Jewish tradition represented Jonah as the son
of the widow of Zarephath, who is said to have called her child "the
son of Amittai" because the prophet Elijah had spoken to her truth
about him (1 Kgs. xvii. 24).

2. *Nineveh.* In the cuneiform inscriptions the name of the city is
written *Ninuâ* and *Ninâ*; in Greek writers Νῖνος. It was the latest
capital of Assyria, situated 250 miles N.W. of Babylon, to which
Assyria was at first subject, Nineveh being originally a Babylonian
settlement (cf. Gen. x. 10, 11). It seems to have been about 1850 B.C.
that Assyria became an independent state; and its earliest capitals
were Asshur and Calah (60 miles and 18 miles S. of Nineveh respectively). The Assyrian court was removed from Asshur to Calah
about 1300, and from Calah to Nineveh about 1100. Asshur-nazir-pal III
(884—860) again made Calah the royal residence; but Sennacherib

---

[1] Cp. Gray, *Heb. Proper Names*, pp. 86—115.

cry against it ; for their wickedness is come up before me. 3 But
Jonah rose up to flee unto Tarshish from the presence of the LORD ;

(704—681) once more restored to Nineveh the dignity of being the
capital city. He greatly enlarged and adorned it, its circumference (it
is said) being no less than 7½ miles. It was destroyed in 612 by the
Medes under Cyaxares (Hdt. I. 106), aided by a Chaldean, Nabopolassar, who had made himself king of Babylon: its overthrow is the
subject of the book of Nahum. Its site is marked by mounds on the
E. bank of the Tigris opposite the present town of Mosul, the principal
being at Kouyunjik and Nebi-yunus (the latter preserving the memory
of the prophet Jonah, to whom a mosque is dedicated).

The reason why the writer of this book took Nineveh as typical
of the heathen world, and represented it as being an object of concern
to God, can only be conjectured. Either there was a tradition connecting
Jonah with it, or else the circumstance that of all the famous cities of
the past it was the one whose inhabitants had done most permanent
injury to his fellow Hebrews (for Assyria had carried the people of
Northern Israel into captivity, whence they had not returned) rendered
it the best illustration of God's comprehensive mercy.

that great city. Compare iii. 3, iv. 11. In Gen. x. 12 the same
description is applied apparently to a group of four cities (including
Nineveh) which lay between the rivers Tigris, Khusur, Zab, and
Gomal.

cry against it. Cf. the similar phrase in 1 Kgs. xiii. 2. The purport
of the cry (or proclamation) must have been the same as that stated
later in iii. 4.

their wickedness. The pronoun refers to the citizens implied in the
previous mention of the city: cf. *v.* 3 (*them*, i.e. the mariners implied
in the reference to the ship): see also Mk. vi. 11, Acts viii. 5, Gen.
xv. 13. For the wickedness of Nineveh as viewed by a Hebrew prophet
see Nah. ii. 11, 12, iii. 1, 19. The LXX. has ἡ κραυγὴ τῆς κακίας αὐτῆς ;
cf. Gen. xviii. 21, iv. 10.

is come up before me. Jehovah is conceived by the writer not as
a mere national deity, but as the Judge of the whole earth (Gen. xviii.
25). The phraseology (which implies that God is seated in heaven) is
similar to that in Gen. vi. 13, 1 Sam. v. 12, Lam. i. 22, Acts x. 4.

3. *Tarshish.* This was a place famed amongst the Hebrews for its
minerals (Jer. x. 9, Ezek. xxvii. 12), and was reached from Palestine by
a long sea voyage (being amongst the most distant localities, 3 Is.
lxvi. 19); so that "Tarshish ships" (Is. ii. 16, 3 Is. lx. 9, Ezek.
xxvii. 25, Ps. xlviii. 7) came to be a term applied to the more sea-
worthy vessels (cf. the LXX. of Is. ii. 16, πλοῖον θαλάσσης). On the
other hand, it is reckoned in Gen. x. 4 among the "sons" of Javan
(probably representing Ionia or Greece), the others being Elishah,
Kittim and Dodanim (1 Ch. i. 7, Rodanim), of which the first may
possibly represent Hellas, and the others more certainly Cyprus (with
its town of Κίτιον) and Rhodes, so that it may plausibly be looked for

and he went down to Joppa, and found a ship going to Tarshish:

in Greek waters. It was especially connected by commerce with Tyre
and Zidon (Is. xxiii. 6, Ezek. xxvii. 12); but as the Phœnicians were
bold sailors, this fact does not throw much light upon its situation. By
Josephus it was identified with Tarsus (on the Cydnus) in Cilicia
(*Ant.* IX. 10, 2), though Tarsus was not a port; whilst in the LXX.,
when it is not transliterated or paraphrased as it is here, it is identified
with Carthage (Is. xxiii. 1, Ezek. xxvii. 12). It is most commonly
thought to have been the same as the Greek *Tartessos*, a name
successively applied first to a river in Spain (the Bætis or Guadal-
quivir); then to a tribe there (the Tartessii); and finally to a Phœnician
colony in the same country (perhaps Gades or Cadiz). The abundance
of minerals in the Spanish peninsula, especially the presence there of
tin, which was obtained from Tarshish (Ezek. xxvii. 12) supports the
view that Tarshish was a locality within it. But since the place may
have been an emporium for metals rather than a mining district, some
authorities favour the conclusion that it was Etruria, whose inhabitants
were *Tyrsenians* or *Tyrrhenians*, a race of Asiatic origin (cf. Hdt. I. 94),
and perhaps represented by *Tiras* in Gen. x. 2 and by the *Tursha*
known to the Egyptians. Others suggest *Tharros*, a place in Sardinia.
The evidence (which is reviewed in *JTS.* vol. XVII., p. 280 f.) is too
conflicting to yield a confident conclusion, though the arguments for
a locality in Spain are perhaps preponderant.

If the narrative is a unity, the mention here of Tarshish as Jonah's
destination anticipates the next clause, and some critics would omit
unto Tarshish. But as there are discrepancies in the book, these clauses,
which suggest respectively that the prophet went to Tarshish by design
and by chance, may be derived from duplicate and slightly variant
versions (p. lxxxvi).

from the presence of the LORD. The phrase (since the book is cast in
an antique mould) probably means withdrawal from Jehovah's land (as
in Gen. iv. 14, 16, 1 Sam. xxvi. 19, 20, Jer. xxiii. 39), though it is clear
that the writer no more entertained a localized conception of the Deity
than did the writer of Ps. cxxxix. The expression, however, may only
signify the abandonment of the position and functions of a minister of
Jehovah (see 1 Kgs. xvii. 1, xviii. 15, 2 Kgs. iii. 14, v. 16, Lk. i. 19).
The motive for Jonah's action is given in iv. 2.

went down. I.e. from his home at Gath-hepher to the coast. The
nearest port would have been either Acco (the modern Acre), or
Tyre.

Joppa. This form of the name is Greek—Ἰόππη: in Hebrew it is
Yapho, in the Egyptian inscriptions of the 15th century B.C. *Yepu,*
and in the Tell-el-Amarna tablets (14th century B.C.), *Yapu.* The
place, now called *Jāfā* or *Jaffa,* stands on a rocky eminence, 50 miles
from Gath-hepher, and affords the only shelter for ships between the
coast of Egypt and Mount Carmel. The harbour, such as it is, "is
formed by a low ledge of rock running out at a sharp angle in a N.W.

so he paid the fare thereof, and went down into it, to go with
them unto Tarshish from the presence of the LORD. 4 But the
LORD [1]sent out a great wind into the sea, and there was a mighty
tempest in the sea, so that the ship was like to be broken. 5 Then
the mariners were afraid, and cried every man unto his god; and
they cast forth the wares that were in the ship into the sea, to
lighten it unto them. But Jonah was gone down into the innermost parts of the ship; and he lay, and was fast asleep. 6 So the

[1] Or, *hurled*

direction from the southern end of the town[1]." In ancient times it
served as a port to Jerusalem (Ez. iii. 7, 2 Ch. ii. 16), though it was
never in the possession of Israel until taken by Jonathan the Maccabee
in 148 B.C. (1 Macc. x. 76), and afterwards garrisoned by his brother
Simon (1 Macc. xii. 33, 34, xiii. 11, xiv. 5). After experiencing some
changes of ownership, it became, during the wars between the Jews and
the Romans, a nest of pirates; and it was attacked, and its inhabitants
were destroyed, by Vespasian in 68 A.D. (Jos. *BJ*. iii. 9, 1—3). It has
undergone various assaults in mediæval and modern times, including
one by Napoleon. Its present population is about 8000. The oranges
for which Jaffa is now famous are said to have been introduced from
China.

went down into it. Compare *v.* 5.

4—17. The arrest of the prophet's flight by a storm and his miraculous
preservation from drowning.

4. *sent out.* Literally, *cast* or *hurled* (see mg. and cf. 1 Sam. xviii. 11,
xx. 33), the word here used suggesting the violence of the wind.

a mighty tempest. It was in the same region that St Paul encountered
the tempestuous wind called Euraquilo (Acts xxvii. 14).

was like to be broken. Literally, *was minded to be broken* (cf. Ps. lxxiii.
16 *was minded to know*), like the French *le vaisseau pensa se briser*.
The LXX. has ἐκινδύνευε συντριβῆναι.

5. *mariners.* The Heb. word (occurring also in Ezek. xxvii. 9, 27, 29)
is equivalent, in etymology, to our "salt" and the Greek ἁλιεύς.

every man unto his god. The crew (like so many crews to-day) were
of various nationalities: cf. Ezek. xxvii. 8 (where the cities of Arvad
and Zidon supply Tyre with rowers).

the wares. Better, *the gear* (LXX. τῶν σκευῶν, cf. τὸ σκεῦος in Acts
xxvii. 17). The Heb. word, like the Greek ὅπλα and the Latin *arma*,
has the double sense of "tackling" and "weapons."

to lighten it unto them. Literally, "to lighten (the calamity) from
upon them": cf. 1 Kgs. xii. 10 (Heb.).

the innermost parts of the ship. I.e. either a lower deck, or else the
hold: LXX. τὴν κοίλην. The word here employed for *ship* is not the

[1] Hastings, *DB*. ii. p. 755.

shipmaster came to him, and said unto him, What meanest thou,
O sleeper? arise, call upon thy God, if so be that God will think
upon us, that we perish not. 7 And they said every one to his
fellow, Come, and let us cast lots, that we may know for whose
cause this evil is upon us. So they cast lots, and the lot fell upon
Jonah. 8 Then said they unto him, Tell us, we pray thee, for
whose cause this evil is upon us; what is thine occupation? and

common term used in *v.* 3, but means a *decked* vessel, from a Hebrew
root meaning "to cover." The English substantive *deck* similarly means
a covering, and was originally regarded as a roof for the hold. So in
Greek a decked vessel was termed πλοῖον ἐστεγασμένον (from στεγάζειν,
"to cover").

was fast asleep. Or, better, *slept soundly.* The LXX. has *and he
slept and snored.*

6. *the shipmaster.* Literally "the chief of the rope-pullers." The
LXX. has ὁ πρωρεύς (i.e. "the look-out man" in the bow of the ship),
but the other Greek translators have ὁ κυβερνήτης, whence the Vulg.
gubernator.

What meanest thou, O sleeper? Perhaps better, *What meanest thou by
sleeping soundly?* (cf. Vulg. *Quid tu sopore deprimeris?*). The last verb
is used of the "deep sleep" of Sisera (Jud. iv. 21), and a cognate noun
of the "deep sleep" sent by God upon Adam (Gen. ii. 21). For the
Heb. construction cf. Is. xxii. 16.

will think upon us. The Aramaic verb *hith'ashshēth* here used (see
p. lxxxiii) takes the place of the common Hebrew verb *hāshabh* occurring
in the same sense in Ps. xl. 17 (18) and elsewhere. The LXX. has ὅπως
διασώσῃ ὁ θεὸς ἡμᾶς.

7. *let us cast lots.* The use of the lot was an appeal to God (cf. Prov.
xvi. 33) to decide upon whom the responsibility for what had happened
rested: cf. the instances of Achan (Josh. vii. 14 f.) and Jonathan
(1 Sam. xiv. 40 f.). Unless the guilty person could be detected and
removed, the whole company were endangered: cf. Æsch. *Septem c.
Thebas,* 595—600. It was through the casting of lots that the Apostles
appealed to the Lord to determine who should fill the place among
them forfeited by the traitor Judas (Acts i. 26): cf. also Hom. *Il.* VII.
171, κλήρῳ νῦν πεπάλαχθε διαμπερὲς ὅς κε λάχῃσιν.

for whose cause. Better, *on whose account.* The Heb. is peculiar, see
p. lxxxiii.

8. *for whose cause.* Better (in order to mark a difference in the Heb.
between this and the preceding), *on account of whom.* This question is
identical in purport with that which, according to *v.* 7, had already
been decided by the lot, and seems otiose after it (though it is, no doubt,
possible to explain it as due to the wish to obtain a confession from the
culprit). It is absent from the Vatican codex of the LXX. and from some
Hebrew manuscripts, and is omitted by Nowack as a gloss on *v.* 7, which
has been accidentally misplaced. It is not unlikely, however, that the

whence comest thou? what is thy country? and of what people
art thou? 9 And he said unto them, I am an Hebrew; and I fear
the LORD, the God of heaven, which hath made the sea and the
dry land. 10 Then were the men exceedingly afraid, and said
unto him, What is this that thou hast done? For the men knew
that he fled from the presence of the LORD, because he had told
them. 11 Then said they unto him, What shall we do unto thee,
that the sea may be calm unto us? for the sea grew more and
more tempestuous. 12 And he said unto them, Take me up, and
cast me forth into the sea; so shall the sea be calm unto you:

two questions proceed from different versions of the story (see p. lxxxvi),
and that in one of these the question in this verse followed directly
upon v. 6, the suspicions of the sailors being aroused by the fact that
Jonah took no part in their supplications to heaven.

9. *an Hebrew.* This was a customary term used in early times to
designate an Israelite in contrast to a foreigner (Gen. xl. 15, Ex. i. 19,
ii. 7, iii. 18, etc.: cf. also Phil. iii. 5). The word *Hebrew* etymologically
means "one from the other side" of some familiar boundary (not
necessarily the river Jordan only, which Israel crossed on entering
Canaan). Instead of the description *a Hebrew*, the LXX. has δοῦλος
Κυρίου, reading *'abhdi* for *'ibhri* and interpreting it as *'ebhedh Yĕhōvah.*
The other Greek translators have Ἑβραῖος.

I fear the LORD. Strictly, "I am a fearer (i.e. a worshipper) of
JEHOVAH" (cf. Dt. vi. 13, Ps. cxv. 11). The expression does not imply
a claim to exceptional piety, but merely describes the cult of which he
was a follower.

the God of heaven. The phrase occurs in Gen. xxiv. 3, 7 (J); but
otherwise only in post-exilic writings (2 Ch. xxxvi. 23, Ez. i. 2, Neh. i.
4, 5, Ps. cxxxvi. 26, and (in an Aramaic form) Ez. v. 11, vi. 9, Dan. ii.
18, 19, etc.).

10. *Then were the men...afraid.* The description of JEHOVAH as
Maker of the sea and the dry land led to the inference that the storm
came from Him.

For the men knew, etc. This points to some prior communication
imparted by Jonah about his flight (v. 3), and reported in one of the
two versions out of which the present narrative seems to have been
compiled, but omitted in the process of compilation. The sentence here
was probably once connected with v. 7; but some words, such as "thou
art the man; thou hast sinned against thy God," have been dropped
between them. In view of other evidence of the composite character of
the book, this appears a preferable hypothesis to that of Wellhausen,
who takes the words *because he had told them* to be a gloss.

11, 12. These two verses seem originally to have followed upon
vv. 8—10ᵃ. Jonah's avowal that he was a worshipper of Jehovah, the
Maker of the sea, led them to ask him what they should do to him to

for I know that for my sake this great tempest is upon you.
13 Nevertheless the men rowed hard to get them back to the
land; but they could not: for the sea grew more and more
tempestuous against them. 14 Wherefore they cried unto the
LORD, and said, We beseech thee, O LORD, we beseech thee, let
us not perish for this man's life, and lay not upon us innocent
blood: for thou, O LORD, hast done as it pleased thee. 15 So
they took up Jonah, and cast him forth into the sea: and the sea

avert the anger of his God. The prophet's declaration in *v.* 12 that he
knew the tempest to have occurred on his account appears unnecessary
after he had been marked out as the guilty individual by the decision
of the lot; and the verse containing it presumably comes from a version
which did not include the episode of the sailors' casting of lots.

13. *Nevertheless the men rowed*, etc. This rendering probably conveys
a wrong impression of the Hebrew, which has *And the men rowed*
(literally *dug*)[1]. Although the conjunction here employed sometimes has
an adversative sense (see p. 63), this *v.* is not a natural continuation
of *v.* 12; and hence Winckler would transpose it to after *v.* 4. But on
the theory that the book is a compilation, the *v.* is suitable enough as
the original sequel of *v.* 10[b]. The sailors, having inferred that Jonah
had gravely offended by fleeing from the land of Jehovah, exerted themselves first of all to restore him to it, for this might turn out to be all
that Jehovah wanted.

the land. More strictly, *the dry land*, as in ii. 10, Gen. i. 9, etc.

14. *We beseech thee, O LORD.* Literally, *Pray, JEHOVAH.* The
sailors naturally address Jonah's God, since they had ascertained that
He had caused the tempest which endangered them, and their own
deities had proved powerless to calm it.

let us not perish, etc. The words are a plea that JEHOVAH will not
avenge the death of His worshipper, if by the latter's direction they
cast him into the sea. The phrase *for* (i.e. for destroying) *this man's
life* has a parallel in 2 Sam. xiv. 7.

for thou, O LORD, etc. Compare 1 Sam. iii. 18, Ps. cxv. 3, cxxxv. 6.
The sailors mean that Jehovah Himself, by sending the storm which
the fall of the lot or Jonah's own admission had shown that the prophet
had provoked, caused them to adopt the course they were taking.

15. *So they took up Jonah*, etc. Various commentators quote a
parallel Buddhist story about a certain Mittavindaka of Benares, who
had gone to sea in disobedience to his mother. As the ship came to a
stop, and could not proceed, the mariners cast lots to discover on whose
account the trouble had happened; and when Mittavindaka was indicated as occasioning, through his fault, the interruption of the voyage,
he was set adrift on a float, and the ship then continued her course.

---

[1] A similar metaphor is common in Latin and English (*æquor arare, to plough
the sea*).

ceased from her raging. 16 Then the men feared the LORD exceedingly; and they offered a sacrifice unto the LORD, and made
vows. 17 And the LORD prepared a great fish to swallow up
Jonah; and Jonah was in the belly of the fish three days and
three nights.

her raging. The word, commonly used of human or Divine anger
(Prov. xix. 12, 2 Ch. xvi. 10, Is. xxx. 30), is here employed of the sea,
just as Ovid speaks of *maris ira* (*Met.* i. 370). The LXX. has τοῦ σάλου
αὐτῆς.

16. *feared the LORD.* This does not necessarily mean more than that
the sailors, influenced by the sudden cessation of the storm in accordance with the prophet's words (*v.* 12), worshipped Jehovah as a powerful
deity whom it was expedient to propitiate, in addition to their own
divinities: cf. 2 Kgs. xvii. 33, 41.

offered a sacrifice. Cf. the act of Noah when the Ark rested upon the
earth (Gen. viii. 20).

made vows. These were presumably promises of further sacrifices, in
the event of their reaching the land safely: cf. Verg. *G.* i. 436, *Votaque
servati solvent in litore nautæ*; *A.* iii. 404, *Positis aris iam vota in
litore solves.*

17. *prepared.* Better, *appointed* or *ordained*; cf. LXX. προσέταξεν;
and so in iv. 6, 7, 8. But the Vulg. has *præparavit.*

a great fish. LXX. κήτει μεγάλῳ, whence the use of κῆτος in Mt. xii. 40.
The Greek term was applied to viviparous marine creatures like seals
and whales; but was also extended to fish, such as sharks. A story not
wholly unlike this figures in Greek legend. The dithyrambic poet Arion,
whilst voyaging to Italy and Sicily, found himself beset by the crew of the
ship, who, coveting his money, demanded that he should throw himself
into the sea; and when, before doing so, he was allowed to play on his
harp, a dolphin came and took him upon its back, carrying him safely
to Tænarus (Hdt. i. 24). It is quite alien to the spirit of the present
narrative to rationalize the fish into a vessel bearing the figure-head
and name of some sea-creature (like the ship *Pristis* in Verg. *A.* v. 116),
and to suppose that it picked up Jonah.

and Jonah...three nights. The passage, as rendered in the LXX., is
quoted in Mt. xii. 40 (see p. xcv). The Hebrew method of reckoning
periods of time was generally *inclusive*; cf. Jud. xiv. 17 with 18, Mk.
viii. 31 with Mt. xvi. 21.

CHAPTER II.

II. 1 Then Jonah prayed unto the LORD his God out of the
fish's belly. 2 And he said,

1—10. Jonah's prayer and his restoration to the land.

1. *Then Jonah prayed.* If the following psalm is an insertion (see
p. lxxxv), the verb here used was probably intended originally to have its
proper sense (see iv. 1 (2), 1 Kgs. viii. 33, etc.), expressing a petition for

I called ¹by reason of mine affliction unto the LORD,
And he answered me;
Out of the belly of ²hell cried I,
And thou heardest my voice.

¹ Or, *out of mine affliction*   ² Heb. *Sheol.*

restoration to the land; but taken in connection with the psalm, which
is an utterance of gratitude for a deliverance already experienced, it
must be understood to mean *gave thanks* (as in 1 Sam. ii. 1) for his
preservation from drowning.

the fish's belly. The Hebrew word for *fish* here is the fem. *dāghah*,
which ordinarily has a collective signification (Gen. i. 26, Ex. vii. 18,
etc.); but in this place must be synonymous with the masc. *dagh*, used
in i. 17 (ii. 1), ii. 10 (11) of a single fish.

2—9. The psalm contained in these verses is written in the Hebrew
elegiac (or *Kīnah*) metre (see p. 143). The lines are arranged in a series
of couplets (seemingly seven), the constituents of each being more or
less parallel in thought or expression, so that any serious departure not
only from the prevailing rhythm but from the normal correspondence
of ideas and wording raises suspicions of textual corruption. The resemblances which it offers to many of the psalms collected in the Psalter
are pointed out where they occur, though it may be true, as Pusey
observes, that no one verse is (wholly) taken from any psalm; and there
are suggestive likenesses subsisting between it and the psalm in Ecclus.
li. 1—12. The submergence in deep waters which is so graphically
described was perhaps meant originally to be figurative of a desperate
situation of a different kind: cf. Ps. xviii. 16, xlii. 7, lxix. 1 f., cxxiv. 4,
Lam. iii. 54, and see p. lxxxv. Parallel metaphors for overwhelming
calamities are common in other languages: cf. Shakespeare's "a sea of
troubles" (*Hamlet*, Act III. Sc. 1), and Æschylus's χειμὼν καὶ κακῶν
τρικυμία (*PV.* 1015).

2. *I called.* The original author of the psalm must have had in mind
an appeal addressed to God in a past emergency, to which a response
had been mercifully granted: cf. Ps. cxx. 1.

by reason of mine affliction. Since the same preposition is used in both
halves of the *v.*, and in the second must signify "withdrawal from," it
is probable that it conveys the same sense in the first half, and that the
mg. is correct—*out of mine affliction*: cf. Vulg. *de tribulatione mea.*

hell. Heb. *Sheol.* For the personification of Sheol (the capacious
region below the earth, whither the human spirit departed at death) as
a monster cf. Is. v. 14, Prov. i. 12, 15, Ecclus. li. 5, and our own metaphor
"the jaws of death." The hyperbolic representation of a person exposed
to extreme danger as being already *in* the nether world has its counterpart in the language of Ps. xviii. 5, xxx. 3. Possibly it was the metaphor
of *belly* that occasioned this psalm (the thanksgiving of one who had
been in peril of drowning) to be inserted in this place by an editor or
reader, who missed the prayer ascribed to Jonah in *v.* 1 and sought to
supply it.

3 For thou didst cast me into the depth, in the heart of the seas,
   And the flood was round about me;
All thy waves and thy billows passed over me.
4 And I said, I am cast out from before thine eyes;
   Yet I will look again toward thy holy temple.

3. *For thou didst.* Literally, *And thou didst*, the Hebrew writer appending by *and* an explanation of the affliction referred to in *v.* 2, where we should use *for* (cf. 1 Sam. xviii. 11, where *for he said* is literally *and he said*).

the depth. The Heb. term rendered *depth* recurs in Ps. lxviii. 22, lxix. 15, Mic. vii. 19, etc. The LXX. has the plur. βάθη. But the first half of the *Kinah* line here is too long, so that the metre suggests some omission. The word that can best be spared is this (*mĕtsŭlah*), which lacks the preposition that is prefixed to the next word, and looks like a gloss explanatory of the following figure *in* (or *into*, for *bĕ* in this sense cf. Is. xix. 23) *the heart of the seas.*

the heart of the seas. The same metaphorical phrase occurs in Ezek. xxvii. 4, 25, 26; cf. also Ex. xv. 8, Ps. xlvi. 2. Cf. the similar phrase *the heart of the earth* (Mt. xii. 40).

the flood. Literally, *the stream* or *river.* The word is commonly employed in connection with rivers (Job xiv. 11), especially large rivers, like the Euphrates (Is. xi. 15) and the Nile (Is. xix. 5); but it also occurs (in the plural) as a parallel to *seas* in Ps. xxiv. 2: cf. the Homeric ποταμοῖο ῥέεθρα Ὠκεανοῦ (*Il.* xiv. 245). The LXX. has ποταμοί and the O. Lat. version *flumina*; and some critics would substitute the plural here.

waves...billows. Literally, *breakers...rollers*; cf. Ps. xlii. 7 (where the phrase is used figuratively of grievous distress).

4. *I said.* I.e. I thought: cf. Is. xxxviii. 11, and the Greek φῆ in Hom. *Il.* ii. 37.

I am cast out, etc. The psalmist in the extremity of his peril felt himself overlooked by God: cf. Ps. xxxi. 22.

Yet I will look, etc. The present Heb. text, by beginning with *Yet* (*'ach*, literally *only*), here marks a transition from despair to hope, due (according to Van Hoonacker) to Jonah's sense of comparative security in the belly of the fish. But Th. has πῶς (*'ēych*) ἐπιβλέψω, κτλ., *How shall I look...?* which agrees better with the circumstance that the description of the speaker's desperate situation is continued in the next verses to the end of 6ᵃ. The LXX. appears to support this reading by having ἄρα (for ἆρα?) προσθήσω τοῦ ἐπιβλέψαι.

toward thy holy temple. The author of the psalm was doubtless a member of the kingdom of Judah or (more probably) of the post-exilic Judæan community, for whom it would be natural to direct his face towards the Temple at Jerusalem (1 Kgs. viii. 29, 30, 48, Ps. v. 7, cxxxviii. 2, Dan. vi. 10); but the words are inappropriate to the historical Jonah, who was a member of the Northern Kingdom, which had its own shrines.

5 The waters compassed me about, even to the soul;
　The deep was round about me;
　The weeds were wrapped about my head.
6 I went down to the bottoms of the mountains;
　The earth with her bars *closed* upon me for ever:
　Yet hast thou brought up my life from ¹the pit, O LORD my
　　God.

¹ Or, *corruption*

5. *even to the soul.* I.e. even to the danger of life: cf. Ps. lxix. 1,
Jer. iv. 10.

The deep. The Heb. word is the same as that occurring in Gen. i. 2,
where it means the primæval chaos of waters that preceded the formation
of the cosmos. Elsewhere (Ps. lxxi. 20, cvi. 9, etc.) it is used to denote
the sea. The LXX. renders it by ἄβυσσος, but Sym. by θάλασσα.

The weeds. The Heb. word, which here denotes sea weed, was used
especially to describe the reeds or flags of the Nile (Ex. ii. 3, 5, Is.
xix. 6) and of the Gulf of Suez, the latter being called in Hebrew "the
sea of reeds" (which are abundant at its northern extremity). The term
was perhaps an Egyptian loan-word.

about my head. Verses 5 and 6 are probably here wrongly divided;
and to the end of *v.* 5 there should be added from the next *v.* the words
at the bottoms of the mountains: see the following note.

6. There is reason to suspect, in the present Heb. text of this verse,
some disorder and corruption. The LXX. includes within *v.* 5 the words
to (or *at*) *the bottoms of the mountains*; and for the first half of *v.* 6 it
has *I went down to the earth* (implying *lā'ārets* for *hā'ārets*), *whose bars
are everlasting detainers* (κάτοχοι αἰώνιοι). The transfer of the words *at
the bottoms of the mountains* to *v.* 5 completes the metre of the final
clause of that verse, which is otherwise defective. For the rendering of
the preposition (*lĕ*) by *at* (instead of by *to*) cf. Gen. xlix. 13, Jud. v. 17.
The mountains are regarded as having their bases in the sea (cf. Ps.
xxiv. 2). By the transposition just explained the remainder of *v.* 6,
which at present consists of three clauses, is reduced to the normal
couplet; nevertheless there must be some textual error in it, as will be
seen from the fact that the R.V. has to supply a word (the Vulg. has
concluserunt me). The textual corruption is probably in the Heb. word
ba'ădhi, rendered *upon* (or *about*) *me* (cf. Jud. iii. 22, Job i. 10, etc.),
which may conceal either a noun or a verb. In place of it Van
Hoonacker, followed by Bewer, conjectures *bolts* (*baddē*), comparing
Job xvii. 16 and rendering the first line of the couplet, *I went down to
the earth, whose bars are everlasting bolts.* (For the irregular use, in the
Heb., of the construct, instead of the absolute, form of the word see
Gesenius, *Heb. Gram.* § 130*a*.)

Yet hast thou, etc. This constitutes the second line of the fifth
couplet.

the pit. The term is sometimes synonymous with *the grave* (Ps. xxx. 9),

9—2

7 When my soul fainted within me, I remembered the LORD:
And my prayer came in unto thee, into thine holy temple.

8 They that regard lying vanities
Forsake their own mercy.

9 But I will sacrifice unto thee with the voice of thanksgiving;
I will pay that which I have vowed.
Salvation is of the LORD.

sometimes, as here, with *Sheol.* The mg. *corruption* (cf. Vulg. *de corruptione*) seems erroneously to associate the word with a different root.

7. *fainted within me.* Literally, *fainted upon me* (the preposition emphasizing, as it were, the sense of oppression): cf. Ps. cxlii. 3, mg., and (with a different preposition) cvii. 5.

thine holy temple. Probably the earthly temple is meant (as in *v.* 4), but possibly the temple in heaven (as in Ps. xi. 4, xviii. 6).

8. *lying vanities.* I.e. false gods. The particular expression here used recurs only in Ps. xxxi. 6; but *vanities* is a common term in Hebrew writings for heathen deities (Dt. xxxii. 21, Jer. x. 15, xiv. 22, xviii. 15).

Forsake their own mercy. I.e. banish from their thoughts the source of the succour experienced by them. The term *mercy* seems to be used here as a title for Jehovah (cf. Ps. cxliv. 2, R.V. *my lovingkindness*), and should be printed with a capital letter. Some scholars, however, render *their piety*, i.e. their duty towards God. For the meaning of the Hebrew root see further on p. 57. The replacement of the word (*hasdām*) by the conjectural emendation *their Refuge* (*mahăsēhem*, cf. Joel iii. 16, Ps. xiv. 6, etc.) seems unnecessary.

The whole of this *v.* constitutes the first line of the seventh couplet.

9. *But I will sacrifice,* etc. Better, *But as for me, I will sacrifice,* etc. (the pronoun being emphatic): cf. Ps. cxvi. 17, l. 14, 23. This clause (down to *thanksgiving*) forms the second line of the seventh couplet. The LXX. expands *thanksgiving* into *praise and thanksgiving.*

that which I have vowed. For the practice, among the Hebrews, of making, in time of need, vows which were to be paid if the desired relief came, cf. Gen. xxviii. 20 f. (Jacob), Jud. xi. 30, 31 (Jephthah), 1 Sam. i. 11 (Hannah), Job xxii. 27.

Salvation is of the LORD. Or, *Help belongs to JEHOVAH*: cf. Ps. iii. 8, Rev. vii. 10.

The concluding two lines of the psalm (*I will pay...of the LORD*), as arranged in the R.V., constitute only a single line in the Hebrew (not a couplet), and this appears to be outside the structure of the poem, which consists of seven couplets (see p. 143). The psalm, though comprising numerous expressions occurring in other psalms, is not a mere cento, but exhibits some originality of phrase (see *v.* 6). Hebrew writers (as has been said) often compared calamitous experiences to immersion in deep waters (see p. 129, and to the examples there cited add 2 Is. xliii. 2). In the light of certain of these parallels, it is not surprising that some have thought that the psalm is really meant to be an ex-

10 And the LORD spake unto the fish, and it vomited out Jonah upon the dry land.

pression of national, and not individual, feeling. This view finds support in the reflection (*v.* 8) upon the folly of idolatry ; nevertheless the vividness of the language in *vv.* 5, 6 rather favours the conclusion that the poem is really a personal thanksgiving for some deliverance from drowning, though effected by less extraordinary means than that whereby Jonah is represented as preserved.

10. *spake unto the fish.* Cf. Gen. iii. 14 (*said unto the serpent*), 1 Kgs. xvii. 4 (*have commanded the ravens*). The word *spake* is literally *said.*

upon the dry land. Presumably somewhere on the coast of Palestine, near Joppa, whence the ship had started, and which the sailors were trying to regain. Josephus, however, describes the fish as carrying Jonah into the Euxine (*Ant.* IX. 10, 2), perhaps because he thought the S.E. coast of that sea would be the nearest starting-point for Nineveh.

CHAPTER III.

III. 1 And the word of the LORD came unto Jonah the second time, saying, 2 Arise, go unto Nineveh, that great city, and [1] preach unto it the preaching that I bid thee. 3 So Jonah arose, and went unto Nineveh, according to the word of the LORD. Now Nineveh

[1] Or, *cry* See ch. i. 2.

1—4. The prophet's discharge of his commission.

1. *And the word...time.* The writer leaves it obscure whether Jehovah's communication reached the prophet on the shore where the fish disgorged him, or at his home, whither he had returned. The despatch of the prophet once more to carry out the duty from which he had previously shrunk recalls the narrative of Elijah at Horeb (1 Kgs. xix., see especially *v.* 4).

2. *that great city.* The reiterated allusions to Nineveh's greatness (i. 2, iv. 11) accentuate the appeal which the number of lives at stake in it made to the Divine compassion.

preach. Literally, *cry* (the same word as in i. 2, 2 Is. xl. 3, etc.); but a better translation would be *proclaim* (LXX. κήρυξον).

the preaching...bid thee. The LXX. has κατὰ τὸ κήρυγμα τὸ ἔμπροσθεν ὃ ἐγὼ ἐλάλησα πρός σε. The word rendered *preaching* (literally, *cry*, in the sense of *proclamation*) occurs only here.

3. *Nineveh was*, etc. The tense does not *necessarily* imply that the city, in the writer's time, had ceased to exist : cf. Joh. xi. 18.

an exceeding great city. Literally, *a city great for God* (cf. mg.), i.e. great even in the judgment of God, Who estimates by a standard higher than human ; cf. Acts vii. 20 (ἀστεῖος τῷ θεῷ), 2 Cor. x. 4 (δυνατὰ τῷ θεῷ), Gen. x. 9 ("a mighty hunter before Jehovah"), Lk. i. 15 (μέγας ἐνώπιον Κυρίου). Somewhat similar are Ps. xxxvi. 6, lxviii. 15 ("moun-

was ¹an exceeding great city, of three days' journey. 4 And Jonah
began to enter into the city a day's journey, and he cried, and
said, Yet forty days, and Nineveh shall be overthrown. 5 And

¹ Heb. *a city great unto God.*

tains of God" for "high mountains"), Is. xiv. 13 ("stars of God" for
"lofty stars"), Ps. lxxx. 10 ("cedars of God" for "tall cedars"), Gen.
xxiii. 6 ("a prince of God" for "a mighty prince"), xxx. 8 ("wrestlings
of God" for "vigorous wrestlings").

of three days' journey. It is clear from *v.* 4 (which represents that
Jonah advanced one day's journey into the city before beginning to
announce his message) that the phrase here is meant to describe the
measure of the city's *diameter*, not its circumference. If a day's journey
be assumed to be 20 miles (Herodotus, IV. 101, reckons it at 200 stades,
a *stade* being about 200 yards), this would imply a diameter of 60 miles.
The actual *circuit* of its ruins, as reported by Felix Jones in 1855
(quoted by Bewer), is about 7½ miles, though the plain which is bounded
by the rivers Tigris, Khusur, Zab, and Gomal, and which embraces the
ruins of Nineveh, Dur Sargon, and Calah, measures about 61½ miles in
circumference. This would naturally include extensive pasture grounds
(cf. iv. 11 end).

4. *a day's journey.* This, according to the estimate of Nineveh's size
in *v.* 3, would carry Jonah almost into the heart of the city.

Yet forty days...overthrown. This is perhaps only meant to be a
summary of what the prophet said: cf. the brief proclamation attributed
to Jesus in Mk. i. 15, Mt. iv. 17. The announcement is couched in
unconditional terms, but it is implied in iv. 2 that Jonah understood
that the destruction of the city was really dependent upon the conduct
of its people, whose repentance could avert it: cf. Jer. xviii. 7, 8, and
p. xxiii. It is not stated how Jonah, a Hebrew, made himself intelligible
to the citizens of Nineveh who spoke Assyrian. If the author had
thought about the matter, he might have explained that the prophet
used Aramaic, which was a medium of international intercourse between
Assyrian and Hebrew *officials* at the end of the eighth century B.C.
(2 Kgs. xviii. 26). Since, however, the religious bearings of the story
were alone of importance, such considerations did not interest the
narrator.

Instead of *forty days* the LXX. has τρεῖς ἡμέραι (the other Greek
translators following the Heb.). Both *forty* and *three* are conventional
periods of time in the O.T. (for the former in connection with *days* see
Gen. vii. 17, Ex. xxiv. 18, 1 Kgs. xix. 8, and for the latter see Gen.
xxx. 36, xl. 13, 19, Ex. iii. 18, x. 22, etc.); so that the variation may be
either accidental or intentional in origin. *Three* may be a copyist's
error, introduced through the nearness of the same figure in *v.* 3; whilst
conversely *forty* may be a deliberate correction in view of the fasting
mentioned in *v.* 5, since 40 days was a period associated with the fasts
of Moses and Elijah (Dt. ix. 9, 1 Kgs. xix. 8). But a decision between

the people of Nineveh believed God; and they proclaimed a fast,
and put on sackcloth, from the greatest of them even to the least
of them. 6 [1]And the tidings reached the king of Nineveh, and he

---

[1] Or, *For word came unto the king &c.*

---

the two readings in respect of originality is not called for, since both are
probably genuine, several features in the book uniting to show that it
has been constructed out of two versions of a single story, one of which
presumably had *three days*, whilst the other had *forty days* (see further
on iv. 5, and p. lxxxvii).

overthrown. The verb and the corresponding noun are used in connection with the destruction of the cities of the Plain (Gen. xix. 25, 29,
Dt. xxix. 23, Is. xiii. 19, etc.). There is nothing said here about the
nature of the contemplated overthrow, which Josephus (*Ant.* IX. 10, 2)
represents as the loss of Nineveh's dominion over other nations.

5—10. The repentance of the Ninevites and their respite by God.

5. *believed God.* Strictly, *believed in God* (as in Gen. xv. 6, Ex. xiv. 31
(Heb.), etc.). The immediate repentance of the Ninevites is doubtless
intended by the writer as a contrast to the indifference or hostility with
which his own countrymen had so often received the warnings of their
prophets. It has been suggested by Trumbull (see Bewer, p. 5) that the
impression produced by Jonah upon the population of Nineveh was the
result of the miracle that had happened to him. One of the deities
worshipped there was a fish-god (called by Berosus, Oannes); and the
ejection of the prophet alive by the fish having been witnessed, the
report of it created among the inhabitants the conviction that it was
one of their own gods who demanded their repentance. Such an explanation presupposes that the narrative has far more historical value
than can reasonably be claimed for it. On the other hand, if any sub-
stratum of fact underlies the account of Jonah's preaching at Nineveh,
the effect represented as produced by him can be in some measure
paralleled. Layard relates "I have known a Christian priest frighten a
whole Mussulman town into repentance by publicly proclaiming that he
had received a Divine mission to announce a coming earthquake or
plague" (*Nineveh and Babylon*, p. 367).

proclaimed a fast, and put on sackcloth. The practice of abstinence
and the assuming of a particular vesture in connection with religious
observances and occasions probably have their explanation in physical
ideas of holiness; see pp. 90, 93.

6. *And the tidings reached the king*, etc. By *the tidings* is meant the
report of Jonah's utterance. There is a lack of plausibility in the
representation that the king received information of the prophet's announcement only after the people had taken action upon it (*v.* 5), and
that he proclaimed a fast, with its usual concomitants (*vv.* 7, 8), when such
was already being observed. The difficulty, which some critics propose
to remove either by placing *v.* 5 after *v.* 9, or by omitting *vv.* 6—9 as
a later insertion, is best solved by the supposition that the book is

arose from his throne, and laid his robe from him, and covered
him with sackcloth, and sat in ashes. 7 And he made proclamation and ¹published through Nineveh by the decree of the king
and his nobles, saying, Let neither man nor beast, herd nor flock,
taste any thing: let them not feed, nor drink water: 8 but let

¹ Heb. *said*

composite, and that the constituent versions out of which it has been
woven together differed in detail here, one assigning the public fast to
an impulse on the part of the collective people, and the other ascribing
it to the initiative of the sovereign.

the king of Nineveh. The king of Assyria is nowhere else called by
this title. The reigning Assyrian sovereign in the time of the *historical*
Jonah may have been any one of five—Ramman-nirari (810—782), Shalmaneser IV (781—772), Asshur-dan III (771—754), Asshur-nirari IV
(753—745), and Tiglath-Pileser (744—727).

covered him with sackcloth. For the wearing of sackcloth as a token
of mourning among the Hebrews see p. 90. The custom is assumed in
Jer. xlix. 3, Ezek. xxvii. 31 to have prevailed likewise amongst neighbouring Gentile nations.

sat in ashes. Compare Job ii. 8, Dan. ix. 3, 3 Is. lviii. 5, Mt. xi. 21
(= Lk. x. 13). Possibly the sitting in ashes, like the casting of earth or
dust on the head (Josh. vii. 6, 2 Sam. i. 2, cf. Hom. *Il.* XVIII. 23, 24¹),
was a survival from a time when contact with the remains of the in-
cinerated or buried dead was a method of bringing the departed into
relation with his sorrowing kinsfolk: cf. Hom. *Il.* XVIII. 26 (of Achilles),
αὐτὸς δ᾽ ἐν κονίῃσι μέγας μεγαλωστὶ τανυσθεὶς | κεῖτο.

7. *And he made proclamation,* etc. Perhaps better, *And one* (i.e. an
official) *made proclamation,* etc.: cf. LXX. καὶ ἐκηρύχθη καὶ ἐρρέθη.

the decree. This sense of the term used in the original is an Aramaism
(p. lxxxiii). The LXX. omits the word and has merely παρὰ τοῦ βασιλέως,
κτλ.

his nobles. Literally, *his great ones* or *grandees:* cf. Prov. xviii. 16.
The decree here proceeds from the king and his nobles together, just as
in Dan. vi. 17 the signets used by Darius are those of both himself and
his lords. The LXX. has παρὰ τῶν μεγιστάνων αὐτοῦ.

Let neither…taste any thing. When Nineveh was beset by the Medes
and Babylonians, the king then reigning enjoined a fast of a hundred
days².

nor beast. In view of the addition *herd nor flock* in the next clause,
the term *beast* must here be limited to draught animals and beasts of
burden (1 Kgs. xviii. 5): the Greek and Latin renderings are τὰ κτήνη
and *iumenta* respectively.

---

¹ ἀμφοτέρῃσι δὲ χερσὶν ἑλὼν κόνιν αἰθαλόεσσαν | χεύατο κὰκ κεφαλῆς.
² Kennedy, quoted by Lanchester, *Ob. and Jonah,* p. 41.

them be covered with sackcloth, both man and beast, and let them cry mightily unto God: yea, let them turn every one from his evil way, and from the violence that is in their hands. 9 Who knoweth whether God will not turn and repent, and turn away from his fierce anger, that we perish not? 10 And God saw their works, that they turned from their evil way; and God repented of the evil, which he said he would do unto them; and he did it not.

let them not feed...water. It is the animals previously mentioned that are chiefly in the mind of the writer, for the verb rendered *feed* is the customary one for feeding in pastures.

8. *let them be covered.* Literally, *let them cover themselves.* The inclusion of the cattle in the king's order enjoining national mourning obtains illustration not only from Judith iv. 10, but also from parallel narratives in Classical authors. Herodotus relates that the Persians, on the occasion of the death of Masistius, clipped their horses and baggage animals (IX. 24); whilst Plutarch states that Alexander did the same when Hephæstion died (*Alex.* 72), and that the Thessalians cut off their horses' manes (as well as their own hair) in mourning for the Theban Pelopidas (*Pel.* 33). Cf. also Eur. *Alc.* 425—429. Funeral trappings on horses are not unknown even among ourselves.

let them cry. Grammatically this applies to the animals as well as to the human beings in the city, but the carelessness of expression scarcely needs to be remedied by emendation. The LXX. in this *v.* has *And they were covered...and cried...and turned*, etc.

turn...from his evil way. The national repentance was not to be limited to outward tokens of sorrow: cf. Jer. xviii. 11, xxvi. 3, 3 Is. lviii. 6, 7, 9, 10, Joel ii. 13.

violence. Aggression upon the rights of others was a feature in the career of Assyria as a nation (cf. Is. x. 13, 14, Nah. ii. 11, 12, iii. 1), and no doubt characterized its citizens in their individual relations.

in their hands. Literally, *in their two palms.* For similar phrases cf. Job xvi. 17, 1 Ch. xii. 17, 3 Is. lix. 6.

9. *Who knoweth,* etc. The expression, which is borrowed from Joel ii. 14, is placed in the mouth of the people by the LXX., which prefixes λέγοντες: see *v.* 8.

10. *And God saw...their evil way.* The repentance of the Ninevites at the preaching of Jonah was contrasted by our Lord with the impenitence of the Jews in spite of His own preaching (Mt. xii. 41 = Lk. xi. 32).

and God repented, etc. The same phrase occurs in Ex. xxxii. 14, Am. vii. 3, Jer. xviii. 7, 8. God's threatened chastisement was conditional; and His relenting from His purpose was consequent upon the offenders' contrition.

he did it not. I.e. at the time which the writer describes. The conversion of the Ninevites from their evil practices on this occasion, if historical, did not finally preclude the subsequent destruction of their city.

CHAPTER IV.

IV. 1 But it displeased Jonah exceedingly, and he was angry.
2 And he prayed unto the LORD, and said, I pray thee, O LORD,
was not this my saying, when I was yet in my country?
Therefore I [1]hasted to flee unto Tarshish: for I knew that thou
art a gracious God, and full of compassion, slow to anger, and
plenteous in mercy, and repentest thee of the evil. 3 Therefore
now, O LORD, take, I beseech thee, my life from me; for it is
better for me to die than to live. 4 And the LORD said, [2]Doest
thou well to be angry? 5 Then Jonah went out of the city, and

[1] Or, *was beforehand in fleeing*   [2] Or, *Art thou greatly angry?*

1—11. Jonah's displeasure at the mercy shown to the Ninevites, and
God's rebuke.

1. *But it displeased Jonah.* The writer doubtless thinks of Jonah's
displeasure as mainly due to the clemency shown to his country's
enemies by God, but possibly also as occasioned in part by mortification
because his prediction was not fulfilled (since this was calculated to
bring discredit and derision upon a prophet, see Dt. xviii. 22, Jer.
xx. 7—8).

and he was angry. The LXX. has καὶ συνεχύθη ("he was upset"),
the Old Lat. *et mæstus factus est.*

2. *my saying.* I.e. my reflection.

I hasted to flee. Or, *I fled betimes* (literally (as in the mg.), "I was
beforehand in fleeing," LXX. προέφθασα τοῦ φυγεῖν, Vulg. *præoccupavi
ut fugerem*).

a gracious God, etc. The phraseology appears to be borrowed from
Joel ii. 13 (see note); cf. also Ex. xxxiv. 6, Num. xiv. 18, Ps. lxxxvi.
15, etc.

3. *take, I beseech thee, my life.* A similar request was made in
despondency (arising from a very different source from that implied
in Jonah's case) by both Moses and Elijah (Num. xi. 15, 1 Kgs. xix. 4).

4. *Doest thou well to be angry?* Cf. Sym. ἆρα δικαίως ἐλυπήθης; Vulg.
putasne bene irasceris tu? According to this translation, Jonah is not
directly rebuked for his anger, but is invited to reflect whether it is
justifiable. The general meaning, however, of the Heb. verb represented by the adv. is "to do (a thing) perfectly or thoroughly" (see
Mic. vii. 3, Dt. xiii. 14 (15), Jer. i. 12), and so is in favour of the
rendering *Art thou thoroughly angry?* and this is the sense given to it
by the LXX. (εἰ σφόδρα λελύπησαι σύ;) and the Old Latin (*si valde* (or
vehementer) *contristatus es tu?*); though such a question attributes to
the Deity a bantering attitude which seems unnatural.

5. *Then Jonah went out.* Literally, *And Jonah went out.* If the
narrative is a complete unity, it must be supposed that Jonah, though
virtually convinced (as his anger showed) that God would spare the

sat on the east side of the city, and there made him a booth, and
sat under it in the shadow, till he might see what would become
of the city. 6 And the LORD God prepared a [1]gourd, and made it

city, yet did not give up all hope of seeing its destruction accomplished.
But the natural implication of the passage is that he had not yet learnt
that the city was to be spared; so that Sellin thinks that this *v.* has
been displaced, and that its original position was after iii. 4. It is more
probable, however, that the *v.* comes from a version distinct from that
whence the adjoining verses have been drawn (see p. lxxxvii). The conjunction *and* probably linked the present passage to iii. 9.

on the east side. Jonah appears to have crossed the city: on approaching it from Palestine, he would naturally enter it on the west
side. In designating the quarters of the sky the Hebrews turned to
the rising sun, so that the east side of a place or thing was the front
(cf. Joel ii. 20).

a booth. The term (equivalent to the σκηνή of Mk. ix. 5) describes
a shelter like the structures of leafy boughs occupied by the Hebrews
on the occasion of the Feast of Tabernacles (Lev. xxiii. 42, Neh. viii.
14—17). That the prophet felt the need of such a shelter clearly presupposes that he expected that the fate of the city would not be
determined until after the lapse of some considerable interval, so that
this passage coheres best with the representation (iii. 4, Heb.) that the
space of time within which repentance was required was *forty days*
(not *three days*, as represented in iii. 4, LXX.). This period was not
yet exhausted.

6. *the LORD God.* Strictly, *JEHOVAH God.* The combination is
rare outside of Gen. ii., iii.

prepared. Better, *appointed*, as in i. 17, iv. 7, 8.

a gourd. Probably a better rendering is *a palm-christ* (*Palma
Christi*)[1]. The Heb. word is *kīkāyōn* (which Aq. and Th. transliterate—
κικεών), and the resemblance between it and the word κίκι, mentioned in
Hdt. II. 94 as the Egyptian name for the σιλλικύπριον and applied by
Dioscorides to the κροτών, a tree producing the castor-oil berry, favours
the view that the castor-oil plant (*Ricinus communis*, Linnæus) is meant.
This is described by Pliny (*Hist. Nat.* xv. 7) as *altitudine oleæ, caule
ferulaceo, folio vitium, semine uvarum gracilium pallidarumque*, and
grows, under favourable conditions, to a height of 30 or 40 feet. It has
broad palmate serrated leaves like those of a plane, only larger, and sometimes measuring more than a foot across. It is a native of the East
Indies, but flourishes in most tropical and semi-tropical countries. The
LXX., which renders the Hebrew term by κολοκύνθη (*Cucurbita lage-
naria*), takes it to be a gourd, which is also of rapid growth and has large

---

[1] A.V. mg. has *palmcrist.* The name is said to be due to the hand-like shape of
the leaves.

to come up over Jonah, that it might be a shadow over his head,
to deliver him from his evil case. So Jonah was exceeding glad
because of the gourd. 7 But God prepared a worm when the
morning rose the next day, and it smote the gourd, that it
withered. 8 And it came to pass, when the sun arose, that God
prepared a sultry east wind; and the sun beat upon the head of

leaves. As this is of a vine-like nature, it has been argued (by those
who assume that the narrative is completely self-consistent) that this
identification suits the account in the text best, since a trailing plant
was more suitable for covering Jonah's booth than a tree, such as the
castor-oil plant, could be. Of the early translators Sym. assumes that
the plant intended was of a trailing nature, and translates it by κισσός,
and the Vulg. (following him) has *hedera*. The text, however, does not
state that the *kīkāyōn* was designed to screen the booth and to render
it more impervious to the sun's rays: the natural sense of *v.* 6 is that
it was meant *by itself* to afford to Jonah the shelter he needed. In
reality, the booth and the *kīkāyōn* seem to serve the same purpose, and
the accounts of them in *vv.* 5 and 6 to be not successive, but parallel,
presumably contained in different versions of the story. Hence, as the
chief argument for considering the plant in question to be a gourd
breaks down, there is no objection to the identification of it with the
Ricinus communis (as the similarity between the Hebrew and Greek
words suggests). This, which in Mediterranean countries is known as
the *Palma Christi*, is normally speedy in its development (it has been
known in America to reach a height of 13 feet in 3 months); but the
present narrative, which describes it as growing in a single night (*v.* 10)
tall enough to shelter Jonah, manifestly implies a miracle.

made it to come up. The Heb. admits of the rendering, *it came up*, and
the LXX. and the Latin Versions have ἀνέβη and *ascendit* respectively.

that it might be a shadow. It is a reasonable inference from these
words that the plant was designed to furnish protection from the sun
independently of any structure like the booth of *v.* 5, though Pusey
quotes from the Talmud passages showing that the kind of booth erected
at the Feast of Tabernacles was not impervious to the sun's heat, which
was kept out by various devices.

to deliver him. The construction (the use of *lō* to express the direct
object) is unusual, and is thought to be due to Aramaic influence, though
it occurs sporadically in early Hebrew. The LXX. for *to deliver* has τοῦ
σκιάζειν (vocalizing differently).

his evil case. I.e. the physical distress occasioned by the heat.

7. *a worm.* The singular is perhaps used collectively, as in Dt. xxviii.
39, Is. xiv. 11. The palm-christ is said to be subject to the attacks of
caterpillars, which strip it of its leaves; but the writer of the book
obviously has in view a process of destruction as miraculous in its
rapidity as the previous growth.

8. *a sultry east wind.* The wind meant is one that blows from the

Jonah, that he fainted, and requested for himself that he might
die, and said, It is better for me to die than to live. 9 And God
said to Jonah, Doest thou well to be angry for the gourd? And
he said, I do well to be angry even unto death. 10 And the LORD
said, Thou hast had pity on the gourd, for the which thou hast
not laboured, neither madest it grow; which came up in a night,
and perished in a night: 11 and should not I have pity on

S.E., called in Arabic *sherkiyeh* (whence "sirocco"): for its scorching
and destructive character cf. Gen. xli. 6, Ezek. xvii. 10 (see Driver,
Par. Psalter, p. 136). The epithet translated "sultry" (*hărīshīth*) occurs
only here, and is of doubtful derivation and significance. The most
plausible explanation connects it with *hōresh*, "autumn," in the sense
primarily of an "autumnal," and secondarily of a very hot, wind (LXX.
πνεύματι καύσωνος συνκαίοντι). As the narrative stands, it must be
assumed that the hot wind is mentioned as something which merely
aggravated Jonah's discomfort; but it is a plausible conjecture that the
compiler has omitted a clause, occurring in one of the alternative versions,
of which the tenor was, *and it tore down the booth*. If the booth and the
palm-christ were originally distinct agencies subserving, in the different
versions, the same end of sheltering Jonah, it is probable that they were
both represented as destroyed, the one by a wind, and the other by a
worm.

and the sun beat, etc. In regard to the heat at Nineveh Pusey quotes
from Layard (*Nin. and Bab.*, p. 366), "Few European travellers can
brave the perpendicular rays of the Assyrian sun. Even the well-
seasoned Arab seeks the shade during the day, and journeys by night,
unless driven forth at noontide by necessity or the love of war."

requested for himself, etc. The resemblance to the language of Elijah
(1 Kgs. xix. 4) is very noticeable here.

9. *Doest thou well to be angry?* See on *v.* 4. Jonah's anger on this
occasion had a different origin: previously it was due to the sparing of
Nineveh; now it is caused by the destruction of the palm-christ.

even unto death. The phrase is used in connection with various emotions to express intensity: cf. Jud. xvi. 16, Mk. xiv. 34.

10. *Thou hast had pity.* The pronoun *thou* is emphatic here, as is
the *I* in *v.* 11. Whilst Jonah had done nothing for the plant whose
fate he deplored, God was the Creator of the living beings in Nineveh.

laboured. The verb here used (*'āmal*) is apparently late (see p. lxxxiii),
and takes the place of the earlier *yāgha'* (Josh. xxiv. 13).

which came up in a night. Literally, "the son (i.e. the product) of a
night." The expression resembles the common idiom employed in Heb.
to express age (e.g. *a yearling* is "the son of a year," Ex. xii. 5).

11. *and should not I have pity*, etc. "God waives for a time the fact of
the repentance of Nineveh" (Pusey), and here speaks only of the appeal
to His compassion made by the tender age of so many in the city which
Jonah wishes to see destroyed. Cf. Wisd. xi. 26.

Nineveh, that great city; wherein are more than sixscore thousand persons that cannot discern between their right hand and their left hand; and also much cattle?

sixscore thousand. Literally, *twelve myriads.* The Heb. for *myriad* (*ribbo*), here used, is confined almost exclusively to late books (see p. lxxxiii).

that cannot...hand. The expression (with which cf. Dt. i. 39, Is. vii. 15, 16) denotes very young children, in whom intelligence had not yet awakened, and who consequently could have no responsibility for the city's wickedness (i. 2). Such would be under two years of age, and the number of them (120,000) is thought to imply a population of 600,000. F. Jones estimated, from the extent of the ruins of Nineveh, that its inhabitants must really have amounted to 174,000.

much cattle? The numerous cattle were as irresponsible as the children. The writer's thought that God has care for animals is found elsewhere in the O.T., see Ex. xx. 10, xxiii. 12, Dt. xxv. 4, Ps. cxlvii. 9: cf. also Mt. vi. 26, x. 29.

The effectiveness of the question with which the book concludes is not allowed by the writer to be impaired by any further particulars about Jonah himself, his reflections upon the Divine remonstrance, or his return home.

ADDITIONAL NOTE BY THE GENERAL EDITOR.

The Book of Jonah has lent itself more than any other of the Minor Prophets to artistic illustration, especially in painted glass. The chief incident represented is that of Jonah's escape from the whale's belly. This is natural, since it was treated as typical of our Lord's Resurrection. In the windows of four Oxford Colleges there are Jonah-scenes; and three of them—those in University, Lincoln, and Wadham Colleges—depict the incident mentioned. But in Christ Church there is another scene (the work of Van Ling) which touches a central thought of the book: the prophet is seated under the gourd, gazing sadly at the city of Nineveh, as it stretches undestroyed and magnificent before his eyes.

APPENDIX I

THE PSALM IN CH. II. RENDERED IN THE RHYTHM OF THE ORIGINAL.

The following will serve in some slight degree to illustrate the rhythm of the psalm in ch. ii. The rendering is necessarily in places a little less close to the original than that which is given in the R.V. or supported in the commentary, and in two passages additional emendations are adopted, for metrical convenience.

1. "Oút of my straíts did I crý | to Jehóvah, who ánswered;
   From the bélly of Shéol complaíned; | thou heárdest my cálling.

2. To the heárt of the seás was I cást; | embráced me their cúrrent;
   Áll of thy bíllows and wáves | went swírling abóve me.

3. Methoúght, I am dríven awáy | from the ránge of thy vísion:
   Hów shall I ónce more behóld | thy témple most hóly?

4. The wáters did clásp me aboút; | the deép did encómpass.
   Twísted was weéd round my heád, | at the báse of the moúntains.

5. I sánk to where eárth with its bárs | imprísons¹ for éver;
   But my lífe thou didst bríng from the pít, | O Jehóvah my Gód.

6. When the soúl that was ín me grew faínt, | my Gód I remémbered;
   And my práyer entered ínto thy coúrts, | thy témple most hóly.

7. Who revére the Vaín and the Fálse | abándon their Réfuge²;
   But Í with the voíce of thanksgíving | will ófferings rénder.
   Whát I have vówed I will páy: | from Jehóvah comes súccour."

¹ Here instead of *ba'ădhi* is substituted *'ātsĕru* "detain," which is translated by κατέχω in the LXX. of Jud. xiii. 15, 16. In the present passage the LXX. has κάτοχοι.

² Here instead of *hasdām* there is substituted (after Marti) *mahăsēhem* "their refuge."

APPENDIX II

CRITICAL ANALYSIS OF JONAH.

The following translation (more literal than the R.V.) of the narrative portion of the book will make plain the tenor of each of the hypothetical sources.

Version A	*Matter common to both Versions*	*Version B*

i. 1 And the word of Jehovah came unto Jonah, the son of Amittai, saying, 2 Arise, go to Nineveh, the great city, and cry against it, for their wickedness hath come up into my presence.

3ª But Jonah arose to flee to Tarshish from the presence of Jehovah.

3ᵇ But he went down to Joppa and found a ship going to Tarshish. And he paid the fare of it, and went down into it to go with them to Tarshish from the presence of Jehovah.

4 And Jehovah had flung a great wind into the sea, and there was a great tempest in the sea, and the ship was about to be shattered.

5ᵇ And they flung the gear which was in the ship into the sea to lighten it from off them.

5ª Then the seamen were afraid, and cried each to his god. 5ᶜ But Jonah had gone down into the hold of the vessel and lay down and slept soundly. 6 And the captain of the sailors approached him and said to him, Why art thou sound asleep? Arise, cry to thy God; perchance God will think upon us that we perish not.

8 And they said to him, Tell us now on account of whom this evil has happened to us. What is thy occupation? Whence dost thou come? What is thy land? And of what people art thou? 9 And he said to them, I am a Hebrew; and I am a worshipper of Jehovah, the God of heaven, who made the sea and the dry land. 10ª And the men feared with great fear.

7 And they said each to his mate, Come, that we may cast lots and know on whose account this evil has happened to us. And they cast lots and the lot fell upon Jonah.

10ᵇ And they said to him, What is this that thou hast done? for the men knew that it was from the presence of Jehovah that he was fleeing, for he had told them. 13 And the men rowed to restore him to the dry land, but they were not able, for the sea went on being tempestuous upon them.

11 And they said to him, What shall we do to thee that the sea may be calm from off us; for the sea went on being tempestuous. 12 And he said to them, Take me up and fling me into the sea that the sea may be calm from off you, for I know that on my account this great tempest is upon you.

Version A   *Matter common to both Versions*   *Version B*

14ᵃ And they cried to Jehovah and said, Pray, Jehovah,

14ᵇ Let us not perish for this man's life,   14ᶜ [and] Do not lay upon us innocent blood,

14ᵈ for thou, Jehovah, hast done as thou hast pleased. 15 And they took up Jonah and flung him into the sea, and the sea stayed from its raging. 16 And the men feared Jehovah with great fear, and they sacrificed a sacrifice to Jehovah and vowed vows.

ii. 1 But Jehovah appointed a great fish to swallow Jonah, and Jonah was in the bowels of the fish three days and three nights. 2 And Jonah made petition unto Jehovah his God from the bowels of the fish. 11 And Jehovah said to the fish...and it disgorged Jonah on to the dry land.

iii. 1 And the word of Jehovah came to Jonah a second time, saying, 2 Arise, go to Nineveh, the great city, and cry unto it the cry that I speak unto thee. 3 And Jonah arose and went to Nineveh, according to the word of Jehovah. And Nineveh was a great city (even) for God, three days' journey (across). 4ᵃ And Jonah began to enter into the city one day's journey, and he cried and said:

4ᵇ (LXX.) Yet three days and Nineveh shall be overthrown. 5 And the people of Nineveh believed God; and they proclaimed a fast and put on sackcloth, from the greatest of them even unto the least of them. 10 And God saw their works, that they turned from their evil way, and God repented concerning the evil which he said he would do unto them, and he did it not. iv. 1 But for Jonah it was evil, a great evil, and he was angry. 2 And he made petition unto Jehovah and said, Pray, Jehovah, was not this my saying, while I was yet on my own soil? Therefore I was beforehand in fleeing unto Tarshish; for I knew that thou art a gracious God and compassionate, slow to anger, plenteous in mercy, and repentant of the evil. 3 And now, Jehovah, take my life from me, for better for me is my death than my life.

4 And Jehovah said, Doest thou well to be angry? 6 And Jehovah God appointed a palmchrist, and it came up over Jonah, to be a shade over his head, to deliver him from his evil state.

4ᵇ (Heb.) Yet forty days and Nineveh shall be overthrown. 6 And the matter reached the king of Nineveh, and he arose from off his throne, and laid his robe from off him, and covered himself with sackcloth, and sat in ashes. 7 And one made proclamation and said in Nineveh by the decree of the king and his great men, saying, Let neither man nor beast, herd nor flock, taste anything, let them not feed nor drink water; 8 but let them be covered with sackcloth, both man and beast; and let them cry with might to God; and let them turn each from his evil way, and from the violence that is in their hands. 9 Who knoweth whether God will turn and repent, and turn from the heat of his anger that we perish not?

iv. 5 And Jonah went out of the city and sat on the east side of the city and there made for himself a booth and sat under the shade until he should see what would happen to

W.   10

Version A

And Jonah was glad with great gladness because of the palmchrist. 7 But God appointed a worm, when the dawn arose on the morrow, and it smote the palmchrist, and it withered; 8[b] and the sun smote upon the head of Jonah and he fainted, and requested for himself that he might die, and said, Better for me is my death than my life. 9 And God said to Jonah, Doest thou well to be angry on account of the palmchrist? And he said, I do well to be angry even unto death. 10 And Jehovah said, *Thou* hast pity on the palmchrist, on which thou didst not labour, neither madest it to grow, which came into being in a night and perished in a night; 11 and should not *I* have pity on Nineveh, the great city, wherein are more than twelve myriads of persons that discern not between their right hand and their left, and much cattle?

Version B

the city. 8[a] And it came to pass when the sun arose that God appointed a sultry east wind; ⟨and it overthrew the booth.⟩

INDEX

CAMBRIDGE: PRINTED BY W. LEWIS AT THE UNIVERSITY PRESS